FOLLOWING THE TON

A career covering Greenock Morton (1974-2010)

Roger Graham

A Bright Pen Book

Text Copyright © Roger Graham 2012

Cover design by Roger Graham ©
Cover picture by James McFadden

Front cover: Andy McLaren on the wing.

All rights reserved. No part of this publication may be reproduced, stored in a retrieval system, or transmitted in any form or by any means, electronic, mechanical, photocopy, recording or otherwise, without prior written permission of the copyright owner. Nor can it be circulated in any form of binding or cover other than that in which it is published and without similar condition including this condition being imposed on a subsequent purchaser.

British Library Cataloguing Publication Data.
A catalogue record for this book is available from the British Library

ISBN 978-0-7552-1513-3

Authors OnLine Ltd
19 The Cinques
Gamlingay, Sandy
Bedfordshire SG19 3NU
England

This book is also available in e-book format,
details of which are available at www.authorsonline.co.uk

About the Author

Roger Graham was born in Greenock, in Scotland, in 1950. He was educated at Greenock Academy and his father, Duncan, first took him to see Morton Football Club in 1961.

He became a journalist in 1970, joining D.C. Thomson & Co in Dundee where he worked for four years. He was then asked to become sports editor designate at the Greenock Telegraph in 1974. He worked there as sports editor up until he was made redundant in 2010.

He is married to Susan, with three children, Colin, Jennifer and Nichola, and what he describes as a brilliant clutch of grandchildren.

FOREWORD

By Allan McGraw

I consider it a great honour that Roger has asked me to write the foreword to his book.

I've known Roger since he started with the Greenock Telegraph back in 1974. I've always valued his opinion given in reports involving Greenock Morton Football Club, not always agreeing with him, but respecting his honesty.

I think he has done a superb job with this book. I know he has taken a lot of time and effort with it. He should feel very proud of himself, but he's too modest to think that.

He has produced a very good book for us all to read. It brought great memories flooding back to me, as I am sure it will do for all Greenock Morton supporters and the people of Inverclyde.

To Roger, thank you for your friendship over these many years.

And to all Greenock Morton fans everywhere – as I know this book will go to many parts of the world – thank you for allowing me to be part of the history of this great club.

Author's Note

THE incentive to write this book was that I felt I had a story to tell after covering Morton Football Club's affairs for 36 years.

My professional involvement with the club as a sports reporter started in 1974 when, coincidentally, Morton secretary Tom Robertson produced his centenary volume on the club. This book, therefore, completes the history from that year to 2010.

In my time covering the club's activities Morton had seven seasons in the Premier League, five consecutively under Benny Rooney's management.

Rooney's side was the best I saw in that time, though Allan McGraw was later to build an excellent team of his own and produce several fine young players.

There was also the Hugh Scott era, when the club almost went out of business altogether, then the revival under Douglas Rae's ownership.

One or two managers, who went on to greater things, cut their teeth at Cappielow, notably Alex Miller and Tommy McLean.

It was an eventful 36 years, mostly thoroughly enjoyable, covering the affairs of one of the friendliest clubs in Scotland. I met some lovely people at Cappielow and throughout the game as a whole. I also saw some great players and feel privileged to have been able to document such a big slice of the club's history.

I have tried to give a faithful account of that period, with its various highs and lows. Everyone will have his or her own favourite moments.

I'd like to thank Allan McGraw, one of the best liked and most respected men in Scottish football, for his kind foreword. It's impossible to think of Morton without thinking of Allan. The club's record goalscorer with 58 league and cup goals in 1963-64 season, no one knows how far he would have gone in the game had it not been for a bad injury sustained during the course of that campaign. He did go on to play well for Hibernian for several years but, as he himself has said, they never got the best of him due to that injury.

He then returned to serve as reserve manager at Cappielow and, later, managed the club for 12 years, setting up the best youth policy the club has ever had. To many he is simply 'Mr Morton'.

I would also like to thank photographers Kenny Ramsay, James McFadden, George Young Photographers and David Bell for the use of their excellent pictures; also Chas Halliday for his help with pictures.

Hopefully, you will enjoy the read, and it may recall your own fond memories.

CHAPTER ONE

Road to the SPL

My father first took me to watch Morton as an 11-year-old in 1961, though it was the dramatic 1963-64 season which really ignited my interest.

That was a term when a new-look side, composed mainly of free transfers, created a real stir in Scotland, racing to the Second Division title in record-breaking fashion. They also reached the League Cup Final against one of the best sides in Glasgow Rangers' history, including world class players Jim Baxter and Willie Henderson, when a record crowd for the competition of over 106,000 attended, half of them from Greenock, its adjacent towns, Port Glasgow and Gourock, and assorted outposts.

Little did I suspect then as I cheered on the team from the packed terracings in the Cowshed that a decade later I would be reporting on the Cappielow club's activities.

I arrived at the Greenock Telegraph in 1974 after spending four years as a journalist at D.C. Thomson in Dundee. I had been brought to the newspaper as sports editor designate, to take over from veteran sports reporter Dick Smith when he retired.

To say that sport in these days in the Telegraph was not much of a priority would be an understatement. In 1974 it was scattered throughout the paper in no identifiable format. It was used as something to fill in the gaps, rather than being a key section of the newspaper. That is not to criticise my predecessor; it was simply the way things had been done up to then. I had to argue my corner for sport to be given greater recognition.

I liked the Greenock Telegraph. My home town paper had a real identity with the towns of Greenock, Gourock and Port Glasgow and outlying villages. Unlike most local papers it was a daily, Monday to Saturday, with two editions – later to become one – and by far the majority of management and staff comprised local people. It was a good place to work, rather like an extended family. Crucially, the staff knew the area, lived in it and had an empathy with it. I was to find it a very different working environment in later years.

Morton were the principal sporting force in the district and when I arrived they were a team of modest accomplishment. Morton secretary Tom Robertson, later to become a director, had just brought out a centenary book on the club. This volume, therefore, by coincidence, takes up the story where he left off. It covers a period of 36 years with its highs, lows and one season in which the club almost went out of business altogether.

I came to the Telegraph at a time which coincided with the start of the Sinclair Street club's best era since the Danish "invasion" of the 60s and arguably that of the star-studded team of the post-war years of the 40's, which included such luminaries as goalkeeper Jimmy Cowan, wing halves Billy Campbell and Tommy Orr, and forward Billy Steel, all Scotland internationalists.

In the summer of 1974 Dane Erik Sorensen was the manager. Sorensen was legendary Morton manager Haldane Y. Stewart's first signing in a notable Danish incursion in the 60s, being introduced as the 'man in black' when he played his first game in goal. He went on to have a short, but illustrious, career with Morton before being transferred to Rangers.

The 1974-75 season was one in which clubs were playing for places in a revolutionary new set-up, which was to include a 10-club Scottish Premier League for the first time. With veteran Dick Smith still writing on Morton's matches that season, I covered few games, but took in as much as I could of what was going on at Cappielow.

Jim Townsend was Sorensen's assistant as player-coach and it was he who, by all accounts, was the football brain, with Sorensen's strengths seen more on the side of fitness and discipline. Sorensen also was an excellent goalkeeping coach.

Morton had a mix of experience and youth, but in truth they were a run of the mill side. Their team in the first competitive match of the season, against Dunfermline in a League Cup tie at East End Park, lined up as follows: Roy Baines; Davie Hayes, Steve Ritchie; Jim Townsend, John Nelson, Stan Rankin; Alex McGhee, Alex Reid, John Hazel, Kevin Hegarty and Kenny Skovdam. George Anderson was a substitute.

The tie ended 1-1, midfield playmaker Reid scoring for Morton. A 3-1 win in the same League Cup section followed against Aberdeen at Cappielow, Alex McGhee, Kenny Skovdam and Kevin Hegarty scoring, before two drubbings – 5-0 at home to Hearts (who included Drew Busby in their side, a player who was to end up at Cappielow in the not too distant future) and 4-0 away to Aberdeen, quashed any premature feelings of optimism.

The League Cup ended disappointingly and the league began with little cause for joy. John Goldthorp, another who would arrive at Cappielow, scored in a 3-0 Motherwell win at Fir Park, a match in which George Anderson was Morton's star man.

Hibs then administered a 5-0 whacking at Easter Road before young John Nelson, an aspiring prospect at centre half, broke an ankle in a reserve game against Kilmarnock.

Morton had gone six weeks without a win when they finally mustered a 3-3 draw at Pittodrie against Aberdeen, forward Ian Harley arriving from Falkirk to boost the Cappielow squad.

There was a more creditable 1-0 loss at Parkhead against a Celtic side including Kenny Dalglish, Danny McGrain, Billy McNeill and Bobby Lennox, but it was clear Morton were going to be hard-pushed indeed to make the next season's new Premier Division.

Charlie Brown, a talented if enigmatic midfielder, was breaking through to the first team but on 14th December, 1974, Morton were stunned by the young Dundee United side Jim McLean was building at Tannadice, going down to a humiliating 6-0 defeat at Cappielow. Andy Gray and Paul Hegarty, the latter a striker at that stage in his career, each grabbed a brace, with Dave Narey and Jackie Copland notching one apiece. Gray was later to head south in a million-pound deal to Aston Villa. It was the money from that transfer which McLean used to transform United, key players such as Paul Hegarty, Dave Narey and Paul Sturrock being fixed up on long-term deals.

The season was becoming a hard slog, brightened briefly by a home 1-1 draw to Rangers, John Hazel's opener being nullified by a Graham Fyfe equaliser. Two men in the Rangers team that day, Alex Miller and Tommy McLean, were to become managers at Cappielow in later years. Interestingly, the crowd was 16,200.

Greenockian Eddie Morrison, another who in future was to make his mark at Cappielow, played a key part in a 2-1 Kilmarnock win over Morton, in which Gordon Smith and Ian Fallis scored, and the season was coming to a disappointing conclusion.

Club chairman Sir William Lithgow donated a handsome silver trophy to be awarded to the Player of the Year and few were surprised when goalkeeper Roy Baines received the lion's share of the votes to become the inaugural winner in a poll run by the Greenock Telegraph.

Ironically, it was two uncharacteristic Baines errors which led to English visitors Preston North End beating Morton 2-0 at Cappielow in a pre-1975-76 season friendly. Preston's manager on the occasion was legendary English internationalist Bobby Charlton, his assistant being another World Cup winning team-mate, Nobby Stiles. I remember thinking it would be difficult to imagine two more contrasting styles of player; Charlton the elegant, graceful, explosive forward, and Styles, the small, aggressive, destructive midfield warrior. Charlton, as ever, came across as a gracious winner. When I spoke to him afterwards he had no airs and graces and genuinely wished Morton well in their new season. He was to resign from what was his first and, as it turned out, only job in football management a few weeks later.

In the league opener at Cappielow against Partick Thistle, Morton gained a point in a scoreless draw. Included in the Jags ranks was midfielder Benny Rooney who would have had no clue as to the huge part he was soon to play in the Greenock club's future.

In March of 1975, Sir William Lithgow stepped down as club chairman, becoming honorary president. His place was taken by Hugh Currie, representing major shareholders Scott-Lithgow and Sir William himself.

Hal Stewart, by now managing director, soon took the painful decision to sack Erik Sorensen as manager, taking over the role himself on a temporary basis. The charismatic Stewart, of course, had created a real stir in Scottish football when he signed Danish international goalkeeper Sorensen for the 1964-65 season as the start of an amazing Scandinavian invasion. Top quality Danes arrived at Cappielow, such as Kaj Johansen, Leif Nielsen, Jorn Sorensen and Preben Arentoft.

If Erik Sorensen had not enjoyed the same managerial success at Cappielow he had as a player, Hal's great days as a manager in the 60s were also behind him by now. He could do little to restore the fortunes of the Sinclair Street club.

Former Ton favourite Eric Smith could not be persuaded to return to Cappielow from his post as manager at Hamilton but by 11 October, 1975, Morton finally had a new man in place. He was Joe Gilroy, a decent centre forward with Clyde, Fulham and Dundee, who had been managing Icelandic club Valur.

Gilroy was one of a new breed of managers who seemed determined to bring a more technical, studious approach to football. Like Don Revie who was in charge of the great Leeds team including Billy Bremner, Eddie Gray, Johnny Giles, Mick Jones and Peter Lorimer, he was an avid compiler of the dossier on opponents' strengths and weaknesses, of blackboard diagrams and technicalities. He expressed a desire to allow individuals freedom to express themselves within the team structure, but his accent seemed more on the organisational side of things. He came from a PE teaching background and perhaps this had a bearing on his approach to the players.

I recall a story told to me by Ross Irvine, an enthusiastic defender, if relatively modest in ability. Gilroy had been explaining to his players with the aid of a blackboard what their various roles would be during the forthcoming Saturday match. To some it seemed more like geometry than football. According to Irvine, upon leaving the dressing room, fellow player Charlie Brown turned to him with a perplexed gaze and asked: "What am I supposed to do?"

"What you always do, Charlie," replied Irvine.

Gilroy, who combined his job at Cappielow with that of a PE teacher, was not yet in control when he watched his new charges going down 4-0 at Dumbarton. The following Saturday he took his side to Dumfries where Queen of the South, bottom of the new First Division, awaited them. A Ricky Sharp goal won the points for Morton.

Gilroy's problems, however, were highlighted the following week when second top Killie, including players of the quality of Ian Fallis, Ian McCulloch, Gordon Smith, later to become chief executive of the SFA, and a youthful Gourockian, Davie Provan, proved too strong in a 3-1 victory.

Before the match there was a minute's silence in respect of the late Bob Williamson, a former Cappielow chairman who had spent 27 years in the role.

The new league set-up had not been wholly welcomed, but it was certainly competitive. I wrote at the time: "We have reached a situation in which a club can leap from the relegation zone to a promotion challenging position with two or three good results."

Morton were gradually improving under Gilroy, whose organisational talents had come to the fore. They suffered a blow when promising winger Raymond Taylor opted to join his family in emigrating to Canada, while a shoulder injury ruled out George Anderson at centre back. Anderson had been sufficiently well thought of by Tommy Docherty for the then Scotland boss to take him on a South American tour the year prior to the 1974 World Cup. When George tackled someone, that person stayed tackled.

Anderson's absence, however, was to prove an opportunity for another bright young star in the making, Neil Orr. At the age of 16, he made his debut as a sweeper in the team which beat Airdrie 1-0 at Cappielow on 22nd November, 1975, excelling the following week at Falkirk in a 3-3 draw.

It is always risky to make predictions regarding young talent. Most fall by the wayside for a variety of reasons but Orr, whose father Tommy had played for Morton and Scotland, always looked set for a big future in the game from the earliest development of his career. The Gourock youngster had gravitated to Cappielow via Gourock Youth Club and Port Glasgow

Rovers. Orr's all-round sporting prowess was highlighted by the fact that, at 16, he was already playing off a golfing handicap of only four.

John Nelson made a comeback after a year out due to an ankle break, but Morton's problems seemed more in the scoring department, having managed just 19 goals in 17 games.

After a 3-2 defeat at Rugby Park on 27th December, in which the scoreline flattered the Greenock men, I wrote: "The sad truth is that Morton were well behind them [Kilmarnock] in the skills of the game and, on this form, there is a grave danger of the Greenock men slipping into the relative obscurity of the Second Division."

First half scorers for Killie had been Eddie Morrison, Ian Fallis and Gordon Smith, Morton replying with two goals in the last three minutes from Ian Harley and the teenage Mark McGhee.

The season was fast becoming a matter of retaining First Division status. In order to improve their chances of survival Morton moved to sign Motherwell striker John Goldthorp who had lost his place at Fir Park to the free-scoring Willie Pettigrew. It was an inspired £10,000 signing, 'Goldie' winning over the fans immediately with the only goal in his New Year's Day debut against county rivals St Mirren, following up with another priceless strike five days later in a 1-0 win at Arbroath, heading in a Charlie Brown cross. That opened up a four-point gap between themselves and second bottom Queen of the South.

In order to bring in Goldthorp, Joe Gilroy had been forced to part with midfield general Alex Reid who moved to Dundee United, veteran winger Tommy Traynor coming to Cappielow as part of the deal. Striker Ricky Sharp moved to Kilmarnock.

Meanwhile highly promising young centre half John Nelson suffered a second leg break in just over a year in a reserve match against Kilmarnock. He was destined to be freed at the end of the season and a future which had looked so bright – Celtic monitoring his development – was virtually over.

Stan Rankin, a mainstay of the Greenock central defence for a decade, received a cheque from Greenock Morton Supporters' Club as part of his benefit year. This uncompromising defender was always popular with the fans whose favoured terracing ditty was "Have a man, Stan, c'mon and have a man". Stan invariably obliged. If you can read a man by his face, Rankin had a nose which spoke volumes of his commitment. An expedition to climb his snout would almost certainly have run into severe trouble just beyond base camp. Stan was almost stupidly hard.

By the time they met Partick Thistle on 7th January, 1976, Morton were still in real relegation trouble. Injuries were piling up and they took the field at Firhill with three new signings. Eddie Morrison, at 29, joined his home-town team from Kilmarnock, where his goalscoring exploits over the seasons had made him a hero with the Ayrshire fans. Accompanying him were ex-player coach Jim Townsend and Birmingham's Scottish centre back Ricky Sbragia, both arriving on short-term deals. Sbragia was especially impressive.

In the event an ultra-defensive Morton performance was not enough to prevent a 2-0 defeat against a Thistle team again containing midfield grafter Benny Rooney.

Morton were berated by Jags boss Bertie Auld, the former Celtic Lisbon Lion, for their cautious display, but in defence of his tactics Joe Gilroy pointed to his side's lowly league position and the fact that Partick did not breach the Cappielow defences until 12 minutes from time.

By 14th January, Morton were facing a must-win match against bottom club Clyde at Shawfield Stadium. Their predicament was eased with a 2-1 win, a result which condemned the Rutherglen team to relegation. John Goldthorp and Tom McNeil supplied the goals. Goldthorp added another crucial strike in a 1-1 draw at Montrose, Eddie Morrison doing the spade work.

Relegation was finally cast aside when the Cappielow men, in front of a delighted home crowd, produced a scintillating display to defeat East Fife 3-0. I described the second half performance as one which belied their lowly league position, adding: "Two-goal hero Eddie Morrison scored his first goals since arriving from Kilmarnock and wore a grin as wide as the Great Harbour." Tom McNeil fittingly opened the scoring after a typically driving display from midfield.

Centre half George Anderson made his comeback, after a lengthy absence due to injury, in the Spring Cup tie which followed against Montrose, Goldthorp adding another two goals to bring his tally to an impressive 10 since signing from Motherwell. It was not enough to prevent a 4-2 home defeat, Eddie Morrison dropping back to a midfield role.

In the return tie, Morton gained revenge with a 4-1 win, Goldthorp and Ian Harley, the latter showing his best form of the season, each hitting a brace.

I had an interesting chat with manager Joe Gilroy on the train journey home after the match. I asked him if he had available his end-of-season free transfer list. He informed me that it was complete with the exception of one decision – whether or not to allow either Ian Harley or Mark McGhee to go. Harley had done his chances no harm with his latest display. The final choice was made after Hal Stewart asked Allan McGraw, who was working with the reserves, for his input. McGraw, the club's record goalscorer with 58 league and cup goals in season 1963-64, felt McGhee had the greater potential and told Stewart so.

McGhee stayed, going on to play for Newcastle, Aberdeen, Hamburg and Celtic, as well as his country. In the process Morton gained a then club record transfer fee from Newcastle. But, back then, it did not seem controversial at all that McGhee should be considered for release. Harley was a forward with real pace, albeit with no great sense of direction. Without wishing to be unkind, the description of a "heidless chicken" was not too far off the mark. McGhee was a youngster who also had pace and a degree of close control, but in those early days he was as likely to beat himself as any opponent. His brain was not always co-ordinated with his feet.

Youngsters Neil Orr, Mark McGhee, Charlie Brown and Barry Evans were all breaking through into the side, John McNeil also beginning to make a claim to a top team place.

Against East Stirlingshire in the Spring Cup, I wrote of Orr's performance: "He indicated his class with one particular move in which he intercepted well, carried the ball out of defence and then sent a beautifully weighted 40-yard pass to Tom McNeil on the left wing. In my admiration I found it hard to believe that here was a 16-year-old playing like a seasoned veteran."

Morton beat their great Paisley rivals, St Mirren, in the Spring Cup quarter-finals at Cappielow, Goldthorp, almost inevitably by this time, scoring, before losing 3-1 to Airdrie in the semi-final, Mark McGhee getting the consolation goal. The St Mirren manager was a certain Alex Ferguson whose principal claim to fame up to then was as a bustling centre forward with Rangers with the sharpest elbows in Scottish football. But already he was showing his managerial ability, co-ordinating a highly talented group of young players at Love Street.

Gilroy finally announced his players to be freed at the end of the season, Ian Harley being joined by the unfortunate John Nelson, Ross Irvine and youngsters George Headley, Mick Hepburn, Charlie Palmer and Gordon Parker.

But the biggest surprise came near the end of June, 1976, when the manager announced his own departure to amateur side Queen's Park. He said he was becoming increasingly concerned about the amount of time he had to devote to both Morton and his full-time job as a PE teacher at Paisley Grammar School.

He explained: "I had to get my priorities right. I found I was never seeing my children at an important stage in their growth and the demands upon my family life were very difficult."

His follow-up statement seemed contradictory as he added: "Not that I'll be putting in any less effort with Queen's Park, but I will be nearer home and will therefore cut down on travelling and have more time at the job and at home."

Years later I was to ask Allan McGraw about what seemed a backward move by Gilroy. "It did seem odd," he replied. "I don't know if it had anything to do with the decision to keep McGhee and Hal asking me about it."

In any event, Joe Gilroy wished Morton well who, by the end of the following month, had moved to acquire not just a replacement, but someone who was to become the most successful manager at the club since the inimitable Hal Stewart.

CHAPTER TWO

Benny Rooney – an inspired appointment

Former Celtic, Dundee United, St Johnstone and Partick Thistle midfielder Benny Rooney (33), who was also the Professional Footballers' Association chairman, was brought in as player-manager, saying: "I'm happy to get this chance to enter football management. My aim is to bring back some of the joy to football and produce a winning Cappielow side. I believe it is essential that players think for themselves again. The joy seems to have gone out of football."

Of Rooney, managing director Hal Stewart commented: "He is management material of the highest order."

Rooney's best days as a player were at St Johnstone in the fine side built by Willie Ormond. He played as a "worker bee" in midfield in a team which included the creative talents of such as Henry Hall, John Connolly, Jim Pearson, Gordon Whitelaw and Kenny Aird. It was the best team in Saints' history. After finishing third in the old Scottish First Division, Saints beat SV Hamburg and Vasa Budapest in the following season's UEFA Cup, Rooney captaining the side, before going out to Zeljeznicar Sarajevo. The Hamburg result was especially pleasing.

Rooney's first signing as Morton boss was to bring Jim Holmes from his old club, Partick. An average midfield player, Holmes was converted by Rooney into one of the top full backs in the country. Defensively he read the play well, while going forward his silky skills were highly effective. 'Homer' had his own soft-shoe shuffle as he skipped past opponents. He should have worn a dinner suit instead of a football strip.

Stan Rankin meanwhile moved on to St Johnstone while there came a goalkeeping crisis, Roy Baines virtually walking out on the club, saying that Morton were preventing his transfer – Celtic being specifically interested – by placing too high a price on his departure. Heaven forfend that Haldane Y. Stewart would do such as thing!

In Baines' place, Rooney brought in Jim Liddell from Hong Kong Rangers, while winger John Hotson arrived from St Johnstone. Hotson was one of those irritating players who clearly have talent, but too infrequently display it. He was a luxury Morton found themselves unable to afford for too long.

On 21st August, 1976, Morton thrashed Cowdenbeath 7-1 in a League Cup tie, young Mark McGhee, so nearly given a free transfer, grabbing a hat-trick, and the ubiquitous Jim

Townsend playing a key midfield role after returning from America. He was given a short-term contract.

The season began inauspiciously with draws against Montrose and Dundee and defeat to Queen of the South, before three successive wins over Falkirk (a), East Fife (a) and Raith Rovers at Cappielow.

The prolific John Goldthorp hit a hat-trick over Falkirk at Brockville in a 5-3 win, Mark McGhee and centre half Barry Evans also scoring, Eddie Morrison grabbed the only goal against East Fife, while Evans, Tom McNeil and Charlie Brown scored in a 3-1 win over Raith. Morton were on the move. Rooney by this time had made the decision to stop playing and concentrate fully on management.

On 29th October, the Roy Baines stand-off was finally resolved when a deal was done with Celtic. Fine goalkeeper though Baines was, it was to prove one of the best pieces of business ever done by Morton in the transfer market. After playing his first game of the season in a no-score draw against Clydebank on Wednesday 28th October, 1976, Baines went to Parkhead the next day, Morton receiving £12,000 and Andy Ritchie in return.

Tall and ponderous in gait, Ritchie was to gain a momentous place in Morton folklore. His close dribbling skills, superb passing range and ability to direct free kicks and corners with deadly precision made him an immediate favourite. He left Celtic after falling out with Jock Stein. Stein had no doubt about his talent, but he was dealing with a young player who was not of a mind to put in the kind of work-rate required at Parkhead. Ritchie knew his own ability and had his own ideas on how he wanted to play the game. There was going to be only one outcome of a fall-out with Jock Stein.

Ritchie's departure from Celtic was to signal a failing which was to haunt his career. He has since admitted to his own mistakes. Kevin Keegan, for example, with less natural talent but an abundance of application, reached the heights of his profession and reaped the rewards. Ritchie, whose footballing imagination was matched by an audacious execution, was left with little but his memories at the end of an unfulfilled career. If it was a squandering of that gift for it not to be applied at the highest levels of the game, then Morton at least were huge benefactors.

In his second appearance for Morton, Ritchie scored the only goal of the game in a derby against St Mirren at Love Street. A legend was born. He scored a second against the same opponents soon after, but this time it was Alex Ferguson's precociously talented young team which triumphed 5-1.

On 6th November at Montrose Ritchie's precise skills were headlined with a fierce 25-yard drive for the opening goal. A typical free kick over the defensive wall followed before Mark McGhee added a third goal. At Dens Park Morton drew 1-1 with Dundee and I wrote: "New signing Andy Ritchie continued to impress and I am sure he will develop into one of the personalities of the First Division. He has an abundance of talent and at times he reminds me of the Jim Baxter of old. A tall, lazy looking player, he strolls past opponents with apparent ease and hits the ball with telling accuracy."

Eddie Morrison capped a good display with a stunning volley, Dundee equalising with a penalty after Gordon Strachan had collapsed more dramatically than a Scottish bank under a

Davie Hayes challenge. By the end of the month Morton were fifth top after a 2-0 defeat of East Fife, McGhee notching a penalty and Ritchie perfectly lobbing the goalkeeper.

After an embarrassing 6-3 New Year's Day defeat at the hands of league leaders St Mirren, Morton bounced back with a 3-1 win at Montrose, the exuberant Ritchie netting a hat-trick.

A 3-2 home defeat followed against Dundee before midfield player Tommy Veitch arrived from Hartlepool, making his debut in a 2-0 win at Methil against East Fife, then Morton were bundled out of the Scottish Cup 1-0 by Ayr at a treacherously icy Cappielow. "The Cappielow club," I wrote, "who started the influx of Danish players to Scotland in the 60s, may well be the first to sign an Eskimo if matches on such surfaces are to become commonplace."

With Andy Ritchie and Mark McGhee supplying the cutting thrust up front, Morton were nevertheless moving upwards. But football isn't all about scoring goals. "George Anderson has been superb in the centre of the defence with young Neil Orr playing like a veteran alongside him," I penned.

At full back, Davie Hayes and Jim Holmes were combining defensive duties with a productive ability to overlap down the wing. Hayes bludgeoned onwards with a claymore while Holmes' incursions were more the subtle manoeuvrings of an expert fencer.

McGhee, at 19, had become one of the division's most dangerous strikers – shedding much of the irritating inconsistencies of the past season – while Ritchie was a breath of fresh air, not just for Morton but Scottish football as a whole.

League leaders St Mirren suffered their first defeat in 29 games at Cappielow on 12th March, 1977, going down 3-0 to goals by Andy Ritchie, John Goldthorp and Charlie Brown. Ritchie was in sparkling form and his winner at Brockville against Falkirk took Morton into third top spot. A second goal against the same opponents within eight days saw Morton go 11 games undefeated.

By this time Roddie Hutchison had arrived from Pollok Juniors to add to Rooney's squad. A tall, robust forward or midfield player given to seemingly contradictory moments of delicacy, he became something of a cult hero at Cappielow. Moments of surprising skill collided with others of extreme frustration. He could be revered and berated by the fans in the same 90 minutes. He lacked nothing in commitment, however, and was fearless; sometimes a bit daft. He would invariably run about until his face glowed like a wood-burning stove.

In a 3-2 Ton win at Clydebank, for whom Davie Cooper was a star opponent, a double by Mark McGhee and a goal by Ritchie extinguished the home challenge. In the second instalment of a double header, this time at Cappielow, the Bankies gained a 2-2 draw.

Morton were irrepressible and crushed Queen of the South 4-0 at Dumfries. Hayes and Holmes were stars at full back, especially the quicksilver Holmes who created havoc down the left flank. A Ritchie hat-trick took him to 19 goals in 25 games. John Goldthorp, despite missing many games through injury, added a fourth to carry him to 11 for the season. With McGhee on 18, Morton were anointed up front.

Ritchie (2) and McGhee were again on target as Queens were beaten for a second time near the end of April at Cappielow, the fans chanting for Ritchie and manager Rooney at the end of play.

By the time the league season ended with a victory at Stark's Park against Raith Rovers,

Morton had gone 16 games unbeaten to finish fourth in the league, Ritchie ending up with 22 goals and McGhee 20.

Tommy Veitch scored his first goal for the club in a 1-0 first leg Renfrewshire Cup Final win against St Mirren, who nevertheless triumphed 5-3 on aggregate after the Love Street leg.

Andy Ritchie was voted Player-of-the-Year by the fans to become the second recipient of the Sir William Lithgow Trophy but, more importantly, Morton had shown their intent on winning their way into the top flight of Scottish football next time round.

During the close season there were enquiries from Rotherham and St Mirren regarding Andy Ritchie and Mark McGhee respectively, neither coming to anything. The club then signed 16-year-old Jim Tolmie from Auchengill Boys' Club.

The 1977-78 league season began on 13th August and Morton quickly got into their stride, beating Kilmarnock 3-0 at Rugby Park, the double act of Ritchie and McGhee (2) again producing the goods. The following week Goldthorp (2), Ritchie, with a penalty, and McGhee scored in a home 4-2 win over Alloa, McGhee emerging as star man.

Noting the success Alex Ferguson was enjoying at St Mirren, now playing in the Scottish Premier League, I wrote: "At Love Street, St Mirren manager Alex Ferguson has shown what can be achieved from virtually nothing, and I have a feeling that Benny Rooney can do the same with Morton."

Birmingham City then began to show an interest in centre half George Anderson who had been outstanding in a 3-2 Morton win over Falkirk in the League Cup. However, an agreed deal for the 24-year-old, with Ricky Sbragia scheduled to switch from Birmingham to Cappielow, was shelved after City's Scottish manager Willie Bell was sacked. On such precarious moments do footballers' fortunes depend. Anderson, often sidelined by injury, never was to get the move his ability and professionalism merited. At times both Rangers and Celtic had shown interest.

Meanwhile, Mark McGhee was turning the heads of other clubs as he and Ritchie continued their scoring exploits. Against Hamilton at Cappielow he gave a virtuoso display, netting all four home goals. It was a team performance which drew praise from Benny Rooney. "If we keep going like that it is hard to see anyone beating us," he enthused. It was also hard to see Morton holding onto McGhee who was growing in stature with every game. While Ritchie may have been blessed with a greater depth of natural talent, McGhee had pace, decent close control and a willingness to work prodigiously at his game. The latter attribute was making him the more saleable asset.

In October, Benny Rooney was voted McKinlay's Football Personality of the Month. It was a tribute to his team being top of the First Division without losing a game. Mark McGhee, Scotland's top scorer with 12 goals, was accorded an honourable mention.

On a Wednesday night in Edinburgh a few days later, however, Morton were well beaten in a League Cup tie by league rivals Hearts, 3-0 at Tynecastle, but on the following Saturday at Cappielow they gained revenge by defeating the same opponents 5-3 in a league thriller at Cappielow. This result prompted Benny Rooney to say: "It [the title] is there for us now. The players believe in themselves. They can make it happen."

Eamonn Lynch and Tom McNeil had excellent games in midfield and at full back respectively, Ritchie was at his supreme best while the goals came from John Goldthorp (2), Mark McGhee (2) and Roddie Hutchison.

All good things come to an end, and Morton's amazing unbeaten run stretching back to January was halted when Queen of the South produced a shock 1-0 home loss. Kilmarnock then delivered a second successive home defeat, by 2-0. The saving grace for Morton was that their nearest rivals also faltered, leaving the Cappielow club four points clear at the top.

In the second leg of the League Cup tie against Hearts, Morton won 2-0, nevertheless going out 3-2 on aggregate. Predictably, McGhee and Ritchie were on the scoresheet, while young Neil Orr was outstanding at sweeper.

Goalkeeper Denis Conaghan was in fine form in a 3-1 win at Alloa, but Morton received a blast from Benny Rooney after an insipid draw at Montrose. If the wheels hadn't come off the motor, one or two of the hubcaps were rattling down the street.

Dundee then made a significant move in the transfer market to enhance their promotion chances, adding Aberdeen pair Jocky Scott and Jim Shirra, and Eric Schaedler from Hibs, to their squad. Ton's other two rivals, Hearts and Dumbarton, were on the lookout for players too.

A draw at Tynecastle, followed by a home defeat to Arbroath, served as a reminder to Morton that they too did not have the strength in depth they might have desired. When Dundee beat them 3-0 at Dens Park, the Dark Blues had gone three points ahead of Morton who, nevertheless, had two games in hand.

Four days later, on 30 December, Morton fans were shocked when the Greenock Telegraph broke the news that star striker Mark McGhee was off to Newcastle for a club record fee of £150,000. Benny Rooney commented: "It was an offer we could not refuse. As I have said all along, I would not sell players unless the offer fell into this category. At the same time it means that there is now money available to me to strengthen the team."

McGhee, who was a trainee architect as a part-time player, would be turning full-time with the Magpies. His 18 goals in 24 games for Morton that season, following upon his 20 goals of the previous term, had awakened interest among several of the bigger battalions.

With Morton having secured just seven points from nine matches, it was a crucial time for the club. Already the cynics were muttering that Morton didn't really want promotion. The reply came in the best possible fashion, with a 4-1 win at Dumbarton, Ritchie returning to his imperious best, masterminding a display in which John Goldthorp and Charlie Brown added to the master's own two goals.

A 5-0 thumping of Alloa followed at Recreation Park, on a day when Hearts and Dundee drew, to answer the doubters as to Morton's title credentials, Ritchie again scoring twice. Goldthorp, Brown and Billy Thomas, the latter promoted from the reserves, added the other strikes.

John Goldthorp, whose contribution to Morton can not be underestimated during their push to the Premier League, weighed in with both goals in a win over Stirling and the Ton were back on an even keel.

Benny Rooney was not going to be rushed into spending the McGhee money, saying: "What I want are players who can hold their own in the Premier League if we get there." Morton were now on the same 36-point mark as Dundee and two ahead of Hearts, having two games in hand over the Dens men and one over Hearts.

A Ritchie strike overcame Albion Rovers in the Scottish Cup third round and honour came to the club when Neil Orr was selected for the Scotland under-21 side to meet Wales in Chester.

John McNeil was now coming more into the frame at Cappielow and starred in a Scottish Cup 3-0 win over Meadowbank which was to set up a glamorous quarter-final tie against Aberdeen. Ritchie (2) and Thomas were the scorers.

Morton finally splashed out some cash on bringing Greenockian Jimmy Miller from Motherwell for £10,000. Rooney said of the midfield man: "Jimmy is aggressive. He's got tons of energy, is very mobile and always makes himself available for a pass." Miller was prominent in a 2-0 win over Kilmarnock at Cappielow, local boys George Anderson and John McNeil each scoring goals made by the peerless Ritchie.

Key games were coming thick and fast, Morton going down 1-0 to Hearts at Cappielow in the league before being knocked out of the cup by Aberdeen in front of a home crowd of 10,500 after a 2-2 draw at Pittodrie. The score was 2-1 to the Dons, John McNeil netting with a 20-yard drive.

Soon after, Bobby Russell was added to the squad, the former Alloa striker netting on his debut against Queen of the South at Dumfries in a 3-2 win in which Goldthorp scored twice with trademark headers. Morton were setting themselves up for the vital run-in for a place at Scottish football's pinnacle.

There was all to play for and very little to choose between the Greenock men and their principal rivals, city clubs Dundee and Hearts. What Morton had was an irrepressible team spirit, exemplified by skipper Davie Hayes, some very good players, and one, Andy Ritchie, capable of uniquely bravura moments of quality.

By the time Morton were due to meet St Johnstone at Cappielow in a midweek match on 5th April, Dundee were leading the First Division table with 50 points from 34 games, one ahead of Hearts who had also played 34 games, and five ahead of Morton who had three games in hand. That night at Cappielow Morton rose to the occasion, beating the Perth Saints 4-1 with goals by Ritchie, Goldthorp and, unusually, two by centre half George Anderson who was enjoying an outstanding season.

On the Saturday they travelled to Dens Park and fought out an excellent 1-1 draw, Ritchie once again obliging with a crucial goal. Jimmy Miller had been a key man in midfield, winning the ball and disrupting the Dark Blues' supply lines. Alongside him Charlie Brown returned to the side as a more creative force. Of a player who tended to blow hot and cold, but with an indisputable talent, manager Rooney commented: "Charlie would always be in the team if his attitude was right. For a couple of games I had kept him out. Apart from anything else, he wasn't doing himself justice."

As the three-team title race continued, Morton enjoyed a superb night on Wednesday 12th

April when they crushed East Fife 5-0 at Cappielow while Dundee lost at Dumbarton. Andy Ritchie gave an exhibition of his full repertoire of skills, 'Beastie' Russell grabbing a hat-trick, Morris scoring an own goal and Charlie Brown netting the remaining goal. It was one of those nights which proved to be a defining moment.

Three days later Hamilton were dispatched 3-0 at Cappielow, Anderson, Goldthorp and Russell scoring, Goldthorp gaining his manager's praise. "He's had a really good season," said Rooney of the striker who had tended to play in the shadow of first McGhee then Ritchie, but whose goals had been crucial to Morton's challenge.

After a Bobby Russell goal was all that separated St Johnstone and Morton in Perth, the Greenock men had fought their way to the top of the table, ahead of Hearts on goal difference. They now needed just four points from three games to gain promotion. I asked Rooney about the side's tremendous spirit in these last few fixtures. He said: "The main thing is to get the players playing for you and, just as importantly, for themselves. They have to be made aware of their full potential and realise that they will benefit from making the most of what skills they have."

Rooney was proving that he was a very fine manager. Not only did he get the best out of his players, he had a knack for bringing the right ones to the club in the first place. At the time I wrote: "He has the respect of his players and, although he can be firm when he has to be, he is never slow to give credit."

Club secretary Tom Robertson, with a key knowledge of the administrative side of football, was made a director of the club on the same weekend that Morton beat Stirling Albion 2-1 at Annfield, John Goldthorp and Billy Thomas scoring. Skipper Davie Hayes was in fine form, as was George Anderson, while left back Jim Holmes was man-of-the-match.

Morton's resolution was holding firm. With two games to go they led the table on goal difference from Hearts, Dundee being a point behind. They also, crucially, had a game in hand over their rivals.

On Wednesday 26th April, 1978, they hosted Airdrie at Cappielow. Two points from a win would ensure promotion from the 14-club First Division to the top-10 elite of Scottish football. It would almost certainly suffice for the title too, such was the superiority of their goal difference over Hearts. Rooney summed up the mood in the home camp when he said: "If we win tonight it will be the perfect end to a long season. The national press have been plugging Hearts and Dundee all season."

With every team meeting each other three times, the omens favoured a Morton side who already had won twice against the Broomfield club. Big games bring big tensions, however, and if the 8,000 crowd was expectant there was also an undeniable frisson of nerves as the match began.

This spread to the players. No one seemed to want to hold the ball and, just before half-time, uncertainty and hesitancy were punished in the home rearguard, Joe Cairney shooting past Conaghan in the Morton goal to send a collective shudder through the Cappielow support. Was triumph to be wrenched from Morton's grasp at the 11th hour?

Six minutes after the interval the hosts gave their reply. Fittingly, skipper Davie Hayes began the move from right back, rampaging down the wing before slipping a pass to Tommy Veitch in front of him and to his right. Veitch crossed and midfielder Jimmy Miller, whose energy and vitality had carried him forward into the box, rose to nod down. The ball fell perfectly into the path of 'Hannibal' Hayes, who had continued his run, and he steered a shot past Poulton for the equaliser. Signal pandemonium on the terracings.

For all that Morton now had territorial advantage, and despite their pressure, the minutes began to tick by. Nerves were once more stretched to breaking point when, with six minutes remaining, reward for an entire season's unremitting effort was finally forthcoming.

Bobby Russell set off on a run which few had attempted all night, forcing Airdrie to backtrack, before sending a perfect pass on to John Goldthorp. There was a suspicion of offside, but the flag stayed down and 'Goldie' slotted the ball into the net. Cue the type of spontaneous glee among the home support which somehow permits gruff, grown men from the west of Scotland, not normally given to extravagant displays of emotion, to embrace each other and generally behave like daft wee laddies. To the ecstasy and excitement was added relief when the issue was decided minutes later, Andy Ritchie converting a penalty right at the death. All the night's tension was released as the friendliest pitch invasion greeted the final whistle.

"What can you say?" asked an emotional Morton boss Rooney as the fans chanted his name in the aftermath. "It was wonderful; it all came right in the end."

He then broke off to hug managing director Hal Stewart as the champagne corks orbited around the dressing room area like miniature mortar bombs. It was a celebration reminiscent of Stewart's great days of the 60s.

Provost Freddie Fletcher commented: "I almost lost my voice. I would like to congratulate Hugh Currie [Morton chairman] and his board of directors, Benny Rooney and his backroom boys and, of course, the players. I will be proposing a civic reception." What opposition politician was going to be brave enough to oppose that?

On the Saturday at Cappielow, there was some anti-climax as Dundee, for so long promotion contenders, beat Morton 3-2. It wasn't enough for the Dens men to pip Hearts to second place and Morton, superior in goal difference to the Edinburgh club, were officially champions. Defeat by the Dark Blues became an irrelevance as the Morton fans applauded their heroes. The players were rewarded with a holiday to Estoril in Portugal and a bonus of £1,000 a man, a not inconsiderable sum in these days for part-time players.

In a quieter moment of reflection I was to write: "While the players who took Morton to the top 10 deserve every plaudit heaped upon them over the past couple of days, there seems little doubt that the team will be strengthened." The most pressing need appeared to be in midfield where Morton, for all their work-rate, looked short of Premier League quality.

Benny Rooney's record in the transfer market had been impressive to say the least, Conaghan, Russell, Miller, Veitch, Lynch, Hutchison and, of course, Ritchie all playing important parts in the promotion battle. I once asked the Ton boss what single attribute was most important to management. His reply was "to bring the right players to the club." His record right up until he left Morton was almost impeccable in that regard given the resources with which he had to operate.

Morton released six players, only goalkeeper Jim Liddell having regular first team experience and, upon their return from Portugal, they began to lay their plans for the big test ahead in the top 10.

Twenty-one-year-old Jim Rooney, an impressive midfield player with Queen's Park, was acquired while Benny Rooney then moved to bring Queen of the South's part-time manager, Mike Jackson, to Cappielow as his full-time assistant. They had been players together at Celtic in 1960.

George Anderson was a worthy winner of the Sir William Lithgow Player of the Year Trophy in a season in which he not only defended with his customary resolution and skill, but scored a handful of key goals, nine to be precise.

Changes were taking place at other clubs too, the Old Firm of Rangers and Celtic bringing in former players John Greig and Billy McNeill as managers, while Alex Ferguson left St Mirren to replace McNeill at Aberdeen.

CHAPTER THREE

Up among the big boys

Benny Rooney and Mike Jackson were to form a profitable partnership. Both knew their football. Rooney appeared cast in the role of the enforcer; the disciplinarian. Jackson was the free dispenser of the witty one-liner, the sunny side of the pairing, though he was quite capable of giving a passable imitation of volcanic eruption.

He told the story of how in one pre-season friendly against Watford he and Rooney watched Andy Ritchie attempt a shot from a free kick fully 35 yards into a breeze. "The stupid big bastard's not going to shoot from there," he recalled his touchline conversation with Rooney, before he and the manager broke off in mid-sentence to throw their arms in the air and shout "Goal!"

Together Rooney and Jackson gelled and began to assemble a new cast for the Cappielow stage. It was to herald the start of one of the best spells in the club's history, arguably since the late 40s, and certainly since the record-breaking Second Division-winning side of 1963-64 had carried Morton into the top league and the start of an influx of Danish stars.

It seems unthinkable now, but Morton made the decision, based on their finances, to continue in the Premier League as a part-time team. Rooney knew they needed to strengthen and they moved to bring ex-Rangers striker Ally Scott from Hibs. Good in the air, hard-working and enthusiastic, Scott did a tremendous amount of selfless running for the team. Follicly challenged in the days when it was not yet fashionable, he became dubbed the 'bald eagle' by the fans.

Bobby Thomson followed soon after in a deal in which Morton paid St Johnstone £30,000 plus utility player Tom McNeil. This was to be a key signing, Thomson bringing height, aggression and pace to the midfield. He was also a goalscorer. Since Mark McGhee's departure, Rooney had now brought in five players – Bobby 'Beastie' Russell, Jimmy 'Scooter' Miller, Jim 'Casper' Rooney, Ally Scott and Bobby Thomson. Writing at the time, I commented: "In two short seasons, he [Rooney] has changed the face of football at Greenock and the team which lines up at the start of this coming season will be very much his own. Conaghan, Holmes, Miller, Rooney, Thomson, Russell, Scott, Ritchie and a young Tolmie are all his signings."

On the way out of Cappielow after a very productive two-and-a-half years was 29-year-old striker John Goldthorp, switching to Airdrie for a fee reported to be £7,000. Meanwhile, goalkeeper Jim Liddell, given a free transfer to go to Hong Kong Rangers, found the move collapsing and re-signed at Cappielow.

Morton were building a side with a very healthy mixture of talented youth and experience, but there was a shock in store for the fans when Andy Ritchie, now of heroic status, revealed through the Telegraph on 25th July, 1978, that he wanted a transfer. Top scorer the previous season with 25 league and cup goals, he was not unaware of his growing reputation and he commented to me that he wanted full-time football and the enhanced wages that went with it. Manager Benny Rooney stated: "I'm obviously very disappointed with this move as there is no way I want the team to be affected. The player wants more money and full-time football and his request will have to be discussed at the next board meeting." As things transpired there were no concrete moves for Ritchie and Morton managed to meet the player's demands by appointing him as the club's lottery agent, a neat way of giving him the extra cash he felt his skills merited.

Watford, key financial contributor Elton John and all, were trounced 5-1 in a pre-season warm-up at Cappielow, Bobby Thomson enjoying an impressive debut, scoring with literally his first touch of the ball for the club when he headed home a Hayes cross in the opening minute. Ally Scott also netted on his debut, while Ritchie smashed home that wonderful free kick from fully 35 yards, as earlier described by Mike Jackson. Rocket Man! … as Elton John might have said. Russell and McNeil added further goals.

Meadowbank were crushed 6-1 in another friendly before Morton beat Raith Rovers 2-1 at Stark's Park in their first competitive outing, the first leg of the Anglo-Scottish Cup, Ritchie's 20-yard drive and a strike by Jim Rooney overcoming the Kirkcaldy men. For the visitors, Jim Holmes was the star man with a polished display. The return leg provided a 4-1 Ton win at Cappielow, Ritchie, Russell, Rooney and Scott scoring, the former with a rare headed goal. For such a big and skilful player, Ritchie's ability in the air was akin to a prosperous, uncoordinated lassie's attempt to jump over a pencil while carrying a haversack of ball bearings. On this occasion he stooped to head home.

It was with eager anticipation, therefore, that the club's supporters looked forward to their first ever Premier match in the fourth season of the new league, at home to the might of Celtic on 12th August, 1978.

A crowd of 16,500 watched as Morton were overcome 2-1. There was some consolation as Andy Ritchie reduced a two-goal deficit with a perfect strike, controlling a Hayes cross with a sublime first touch before hammering a shot on the volley past Peter Latchford. If it was not enough to give the hosts a point, it at least silenced the Celtic fans' taunts of "Ritchie's a reject".

The following week Morton were outplayed at Pittodrie as Aberdeen, under new boss Alex Ferguson, won 3-1. The home heroes were Inverclyde duo Joe Harper, with a hat-trick, and midfield general John McMaster whose sophisticated left foot continually probed and dissected to telling effect. Harper, of course, had begun his senior career at Cappielow, enjoying a second spell there after a move to Huddersfield. Neil Orr was Morton's best player, with goalkeeper Denis Conaghan not far behind, while Ritchie slid a shot past Jim Leighton after slipping out of Willie Miller's back pocket.

There was some concern when a very talented St Mirren side with Iain Munro, Tony Fitzpatrick, Billy Stark, Frank McGarvey, Jackie Copland and Lex Richardson in their ranks, made it three consecutive defeats with a 3-1 derby win in Greenock, Ritchie by now almost inevitably scoring for the home side. Manager Rooney may have been disappointed, but he was not dismayed and said: "We're playing well and the boys are giving me everything they've got. I couldn't ask any more of them."

The following Wednesday night, Morton's fortunes at last turned when they beat Hearts 3-1 at Tynecastle in the League Cup, Ritchie maintaining his goal a game record with a penalty, Scott and McNeil adding the others. In the return on the Saturday they completed the job with a 4-1 win, Russell (2), Ritchie and Anderson netting to give them a 7-2 aggregate triumph.

Morton were finding their feet and on the following Saturday they beat Scotland's UEFA Cup representatives, Dundee United, 2-1 at Tannadice minus injured pair Andy Ritchie and George Anderson. Bobby Russell and Jim Rooney, with a penalty, were on the mark.

Skipper Davie Hayes was outstanding in a 3-0 victory over Oldham at Cappielow in the Anglo-Scottish Cup, Scott with a double and Thomson scoring.

Thomson netted again in a 1-1 home league draw with Hearts, Morton fielding new signing Billy McLaren from Queen of the South. Football teams comprise many elements, among them finesse, pace and hard work. McLaren provided calculated aggression. Off the field he was a quiet, pleasant and intelligent personality. On it he was fearsome. Alex McLeish was to tell a story of how after one Morton-Aberdeen clash in which the youthful Alex, then playing in midfield, had barged McLaren off the ball, the latter had approached him at the final whistle. McLeish was apprehensive, only to discover that a softly spoken McLaren had merely come over to introduce himself as a distant relative.

A creditable 2-2 draw with Rangers at Cappielow bolstered Morton's growing confidence, goals by Ritchie and Scott sandwiching strikes by the two Dereks, Parlane and Johnstone. Jimmy Miller fought valiantly in the midfield, outshining Ibrox counterpart Alex MacDonald.

Emerging pride was dealt a severe blow, however, when an abject display saw Morton tumble out of the Anglo-Scottish Cup, Oldham gaining revenge in the second leg of the tie with a 4-0 win to edge through 4-3 on aggregate. "We let the fans down," said Benny Rooney. "It was a disaster. We just didn't play at all."

Morton grabbed a thoroughly deserved point at Easter Road against an in-form Hibs, only to lose the first leg of a League Cup tie at Rugby Park against First Division Kilmarnock by 2-0. A 1-0 league win followed at Firhill before Morton gained revenge over Killie with a 5-2 victory before an enthralled Cappielow crowd of almost 5,000.

Changes were continuing in the squad, Charlie Brown's transfer request being accepted. Brown joined fellow midfielders Tommy Veitch and Eammon Lynch on the available list. Schoolboy international Brown (22) had made a name for himself when he played as a 15-year-old against Celtic in a 1-0 League Cup section tie win at Parkhead. But his talent was considered too fluctuating in its appliance. Veitch and Lynch had been valuable contributors at various times, but the arrival of Jim Rooney and Bobby Thomson had relegated their roles at the club to bit-part players.

Morton then welcomed New York Cosmos pair Dave Brcic (pronounced Birsik) and Ron Atanasio on a loan arrangement until the start of the American soccer season. Atanasio, a frail winger, was found wanting and soon returned to America, but goalkeeper Brcic quickly became a favourite of the fans.

Meanwhile Neil Orr and Bobby Thomson were selected by Scotland boss Jock Stein for the Scottish League squad to meet Ireland.

Orr gave an outstanding display in a 0-0 draw at Parkhead against Celtic, who included fellow Gourockian Davie Provan in their ranks.

Orr was to play a key role in Scotland under-21s' 5-1 destruction of Norway's young side, before the Greenock team proved their top league status yet again with a 2-1 win over Fergie's Dons at Cappielow. The unique Ritchie propelled home a wonderful strike from an acute angle, Jim Leighton only managing to help the ball on its way into the net, before Bobby Russell provided the winner with a headed touch to Ritchie's 40-yard free kick. Ritchie chirpily described his own goal as 'a topper'. The game, before a crowd of 6,650, marked the entrance, as a sub, of 17-year-old Jim Tolmie into the top team environment.

Bobby Thomson then put in a decent performance in a 1-1 draw between the Scottish and Irish Leagues, Neil Orr being on the bench as Morton's progress began to be recognised.

CHAPTER FOUR

The genius of Ritchie

Morton's growing reputation was enhanced against league leaders Dundee United who succumbed 3-1 at Cappielow. Ritchie's genius was again to the fore. He scored all three goals, prompting his picture to appear in the Greenock Telegraph with the match ball in hand, on top of which was perched Hal Stewart's trademark Tweed Trilby hat.

At the time I wrote: "Exaggeration and cliché are too often used to describe the display of our professional footballers each week, but on Saturday at Cappielow Morton's Andy Ritchie gave a genuinely remarkable performance worthy of superlative.

"In an age when workrate and the ability to run oneself into a lather are venerated, it is refreshing to see natural talent flourish so profusely." When Ritchie was in the mood it all looked so irritatingly easy for him. After the match, United boss Jim McLean, rarely given to rash bouts of complimentary remarks, said: "You never like to get beaten, but when you lose to class like Ritchie's it makes it that bit easier to take."

Ritchie's first strike was a powerful, swerving drive from the right wing which flew into the far corner of the net. He was later to admit that it might well have been intended as a cross. A penalty provided the second goal, while the third was a piece of pure genius.

United, at 2-0 down, had switched centre half Paul Hegarty up front where he had begun his career, moved Dave Narey from his then midfield position back to defence, and brought on Graham Honeyman in midfield. They began to take control, moving the ball sweetly from man to man in their characteristic style, an Addison goal being their reward. Neil Orr cleared off the line from Paul Sturrock as the pressure mounted.

Then Ritchie put a serious spoke in the wheel of their comeback; not so much a spoke as a conductor's baton. Collecting a long ball from defence on his left thigh, he turned deftly in the same movement to avoid Narey's challenge, before lobbing perfectly with his right foot over United goalkeeper Hamish McAlpine who had come off his line, no doubt anticipating a passback from Narey. The strike was from just inside the centre circle in the United half. It is the only time in my press career that I can recall the entire assembly of normally cynical scribblers rising to a man to applaud. Ritchie's own comment on the goal was typical. "Aye," he quipped with that gallus air that defined his joy at the spectacular, "you don't get many of these in a half dozen."

The late Ian 'Dan' Archer, then of the Glasgow Herald, and a marvellously descriptive writer, was later to depict Ritchie's wizardry with the ball as being akin to him possessing one of those old-fashioned children's toy rifles which could shoot round corners. Archer adored coming to Cappielow, for he was a devoted enthusiast of the artistic in football. The top football writer in the country at the time, he occasionally forsook the match of the day on a given Saturday, usually involving one of the Old Firm, to come to Cappielow. He loved the traditional old ground with its backdrop of the shipyards and its warm hospitality. Archer once told me I was the luckiest football writer of the time in being able regularly to watch Andy Ritchie.

The irony, however, of so many supremely gifted footballers is that where they find the extraordinary to be a matter of course, it is the mundane, if exhausting, aspects of the game which they are so often reluctant to embrace. I'm not sure if it is arrogance, or simply that a footballing genius can't see the point of expending energy on the commonplace. Just a canter or two, not even a gallop, and Andy would have adorned much greater stages than Cappielow. As Jim McLean said when I asked him if he would have Ritchie in his own multi-talented squad: "Oh aye, I'd have him no problem, but I wouldn't pay money for him." By that McLean meant any considerable sum of sponduliks.

It was a telling, prophetic remark. Ritchie's unwillingness to put in the hard graft alongside his undoubted genius was to prove fatal to any ambition he might have had of playing at the highest levels. On one notable occasion Arsenal's Frank McLintock and Oldham Athletic's Jimmy Frizzell came to Cappielow to cast their expert eyes over the big fellow. He impressed as usual with his skill but McLintock, while readily admitting to Morton reserve manager Allan McGraw that Ritchie was blessed with ability, said: "He wouldn't do for us. He does no running at all."

Relating the instance years later, McGraw told me: "I said to Andy 'they don't want you to be a workhorse, they just want you to do some running', but Andy just shrugged and said: 'Ach, that's just me.' It was frustrating but you couldn't change him."

McGraw related one instance in a game at Cappielow which summed up the exasperation Ritchie could engender. He said: "Andy had the ball on the edge of the opposition penalty area. He tried to sell a dummy to a defender, but the boy was too stupid to take it and the ball broke off him and he ran on to it. Instead of tracking back, Andy shouted at Jimmy Miller "get him" and off Jimmy went to win the ball back. I said to Andy after the game: 'If that had been me [instead of Miller] I'd have belted you one', but that was just Andy for you."

How frustrating it is that the most sublimely gifted so frequently fall short. How often do lesser talents achieve so much more for themselves simply through a willingness to work harder? Anyone can perspire; few can inspire. Just a touch more perspiration and Andy could have played for anyone.

For all that, I was privileged to have seen Ritchie in his prime. He brought such joy to the game. His best moments were truly great; priceless in fact. When you compare the clamour which has accompanied David Beckham over the years, you can only imagine what homage might have been paid to Ritchie's superior ability. Where Beckham would produce moments of brilliance at free kicks and with his crossing, Ritchie did it astonishingly regularly, and in a variety of ways. Throw in his excellent close control, superb range of passing and ferocious shots to produce goals from open play and it seems criminal now that he did not shine at the top levels of football. We are all flawed to varying degrees and perhaps it is just that the geniuses' defects are highlighted so much more by the very brilliance of their talent. We should enjoy the great moments when they occur, and maybe that is enough.

Ritchie was a genuine character too. I recall one time at Cappielow as he lingered out on the left wing, no doubt trying to catch his breath, him leaning over the perimeter wall on the Cowshed side of the ground to take a drag from a spectator's cigarette. On another occasion, before an important SPL match, I was chatting to manager Benny Rooney outside the home dressing room. Andy ambled past …. the amble, after all, was his forté …. and Rooney broke off our conversation to ask: "Andy have you seen Archie (a helper behind the scenes at Cappielow)? I want him to do a wee job in the dressing room for me this afternoon."

"Hivnae seen him," came the reply, "but don't worry, I'll do it for you … I won't be doing anything else this afternoon anyway."

As Ritchie strolled on, Rooney turned to me with a shake of his head and said: "The trouble is, the big bugger means it."

On another occasion as Ritchie was coming off the pitch having been subbed, the sweat lashing from him, Morton assistant Mike Jackson said to him: "Christ, Andy, you must have been working hard today."

"Naw," replied Ritchie, "I fell in a puddle."

Always there was that lack of consistent application, something in which he almost seemed to revel. Ritchie was, and still is, a lovely big man, but he enjoyed being a rebel – or perhaps just being himself – and he wasn't going to change for anyone. In the end it cost him the career he ought to have enjoyed.

Morton's impact on the SPL was drawing admiring glances also towards their manager and Benny Rooney issued a denial that Partick Thistle were seeking him as a possible replacement for Bertie Auld who was thought to be on the move.

On 16th December at Fir Park, Dave Brcic made an impressive debut in goal in a 1-1 draw, following up with another top display in a 1-0 home win against Celtic, Ritchie netting a penalty against his old club. Morton had proved they could live in any company in Scotland, made all the more meritorious in that they were a part-time club.

Ritchie and Morton were to become the bane of Alex Ferguson's life and also a considerable thorn in the flesh of Jim McLean. These two superb managers were to form a challenge to the Old Firm of Rangers and Celtic at Aberdeen and Dundee United respectively which made the Scottish Premier League dangerously competitive for all others. For that reason it was an exciting, and highly demanding, time in Scottish football. Both the "New Firm", especially the Dons, were to win titles and trophies with such regularity as to shatter the Old Firm monopoly.

When the truly great Scottish managers are mentioned, the elite invariably includes Jock Stein, Alex Ferguson, Matt Busby and Bill Shankly. On his 25th anniversary with Manchester

United in 2011 it was generally conceded that Ferguson, now Sir Alex, had established himself as probably the best ever on the planet. Other Scots, such as Scott Symon, Bill Struth, Eddie Turnbull, George Graham and Walter Smith also rate a mention in the pantheon of British greats, but no one should forget the contribution of Jim McLean. He always had a reputation as a dour, often irascible, character – with good reason – but his input to Scottish football has been remarkable. I would argue that what he accomplished with Dundee United is as good as anything any manager has ever achieved.

I worked in Dundee, with D.C. Thomson & Company from 1970-74. In that time Dundee United – for whom Walter Smith was a journeyman defender/midfielder – were still the Cinderellas of football in the city of jute, jam and journalism. They attracted crowds of around two to three thousand, while rivals Dundee were a considerably bigger club with real history, having reached the semi-final of the European Cup after winning the old Scottish First Division in 1962.

McLean was to take United to an SPL title, two League Cups and regular successful forays into Europe, including one UEFA final and a European Cup semi-final; this with a club who had just avoided relegation – on goal difference – in the very same season as Morton were to win promotion to the SPL. On the back of these successes the club also built an impressive new stadium. What 'wee Jim' accomplished will, simply, never be repeated again at a club of such modest background and support. It is right up there with the greatest achievements at club level in the British game.

The winter of 1978-79 was severe and Morton's first game of the New Year was played on 20th January when Rangers beat them 2-0 at Cappielow.

American goalkeeper Dave Brcic was voted McKinlay's Whisky Distillers' Player of the Month as the issue of summer football reared its head. Ah yes, even then it was a major talking point. At a meeting of the 38 league clubs on 15 February, 1979, the decision was taken not to have a winter shutdown. Some things never change.

At a frozen Cappielow on 17 February Morton and Partick slid to a 2-2 draw, literally, in their flat-soled boots. It was the sort of surface that would not be tolerated for a game nowadays.

Brcic departed for America, his loan period expiring, and was to tell the Greenock Telegraph: "I've thoroughly enjoyed my stay here. Football-wise it was a great experience to play in a country such as Scotland where soccer attracts so much interest." He had proved himself to be a class act. Had he stayed longer I believe he would have been recognised as the best Morton goalkeeper since Danes Erik Sorensen and Leif Nielsen. I still think Nielsen was one of the best goalkeepers I have ever seen, certainly the best I ever saw playing for Morton.

In a third round Scottish Cup replay at Muirton Park, Morton overcame St Johnstone 4-2, a hat-trick by the maestro Ritchie and a goal by that most honest of professionals, Ally Scott, proving too much for the Saints to overcome. In the fourth round against Hearts, after a 1-1 draw at Cappielow in which Roddie Hutchison and Bobby Thomson were sent off, Hearts' Drew Busby scored the only goal of the replay at Tynecastle.

March heralded the start of better weather and a key signing for Morton. On the ninth of the month the club announced to the Telegraph that goalkeeper Roy Baines would be returning to Cappielow. After a spell in Celtic's top side, he had been unable to oust fellow Englishman Peter Latchford from the number one position. Morton paid £10,000 for Baines' return, £2,000 less than they had received for him from the Parkhead club in addition to the transfer of Andy Ritchie to Greenock. The club will never do better business than that.

Dundee United crushed Morton 4-1 in Baines' first game, at Tannadice, only for Morton to administer a 6-0 whacking of Motherwell the following Wednesday. The star of that trouncing was teenager Jim Tolmie, who set up the first two goals, scored by Bobby Thomson, then added two of his own, Ritchie and Russell completing the scoring. Tolmie's touch in supplying the passes for 'Tommo' and his lob for his first goal showed that he was just a bit special. He was making his mark.

Despite a goal direct from a corner from Andy Ritchie, the derby clash against a fine St Mirren side on 17th March at Love Street was lost 3-1. Morton, however, bounced back against league leaders Dundee United at Cappielow a week later. For the third time in their inaugural SPL season they beat the Taysiders. At the time I wrote: "After a most impressive opening 25-minute spell by the Dundee side, during which they took the lead and played some delightful football, few would have given Morton much chance of salvaging even one point. United were at their best, always supporting each other and moving the ball about quickly and accurately.

"Yet the Cappielow side hung on and, when United failed to deliver a second goal and what would have been a killer blow, they battled their way back into proceedings."

John McNeil grabbed an equaliser for the hosts and suddenly Morton, whose midfield ran tirelessly, seized the initiative. Rugged defender George Anderson, back in the side after a lengthy absence due to an ankle injury, gave the home team the lead and young Jim Tolmie made the points secure when he raced onto a long clearance and smashed a volley past Hamish McAlpine from 14 yards. It was a triumph of determination and an indication of the spirit within the squad.

Greenock boss Benny Rooney was to appeal in the local press for more support in the immediate days after the victory, making the point that a crowd of 5,500 against the league leaders was not proportionate to his team's efforts. The following Wednesday his men went down 3-0 at Parkhead to Celtic. Despite that loss, Rooney's point was valid. Time has a great habit of adding feet and legs to past glories. I have sometimes heard people in current times talk of Morton having the potential to attract home crowds of seven or eight thousand if only they were back in the Premier League. Those days are long gone. In truth they were disappearing fast in 1979. And since then population decline has continued and the economy has become more fragile than a Ming Vase.

Andy Ritchie, with a penalty, and Bobby Thomson scored in a 2-2 draw with Hearts at Cappielow on the last day of March. On the following Wednesday Aberdeen came to Cappielow and managed a 1-0 win with a side including ex-Cappielow legends Joe Harper and Mark McGhee, the latter having swapped the north-east of England for the north-east of Scotland.

As the season drew towards its conclusion, Morton regained some momentum with a fine 1-1 draw at Ibrox, Bobby Russell getting the goal. It was a performance that owed much to the strong physical presence of Billy McLaren and Roddie Hutchison in midfield.

That was followed up in midweek with the Greenock club's first derby success of the season when a swerving Andy Ritchie free kick from 25 yards flew past Billy Thomson in the Buddies' goal. It was also Roy Baines' first shut-out since returning to Cappielow from Celtic.

Despite Ritchie's strike, the match was to draw a bitter comment from St Mirren manager Jim Clunie who said that he "wouldn't have Ritchie if he won him in a raffle". It was a needless remark as daft as it was ungracious.

Hibs were the next opponents in a Cappielow double-header necessitated by the winter freeze, Bobby Thomson and Andy Ritchie (penalty) netting in a Saturday 2-2 draw before 6,743 fans, then beating the Edinburgh men 3-0 in one of their finest performances of the season on the following Wednesday. Russell, McNeil and Ritchie were the scorers. Ritchie's goal, after an earlier lobbed attempt from 40 yards struck Hibernian goalkeeper Jim McArthur's post, was his 27th of the season.

Man-of-the-match, however, was left back Jim Holmes with a faultless display. It prompted his manager, Benny Rooney, to say: "Jim Holmes epitomises the good professional. He does a good job every week, and his skill is tremendous for a full back. He has had a great season." Rooney was too modest to remind us that it was he who had converted Holmes from an average midfield man to an outstanding full back.

Jim Tolmie then hit the net for Scotland under-18s in an excellent 2-2 draw against West Germany before Andy Ritchie scored his 28th goal of the season in a 3-2 defeat at Firhill against Partick.

The Tuesday after that Thistle defeat was marked by Ritchie being voted the Scottish Football Writers' Player of the Year, the first non-Old Firm player to be accorded the accolade for eight years. On being informed of the news, Andy told me: "I'm obviously delighted to win this award. I honestly didn't expect to win, though some people did think I had a good chance. It would be nice now to go on and score two more goals this season and end up top scorer." This was in reference to the fact that Aberdeen's Joe Harper was on 29 goals, his season effectively being over after being dropped by Alex Ferguson.

Benny Rooney commented: "We're all very pleased for Andy. It's a great honour also for the club, and I am sure not many people thought a year ago that a Morton player would win something like this." In second place was Dundee United's Paul Hegarty, with Aberdeen goalkeeper Bobby Clark third. Not one Old Firm player in the top three!

After going two ahead through a Bobby Thomson double, Morton were eventually held to a 3-3 draw at Fir Park against relegated Motherwell, Ritchie moving onto the same 29-goal total as Harper.

There then followed a satisfying Renfrewshire Cup Final win over St Mirren at Cappielow, 3-2 on penalties, when the score was tied at 1-1 after 90 minutes. Roy Baines, who had had a sticky start to his return to Cappielow, was the hero with two excellent penalty saves.

Bobby Thomson rounded off an excellent first season in the Scottish Premier League, the club finishing seventh, when he notched the only goal of the final league match of the season against Hearts at Tynecastle.

Meanwhile the Morton support had named Jim Holmes as their Player of the Year and recipient of the Sir William Lithgow Trophy in a poll run by the Greenock Telegraph. Manager Rooney was delighted, saying: "That's great news. The honour is obviously deserved. I don't think I can remember Jim having a bad game this season."

Jock Stein selected Neil Orr once again for the international under-21 side for a match against Norway in June while, on 24th May, Jim Tolmie was in the under-18 team which beat Poland 3-2 in Austria in the European Championships.

It had been a fine debut season in the SPL for the Cappielow men whose reward was a holiday to Mallorca.

CHAPTER FIVE

A parcel of rogues top the league

A tremendous capacity for sheer hard work, allied to the skill of players such as Jim Holmes, Bobby Thomson and the virtuoso Andy Ritchie, had been rewarded with a better than expected final seventh place in their first season in the Scottish Premier League.

There was also a tremendous camaraderie within the squad. They were known to 'take a few refreshments' together – if memory serves me correctly a Monday was a favourite meeting time in the watering holes of the west coast – and, as Allan McGraw told me with a smile: "They were a bunch of rogues. I don't know how Benny [Rooney] managed them at times."

On one trip back from the east coast in the loo-less team bus, there was a stop for a comfort break. I joined the group irrigating the grass verge beside the coach. After a brief interval, passing cars began to hoot their horns and I looked round to see a group of players, trousers down, mooning at the passing traffic at the rear of the coach. In the gathering dusk I couldn't possibly say with certainty who they were, but the names Rooney, Thomson, Hutchison and Ritchie somehow spring to mind. I quickly zipped myself up and clambered back on the bus. "What's going on out there?" Benny Rooney enquired, a steely gaze beneath brows that glowered menacingly. "Oh, nothing," I replied, as convincing as a coalman in a tutu.

But, if the players knew how to enjoy themselves and stretch acceptance to its limits, they also worked flat out on the training ground. They could enjoy themselves there too. On one evening session I had gone out to Cappielow to talk to the manager. As I watched the last few minutes of a training game under the floodlights, the ball flew out towards where I was standing near the right wing. "My big chance," I thought to myself and moved to cross into the crowded penalty box at the Sinclair Street end. I struck the ball and it flew over the crossbar, obviously caught by some rogue zephyr.

"Davie Hayes, Davie Hayes, Davie Hayes" chanted the players, for the skipper was known occasionally to over-hit a cross.

Despite a successful first Premier season, there would be no attempt to switch to full-time football and it was made clear that finances at Cappielow were such that any further incoming transfers would have to be accomplished by clever dealing in the market.

Upon the club's return from holiday, centre back George Anderson turned down a chance to move to Hearts, preferring to stay at Cappielow and fight for his place in the side. The 25-year-old, once the target of several top English and Scottish clubs, had suffered badly from injury at various key times, eventually losing his place in the team towards the end of the season.

Morton had made their impression in Scotland's highest echelon. The question now was, could they keep the momentum going?

July, 1979, saw Morton record an interest in Drew Busby of Hearts. Nothing was to come of it over the close season.

Then, on 11th July, the club rejected two bids by Oldham Athletic for star midfielder Bobby Thomson, the first for £75,000 and the second upped to £130,000. Managing director Hal Stewart told the Greenock Telegraph: "We need the money, but our need for the player is greater." This was an interesting statement. It explained that, while finances were constrained, the board were nevertheless not in a position in which they felt they had to sell. Thomson, after all, had cost the club just £30,000 a year earlier when he moved to Cappielow from St Johnstone. Benny Rooney commented: "This shows the supporters that, as long as I am at Cappielow at least, we mean business."

With Neil Orr, Jim Tolmie and Bobby Thomson all playing for their country at various levels, and Andy Ritchie providing moments of sheer brilliance, the manager was creating a fine side. Jim Holmes was arguably the best full back in the country, George Anderson and Davie Hayes solid defenders, young Joe McLaughlin was beginning to make his claim for the first team, and Roy Baines was a fine goalkeeper.

Morton's first pre-season friendly was against English side Watford who, under the management of Graham Taylor, later to become England boss, had won promotion for the second successive year, this time to the English Second Division. The Englishmen, still under the ownership of pop legend Elton John, succumbed 2-1, an own goal and one by Bobby Russell nullifying a strike by aspiring young star Luther Blissett who would go on to play for England.

The following Tuesday Morton went down 1-0 to Swindon Town, who had narrowly missed out on promotion to the English Second Division along with Watford, the game being notable for the debut of midfielder John Craig from Hearts, a free transfer signing.

The opening competitive salvoes were fired against Berwick Rangers in the Anglo-Scottish Cup, Morton winning 8-1 on aggregate, before the league season began in the most glamorous fashion with a meeting at Parkhead against champions Celtic. The Glasgow giants had been led to the title in Billy McNeill's first season in charge and the Lisbon Lions' skipper told me: "I have the utmost respect for what Morton have done under Benny Rooney. Their strength is that they have a good all-round team, with all the players working for each other, and the players' styles complement each other.

"At the same time they have players who can provide the flair when needed; players like Andy Ritchie who has tremendous skills and can score vital goals for them."

Despite ex-Celt Andy proving how right McNeill was, by scoring a double, it was Celtic who won the game 3-2. The fact that the Greenock side felt they had let themselves down showed how far they had, in fact, come.

Partick were beaten 2-1 in the next outing, at Cappielow, Ritchie corners supplying the ammunition for headed goals by Bobby Thomson and Ally Scott. The game also marked the debut of young centre half Joe McLaughlin and he performed, in his manager's words, as well as one could have hoped. McLaughlin had all the physical attributes, but he was very much raw material. However, he had an exemplary will to learn and was making great strides in the reserves. He often used to stay behind with reserve coach Allan McGraw to work on his game, especially his heading. He got his place against the Jags only after skipper Davie Hayes sustained a freak pre-match injury when he slipped into a fence getting out of Roy Baines' car and required five stitches in a hand wound.

Next Saturday Morton improved their league position with a highly satisfying 3-0 win over derby rivals St Mirren at Love Street, Thomson and Ritchie (2) supplying the fatal blows. Joe McLaughlin again impressed. For Ritchie, his brace was no doubt especially pleasing after St Mirren manager Jim Clunie's silly statement towards the end of the previous season.

Soon after the game, Oldham again returned with a bid for midfielder Bobby Thomson, increasing their offer to £150,000. Yet again, chairman Hugh Currie and the Morton board chose to back their manager who wanted to keep his best players. It was a surprising, if welcome, decision. The board, after all, were rejecting a profit of £120,000 in just over a year. Managing director Haldane Y. Stewart, not one to turn down a bob or two, must have been chloroformed, gagged and locked in a cupboard in a straightjacket when the directors made that decision.

Queen of the South were beaten 5-0 on aggregate over two legs in the League Cup first round, Ritchie inevitably supplying three of the goals, one direct from a corner.

But just two days later Ritchie delivered a major shock to the Sinclair Street club's system. On Friday 7th September he exclusively told me that he had kicked his last ball for Morton. The Telegraph front page headline screamed out 'A bombshell from Ritchie'. In the story Andy said: "I've sent a letter to the club telling them that I'll not be going back until I get a reply to say that a transfer has been arranged.

"As you know, I have asked for a transfer several times over the past couple of seasons, but this time I mean to stay away until something has definitely been fixed up. The main reason is my desire to play full-time football again. I've been four seasons at Cappielow and that's as long part-time as I was full-time at Celtic."

The news was a massive blow to Morton. Manager Benny Rooney commented: "Until we get the letter from Andy we can't really say what action will be taken. I will say that Andy has been good for Morton in his time here, but we have done well by him.

"As far as any moves by other clubs for Ritchie are concerned we have had only one, and that was the enquiry Partick Thistle made for him some time ago. Certainly I, as manager, have had no other enquiry from any other club regarding the player."

It seemed that the player, having been voted Scotland's Player of the Year the previous season, was flexing his new-found bargaining power. He was clearly frustrated. Benny Rooney called on the fans to give the team their full support in the match the next day at Cappielow against Aberdeen.

By the morning of the match, however, there had been a complete U-turn. The board had met with Ritchie and peace had been restored. In a statement made to me, Benny Rooney said: "The club have now decided to list him officially for transfer and will listen to any club willing to make an offer. We will not stand in the player's way if a suitable offer for his transfer is received.

"Both Andy and the club will benefit by his playing for Morton until that time. Andy realised that staying away was not the answer to his wish for full-time football."

All was forgiven by 4.40 in the afternoon when Aberdeen were beaten 3-2, giving Morton their third consecutive victory and joint top place in the league with Celtic. Bobby Thomson hit two goals and, of course, Mr Andrew Ritchie was also on the scoresheet. The fans were generous in their praise of the club's 'idle idol'.

In effect, Morton had lost nothing in the negotiation. Despite their laudable stand to retain Bobby Thomson, any player was for sale at the right price. But the fact was that none of the big spenders was prepared to take a risk on Ritchie. There was plenty of admiration for his ability, but precious little enthusiasm for shelling out serious cash for someone managers felt had too much of a mind of his own, and little of it devoted to any semblance of prodigious effort.

A 4-3 loss in a thriller at Dens Park against Dundee saw the team stumble in their next game before Preston North End, managed by World Cup winner Nobby Stiles, were dismissed 3-1 away from home in the Anglo-Scottish Cup second round.

Ritchie continued to entertain the throng when he scored a penalty in a 3-1 win over Kilmarnock at Cappielow during which he took time out to wave good naturedly to the visiting fans, though the star man was the highly polished Jim Holmes.

In the third round of the League Cup, Partick were beaten 1-0 at Firhill due to a Jim Rooney strike, and the month ended with a key home league game against Dundee United. The Taysiders had ex-England goalkeeper Peter Bonetti in their line-up in a match watched by Scotland boss Jock Stein. United's Dave Narey and Paul Hegarty were his principal concerns, though he was able also to size up Morton's under-21 cap Neil Orr, as well as Andy Ritchie.

In the event, it was Jim McLean's men who took the lead just after the interval when Hegarty's shot spun off Neil Orr and flew over Roy Baines. It took Morton all of 30 seconds to restore parity when Ritchie stabbed home a Hutchison cross at the near post.

Perhaps the big fellow was keen to make a point to Stein, his ex-boss at Celtic Park with whom he had fallen out. Ally Scott supplied the finishing touch to a Joe McLaughlin header to put the hosts in front and then Ritchie swerved home a superb free kick from 25 yards with Bonetti just as impotent as a succession of Scottish goalkeepers before him. Ritchie later completed his hat-trick to finalise a 4-1 victory and send Stein away with something to ponder.

Morton then notched up a 2-0 Anglo-Scottish Cup win away from home over Preston for a 5-1 aggregate success, Roddie Hutchison emerging the hero with a brace in a match minus injured trio Bobby Thomson, Andy Ritchie and Bobby Russell.

The bold 'Hutch' followed this up with the goal in a 1-1 draw against Hibs at Cappielow.

Morton were playing well and a 4-1 victory over Patrick Thistle at Cappielow saw them through to the League Cup quarter-finals on a 5-1 aggregate. John McNeil was his side's top man with a cultured display, Charlie Brown also doing well in a by-now rare appearance. The goals came from Thomson (2), McLaughlin and Ritchie.

Benny Rooney's men were showing great self-belief, typified by a well deserved 2-2 draw at Ibrox. Brown hit a superb opener with a perfectly timed volley before Rangers swept into a 2-1 lead. Back battled Morton, Neil Orr blasting home an equaliser. Jimmy Miller had worked impressively in midfield in a performance which helped boss Rooney win the MacKinlay's Personality of the Month Award for the second time.

The following Saturday it was the turn of the other half of the Old Firm to feel the sting in the Cappielow tail, Bobby Thomson scoring the only goal of the game in a 1-0 Cappielow victory. It came from a marvellously creative piece of football straight from the training ground. Morton had won a free kick outside the Celtic penalty area and to the left of the six-yard box. Everyone expected Andy Ritchie to go for goal. John McNeil ran over the ball and on towards the left byeline, Ritchie stroked it into his stride, McNeil cut it back inside and there was Thomson to steer the ball into the Celtic net.

Morton were now just one point behind Billy McNeill's men at the top of the table. And they were proving that they were able to live with any side in Scotland's elite league.

When they disposed of Partick 4-1 at Firhill on the final Saturday of October with goals by Ritchie, McNeil, Thomson – and a rare Holmes effort – it was ideal preparation for the League Cup quarter-final first leg tie against Kilmarnock at Cappielow the following Wednesday night. Spirits were as high as a Hippie commune. Manager Rooney commented: "Our support at Firhill was simply terrific and I hope it continues at home. We're beginning to get a bit of recognition."

The atmosphere was sizzling as Bobby Thomson gave Morton the lead, only for Killie to hit back in stunning fashion with goals by Stewart McLean and Bobby Street. Then came an Andy Ritchie-inspired comeback. First, Roddie Hutchison headed in an inch-perfect cross from the King of Cappielow, then the man himself weaved his way through the visitors' defence before slotting the ball through the legs of goalkeeper Alan McCulloch – a peach of a nutmeg. Birmingham City boss Jimmy Smith was an interested spectator, having come north to have a look at Ritchie.

Morton were buzzing, and a 0-0 draw at Cappielow on the Saturday against derby rivals St Mirren was enough to see them go top of the Premier League, having scored more goals than Celtic who were on the same number of points.

The Greenock side's momentum seemed irresistible and, in the first leg of the Anglo-Scottish Cup semi-final, they gained a 2-2 draw at Bristol City, a trademark Ritchie free kick and a strike by Bobby Russell gaining them parity. Included in the City team were ex-Morton players Gerry Sweeney and Donnie Gillies.

Aberdeen were next up, at Pittodrie. Would Fergie's men upset the Ton applecart? The answer was 'no' as Morton fought back from a 1-0 deficit after Alex McLeish fired home a long range drive. Bobby Thomson equalised in 18 minutes, Andy Ritchie supplying, for him, a fairly ordinary winner with 10 minutes to go. It was described by Benny Rooney as his team's "hardest match of the season" and it kept them top of the league.

The reward for such prominence by what was, after all, a part-time club, was selection in the Scottish under-21 side for Neil Orr, John McNeil and Andy Ritchie, the latter as an over-aged player. They were picked for the squad to meet Belgium in Brussels in the European Championships.

Brighton and Birmingham had shown interest in Ritchie, but there was to be no follow-up. In the same month, Freddie Fletcher joined the board at Cappielow and then Morton continued on their joyful path with a 2-0 home victory over Dundee, Ritchie and Anderson, from a Ritchie cross, netting. Baines also brought off a superb save to deny Billy Pirie a goal from the penalty spot.

Ritchie and Orr then both played in the Belgian under-21 match, won 1-0 by the Scots through George McCluskey, Ritchie forcing a fine save from the home goalkeeper following a free kick.

On Saturday 24th November, Morton travelled down the coast to tackle Kilmarnock in the second leg of their League Cup quarter-final, holding that slender one-goal lead. The prize was a semi-final tie against Aberdeen. And Morton had already beaten the Dons twice during the season, fast becoming the bane of Alex Ferguson's managerial life.

In the event it was a cup clash which fizzed more than a bottle of Dom Perignon. It was as good as it gets, before 8,500 fans, 3,000 of whom had travelled from Greenock to Rugby Park. On a scintillating afternoon on one of the best playing surfaces in the country, Morton won through on penalties after extra time. I wrote: "This was Scottish football at its most exciting and, while Morton deserved to pull through, one can't help but feel some sympathy for a spirited Kilmarnock team which fought so hard."

Man-of-the-match was the unfashionable Roddie Hutchison who toiled tirelessly throughout two hours of football. I wrote: "His ability to collect the ball, hold it and then dispatch it accurately to a colleague in space made him the Greenock side's key man." Not far behind came the immaculate Jim Holmes, Scotland's most consistent full back. Ally Scott and Jimmy Miller worked themselves to a stand-still in support of their team-mates while substitute Jim Tolmie showed breathtaking pace and skill.

A goal by the home side's Clarke levelled the scores 3-3 on aggregate and took the game into extra time. Cairney then gave Killie the lead to the delight of their big support. Morton hit back with a Hutchison header from a Ritchie cross before young Tolmie hit the goal of the tie. Collecting the ball near halfway, he zipped past two home defenders, squeezed between two more and then whipped a superb, low shot past McCulloch. It was a goal fit to win any game. But Killie weren't finished in an electrifying tie, Gibson netting with five minutes to go to take the match to penalties. This was gladiatorial football and the tension was extraordinary.

Jimmy Miller, Andy Ritchie, Roddie Hutchison and Jim Tolmie all netted from the spot. When Killie's Bobby Street missed his attempt, it left Jim Holmes with the task of winning the tie. He did the business and the Morton camp reacted as if they had all just sat down on a gigantic ant-hill. Holmes later confessed: "The last penalty I took was in junior football when I hit the ball into the same corner."

With the League Cup semi-final in mind, Morton fielded basically a reserve team against St Mirren in the first leg of the Renfrewshire Cup at Love Street and, unsurprisingly, went down 4-1 (they were eventually to lose 10-1 on aggregate), but all eyes were on the following Saturday for the big game with Alex Ferguson's Dons.

Benny Rooney's men were in splendid form and heart as they got on the bus for the trip to Hampden. A passenger myself, I recall the journey well. The spirit could not have been better and the players were singing Morton songs as the bus approached the stadium, blue and white bedecked supporters in the streets waving and applauding.

I climbed up into the famous old press box, perched on top of the main stand roof, with its angled windows and subbuteo-like view of the pitch below. There was a sense of expectation among the hacks that this might well be Morton's day. It wasn't a daring gamble to back the Ton. Aberdeen, after all, had been beaten twice in the league thus far by the Greenock men.

In the event it was to be a severe anti-climax. Aberdeen went on to win 2-1, despite a brave second half comeback by Morton. All the confidence from a wonderful run of games seemed to count for nothing. The players looked star-struck, sucked dry by nervous energy. I commented: "Nerves and the fear of making a mistake led to Morton's most disappointing 45 minutes of football all season at Hampden Park on Saturday, where they were deservedly beaten by a more experienced Aberdeen team. That first half was a nightmare for the Greenock men for whom the occasion seemed too much.

"They could scarcely string two passes together, lost the battle for possession, and badly needed someone in midfield to give them the direction and composure they lacked. By half-time they were two goals in arrears and the match virtually was over.

"To Morton's credit, however, they came out a much rejuvenated side in the second half and, playing with far greater drive and aggression, they controlled the game for long spells."

Neil Orr had a 20-yard drive into the net disallowed for offside, given against George Anderson who hardly could have been interfering with play. Andy Ritchie did claw a goal back nine minutes from time from the penalty spot and also saw a fierce drive hit the junction of post and crossbar. But it wasn't enough.

Earlier, Aberdeen had taken a firm grip from the kick-off, pouring forward like an irresistible red tsunami. Ian Scanlon tormented Morton on the left wing, and a goal followed through former Cappielow hero Mark McGhee. Then Greenock lad John McMaster embarked on a lung-bursting run down the left flank. His cross hit Davie Hayes on the hand and the referee awarded a penalty. Gordon Strachan converted it just before the interval. Morton were flattered to go in just two down.

Ritchie was withdrawn into a deeper midfield role in the second period, and that made a difference to the Greenock men, but the biggest alteration was in their own collective mind-set. It was a defiant, if ultimately unavailing, response.

After the match, it was a subdued bus down the M8 to Cappielow, in stark contrast to the buoyant trip to Hampden. Local boys George Anderson and Jimmy Miller sought me out on the homeward journey, Anderson saying: "Our fans [who numbered over 8,000] were great in that second half and gave us a real lift. Please say how much we appreciated it. I feel we have let them down." His comments were echoed by Miller.

Skipper Davie Hayes said: "A couple of times when I got the ball in the second half I could hear shouts of 'Morton-Morton' and I felt we had to do something for them."

It was the start of a slide, perhaps as much psychologically as anything else, for Morton. It was, frankly, unrealistic to expect a part-time club to maintain a serious league challenge throughout the season. Their limited squad was often stretched by injury and suspension, but one can't help but wonder what might have been achieved with a full-time set-up.

On the following Saturday Morton lost their unbeaten home record, and their discipline, in a bad tempered 1-0 home defeat against Rangers. It was almost as if the frustrations of the previous week had spilled over, though the Ibrox men were hardly blameless.

Bill Anderson was the referee and his performance throughout the afternoon was varied to say the least. But the most controversial moment came seven minutes before the interval. Bobby Thomson fouled Rangers' Sandy Jardine near the touchline in front of the main stand. Jardine remonstrated with Thomson who then appeared to head-butt the Ibrox player, causing him to collapse. Out came the red card and off went Thomson amidst angry scenes. I wrote at the time: "It was later adamantly claimed in the Morton camp that no contact had been made. This was clearly felt to be the case by the crowd at the front of the main stand nearest to the incident who howled "cheat, cheat" at Jardine every time he touched the ball thereafter."

At the time I made the point that, contact or not, the violent gesture in itself warranted an ordering-off. Certainly the referee should not be blamed. A touchline photographer in close proximity to the incident was later to claim that no contact, indeed, had been made. Others close by confirmed that claim. If that was the case Jardine's reaction was undoubtedly regrettable, albeit out of character, but I could not find it in myself to sympathise with Thomson who had played just two games after coming back from a three-match suspension. He had a problem with his temper and on this occasion it cost Morton dear. It was an offence that was to rule him out for a further six matches. Jardine? A player whose actions were invariably exemplary on the pitch probably panicked. In the same situation I might well have instinctively fallen back in anticipation of a severe thud on the dome. But did he need to roll about holding his face? He didn't have as much as a mark on his face after the game. Neither player came out of the incident well.

Morton's anger was not helped by Mr Anderson denying the Cappielow men a clear-cut penalty when Gers' centre half Colin Jackson sent Ally Scott tumbling in the box. It is often said by non-Old Firm fans that referees give decisions too readily in favour of Rangers and Celtic. On balance I agree, but not because of the commonly held view that officials are biased. They aren't in my view. But I do believe they can be subconsciously affected by the crowd. If a massive majority of the supporters in the stadium continually appeals for penalties, free kicks etc, it takes a strong personality to always remain objective; not to be swayed.

My phone line was red hot during the week following the controversial encounter, at least one Rangers fan informing me that I was a 'Fenian bastard' for daring to suggest that Sandy

Jardine would have gone down without being touched, while several Morton fans accused me of being a 'Hun' for saying that Thomson deserved to go off. This newly bestowed Fenian Hundom persuaded me to believe I may have got the balance right. I recall former referee 'Tiny' Wharton once revealing in an after-dinner speech in Greenock that mysteriously his religion seemed to change depending at which end of the park he found himself in an Old Firm game. Ah, the joys of footie.

CHAPTER SIX

When Ritchie almost came face to face with Best

Suddenly a season which had looked so bright for Morton had become seriously overcast within the space of eight days. Jim Tolmie and Neil Orr were included in the next Scotland under-21 squad to meet Belgium in a return tie, though there was no place for a disappointed Andy Ritchie who had played in the first leg.

There was a feeling among some that Jock Stein had picked Ritchie in the first leg simply to placate the sportswriters' clamour for his inclusion in a navy blue simmet. Somehow I doubt Jock Stein ever would have pandered to the press.

On Saturday 15th December, Morton had the opportunity to put the defeats by Aberdeen and Rangers behind them with a fixture which promised much in the way of entertainment. Hibs were to be the visitors, but it was a Hibernian side who included a rather special Northern Irishman in their ranks. George Best had agreed a deal a few weeks before at Easter Road for a match fee reported to be £2,500 a game, attempting to resurrect a once glorious career. Hibs' chairman Tom Hart had taken a chance on signing Best. It was always going to be a precarious gamble, given Best's fondness for a 'wee sensation', and on one occasion he missed a Sunday cup tie against Ayr after going on a spectacular bender overnight with the French rugby team who were playing Scotland in Edinburgh. But his presence in our capital had trebled the gates at Easter Road, and no doubt quadrupled the bar takings in the city's more fashionable establishments.

In anticipation of the possible clash of messrs Best and Ritchie, I contemplated: "The meeting should be fascinating. At this advanced stage in his career, Best does not believe in over-exerting himself, something Ritchie at no time has ever held faith in." I concluded: "It could be one occasion when George has to be content with second Best."

On the day, Best did one of his infamous disappearing acts, the official line – as believable as fairies at the bottom of the garden, reformed bankers and Tony Blair's weapons of mass destruction – being that he had aggravated an injury. George pulled off the same stunt in the return match at Easter Road, one of my major regrets, and I'm sure one of Ritchie's too, not to mention the Morton fans. Begorra! Was George frightened to go head-to-head with Ritchie? More likely a lake or two of white wine spritzers won the day.

As Christmas loomed large, Morton found themselves two points adrift of leaders and champions Celtic who were the visitors to Cappielow on 22nd December. Yet again, Morton lost their composure and the game, 3-1. Of all people, Jim Holmes was sent off for dissent towards a linesman after a controversial goal by Johnny Doyle, the Morton players claiming a suspiciously offside Dom Sullivan had dragged the ball over the byeline before crossing for his team-mate to score. When Partick completed Morton's festive misery with a 3-1 home defeat, the conclusion was that the high points of the season had been and gone.

Morton's sense of injustice over two meetings with the Old Firm seemed to permeate the camp at a time when a more experienced side would have channelled this into a concentrated focus. Nevertheless, it is hard to imagine any similar provincial team these days managing anything comparable, especially given Morton's part-time status and the fact that they had not only the Old Firm to compete with, but the best two teams – Aberdeen and Dundee United – ever to compete consistently with Rangers and Celtic since the inception of the Premier League. All this in a 10-club division.

It was around the heady November days of Morton's pomp that a feature writer from one of England's broadsheets turned up at Cappielow. He had been sent north into the Caledonian wilderness to do what is called a 'colour piece' on the phenomenon that was Andrew Ritchie. I remember hoping that he had brought a tartan pencil. He wanted to know as much background about the big fella as he could and I tried hard to oblige. He was a pleasant observer, if not quite au fait with our most popular sport.

After the match, in which Andy had served up numerous offerings of outrageous talent, our man from down south asked at the press conference: "And tell me Andy, are you one of the breed of 'new men' who help with the ironing and the washing-up?"

Andy looked genuinely bewildered. I almost fell over and a whale could have swum into my open mouth. "No," Andy replied. "After all, I don't ask Rena to take a corner for me on a Saturday afternoon." Rena quite often would come down from Glasgow to Cappielow along with young son Mark to see hubby perform. They would sit just in front of the press benches where Mark's squeals of encouragement were directed out onto the pitch like a castrated air-raid siren. I don't, incidentally, recall one instance when Rena took a corner.

We didn't know it at the time, but the last months of 1979 were to be as good as it got for Benny Rooney's fine team. There was to be one more cup semi-final the following season but, unlike Dundee United who were going from strength to strength from a relatively similar position, the club were about to begin a slide back down the hill they had striven so determinedly to ascend.

When I compare Dundee United with Morton at that time, it is not fanciful. United were very much the bridesmaids to the Dark Blues across the road at Dens in Dundee in the early 70s. With no bigger support than Morton, they managed to get themselves into a position of becoming one of the country's principal clubs. What happened at Tannadice, however, as I have touched on earlier, will never be repeated again. It was an incredible achievement, born of a variety of circumstances. But I am left wondering what Morton might have accomplished had they taken the gamble to go full-time under Benny Rooney. The board at the time knew more than anyone else about the financial structure of the club, but the observation is worth making. If full-time football was never on the agenda, then Morton's ambitions necessarily were going to be restricted. No one could keep a part-time team in the top 10 indefinitely.

In a Ne'erday derby at Love Street, Morton and St Mirren battled out a 2-2 draw before a crowd of around 10,000. Doug Somner, who was enjoying a marvellous season for the Saints and was to finish top league scorer with 25 goals, headed a Peter Weir corner into the net to give the hosts the lead in six minutes. Four minutes later Roddie Hutchison equalised with another header, Billy McLaren supplying the cross. A Ritchie penalty nudged Morton ahead before Somner again pounced to equalise.

Next up were Aberdeen at Cappielow, memories of the League Cup semi-final defeat still raw. Morton took considerable satisfaction in their third league win of the season over Fergie's men when Ally Scott flicked on Andy Ritchie's corner and Billy McLaren dived low to head past Bobby Clark.

Then, on 11th January, 1980, Morton announced that Ritchie had signed a new four-year deal. Boss Rooney commented: "This is a good thing for the player and the club. There has been a lot of transfer talk this season concerning Andy and it is good to get it all settled. We've done our bit to keep the player at Cappielow and it is now up to the fans to rally round and support the club."

Morton, technically, were still in the title hunt but consecutive league defeats, to Dundee away by 1-0 and Kilmarnock at home 3-1, were to end any realistic hope of a sustained title challenge. In between these losses the team were also beaten 1-0 at Cappielow in the second leg of the Anglo-Scottish Cup semi-final, going out 3-2 on aggregate to a Bristol side containing ex-Cappielow men Gerry Sweeney, Donnie Gillies and former St Mirren captain Tony Fitzpatrick.

The targets now were a place in Europe and the Scottish Cup. Cowdenbeath were beaten 1-0 at Cappielow in a modest third round cup win in which Charlie Brown had his best game for a long while.

At this time the club welcomed back to Cappielow former player and Danish international Bjarne 'Barney' Jensen in a coaching capacity. It was also announced that the club would let Roddie Hutchison go if a fair offer were received.

On 9th February it was off to the capital to meet Hibernian. Once again, George Best disappointed the travelling fans. He had gone AWOL from training and was suspended by Hibs chairman Tom Hart. In the event the hosts won 3-2, Joe McLaughlin and Bobby Thomson scoring for the visitors. George Best may well have been scoring somewhere else, but it wasn't on a football pitch.

First Division Dunfermline were then trounced 5-0 at Cappielow in the fourth round of the Scottish Cup to set up a meeting with Celtic, who beat St Mirren after a replay. In the Pars team were ex-Morton men Kevin Hegarty, Ricky Sharp and Walter Borthwick.

Rangers strolled to an unusually comfortable 3-1 win over Morton at Ibrox, Ian Redford making his Ibrox debut after a £210,000 move from Dundee. When Celtic added further discomfort with a 1-0 win at Cappielow, Morton were left not only with no realistic prospect of title success, but a diminishing one of European qualification.

In March Bobby Russell was transferred to Airdrie for a fee of £15,000 before Andy Ritchie, Neil Orr and Bobby Thomson were all picked by Jock Stein for the Scottish League squad to play against the League of Ireland in Dublin and the Irish League in Belfast.

On 8th March Morton travelled to Parkhead to meet Celtic in the quarter-finals of the Scottish Cup. In the event it was a particularly lacklustre performance by Morton, so much so that Celtic manager Billy McNeill commented: "We won the match without ever really having to stretch ourselves." An admirer of Morton's, McNeill genuinely was surprised at the relative lack of fight in the Greenock ranks. There seems little doubt that there was a lingering hang-over from that Hampden defeat by Aberdeen and the subsequent losses to the Old Firm. There were not the resources to freshen up the side and it may be that some players were just a bit stale.

Next up were Kilmarnock at Rugby Park in a 1-1 draw before Jim Tolmie was also called up by the Scottish League for the Irish trip, making it a quartet of Morton players in the pool. Give that Scotland were still a force in international football in these days, this was quite a fillip for the part-timers from Greenock.

Joe McLaughlin was man-of-the-match in a 2-1 win over rivals St Mirren at Cappielow. The big centre back was making huge strides in his development as a player. With George Anderson often playing alongside McLaughlin, and Neil Orr acting as a sweeper, it may appear that Morton were a defensively minded team. In fact, Orr's superb reading of the game and ability to break forward into space in midfield, together with the excellent overlapping of full backs Hayes and Holmes, made it anything but a cautious formation.

However, aspirations of European football at Cappielow the following season were finally dashed when Aberdeen, having lost three league games to Morton, finally broke their duck with victory by a solitary goal at Pittodrie.

Ton managing director Hal Stewart received a Special Merit Award at the Scottish Professional Footballers' Association Awards as the season began to draw to a close. It was a fitting gesture for a man who, in the 60s, was sufficiently far ahead of his time he could have been travelling by Tardis. Doctor Hal!

Dundee drew 1-1 at Cappielow with Jim Rooney netting a penalty, Andy Ritchie being an absentee due to flu, and the run-in had become anti-climactic.

April began with two consecutive away wins over Partick, 1-0 courtesy of Ally Scott, and Kilmarnock with goals by Bobby Thomson and Andy Ritchie. Scott, for so long having to be content with a place on the bench, was a star man in both games, his selfless running creating so much for those around him. Any faint hopes of European football, however, were soon extinguished with defeats by Dundee United and Rangers, 2-0 away and 1-0 at home respectively. Benny Rooney summed up: "We want to finish in as high a position in the league as possible.

Dundee United inflicted another defeat, again by 2-0, at Tannadice to leapfrog above Morton in the league and, after a 1-1 draw with Hibs, now permanently minus George Best, Morton had slumped to sixth place in the top 10, behind Aberdeen, Celtic, St Mirren, Dundee United and Rangers. Dundee United, Rangers and Morton were all on 35 points, nine behind Fergie's Dons.

The season ended with yet another meeting with Dundee United at Cappielow in a typical end-of-season affair which ended 0-0. I commented: "If one judges the highlight of a game by the biggest cheer from the crowd, then this match reached its zenith in the 80th minute when a policeman, striding dutifully behind the goal at the Wee Dublin End, had his hat blown from his head."

Miscues and fresh air shots proliferated, even Andy Ritchie falling on top of the ball at one stage. "It was strange," I wrote, "to reflect that we were watching two teams who, at various stages of the season, have provided a good deal of entertainment in the purely footballing sense."

Morton had finished sixth in the Premier League. They also had reached the League Cup and Anglo-Scottish Cup semi-finals. For one of the lesser clubs that would be considered a marvellous achievement in modern day terms; spectacular for a part-time team. Then it carried a sense of slight disappointment among the support. This was born out of the team's own incredible achievement in the first half of the season which had promised so much only, ultimately and perhaps inevitably, to fall short.

The curtain came down on the season with a testimonial match for Hal Stewart, the legendary Morton managing director whose involvement with the club had carried on to two decades. His select side beat an all-star select, skippered by Scotland's Archie Gemmill, 3-1 at Cappielow. Ritchie (2) and Holmes were the scorers for Hal's side, Stevie Archibald netting for the all-stars. Hal Stewart summed up simply: "Thank you for the greatest day in my life."

Joe McLaughlin was voted the fans' Player of the Year while Jim Holmes signed a new two-year deal, meaning all the first team squad were fixed up at least until the end of the following season.

One close season surprise was Benny Rooney's revelation that he had entered talks with Bertie Auld of Partick Thistle with a view to swopping young striker Jim Tolmie for Jags' talented midfielder Ian Gibson. It was a move that never materialised. Gibson was to move on to Dundee United.

CHAPTER SEVEN

A fine side begins to break up

Morton's third consecutive season in the Premier League could hardly have had a stiffer opening. Their first four league games were against Scotland's representatives in Europe – Celtic, St Mirren, Dundee United and Aberdeen. It prompted Hal Stewart to say: "Just quote me on this; if Benny [Rooney] can get eight points out of that lot, I'll buy him a drink." Hal, as ever, knew what he was doing, and his wallet was to stay deep within his pocket.

The manager meanwhile tipped Joe McLaughlin for Scotland under-21 honours and also explained his attempt during the close season to swop Jim Tolmie for Partick's Ian Gibson. "I spoke to Jim about this," said Rooney, "and he understood the situation. If you're after a good player you must put up a good player." This was in reference to Morton's lack of resources to go into the transfer market. Rooney concluded: "I've told him [Tolmie] that I expect him to really come through next season."

Soon after, centre back Barry Evans moved on to Clydebank for a fee reported to be around £10,000 while midfielder Charlie Brown was given a free transfer and was later to join Clyde. Charlie's early promise was never fulfilled and it wasn't long before he was back playing junior football with Port Glasgow.

Speculation surrounded Newcastle United interest in John McNeil and then there was frustration when Bobby Thomson was ordered off against Aberdeen in a 4-2 Drybrough Cup semi-final defeat at Cappielow for kicking Doug Rougvie. Coming on top of his six-match ban towards the end of the previous season it was yet further evidence of the player's fiery temper and his difficulty in controlling it. Benny Rooney kept the details in-house, but admitted to the press that the player would be disciplined.

In the Anglo-Scottish Cup, Morton defeated Second Division champions Falkirk in the preliminary stages 7-3 on aggregate before the league opener against Celtic at Parkhead on 9th August. With Neil Orr their top player, Morton fell to a 2-1 defeat, Ritchie nullifying George McCluskey's opener when he beat two defenders before side-footing past a young Pat Bonner in goal. Murdo MacLeod netted the home winner in a deserved victory.

It was the start of a depressing run of results for the Sinclair Street club. The following Saturday they went down heavily at home to derby rivals St Mirren whose silky skills saw them triumph 4-1, the prolific Doug Somner grabbing a hat-trick, including two from the penalty spot.

First Division Ayr United caused an upset by dumping Morton out of the League Cup 3-2 on aggregate, including a 2-0 loss at Cappielow.

Some equilibrium was re-established with a 1-1 draw at Tannadice against Dundee United, George Anderson capping a man-of-the-match display with a fine headed goal.

A week later, Morton beat St Johnstone 2-0 at Muirton Park in a friendly match, an occasion notable for the scoring debut of striker Ian Cochrane, a £10,000 signing from Preston North End, the other goal coming from Jim Tolmie.

As predicted by Benny Rooney, Joe McLaughlin won his first under-21 cap, the game taking place in Sweden.

Ally Scott and Jimmy Miller then left Cappielow for Partick and Clyde respectively as Benny Rooney sought to wheel and deal in the transfer market. It was future Scotland boss Craig Brown who took Miller to Shawfield. 'Scooter' was not always enamoured by some of Brown's training methods and was later to tell me: "He had this thing where the players lined up in a circle like the numbers of a clock, and he would shout one o'clock to eight o'clock and that player had to run to that number. Well, that was bad enough, but then he went over to a 24-hour clock. Well, you can imagine…some of our boys couldn't tell the time on an ordinary clock. There were lads running into each other all over the place."

Morton, who for so long had been the Dons' bogey team, were to suffer a dramatic swing in the fixture's fortunes when they travelled to Pittodrie on 6th September. They were not just beaten but systematically dissected by Fergie's champions who had a new swagger and sense of self-belief to their step. Ian Cochrane could hardly have wished for a more disappointing league debut as Aberdeen swept to a hugely convincing 6-0 win.

With Evans, Brown, Miller and Scott all departed, and only Cochrane arriving, fears began to grip the Morton support. Could they continue to feast at the top table? Were they being found out?

Some calm and sense of proportion were restored with a 2-0 home win against Kilmarnock, Cochrane and John McNeil grabbing the goals to give Morton three points from their opening five matches. On the same day, however, the club lost another player when centre half George Anderson (27) was sold to Airdrie for £33,000, having been at Cappielow since 1970.

Of a stalwart whose career so often had been blighted by injury at just the wrong times, I wrote: "Since the introduction into the first team of young centre half Joe McLaughlin, Anderson has not been able to command as regular a place as many believed his talents deserved. Always an admirer of the player, I can nevertheless understand the decision to transfer him. Morton are well served in the central defensive positions and at present their need for money to bring in new faces to the club has top priority."

A move into the market was made at the end of the following week, following a 2-0 Anglo-Scottish Cup loss at Notts County, when Rooney offered Dundee £20,000 for winger Jim Murphy, a bid the Dens club were to turn down days later.

Meanwhile there was shock news when Andy Ritchie was dropped altogether from the squad to face Hearts at Tynecastle. A lack of work-rate can be tolerated when the goals are going in, and the assists being made, but the decision showed that even the most naturally talented player in the country could not be assured of his place. John McNeil scored the only goal of the game to give Morton two key points. The following week, the Morton boss commented on the Ritchie situation: "The good thing is that Andy has taken it in the right way. He's been training hard all week."

The big man was back in the side the next Saturday. The kick in the bahoochie seemed to have had the desired effect as he scored against Partick at Firhill, but it wasn't enough to prevent a 2-1 defeat.

Following the departures from Cappielow, some redress was made when the club acquired Drew Busby from Hearts, a player in whom previously they had shown interest. Originally a striker, Busby had been converted into an abrasive midfielder at Tynecastle. His first appearance came in the second leg of the Anglo-Scottish Cup tie against Notts County at Cappielow, a penalty by Andy Ritchie, restored to the side, giving Morton a 1-1 draw at Cappielow, not enough to prevent the English side going through on a 3-1 aggregate.

The following Saturday, 4th October, 1980, Busby made his league debut against Rangers at Cappielow, the only side Morton had failed to beat since reaching the Premier League. That record seemed to be coming to an end when Morton went ahead courtesy of the new 'boy' when Peter McCloy spilled a Ritchie cross and Busby bundled the loose ball into the net. In the 27th minute John McNeil was tripped by Gers centre half Colin Jackson and Ritchie did his usual efficient job from the penalty spot. Morton were the better side, but an Alex Miller penalty breathed new life into the Ibrox men who went on to snatch a late equaliser through Colin McAdam.

Morton targeted Hearts winger Malcolm Robertson, only to fail to secure his services, while their own ex-Tynecastle midfielder John Craig was told he could find another club.

It was an unsettled period for the Greenock club who lost 1-0 at Broomfield to new Premier arrivals Airdrie before going down 3-2 at Cappielow to an effervescent Celtic team. The scoreline flattered the hosts who found themselves 3-0 down to goals by Davie Provan, Roy Aitken and Charlie Nicholas before providing consolation strikes through Andy Ritchie and Ian Cochrane.

Aberdeen then became the latest club to show an interest in Ton midfield man Bobby Thomson. Forward Stewart Mauchlen was released and young Martin Doak was called up from juvenile club Shamrock Boys' Club while, in a derby against St Mirren at Cappielow, Morton were fortunate to escape with a 1-1 draw after a very soft penalty award allowed Jim Rooney to equalise.

Morton were a shadow of the side who had competed so vigorously in their first two Premier seasons, Andy Ritchie again finding himself surplus to requirement in a 2-0 away defeat at Tannadice, then a 0-0 draw at Firhill. Partick Thistle came in with a £100,000 offer for Bobby Thomson which was turned down, unsurprisingly as Oldham's offer of £150,000 had been rejected the previous season. But, for the first time, Morton were finding it a struggle in the top flight, manager Benny Rooney explaining the need for results over flair by saying:

"That is partly the reason why Andy Ritchie and, to a lesser extent, John McNeil, were not in the team at Firhill on Saturday."

Rooney then went on to voice his reservations of the top 10 league, views which echo to this day. "There's too much fear in the top 10. The game is in danger of slipping to the level of Irish football."

Morton were third bottom in the league with just eight points from 13 games and, of the absence of dropped star player Andy Ritchie, the Cappielow manager said: "The real Andy Ritchie is obviously the player we need in the team; somebody who can score goals and get things going. But we haven't seen the real Andy Ritchie since the start of the season, have we?" It was a rhetorical question.

Hearts went two up at Cappielow on 15th November only for Joe McLaughlin and Jim Rooney to peg them back, Ritchie regaining his place in the team, but with no great improvement in his form. That midweek, Joe McLaughlin was part of the Scottish under-21 side who beat Denmark 2-1 and then, on Wednesday 19th November, Benny Rooney looked as if he may leave the club when speculation grew that Partick Thistle were going to make a move for him to replace Bertie Auld who had switched to Hibs.

Rooney came out with the kind of denial all managers make in the circumstances. "There has been no contact with Partick Thistle. I am more concerned with Morton Football Club," he said; enough to send a tremble through the Cappielow ranks. In fact, Thistle made their move for Rooney on the Friday afternoon. In the event Rooney decided to stay put, but only after being offered a much improved new three-year deal by the Cappielow board. It was a settlement which made Rooney one of the highest paid managers in the country.

The Ton boss later commented: "There is no doubt I was interested in the Thistle offer. I was contacted by Partick on Friday afternoon by telephone and admitted I was quite keen. However, the reaction from my own board of directors on learning that I could be leaving was tremendous.

"That more than anything helped me to make my decision. I suddenly realised that everything I had helped to build up over the past few seasons was not to be thrown away lightly." The Morton gaffer also said that he had been swayed by the reaction of fans to the speculation surrounding Thistle's interest after a visit to the Morton Supporters' Club on the Thursday evening.

The Morton directors were to be commended for the speed and decisiveness of their action in face of a hostile bid, though Partick were somewhat miffed that Rooney had not even agreed to meet them. The Morton boss's explanation was that he did not want to set one club against another.

Rooney told the players of his decision on the Saturday morning before the home game against Airdrie and it was clearly significant in a vastly improved team performance. Morton went on to win 3-1 through goals by Jim Tolmie, Bobby Thomson and Andy Ritchie. Ritchie did the groundwork for Thomson's goal and gave a revitalised display as Morton widened the gap between themselves and third bottom Hearts to three points.

Suddenly the Tail o' the Bank side appeared a completely different proposition.

Next up were Rangers at Ibrox, the only side Rooney's men had not beaten since moving up to the Premier League. Against the odds, Morton gave a composed performance to win 1-0 with more than a dash of style. With Andy Ritchie suffering from a hamstring strain (how is that possible? I hear you ask), they played two up front, Jim Tolmie and John McNeil, with Ian Cochrane tucking in behind. The trio gave a tireless display of running, Tolmie, his side's most effective player, getting on the end of a delicate McNeil lob to round goalkeeper McCloy and score the only goal in 55 minutes. It was fully deserved. Benny Rooney also singled out skipper Davie Hayes as a key man after missing much of the early part of the season.

Hardly had the dust settled on a fantastic result, than Billy McLaren was on his way to Hibs, the 32-year-old moving for a fee of £12,000. Benny Rooney said: "In many ways I'm sorry to be losing him. Since Billy came to Cappielow he has been an ideal professional for us. It was a good bid for a player his age." Given that a five-apartment detached bungalow was selling in Skelmorlie at the time for £30,000, that was true enough. Today's figures would have to be multiplied by some seven times. It was, however, yet another departure, McLaren joining Brown, Scott, Miller, Evans and Anderson through the exit door, only Cochrane and Busby coming in the entrance.

Another big test was to come the following Saturday when league champions and league leaders Aberdeen were the visitors to Cappielow. Fergie's men, for whom Morton had been a particularly sore thorn in the side for so long, appeared to have laid their bogey in spectacular fashion with a 6-0 trouncing at Pittodrie earlier in the season and arrived full of understandable confidence.

Once again they were to limp away from the tight wee Greenock ground with their tails between their legs. Andy Ritchie, so often Aberdeen's nemesis, came off the bench with devastating effect after having recovered from the injury which had ruled him out of the win at Ibrox. His driven free kick into the box was met perfectly by a diving Jim Rooney who deflected the ball past Jim Leighton.

Gordon Strachan and Mark McGhee blasted efforts over the crossbar in the dying minutes, but it was Morton who deserved the victory with another vastly improved display to shatter the Dons' 31-game unbeaten run. Suddenly, Morton were right back to their best. Three successive wins had taken them from third bottom place to one point off fourth spot, highlighting the precarious nature of the top 10.

Draws followed against Kilmarnock at Cappielow (3-3 Thomson 2, Busby) and Hearts (0-0) at Tynecastle and Morton had taken 10 points out of a possible 14 in their last seven outings. The year ended with a good 2-0 home win over Partick, Jim Tolmie once more showing his composure in a one-on-one situation when he rounded Alan Rough to net, before an outrageous Andy Ritchie dummy set up Roddie Hutchison for the second.

Morton meanwhile announced a net profit of £4,820. Over two years they had broken even without having to sell big name players and morale had been well and truly restored. The turning point in the season undoubtedly had been Rooney's decision to stay on at Cappielow.

St Mirren, however, proved too good for Morton in the traditional Ne'erday derby, the Paisley men going three ahead in the first half with some slick football at Cappielow. Andy

Ritchie got one back via the penalty spot in 48 minutes, but there was to be no comeback. Two days later Morton were still suffering when Celtic's new £250,000 signing from Liverpool, Frank McGarvey, hit a double in a 3-0 win, again in Greenock. A third consecutive Cappielow defeat, by 2-0 against Rangers, followed. Morton fielded new signings winger Bobby Houston and midfielder John Marr from Kilmarnock and Partick respectively, but Andy Ritchie was left on the bench. The additions were much needed to complement a squad that was down to the bare minimum.

Virtually a Morton reserve side lost in the Renfrewshire Cup Final, held over from the previous season, 6-2 on aggregate to St Mirren as the third round of the Scottish Cup drew near. A 0-0 draw at Cappielow against Hearts looked ominous but, in the midweek replay at Tynecastle, goals by Jim Tolmie, Jim Rooney and Bobby Thomson, against one by Alex MacDonald, saw the side go through to the fourth round. Roy Baines in goal, and centre half Joe McLaughlin, were outstanding as the visitors repulsed several attempts by Hearts to get back into the game before a crowd of 9,782.

In the league, Morton defeated bottom club Kilmarnock with a Jim Rooney strike at Cappielow before travelling to Pittodrie on Saturday 7th February. Andy Ritchie was by this time back in the side and in his best form as, in a rehearsal for their fourth round Scottish Cup meeting the following Saturday at Cappielow, they once again humbled Fergie's men, Drew Busby getting the only goal. The Morton side, in 4-4-2, formation was Baines; Hayes, McLaughlin, Orr, Holmes; Rooney, Busby, Marr, Thomson; Tolmie and Ritchie. Manager Benny Rooney said of Ritchie's reappearance: "Andy has certainly been showing more application in the last few games and in his training too."

The question was whether or not Morton could maintain their hoodoo over the Dons twice in eight days. They did, and it was due to a marvellous Ritchie goal when he trapped the ball on his chest facing away from the Dons' goal, knocked it over his own head and that of Aberdeen defender Doug Considine, turned to bring it back under control, deceived both Alex McLeish and Willie Miller, and directed it with the outside of his right foot from an angle on the right into the left corner of the net past Leighton. His manager commented: "It was a fantastic goal. The most pleasing thing is the way he is applying himself." Roy Baines had also done his bit with two or three great saves to keep a blank sheet. For the Aberdeen players and their manager, faces redder than the team's jerseys, it was another silent journey all the way back to Pittodrie.

Baines was again in top form a week later at Tannadice, but it was not enough to prevent a 1-0 home win. When Celtic again proved too good for Morton with a 3-0 Cappielow win, McGarvey again hitting a double, Davie Provan getting the other, the Scottish Cup was very much the Greenock club's priority.

The quarter-final against Clydebank was postponed on the Saturday and, on the following Wednesday, the First Division side held Morton to a goalless draw at Cappielow after successfully defending in depth.

On the Saturday Airdrie beat Morton 1-0 in Greenock before the cup replay at Clydebank on the Monday evening. Any hopes Bankies had of creating a shock were swept aside as

Morton literally hit them for six, a Bobby Thomson hat-trick and goals from John McNeil, Jim Tolmie and Jim Rooney emphasising their superiority. Ritchie was the playmaker supreme, back to his brilliant best. The prize was a semi-final tie against Rangers.

Meanwhile the board had held a meeting along with the manager at Sir William Lithgow's Argyllshire home to discuss the club's finances, with Benny Rooney commenting: "I would like to think we are getting nearer to a full-time situation at Cappielow." Also on the agenda was the fact that for the following season the clubs had voted to keep their home gates. Morton, originally opposed to the idea, had changed their minds and voted to support it. The reason given by Hal Stewart at the time was that it afforded greater flexibility as to the setting of prices. Against that, however, there would be no more sharing gate receipts for visits to Ibrox and Parkhead. For clubs such as Morton that was a big slice of revenue and one can't help but look back on their position, as well as several other smaller clubs', as a massive mistake.

On the Saturday after the demolition of Clydebank the confidence carried over into a 3-1 home win against Hearts, John McNeil the star with two excellent goals as well as supplying the cross for Drew Busby to net against his old mates.

McNeil and Neil Orr were excluded from the next match, a 3-1 loss at Firhill against Partick, in order to protect them from further bookings which would have ruled them out of the Rangers cup semi. That tie, scheduled for Parkhead, was now very much the focus of the season.

CHAPTER EIGHT

Cup semi v Gers turns into a war

On Wednesday 1st April, 1981, Morton travelled up to Ibrox to meet Rangers in what was a dress rehearsal for the Scottish Cup semi-final in 10 days' time. The Cappielow men were third bottom of the league table, but were nevertheless virtually safe from relegation. Prior to the Ibrox match, Benny Rooney said: "It's ridiculous that we are third bottom. I've had a talk with the players and I'm looking for something from them tonight.

"I'll have what I consider my best team out tonight. It's up to the players to show me that they are the best team." That side was as follows: Baines; Hayes, McLaughlin, Orr, Holmes; Rooney, Busby, Thomson, McNeil; Tolmie, Ritchie. The challenge had been put before the players – play for your semi-final places.

The best laid plans o' mice and men gang aft agley, and so it was for Rooney as he saw Neil Orr limp off in just three minutes holding his right thigh. On came John Marr who then also had to go off to be replaced by Bobby Houston. It ended up a comfortable night for John Greig's Light Blues who coasted to a 4-0 win. On the Saturday Aberdeen at last overcame their Cappielow hoodoo with a 3-1 victory, Jim Tolmie netting for Morton with a spectacular header, giving the Greenock club a week in which to lick their wounds and plan for cup success.

It was the club's ninth Scottish Cup semi-final, and third against Rangers. Despite their league form, Benny Rooney was highly optimistic in the run-up to the tie at Parkhead, saying: "If the players are confident and play as we know they can then we will win." There were no ifs and buts about the statement. Morton's sole worry concerned the fitness of sweeper Neil Orr and Rooney said: "At the end of the day it will be up to the player."

Looking ahead to the tie, Gers boss John Greig, who had taken his players to the Inverclyde Centre in Largs, commented: "On Friday we'll be doing very little, just sharpening our reflexes, doing some speed work and getting our tactics right. Morton have proved they are a capable side and they will command our utmost respect."

The other semi-final was between Celtic and Dundee United at Hampden Park and Gourockian Davie Provan, in Billy McNeill's line-up, commented: "I'd love to see Morton winning but on present form I'd have to go for Rangers. But anything can happen in a cup tie and hopefully Benny Rooney can lift his players."

There was a steely determination among the Morton players as they travelled to Glasgow. There would be no early nerves as there had been in the League Cup semi-final the previous season against Aberdeen. As it happened, the tie was little about football and more about brute force and it was the Ibrox men who ended up on top 2-1 after 90 bruising minutes.

The headline of my report in the Greenock Telegraph stated simply "Football takes a back seat". I wrote: "Unfortunately this hard, fiercely contested Scottish Cup semi-final match at Parkhead will be remembered in years to come for the incredible number of bookings and dismissals."

Referee Brian McGinlay booked eight and sent off two. Both ordering-offs and five bookings were in the Morton ranks.

I continued: "Obviously the players – and by that I mean the players of both teams – must take their share of blame. At times they quite lost their heads and some of the tackling was ridiculous." It must have been bad, because in these days there was a greater tolerance for the physical side of the game than there is now.

The two managers' selections should have given us a hint of how they felt the tie might go. Morton lined up as follows: Baines; Hayes, McLaughlin, Orr, Holmes; Rooney, Busby, Thomson, McNeil; Tolmie, Cochrane. Subs: Ritchie and McNab.

Rangers: Stewart; Miller, Jackson, Forsyth, Dawson; McLean, Russell, Bett, Johnston; Johnstone, Redford. Subs: McAdam, Jardine.

That Andy Ritchie was on the bench and Davie Cooper not even in the Ibrox 13 said it all. The battle lines had been drawn up, and the emphasis was clearly on the word 'battle'. And so it proved. The opening stages were akin to a Highland charge between warring clans, and the referee failed to stamp his authority on the tie from the word go. I commented: "Brian McGinlay's performance in the opening 15 minutes was, to be generous to the man, inadequate."

McGinlay was to become one of our top officials, but on that afternoon he was taken a loan of. "He totally failed to take a firm grip of the game early on and several bad tackles were perpetrated without any action being taken against the offenders," I observed.

Three players in particular were fortunate not to be booked in that first quarter of an hour; Colin Jackson for persistent fouling, Willie Johnston for dissent and the sort of play-acting football can well do without, and Morton's Drew Busby for a tackle on Tom Forsyth that would have halved the Inverkip Power Station chimney. That unfortunately set the pattern and when Mr McGinlay finally decided to take action he had, frankly, lost control of the game.

Morton began the game the better in terms of its football content, though it was Colin Jackson, with a header, who produced the first save, low down by Roy Baines. Ton skipper Davie Hayes had meanwhile been most unfortunate to be cautioned when he fouled Willie Johnston. The winger, in the worst continental tradition, extracted the maximum advantage, rolling on the pitch as if lassoed by an electrified wire, only to recover magically after Hayes had been booked.

Drew Busby replied with a 20-yard drive held by Jim Stewart before Morton appeared to take the lead in 24 minutes. Jim Tolmie twisted past a defender and sent a short pass to Bobby

Thomson who swept the ball into the net. He was marginally offside, however, and the strike, correctly, was disallowed.

Still Morton looked the more cohesive of the two teams, but in 39 minutes Rangers grabbed a goal against the run of play. Roy Baines was stranded in no-man's land as Tommy McLean's corner came over and Colin Jackson, at the back post, looped a header over the goalkeeper into the net, despite the efforts of Joe McLaughlin to clear. It was a bad goal to lose from a set piece.

Tempers were fraying and Orr, McNeil and Busby were all booked for Morton, Jackson and Miller (Rangers) and Thomson (Morton) following them into the wee black book.

Andy Ritchie came on for Neil Orr, who had been doubtful before the match, and the referee then called over both captains to warn them about their players' behaviour.

Shortly after came the game's decisive moment. Derek Johnstone headed on to Bobby Russell and his 16-yard drive hit Joe McLaughlin and spun past Baines.

Morton appeared to feel a sense of injustice and Jim Holmes sent Ally Dawson to the turf as the Rangers right back ran up the right touchline. In view of the warning issued to both captains, the full back was sent packing. If Holmes, of all people, was losing the plot, it was indicative of the state of play. It was clear that Morton's discipline was fraying severely at the edges. There was a lifeline when Ian Cochrane was nudged off the ball by Jim Bett in the box and Ritchie slotted home the penalty.

Any chance of an equaliser faded soon after when Bobby Thomson sent Ibrox sub Colin McAdam sprawling. Having already been booked, he was now sent off by Mr McGinlay and the tie as a contest was over. Morton had lost their self-discipline and, with it, the game. They had been drawn into a physical confrontation when they should have been concentrating on their football and they paid the price.

That Rangers went on to beat Dundee United to lift the trophy after a replay emphasised the opportunity which had been lost, for this was not the greatest of Ibrox teams. But, in three seasons of Premier contests, Rangers definitely seemed to have the measure of a Morton side who had managed to beat them only once.

The season was over for Morton. They had the dubious distinction of taking part in a 0-0 draw at Rugby Park which produced the lowest crowd in Premier history, just 973 attending. Meanwhile John McNeil had been involved in a car crash which was to rule him out of the remainder of the season.

There was some light relief when Dundee United were beaten 2-0 at Cappielow with goals by Busby and Tolmie, the same afternoon on which Celtic claimed the title after a win over their Old Firm rivals. St Mirren inflicted another loss on a Morton side who had failed to beat them all season, by 2-0, before Airdrie completed a disappointing term with a 3-2 win at Broomfield, consigning Morton to eighth place in the league.

Worse was to follow for Morton when Jim Tolmie, out of contract, travelled to Belgium to discuss a move to FC Lokeren. Under the newly adopted freedom of contract ruling applying to all EEC clubs, he was now within his rights to discuss his future options. Manager Rooney commented: "The player has been given a good offer by Morton and it is now up to him.

Obviously we just have to accept this freedom of contract and we're not going to chase after him. Having said that, we don't want to lose him but I'm not too concerned. I'm still confident he'll sign for us."

There was some small consolation for Morton at the end of a hard, largely unrewarding season, when they beat St Mirren on penalties in the Renfrewshire Cup Final after the teams had drawn 2-2 on aggregate. Roy Baines was the hero with a penalty save from Alan Logan. Baines then came under the scrutiny of Hibernian, who wanted to take him to Easter Road, while Queen's Park Rangers took an interest in Joe McLaughlin.

On 26th May the news was finally given to Morton fans via the Greenock Telegraph that Jim Tolmie would be leaving the club. Director Tom Robertson told me: "Jim Tolmie has, in fact, signed for Lokeren. Only certain financial arrangements between him and them have still to be sorted out."

Under new legislation it was up to the clubs to agree a compensatory fee. If no agreement could be reached then arbitration would be utilised. Either way Morton would certainly not get the sum they felt the player was worth.

A close season bid for Hearts' veteran midfielder Alex MacDonald failed and then, on 6th May, 1981, it was announced through the Telegraph that Morton would receive a fee of £73,000 for Tolmie from Lokeren. The fee took into account the player's age and wages among other factors, but it was approximately half of what the young under-21 cap would have been worth in normal market conditions.

Tom Robertson commented: "We're sad to lose the player and sad also from the financial point of view. The experience also highlights the abuses and pitfalls into which clubs can fall, particularly if an agent gets involved."

It was a look into the future. Player power was on the rise and agents were to be very much to the forefront, much to the chagrin of the clubs. Those same clubs, however, had for far too long been happy to see players reduced to a role of mere chattels to be bought or sold at their whim. The times they were a-changing.

Tolmie's departure was to signal the start of the real break-up of the side Benny Rooney had built. There were no additions to the squad over the close season, though money was spent on putting in seating, donated by Rangers, at the Wee Dublin End of the ground. It was completed just in time for the opening League Cup tie of the 1981-82 season, against John Greig's Ibrox men.

The tie finished in a 1-1 draw and I wrote: "Would that all games were as entertaining as the first half at Cappielow on Saturday. Having feared a repeat of some of the intensely physical encounters of recent meetings between the two sides, it was a pleasant surprise to see a spirited but fair match, keenly fought and containing some passages of excellent football."

Morton began brightly but in 22 minutes a recovering Ibrox side should have taken the lead. Davie Cooper had set off on a meandering run which carried him into the home penalty area when his progress was abruptly halted by Joe McLaughlin. It was a clear penalty, but Alex Miller hit the spot kick wide of Roy Baines' right-hand post.

Rangers were coming back into the match and they took the lead in 41 minutes when Colin McAdam headed in a Willie Johnston cross.

Morton were to gain parity, however, with just four minutes remaining when an Andy Ritchie free kick was headed home by Roddie Hutchison, "It was a deserved reward for the team and Hutchison who had put so much work into the match," I commented.

Neil Orr again had shown his class and I said: "Playing as a sweeper, Orr had time to read the play and choose his moments to surge forward. Comparisons between him and the famous West German sweeper Franz Beckenbauer are perhaps unfair to Orr, but there is no doubt in my mind that there is no better exponent of that style of play in Scotland today."

First Division Raith Rovers and Premier League Dundee were beaten 5-2 and 2-1 respectively in two successive away ties in the same competition, but it was Rangers who topped the group when the two met again at Ibrox, a Derek Johnstone goal being the difference.

By the time Morton completed the section by beating Dundee 3-2 in a fine display at Cappielow, Andy Ritchie was out in the cold once more. Bobby Thomson had been moved up front and there was a place in midfield for the hard-working youngster Danny Docherty. John McNeil managed to get himself sent off twice in this match, the second for dissent, but Benny Rooney commented: "I don't want this incident to take away from the football we played against Dundee."

CHAPTER NINE

Record fees with departure of Thomson and Orr, and Fergie's misery continues

St Mirren produced a 2-0 win at Love Street in the league opener of season 1981-82, both goals coming from ex-Aberdeen winger Ian Scanlon and, when Morton beat Dundee United 1-0 at Cappielow in the next match, there was still no Ritchie. Significantly for the club's finances, the attendance was under 4,000. After the game Jim McLean, manager of a distinctly under-par United side, said tersely: "I've no complaints about the result."

Joe McLaughlin then confirmed his promise with a good display in a Scotland under-21 4-0 win over Sweden.

The Greenock men then fell 2-1 to Celtic at Parkhead. In a performance by the hosts which was a mixture of the excellent and the frustrating, goals by Murdo MacLeod and Tom McAdam carried the day, Bobby Thomson heading a consolation for the visitors.

It was then announced that Middlesbrough, managed by ex-Celt Bobby Murdoch, would provide the opposition for a testimonial game for Morton legend Allan McGraw. I commented: "In an age when the rule of the testimonial match seems to be 'to them that hath shall be given more' it is good to see a man such as McGraw being given the chance to make some money from the game."

There was still no appearance of Andy Ritchie by the time the eve of the Partick home match on 19th September came round. Asked about the man who had been the Player of the Year two seasons before, Benny Rooney said bluntly: "The team is playing well at the moment and I don't want to talk about other players."

The Thistle game produced two valuable points, young Danny Docherty grabbing the only goal. Ironically, where Morton had gone up one place the week before following defeat at Parkhead, they slipped down a place after the Jags win. Andy Ritchie came on as a substitute late on after Bobby Thomson was reported to have sustained a knock.

Of the Partick performance, one of their long-suffering fans commented in the direction of the press: "If we had to apply for re-election I'd vote against it!"

On the following Thursday the news hit the streets that Bobby Thomson had been sold to Middlesbrough for £170,000, a club record fee. It was obviously a deal that had been done on the quiet the week before when the testimonial match for Allan McGraw had been arranged against the English side. It explained why the player had been withdrawn late on against Thistle with no obvious sign of injury.

What was of even more concern to Morton fans than the departure of another of their top players, following as it did upon the exit of Jim Tolmie, was the news that there would be no money available to the manager for any replacements. Rooney himself explained: "This deal has been done to keep things going at Cappielow. With falling gates and one thing and another the club needed the money. I'm disappointed to lose him but wish him every success."

Chairman Hugh Currie spoke in a highly critical manner of the decision taken by the clubs to retain their home gates. The irony was that Morton had voted for precisely that very thing. Asked how long it would be before the club had to sell again, Mr Currie replied: "It really depends on having a good run in the cup. Last season we tried to hold onto the team for as long as we were in the cup.

"Our income comes from three main sources – through the turnstiles, from lotteries and the like, and from transfers. We are not getting the money through the gates, lotteries are not going so well in the economic climate, and that leaves us with transfers."

If anyone was in any doubt, the Morton bubble had well and truly burst. The First Division championship win and three highly respectable seasons in the elite Premier Division had not brought in the hoped for revenue. Commercially the club was struggling and it was now a matter of survival. It had only been a few months since manager Rooney had been talking hopefully of full-time football. That was now a pipe dream. The shock to the public was that it all appeared to happen so suddenly.

In such a setting crowds were only going to diminish further and when Morton beat Dundee 2-0 on a typically dreich Greenock day, with goals from John McNeil and Bobby Houston, only 2,763 bothered to turn out.

The following Monday the almost inevitable news broke that now Andy Ritchie was for sale. Ritchie, still only 25, was out of favour and manager Rooney said: "Ritchie came to see me on Thursday night [at training] and he said he was not prepared to play reserve football. I told him he wasn't producing the goods and that I could not guarantee him a place in the first team.

"In fairness to the player, he has worked hard in training and has lost weight, but it is just not happening for him on the field of play. At this moment we need a team with everyone prepared to work. Having said that, there would still obviously be a place for him if he were playing to form.

"Maybe the time has come when the only answer is for him to move on."

That was all very well in theory but, as I commented: "Quite who would be prepared to gamble on buying Ritchie is another matter. Even when he was at his peak two seasons ago, and available for transfer, there were precious few enquiries and no concrete offers."

The old ghosts of Andy's lack of application had drifted through the walls of football club boardrooms across Britain. Ritchie had made himself a wonderful star with his ability but at the same time a potential liability with his failure to heed the warnings issued on the need to embrace the grubbier, more committed aspects of the game. For all his genial manner, his manifest talent and his superbly entertaining antics, he had virtually become a spent force at the age of 25. Everyone thrives on confidence, but it seemed Ritchie had become more susceptible to mood swings. Without it becoming a conscious decision, he was drifting on a downward spiral. When the magic became less and the work-rate no greater he left the manager with little choice.

On 3rd October, 1981, a downbeat Morton travelled to Pittodrie where Aberdeen beat them 2-0, a largely defensive display being necessitated by available resources. Hibs, with old Ton veteran Billy McLaren in their ranks, were next up at Easter Road where Rooney's men were outplayed and lost 4-0, John McNeil being the sole stand-out.

Asked about the situation with Andy Ritchie, again an absentee, Benny Rooney said: "There have been no enquiries from other clubs for Andy. I have heard a lot of rumours about there being a personality clash between the player and myself, but there is no truth in that."

Ritchie did return seven days later at Cappielow where Airdrie were dispatched 3-0, Roddie Hutchison grabbing a brace and Ritchie the other. Young Bernie Slaven came on as a substitute and some morale had been restored after a difficult period.

That was followed up by a meritorious 1-1 draw at Ibrox. Against a Rangers team which lined up in an adventurous 4-2-4 formation, Morton's 4-3-3 gave them midfield control where Danny Docherty, Drew Busby and Jim Rooney were prominent in the first 20 minutes. At the time I wrote: "Docherty, Busby and Rooney were immense, even if Busby's challenges occasionally tend to be of the early Neolithic variety."

Rangers began to rally but, against the run of play at the time, Morton scored on the stroke of half-time, Ritchie and McNeil setting up Rooney who netted from an angle on the left past Stewart.

Rangers then brought on Ian Redford for Willie Johnston to match Morton's 4-3-3 and that proved a significant factor, most of the play now flowing to the visitors' goal. The Ibrox men were most unlucky to be denied two penalties, the first when Neil Orr fouled Jim Bett inside the box only for a free kick to be awarded outside the area, then when Joe McLaughlin appeared to divert a cross with his hand.

With eight minutes left, and Morton hanging on, John Greig's side finally gained a worthy equaliser when Davie Cooper beat Davie Hayes on the left, crossed and Bobby Russell's shot was deflected past Roy Baines.

The mood in Greenock and its associated towns and villages continued to be subdued, however. The decision of Morton not to go full-time, allied to top players being sold, brought with it the realisation that there was only one direction in which the club realistically could now travel. St Mirren arrived at Cappielow to further add to that atmosphere by inflicting a 2-0 defeat before just 4,800 fans.

Dundee United were hardly likely to improve the situation as next visitors to the Sinclair Street ground, having just recorded a magnificent UEFA Cup victory over Borussia Monchengladbach at Tannadice on the previous Tuesday. Not only did they overcome a 2-0 first leg deficit, they swept the Germans back home with five unanswered goals in a quality performance. I always felt the United side of that time played the best football of any Scottish team when they were in the mood. And, unlike others, they played just the same meticulous style in Scotland as they did in Europe. They kept possession and had a patience alien to other Scottish clubs. How often in Scotland have we heard the cry going up from a crowd 'get the ball up the park' whenever a team attempts to keep possession? Somehow United managed to educate their support, and those fans displayed a tolerance seldom seen at other grounds.

On the day at Cappielow, United continued their European form with a thoroughly convincing 3-0 win, courtesy of goals by Billy Kirkwood and Davie Dodds (2). One could not help but compare the two clubs' fortunes. Three seasons before, Morton were on the verge of emerging, just as United had done, as a provincial side of real force. Since then the two clubs had gone in opposite directions from similar backgrounds and levels of support. The reasons were varied and no doubt arguable.

Asked after the match about his own team's likely representation in the forthcoming Scotland side to travel to Portugal for a World Cup qualifying tie, United boss Jim McLean commented: "Every manager is biased towards his own players but, yes, I would expect a couple of my players to be in the pool. But, if I were the Morton manager I would want to know why Neil Orr is not in the Scotland team. He's a class player. McLaughlin [Joe] too is a very good stopper. He's maybe a wee bit raw yet when the ball is on the ground, but a great prospect."

This was at a time when Aberdeen had the Alex McLeish-Willie Miller partnership and Dundee United themselves had Paul Hegarty and Dave Narey at the heart of their defence. It was praise indeed from a quality coach and someone whose standards were almost impossibly high. Orr surely would have been capped had he come from a more fashionable club, or perhaps it was simply Morton's part-time status that militated against him.

The United defeat was exacerbated by a ligament injury to Jim Rooney which further reduced Benny Rooney's squad. With his pool stretched to the limit the Morton boss was gratified to see his men gain a very creditable 1-1 draw at Cappielow against Celtic, Andy Ritchie nullifying an earlier George McCluskey strike with a penalty before a crowd of just under 13,000 fans.

There was a break from the unrelenting business of trying to preserve Premier status when Morton met Middlesbrough at Cappielow on the following Tuesday night in a testimonial match for record goalscorer Allan McGraw. Prior to the main event, a Morton Old Crocks select met the Lisbon Lions, nine of whom turned out. The only absentees from the famous team who beat Inter Milan in the European Cup Final in 1967 were goalkeeper Ronnie Simpson and Bobby Murdoch who was managing the Middlesbrough team. The side was: Fallon; Craig, Gemmell, Wallace, McNeill, Clark, Johnstone, McBride, Chalmers, Auld and Lennox.

The Lions won their game 4-1 while Morton went on to beat Boro 2-1 with goals from Davie Hayes and John McNeil. There was a nice touch when Allan McGraw received a telegram from Jock Stein and the Scotland squad in Portugal, wishing him well on his big night. Almost 5,000 fans turned out on what was a miserable Greenock night.

Morton continued to scrap away and picked up another point at Firhill against Partick

Thistle for whom a youthful Maurice Johnston opened the scoring. Two down at the interval, Morton fought back to equalise with goals by Bobby Houston and John McNeil who had taken over the mantle of the main attacking force in the side. I asked one of the players if the manager had delivered a "Jim McLean type team talk at half-time."

"No," came the reply, "it was a Benny Rooney type team talk", the implication being that that was even more severe. Having heard both at full volume I would have to come down on the side of the Tannadice manager's wrath being the warmer. He could have blasted paint off the side of a liner, and then found time to fill up a hot air balloon.

As the year ground on, Dundee gave the men from Greenock a 4-1 smacking at Dens Park, Roddie Hutchison scoring the team's consolation goal.

Surely Aberdeen would overcome their normal Morton bogey at Cappielow in the next game. Nope. Once again Morton beat the Dons, 2-1 on this occasion, with a superb goal from John McNeil and another, scrappy effort, by Bobby Houston. "The second half," I wrote, "provided all the dash, élan, goals and determination so lacking in the first. If Neil Orr once more oozed elegance there were other fine displays in the home ranks. Right back Davie Hayes must have had a contract on Dons' left winger Peter Weir such was the latter's ineffectiveness. Roddie Hutchison battled nobly up front and John McNeil took his goal beautifully."

After the game Alex Ferguson wore the sort of expression that made you delighted not to be an Aberdeen player or his wife. One look at his face made words superfluous. If he hated coming to Cappielow, his players loathed even more the long, silent journeys back home. "It's like riding in a hearse," one Dons player told me.

Pitches were freezing over as the winter weather began to bite and, in an interview with Jim Tolmie, the young forward expressed some misgivings at having left Cappielow for Belgian club Lokeren. "I now have a little bit of regret," he said, "at leaving Morton. There were a couple of big English clubs interested in me. I went too early. I maybe should have waited a couple of years." It was little consolation to the Cappielow support, and confirmation of director Tom Robertson's views on the difficulties created by the advent of agents within the game. Tolmie was, of course, later to move to Manchester City after Billy McNeill had switched from Parkhead to Maine Road.

The winter of 1981-82 was severe, but on Sunday 3rd January, Love Street, Paisley, was passed fit to play. Once again St Mirren had the better of the derby encounter, winning 3-1 with goals from Frank McAvennie (2) and Ian Scanlon, against one by Bobby Houston.

By the following Friday the game scheduled for Cappielow against Dundee United had already fallen victim to the weather and provoked a financial crisis for Morton. It was the third successive home match postponed. I had heard strong rumours leaking from the Greenock club that all was not well. I wrote: "The situation is precarious. It would not surprise me greatly if Morton were forced very soon into the position of having to sell another of their star players. Jim Tolmie and Bobby Thomson have already gone and at this rate it is surely only a matter of time before a player, possibly Joe McLaughlin or Neil Orr, completes the hat-trick of departures."

On the Monday the rumours became reality. Neil Orr, capped nine times for the Scotland under-21s, was on his way to West Ham. For a club record fee, said by managing director Hal Stewart to be "around £400,000", the Hammers had plucked away another jewel from Benny Rooney's crown in a deal concluded on the Saturday night.

It transpired that the bold Hal had been in negotiations with two English clubs and Glasgow Rangers. Rangers had come in with an offer of £150,000 before being trumped by West Ham, Stewart exploiting the situation with his usual canny aplomb.

It smashed the transfer record set by Bobby Thomson's £170,000 move to Middlesbrough. It also left the fans in no doubt as to their club's parlous fiscal well-being. Chairman Hugh Currie, aware of the furore the news would cause among the support, came out with the statement: "It is a deal which is going to save the club."

Asked if any of the money would be used for replacements, he continued: "I don't want to talk about that. The money is there to ensure the future of the club. We can always rebuild."

I commented: "Orr was bound to leave Cappielow sooner or later, but the timing of his departure, so soon after the transfers of Tolmie and Thomson, indicates the seriousness of the money worries at Cappielow."

Manager Benny Rooney said: "At the immediate time there is no cash available for new players. I'm obviously very disappointed to lose a player of Neil's ability. Still, you've got to get your head up and get on with the job."

Hal Stewart was quite blunt in a prepared statement, saying: "The position at Cappielow was becoming so untenable with no income over an extended period that we had no option but to sell our best player. To date this season gate receipts have fallen far below operating costs and there was just too big a hole in the bucket to carry on without taking drastic action. The loss of Neil Orr is too drastic for words.

"Ground improvements arising from the Safety of Grounds Act have led to huge commitments and, while in the years ahead the club will have the benefit of an improved stadium, something had to go to pay the bills. Unfortunately it was Neil Orr.

"It was a bad blow to manager Benny Rooney and his assistant Mike Jackson who have worked miracles to keep the club in the top bracket, but they are such a great partnership that we have no fears for the future, especially with so many good young players coming through."

Survival was now the name of the game in Greenock. The club had gone from issuing statements to the effect that transfers were being made to "balance the books" to transfers being made to "save the club".

The fact was that Morton, in the top flight of Scottish football, were attracting crowds no bigger than most English Fourth Division clubs. Add the other rising costs – safety at grounds, policing, EEC legislation regarding transfer fees, and the retention of home gates – and the combination financially was what now would be termed 'highly toxic'. Football boards are first to be castigated when things go wrong. The decision, backed by Morton, to retain home gates was disastrous for all the smaller ambitious provincial clubs. That said, however, there wasn't sufficient support within the community to sustain a Premier side indefinitely while the stadium also required serious upgrading.

When St Mirren inflicted their fourth defeat of the season over Morton in the third round of the Scottish Cup at Love Street on 23rd January, 1982, by 2-1, the picture was crystal clear. No further cup income simply aggravated an already desperate situation. The majority shareholding in the club was held by William Lithgow Holdings Ltd and Sir William Lithgow himself. But there was no treasure chest of cash to fill the coffers; no donations to offer relief. The club had to earn what it spent. The accounts had to balance.

Morale clearly was going to be an issue. You cannot continually sell your best assets without it having an adverse effect both on results and confidence. Morton were now, even at that early stage in the season, looking at a relegation battle.

At the end of January the side ground out a no-scoring draw with similarly threatened Partick Thistle at Cappielow. Making his debut was young Celtic defender Jim Duffy, on loan, and I described his performance as having "played very competently alongside centre half Joe McLaughlin."

Duffy's signing was completed days later for a fee of £25,000 and Benny Rooney said: "He's a good signing for us. It's no stop-gap measure. At 22 he's desperate to prove himself and he showed against Partick Thistle last week that he can play." As things turned out it was to be another top acquisition by Rooney.

CHAPTER TEN

Alex Ferguson's praise for McLaughlin

On 6th February, 1982, Morton travelled north to Aberdeen and managed to gain a fantastic point in the circumstances in their fight to avoid the drop. The side showed great spirit and determination in the face of adversity and I reported: "It was no fluke result. Certainly the home team exerted the greater pressure throughout the 90 minutes. But, they created no more clear-cut opportunities than their less illustrious opponents.

"The Greenock men's heroes were principally found in defence. Centre half Joe McLaughlin was quite simply outstanding, once again this season outshining his international counterpart Alex McLeish in the home line-up. Alongside him new signing from Celtic, Jim Duffy, played like a seasoned veteran. His positional sense was faultless and a continuation of this sort of form will do much to lessen the impact of Neil Orr's departure to West Ham."

McLaughlin's performance drew the comment from Dons boss Alex Ferguson: "That was the best display I've seen from a centre half this season." Praise indeed, considering his own centre backs were Scotland partnership McLeish and Miller. McLaughlin had matured considerably. Commendably, he seemed to relish the added responsibility that had come with losing his partner Orr.

Davie Hayes did well to snuff out the threat of Peter Weir on the left wing, while Andy Ritchie showed that he could apply himself to hard work when he had a mind to.

In the following week John Marr, who frankly had been very disappointing since his arrival from Partick, was told he could find another club. Meanwhile young striker Bernie Slaven was beginning to break into the side. He was not really ready for first team football, but Morton were in no position to pick and choose their times given the paucity of their resources.

It was the youthful Bernie who netted in a 1-1 draw with Airdrie at Broomfield, the match being an example of the fear factor that such a tight league necessarily involves. Both managers, Benny Rooney and Airdrie's Bobby Watson, made that point afterwards. Watson said: "We're hardly halfway through the season and relegation is an issue."

The point saw Morton retain fourth bottom spot on 16 points, two ahead of Airdrie and five above Partick and Dundee.

Meanwhile Joe McLaughlin's form meant he was a shoe-in for the Scotland under-21 team again, this time travelling to Italy, while managing director Hal Stewart was behind a new proposal for league reconstruction, suggesting three divisions of 16,12 and 12. While there was no doubt that having half a league of 10 clubs involved in a fight to avoid the drop from the word go was neither conducive to attractive attacking football nor the development of talented youngsters, the trouble with a 16-club league was the lack of fixtures if clubs were to play each other just twice. It is a problem to which no one has provided an entirely satisfactory solution to this day.

On the third Saturday of February Morton produced two valuable points in a 2-0 home win over Dundee, goals coming from Danny Docherty and Roddie Hutchison. They were scored at excellent psychological moments in the game, either side of half-time. Once again McLaughlin and Duffy were immense, Hayes and Holmes not far behind in a sterling back four. As I wrote: "Morton eased, if not removed, their relegation worries."

Jim Duffy was a completely different style of player to Neil Orr, rugged and ungainly looking in comparison to Orr's air of finesse and flair. But, by God, he was effective. He may not have had Orr's attacking expertise in breaking forward from deep positions, but as a defender he was unyielding and defiant. He was also wholly reliable. Not the biggest, he made up for that with a totally uncompromising, focused approach and an excellent timing in the tackle.

Orr meanwhile was settling in at West Ham. In an interview with him he gave credit to his former manager at Cappielow. "Benny Rooney improved me 100% as a player. He was always interested in me. He would take me aside and tell me what I should be doing, point out little things to help me. Benny and Mike Jackson have done a lot for me as has everyone at Cappielow."

At that stage he was playing left side in a centre back partnership. He expressed a modest satisfaction with his form thus far. On the quality of opponents he singled out two English internationalists and said: "The best player I've played against so far is Frank Worthington. Another is Kevin Keegan. He gets through a lot of work. For someone who has made a lot of money out of football he obviously still has a lot of pride in performance."

Orr went on to enjoy a good career in England, but I believe he suffered at times by virtue of his versatility. After overcoming injury problems early in his London career, West Ham often played him in midfield, such was his composure on the ball, but I always felt he was a supreme sweeper. Had he played regularly there he surely would have won a place in the senior Scotland side. As Jim McLean had said, he was a class act.

The ever present transfer issue with Andy Ritchie again reared its head as March began. The big man still wanted away, but by now he was a rather forlorn figure at the club. There can be little doubt that his disenchantment was exacerbated by seeing the cream of his team-mates depart for greener pastures, but his manager was quick to point out the solution. Rooney said: "There are still two years to run on Ritchie's contract. It's up to him to get clubs interested in him. It seems obvious he wants away. But he has been available for transfer off and on for some time and there have been no enquiries."

I also feel Ritchie's effectiveness in his best seasons was at least partly due to the tremendous work-rate of those around him which allowed him to express himself. If he was understandably disillusioned by the exit of quality players such as Tolmie, Thomson and Orr, he no doubt suffered also from the absence of men such as Jimmy Miller, Billy McLaren and Ally Scott who did so much of the leg work for him.

It was on to Parkhead where a 1-0 defeat by Celtic was creditable enough, Frank McGarvey netting after Roy Baines had earlier produced a brilliant penalty save from the same player.

That was compensated for by the collection of three key points in a 1-0 win over relegation rivals Airdrie, courtesy of an Andy Ritchie penalty, then a 2-2 draw at Easter Road against Hibernian. Morton took the lead at Easter Road against the run of play when a Hutchison knock-down was struck home beautifully by John McNeil. Hibs hit back to take a deserved second half lead with goals by Rae and Murray and looked set for both points. Then came a touch of controversy. Home centre half Craig Paterson dumped John McNeil who fell injured in front of the home grandstand.

In those days a particularly vociferous group of Leith natives occupied a terracing in front of the stand. They had a reputation for being just a wee bit less than cultured. A posh Edinburgh girl would no more have taken one of their number home to meet mother than she would have gone to a Glasgow pub for a girls' day out. I described the scene thus: "As John McNeil received treatment for a foul by Paterson near the standside touchline, Morton boss Benny Rooney and trainer Willie Gray were subjected to a shower of spittle interspersed with the occasional stone or bit of rubbish. Rooney approached the police and he and his staff were subjected to more abuse [by the supporters]."

The police took no action, for which I am indebted, as it gave me the best caption I have ever placed beneath a picture. The photographer had caught a smiling Benny Rooney and Willie Gray turning away from the unimpressed cloth-eared constables and when the picture appeared in Monday's paper I was able to pen "The Leith police dismisseth us". Well done the Embra polis!

Morton were hanging on to fourth bottom spot and were now five points clear of Airdrie, six ahead of Dundee and seven in front of Thistle.

On Wednesday 17th March, in a rearranged fixture against Rangers, a mighty point was secured in a 0-0 draw before surely the lowest crowd ever to watch a match against the Light Blues at Cappielow – 4,579 souls. In a purple 10-minute patch in the second half, Peter McCloy produced three excellent saves to deny the hosts while, at the other end, Jim Holmes cleared off the line from a John McClelland header. Honours were even when the final whistle blew.

On the Saturday St Mirren completed a depressing fifth competitive defeat of Morton, a Lex Richardson drive being deflected past a helpless Roy Baines. For once that season the strike had come against the general run of play in the fixture.

A bizarre story in one of the Sunday papers that Texan outfit Dallas Tornadoes were interested in purchasing Morton turned out to be based on no more than a mission by Hal Stewart to discuss possible player acquisitions, before March drew to a close with a Motherwell bid for Andy Ritchie being turned down out of hand by Ton manager Benny Rooney. Said a weary Rooney: "Motherwell came in with a bid for the player of £30,000 which I have refused. It is well below my estimation of the player's value."

It was then announced that the Hal Stewart instigated move to change the leagues to a 16-12-12 format had been voted down by the clubs, 18 in favour and 20 against. Differing views in the Morton camp were highlighted by director Tom Robertson's statement. "I have no doubt," he said, "that a 16-club league would have cost Morton some £45,000 a year in lost gate receipts." Given that Hal Stewart also had been in favour of clubs retaining their own home gates, something of which his chairman Hugh Currie was vociferously critical when it was voted through, it was evident that the Morton board did not always sing from the same hymn sheet.

The final Saturday of March brought with it a result which signalled the road ahead for Morton when they were soundly spanked 5-0 at Tannadice, Paul Sturrock tormenting them with a hat-trick and Ralph Milne adding two more.

Benny Rooney was aware of his team's goalscoring deficiencies and moved to bring in young Brighton striker Mike Ring on a month's loan. But, in the next match, against Celtic at Cappielow, it was Andy Ritchie who struck in a 1-1 draw in which most of the entertainment came in the second half.

Young Celt Danny Crainie had opened the scoring two minutes before the interval, a lead Billy McNeill's men merited on pressure. Eight minutes after the break, the hosts gained parity. Ritchie bamboozled two Celtic defenders and slipped a pass on to Roddie Hutchison. Pat Bonner did well to block but Ritchie was following up to guide the ball home. Bonner then produced a tremendous save to tip a John McNeil effort over the crossbar.

New boy Ring had a quiet debut, Jim Duffy doing well against his old teammates and Andy Ritchie showing glimpses of fine form.

Another 1-1 draw followed against Dundee United at Cappielow, Drew Busby deflecting a Jim Rooney shot past McAlpine three minutes from time to nullify a strike by Ralph Milne in the 71st minute. Rooney had been in tremendous form, tireless in covering the pitch as well as hitting the post with an early attempt, while the ever enthusiastic Hutchison had worked his socks off. I wrote: "If Roderick gives 100% in a match he isn't really trying."

Just as Morton were showing some real form came a major slump. In an encounter against Partick Thistle in Maryhill the Greenock side went down 4-0. It was a lamentable display. "Morton turned up at Firhill on Saturday … but that is just about all they did," I commented. "This was quite the worst display by the Greenock team I have ever seen."

The season was drawing to its close and goals by Ian Cochrane and Roddie Hutchison gave Morton a 2-1 home win over Hibs before Aberdeen were the visitors on 17th April.

Morton's incredible jinx on Ferguson's men continued as they took the points in a 2-1 win. John McNeil opened the scoring in the first half, but in the second period the Dons began to turn the screw and their dominance was rewarded with a goal by old Ton favourite Mark McGhee.

Morton rallied in the closing stages and their fans erupted when Jim Rooney netted a winner in injury time. John McNeil's shot hit referee Brian McGinlay and Jim Leighton did well to parry, but only as far as Rooney who swept it into the net. Once again centre half Joe McLaughlin was outstanding, increasing the speculation that he would be the next to leave for greater things.

The club had virtually ensured Premier football for a fifth season, though successive defeats to Dundee (2-1 at Dens Park) and Rangers by 3-1 at Cappielow followed. Once again an abysmally low crowd turned out for the match against John Greig's team, the official attendance being 4,859. In two home league games against the Light Blues – one in midweek – less than 10,000 fans had turned out. The season before the equivalent number had been 26,000. "These are incredible all-time low figures," I wrote, "which must send a shiver down the back of all concerned with the club."

Morton then drew 1-1 at Airdrie in their final away match of the season, meaning they had not recorded one single league victory on opposition soil. Amazingly, Jim Holmes lined up in a striking role alongside Ian Cochrane, winger Bobby Houston dropping back to full back, the manager explaining that it was "to keep the players interested and freshen things up."

Rooney then announced that eight players would be given free transfers, among them Drew Busby, John Marr and Jim Wilkie. Like an old shire horse, Busby's legs simply had come to the end of their productive use.

There was talk that the club had put a £200,000 transfer fee on Joe McLaughlin's head, something Benny Rooney denied when he said: "It will have to be a fee of well over £200,000 before we deal with anyone."

The season ended with an insipid, scoreless draw at Cappielow against Hibs. Of the season as a whole, in which Morton finished seventh on 30 points, I said: "Morton's survival in the top 10 this season is, I believe, rather remarkable. At various stages they lost three key players – Jim Tolmie, Bobby Thomson and Neil Orr. Their transfers netted the club around £600,000. Yet of that, only £25,000, for the purchase of Jim Duffy, could be made available to manager Benny Rooney for replacements.

"No team in the league could lose three star players and remain as attractive or competitive a proposition as they were before," I continued. "This applies particularly to a part-time outfit like Morton who are losing money hand over fist and who must sell to survive."

Joe McLaughlin was voted Player of the Year for the Sir William Lithgow Trophy, the only player to have won it twice since its inception in 1975. Previous winners were Roy Baines, George Anderson, Tom McNeil, Andy Ritchie, Jim Holmes, Joe McLaughlin and Jim Tolmie.

As the close season began, Benny Rooney denied any link with the managerial post at Motherwell while his assistant, Mike Jackson, confirmed that the Greenock club were interested in St Mirren midfielder Lex Richardson. Motherwell eventually appointed former Rangers boss Jock Wallace as manager while a deal with St Mirren involving an exchange between Lex Richardson and John McNeil came to nothing. Benny Rooney explained: "It would have been a straight swap, but there wasn't enough money in it for the players. To come here Richardson would have had to take quite a substantial drop in wages and we couldn't afford to compensate him."

Rooney knew full well the ability that local lad McNeil possessed, but at times he was frustrated by the player's apparent lack of drive or consistency. He continued: "We must now motivate John and make sure we get the best out of him here at Cappielow."

As the pre-season posturing and bartering began among the clubs, Hibs expressed interest in Morton centre half Joe McLaughlin, knowing that Rangers were on the verge of taking Craig Paterson to Ibrox. But the price tag of over £250,000 was more than Bertie Auld had a mind to pay. Auld, however, did tie up an ex-Cappielow player when he bought Bobby Thomson from Middlesbrough for a fee reported to be around £80,000, less than half what the English club had paid Morton for the player. Thomson hadn't even been a year down south, but it had been a curiously disappointing venture for him.

Morton, with no money to splash, did bring in former Hibernian and Partick midfielder Tony Higgins on a free transfer and his first outing was in a friendly at Cappielow against Clyde after playing in a closed door game against Clydebank at Largs. "I was pleased with his performance," said manager Rooney. "We are very short pool-wise. I need players but we haven't got the money to buy and I can't afford to let any others go."

Higgins made a scoring home debut against Clyde, but the highlight was an Andy Ritchie goal straight from a corner kick, not the first time he had recorded such a feat. John McNeil grabbed the other goal against a Bully Wee team including Pat Nevin who was to go on to play for Chelsea and Scotland.

Ritchie was on the mark again in another friendly at Cappielow, against Second Division Newcastle for whom Chris Waddle lined up on the left wing. The Geordies, however, won 3-1 and it would have been more had Roy Baines not saved a penalty.

CHAPTER ELEVEN

Relegation

The 1982-83 season proper began for Morton at Cappielow with a League Cup section tie against league runners-up and Scottish Cup winners Aberdeen on 11th August. It ended 2-2, the visitors scoring through Gordon Strachan, from the penalty spot, and Mark McGhee, Morton replying with a Roddie Hutchison header from a perfect Andy Ritchie cross and a penalty from Ritchie himself.

I wrote: "After the match Aberdeen manager Alex Ferguson was generally satisfied to get a point at a ground at which his men have been notoriously unsuccessful in recent years."

What was worrying from a Morton point of view was the fact that just over three thousand fans turned out for a tie against one of the top sides in Scotland. Rooney and his diminishing squad had done a superb job to remain in Scotland's top league in the previous season but, with no money to spend, no benevolent benefactor and losses accumulating like midges on a dank summer evening, the future was not hard to foretell.

Dumbarton were beaten 3-1 in the next League Cup tie before Benny Rooney moved to fix up released Rangers centre half Colin Jackson on a short term deal. Meanwhile Joe McLaughlin received an accolade when Coral Bookmakers awarded him their Daily Star Award as Scottish Premier Player of the Year.

The energetic midfield of Jim Rooney, Danny Docherty and Ian Cochrane were the basis of a convincing 4-1 League Cup tie win over Dundee at Cappielow. If they were the driving force, it was also good for the home fans to see Andy Ritchie back to the kind of form which had made him such a force in Scottish football. One young Dark Blues' fan in the stand near the press benches was heard to say: "That Ritchie's a big dumpling." His elderly companion retorted: "Aye, son, and I wish we had a dumpling too."

Dundee United were next to enquire about a Morton player, but a proposed straight swop between Jim Rooney and Ian Gibson – a former Morton target when at Partick – was rejected after Benny Rooney felt that his club should also receive cash in the deal.

In the return League Cup clash at Pittodrie, Aberdeen were too strong for Morton in a 3-0 win, with goals from Dougie Bell (2) and Doug Rougvie. The section ended with a 4-1 win over Dumbarton and a 3-3 draw with Dundee at Dens Park, not enough to overcome the Dons' lead.

Two of Morton's squad still to sign new deals finally put pen to paper, Joe McLaughlin being assured that if a club came in for him he could go given a reasonable offer, and Danny Docherty renewing his contract. That left Jim Holmes, the full back who had been stand-in skipper for injured Davie Hayes, ruled out for a couple of months due to knee surgery. And Holmes was to supply the next shock to the system when he announced he would not re-sign. His manager commented: "I'm very disappointed with his attitude. He knows the financial position at the club and the injuries we have. He received a substantial sign-on fee two years' ago and he knows the money isn't there for a similar arrangement."

Colin Jackson and a young Martin Doak were added to the squad for the Aberdeen league opener at Pittodrie, Jim Duffy taking over as captain. With the game tied at 1-1 Duffy was sent off in a bad tempered game and with him went Morton's chances, the Dons running out 4-1 winners. For Colin Jackson it was his debut appearance as a sub.

By the time the return leg against Dundee came round, Jim Holmes had settled his differences with the club and was back in the side, but the hosts won 2-0, prompting Benny Rooney to say of his front pairing: "We are going to have to get a lot more out of John McNeil and Andy Ritchie if we are to survive this season."

Thus chastised, Ritchie produced a perfect riposte against Motherwell at Cappielow. I reported: "Six minutes before the interval the home side broke the deadlock. Eddie McNab wandered across the edge of the penalty area before sending a harmless looking pass to Andy Ritchie, standing on the right corner of the box. Andy put on his wizard's hat, waved his wand, and sent a beautiful, bending shot with the outside of his right foot into the right hand side of the goal." Further goals from Eddie McNab and Jim Rooney were to lead to a 3-1 scoreline and enrage Well's new gaffer, Jock Wallace. The ex-Rangers manager's after-match debriefing could have been heard across the river in Helensburgh.

The attendance was once again abysmal, just 2,804 turning up. Some fans from those days appear to look back at crowds then with rose-tinted spectacles. The fact is that Morton were haemorrhaging money. Whether low attendances were due to disillusion over star players being sold or not, the situation was unsustainable.

October,1982, began with Morton occupying fourth bottom spot in the SPL table after four games and with midfield player John Marr being banned from Cappielow. A player who had shown promise in his early career at Partick, Marr had been a big disappointment at Greenock and Benny Rooney stated bluntly: "He's just going through the motions. He's a bad influence on the young players and I've told him to stay away."

On Saturday 2nd October spirits were raised at Cappielow when Morton recorded their first away win in the league since they had beaten Aberdeen in February, 1981. Hibernian were the victims, going down 2-1 at Easter Road, Andy Ritchie and young Eddie McNab grabbing the vital goals.

New Hibs boss Pat Stanton, who had seen his team dominate possession, was frankly honest in his summing up. He said: "It's goals that count and you can't put them away any better than Morton did."

Stanton's side had taken a deserved lead through old Mortonian, Bobby Thomson. He had cut in from the left with that familiar springy stride to rifle a shot past Roy Baines, reminding his old club of the goal threat he so often posed from midfield when in the blue and white hoops.

But it merely prompted his old mucker, Andy Ritchie, into a reply of his own. Alan Sneddon had barged Eddie McNab off the ball on the edge of the home penalty area, very much Ritchie territory. I described the ensuing scene thus: "Andy Ritchie, as conspicuous up until then as a recumbent polar bear in a snow storm, stepped up to supervise. Hibs goalkeeper Jim McArthur was meanwhile organising his defensive wall. Ritchie politely waited until he had finished and then bent the ball superbly round the human barrier and into the goal."

Worse was to follow for the Hibees when young McNab added a winner later in the match. I wrote: "He accelerated in the way I wish my car would past three home defenders before crashing a perfect shot from an angle past a motionless McArthur." It was a commendable reward for Morton's best player on the day.

The side then gained a key point against Rangers at Cappielow in a goalless, but entertaining, draw. Ibrox boss John Greig said: "Both sides tried to win the game. All it needed was goals to make it an excellent match."

There was agreement from Benny Rooney who commented: "I thought it was a very good game. Both sides missed chances but the first half was as good as I've seen for a while." One of Morton's better players was ex-Rangers centre half Colin Jackson before a crowd of 11,370.

Andy Ritchie adorned the match with some lovely passing, not always rewarded with due anticipation by his teammates, while Danny Docherty struck the crossbar with one effort. These results carried the team up to sixth place and gave some reason for renewed optimism.

With a full squad again at his disposal, manager Rooney took his charges to Tayside the following week and a clash with in-form Dundee United. High hopes were shattered by the Tangerines who trounced the visitors 6-0 with an exquisite performance. In my report I said: "In United manager Jim McLean's office after play the lights fused, plunging the assembled press corps into darkness. 'The lights went out on Morton a lot earlier', quipped a contented James, shedding his dour image. 'That first half was as good as anyone could hope to see. Some of the stuff our boys played was brilliant, unbelievable.'"

Unusually for him, McLean picked out one player, Dave Narey, for special mention. The defender had scored as well as giving a flawless display. Davie Dodds contributed a hat-trick, Paul Sturrock and Billy Kirkwood getting the remaining goals.

Asked what he had said to his players after the match, McLean replied: "Probably all the wrong things after their second half performance. But, really, they were superb and no team could be expected to play as they did in the first half for the full 90 minutes."

Benny Rooney was left to say: "We didn't compete. We stood back and let them play." He had a point, but few could live with United in that type of form, and that included some very fine European outfits.

Another defeat was served up, this time at Cappielow, where champions Celtic never had to get out of second gear on a lovely Autumn day to dispatch their hosts 2-1 with goals by

Frank McGarvey and Charlie Nicholas, Jim Rooney getting a consolation strike for Morton. Celtic's best player was their youngest, 18-year-old Paul McStay giving a cultured display. "It will be odd indeed," I wrote, "if he is not a key man for Scotland by the time the next World Cup comes round."

Morton's cash-strapped circumstances were exposed by the fact that when Colin Jackson's loan period expired he was whisked off to First Division Partick Thistle who could afford greater remuneration than the Greenock club.

Some momentum was regained when Morton travelled to Love Street and gained a point in a 1-1 draw, a decent result given that they had lost five competitive fixtures the previous season to their derby rivals. Ian Cochrane gave them the lead with a well struck 25-yard drive, the equaliser coming when Frank McAvennie shoulder-charged Ton goalkeeper Roy Baines, forcing him to drop the ball over the line before falling into the goal himself.

Injuries and suspensions were creating problems for an already tight Ton squad and Kilmarnock cantered to a 3-1 win at Rugby Park in a key match near the bottom of the table. Killie were now in second bottom place, one point behind Morton in fourth bottom spot. With that as a background, few expected the threadbare Greenock side, minus centre backs Joe McLaughlin and Jim Duffy, as well as the charismatic Andy Ritchie, to gain anything against Aberdeen at Cappielow. The Dons were in top form, having dismissed New Firm rivals Dundee United 5-1 in their previous fixture. A defiant Morton, however, grabbed a massive point in a 1-1 draw. It was, I said, a performance which "defied all the odds." Morton took the lead through Eddie McNab before Neil Simpson snatched a draw six minutes from time. Top player for Morton was stand-in centre half Roddie Hutchison who had to be implored by his manager not to gallop upfield such was his enthusiasm for the cause.

There was an honour for club doctor Craig Speirs when he was picked to accompany the Scotland under-21s, including Joe McLaughlin for his 10th cap, to Switzerland for a game won 4-3 by the Scots who had, at one time, been three up and coasting. In the Scottish ranks were players of the calibre of Charlie Nicholas, Paul McStay and Richard Gough.

Still Morton were struggling with injuries and after two successive defeats to Dundee, 2-1 at Cappielow, and Motherwell, 3-1 at Fir Park, the alarm bells really began to ring. The side were now second bottom on eight points, just one ahead of Hibernian. Martin Doak had come on as a substitute against Motherwell as Morton sought to paper over the cracks of their depleted pool and had done well.

It was Hibs next up at Cappielow in what was clearly a massive game. In the event, the scratch Ton selection did more than just grind out a scoreless draw to keep them marginally above their relegation rivals from Edinburgh. Allan Rough, transferred to the capital club from Partick, was the Hibs hero in goal before a crowd of just 1,800 hardy souls.

The injury situation was at last clearing, however, and on Saturday 11th December an excellent home point was garnered against Rangers, Jim Rooney's opening goal being cancelled out by a Robert Prytz penalty. Joe McLaughlin was the outstanding player of the game and again was called up by Scotland under-21s for a 2-1 win in Belgium.

It was with some trepidation that Morton welcomed Dundee United to Cappielow, just a few weeks after that 6-0 demolition at Tannadice, but on this occasion, although beaten again, the score was a more respectable 2-1, goals by Reilly and Sturrock negating one from Eddie McNab.

On Christmas Eve the club held their AGM when they announced a profit of £295,350. Had it not been for transfer fees it would have been a loss of £177,000. Bank borrowing was also reduced by £142,000.

Celtic provided little cause for festive cheer when they walloped their fellow hoops 5-1 at Parkhead in a thoroughly convincing display. Even the Morton counter was an own goal by Murdo MacLeod.

As the year drew to a close it was announced that a swap loan deal had been agreed between Morton and Dundee United involving United's Ian Gibson and Graeme Payne, and the Cappielow club's John McNeil. Benny Rooney had been keen on midfielder Gibson for some time. It was agreed he would play for Morton until the end of February, as would McNeil at Tannadice, while Payne would be a Morton player until the end of the season.

For McNeil it was a chance to impress under the full-time regime on Tayside. His ability was not in dispute, but always there was a question mark over his resolve and consistency. He was going to a club with thoroughbred players and a meticulous manager where any flaws would be thoroughly examined. For Morton it was hoped that the incomers would provide fresh impetus and the spark to carry them away from the prospect of relegation.

With Gibson and Payne in the side, Morton had an impressive start to the New Year with a 3-0 win at Cappielow over fellow strugglers Kilmarnock. Rooney, McNab and Hutchison were the scorers, with Payne, Rooney and Cochrane their best players on the day. It kept Morton in fourth bottom place, albeit only one point ahead of Hibs and Motherwell.

Aberdeen then reintroduced some realism with a comfortable 2-0 victory at Pittodrie before Motherwell came in with another bid to take Andy Ritchie to Firhill. This time they offered £15,000 plus former Celtic midfielder Brian McLaughlin. It was an offer Morton rejected, no reason being given. But the Greenock club scarcely needed another midfield player. A striker was their priority.

Ritchie was not in the squad for the trip to Dens Park to meet another relegation threatened side, Dundee. Benny Rooney commented: "Andy isn't in a state of mind to be playing for Morton, which is unfortunate. We are prepared to listen to offers for him."

The pity was that it was Ritchie who had the ability to score the goals that the club so desperately needed.

In the event, the match at Dens was one of the most extraordinary I have ever seen. At the time I wrote: "Never have I seen a Morton side away from home in Premier competition exert such control. They started the game confidently, suffered a dreadful five-minute spell when they seemed intent on committing soccer suicide, and then totally dominated the game."

It ended up 3-3 after Dundee bizarrely had taken a three-goal lead. Dens boss Donald MacKay summed up: "We were three up without having played. My players began to think that they must be good and they could sit back. If I'm being absolutely honest, we should never even have got a point."

Morton skipper Jim Holmes said after the match: "We started well and I remember looking at the clock at quarter past three and thinking that all we needed was a goal. I looked at the clock at twenty past three and we were three down."

After a dominant opening spell by the visitors, Dark Blues' striker Ian Ferguson took advantage of a huge hole in the Greenock defence to score an opener quite against the run of play. A rare mistake by Holmes again let in Ferguson, his drive struck team-mate Sinclair and spun past a stunned Roy Baines for number two. Hardly had Morton recovered from that when they were three down, Stephen cutting inside and, with enough time to paint a landscape and smoke a Cuban cigar, he planted the ball into the net.

It was a bewildering opening. Morton, however, continued to dominate the play and were rewarded three minutes before the interval when Graeme Payne's shot was spilled by goalkeeper Kelly and squirmed over the line. Jim Rooney, a stand-out for the visitors in midfield, brought it back to 3-2 at which point I described the action as being "almost embarrassingly one-sided."

It was Rooney again on target with 12 minutes to go when he headed in a Payne cross but, despite a further onslaught, Morton had to be content with a point. The bottom of the table could hardly have been tighter, Hibs on 16 points, St Mirren, Morton and Motherwell all on 15, and Kilmarnock bottom on 10 points. Everyone had played 21 games. Killie were already beginning to look isolated, but there was going to be a desperate scramble to avoid being the club to join them in the drop to the First Division.

Next up were Motherwell at Cappielow and no one needed to point out the importance of the game. It turned out to be a demanding physical scrap. Under Jock Wallace, Motherwell were not lacking in resolution. At Ibrox his renowned speciality for imbuing fitness in his players was to send them galloping up and down the sands at Gullane on the east coast. His military background also was often the subject of metaphors as to his footballing philosophy – trench warfare, displays of fortitude, determination, standing shoulder to shoulder etc. I commented: "The first half was virtually all Morton, and three excellent chances were created. None was taken. Certainly Motherwell's aggressive tackling didn't help matters. Jock Wallace has often sung the praises of character and commitment. To that Motherwell also added a third 'c' – that good, old-fashioned word clugging."

With Morton left to rue missed opportunities, it was Well who grabbed the only goal of the game before a crowd of just over 3,600 to take two very important points.

After the fray was over Wallace strode to the press conference, took a look at the tallest member of the hacks and barked at the poor fellow: "Can you score goals?" He was still looking the young lad up and down when he continued at top volume: "Yer no a paratrooper til you've jumped out the plane!" before striding off down the corridor. We smiled vacantly, pens poised in mid-scribble. As I wrote afterwards: "You don't interview Jock. You are on parade."

Benny Rooney was more conventional, and comprehensible: "Motherwell aren't safe," he said, "and we're not going to go down as a result of this game."

But it was a warning to Morton. I concluded: "Wallace favours the bayonets fixed approach and, referees willing, it may be Motherwell's salvation this season."

There was some relief from the pressures of football at the bottom of the SPL when Morton travelled to Recreation Park to meet First Division Alloa in the third round of the Scottish Cup. A Roddie Hutchison goal was the highlight of the first 45 minutes. I reported: "The half ended without further scoring, though with some light relief when the irrepressible Roderick Hutchison paused before the stand on his way in to a half-time cuppa and announced to all and sundry: "Clinical …clinical finishing!" This caused some mirth and provoked the response from one elderly home fan: "Awa and bile yer heid!"

Having presumably biled his heid, Hutchison came out for the second half with his chums, Eddie McNab adding a second goal before the hosts scraped a consolation of their own.

It was back to the relegation battle on Saturday 5th February when Morton travelled through to Edinburgh where they lost 2-0 to Hibernian. There was a concerning lack of spirit about the display. Next up were Rangers at Cappielow and Morton were now second bottom in the table, two points behind Motherwell.

The Ibrox men were incurring the wrath of their own supporters, finding themselves chasing the leading pack of Aberdeen, Celtic and Dundee United. On this occasion they sent their fans home more than happy with a 5-0 dismissal of their hosts. Under the headline "Morton show the white flag" I wrote: "Rangers manager John Greig admitted after his side's demolition of Morton that he could not remember when the Ibrox men had such a comfortable victory at Cappielow."

Greig said: "I don't want to use the word easy," as if in sympathy to a fellow manager. "It's a tribute to Benny's handling of his side that you normally don't get anything at Cappielow."

Rooney in turn said: "We failed in the basics. We couldn't control the ball and we couldn't pass it. But the most worrying thing was that when we went one down the players showed no spirit." One notable exception was centre back Jim Duffy who once again gave everything for the cause. "It would not be a bad idea if he were made captain for the rest of the season," I commented.

St Mirren then dismissed their Renfrewshire rivals from the fourth round of the cup with a 2-0 win at Cappielow, Frank McDougall grabbing a brace before a crowd of 6,045. By this time Ian Gibson had returned to Dundee United, John McNeil making the opposite trip to Greenock. "Gibson did well at the start," said Benny Rooney, "but he's not shown much in the last couple of games." For McNeil it was a disappointment not to make an impression at Tannadice, but one would have to say not entirely unexpected.

Ironically the next match was between the two clubs on Tayside where Morton found the resolve lacking in recent displays to grind out a 1-1 draw with a much more determined display. "I can't ask for any more commitment than I got today," said manager Rooney.

By contrast, United boss Jim McLean was almost purple with rage. "I am so angry," he spluttered. "Words can't describe that performance. It was an insult to the people who paid to watch." It was strange to reflect that here was a United side competing for the title in front of just 5,986 fans.

Morton were still in very real trouble, however, and Celtic cruised to a 3-0 win at Cappielow with goals by Sullivan, MacLeod and McCluskey. It caused me to write: "It is noticeable that visiting managers now use the past tense when they talk of the difficulty of collecting points at Cappielow." Billy McNeill summed up: "Once we got the first goal I never felt we were in any bother." It was shades of Rangers' recent visit.

Amidst the despondency, there were still glimpses of hope. At Love Street Morton fought for every ball in a well earned 3-2 victory over rivals St Mirren. But it still left them three points behind third bottom Motherwell, even if they had a game in hand.

That game to the good, however, was against bottom club Kilmarnock at Rugby Park. There was genuine hope that the gap could be narrowed as the team made the short trip to Ayrshire. It was to be an awful afternoon for the travelling support. Morton were trounced 4-0 and I wrote: "It would not be difficult to assume that the meagre 1,200 crowd was watching a meeting between the two clubs who will go down to the First Division." Killie boss Jim Clunie acerbically commented: "You've got to be pleased when you win 4-0, though Morton's performance has to be taken into account."

On the final Saturday of March it was time for another visit of Alex Ferguson's Aberdeen, going strong in the league and exceptionally well in the European Cup Winners' Cup. Cappielow was a nightmare venue for the Pittodrie men but on form and league placings they had to be supremely confident.

Poor Fergie must have been asking himself what he had to do to watch an Aberdeen win in Greenock when he saw the architect of so many of Dons' downfalls, Andy Ritchie, once again strike a wonderful goal to put the home side into the lead. Neil Simpson had fouled Ritchie fully 35 yards out from goal and to the right of the Wee Dublin End goal. I commented: "With no apparent danger Andy stepped up and crashed a superlative and unstoppable drive past a motionless Leighton into the top right hand corner of the goal."

Alex Ferguson later said: "All my players swore Ritchie's free kick was going over the bar. Of course, it wasn't. But that's Andy for you."

Nine minutes were left for play as Aberdeen launched attack after attack on the Morton goal. Roddie Hutchison was in inspired form as a stand-in for the injured Jim Duffy alongside the defiant Joe McLaughlin, while young Graham Kyle was giving a flawless display as a replacement for flu victim Roy Baines in goal.

I reported: "In the stand young Mark [Ritchie] shrieked like a set of out-of-tune bagpipes while his dad, back on centre stage, adorned a frantic match with subtle skills and a truly magnificent goal."

It all looked to be heading towards another incongruous triumph over the Pittodrie side when, with eight minutes remaining, Andy Watson broke standard practice by grabbing an equaliser after relentless pressure. That would have been reason enough to send Fergie home happy. But, in the final minute of play, Peter Weir flung over a cross from the right and there was Eric Black to hook the ball athletically on the volley past Kyle for a top class winning goal. I reported: "In that one moment all the joys and despairs of football were encapsulated, the Aberdeen players running to swamp Black with congratulations while their Morton counterparts stood dumbstruck, their world having fallen in on top of them."

Alex Ferguson revealed afterwards: "I told the players before the game that a point would be a victory given our record in Greenock. I'm delighted!"

He was too. The following month his side was to compete famously against Real Madrid in the final of the European Cup Winners' Cup. I offered the remark: "If you can win here, Real Madrid in Gothenburg should be a dawdle." He grinned and replied: "Aye, well you're maybe not wrong there." For once Aberdeen players could dare to speak on the journey home to the Northern Lights; perhaps even enjoy a game of cards.

Morton were now four points behind Motherwell and time was running out in their pursuit of survival. But flames still flickered in the Greenock campfires and a John McNeil goal won three priceless home points against Dundee, Hutchison again standing in at centre back. His high-risk style agitated the Cappielow support and I wrote: "I would describe Roddie as a valium player. You need at least two bottles before you can watch him in comfort."

It all set up a huge game against Motherwell on Saturday 9th April at Fir Park. The Lanarkshire men were two points clear of Morton. Abba might well have penned The Winner Takes It All with this sort of scenario in mind. Despite a Graeme Payne penalty, Morton were overwhelmed 4-1 to give their opponents a four-point advantage with five games to go. It was a gut-wrenching defeat for all with the Cappielow club at heart. Motherwell had fronted up when it was most needed; Morton had been found wanting.

A demoralising 1-0 home defeat followed against Hibs and, while not statistically down, everyone knew then that the five-season Premier League jaunt was all but over. Benny Rooney certainly thought so in the aftermath when he said: "We're just not good enough. We've not shown sufficient application and several individual players are not good enough to be in the Premier League."

There was a further revealing insight, which carried considerable truth, when he summed up the battle to preserve their Premier status. "They've heard it all before from me," he commented on his players. "Some seasons ago I could hold forward the carrot of full-time football. We were a team with ambition, going places. Then players had to be transferred out. In a way I don't blame some of the others for becoming a bit stale."

There wasn't bitterness in his tone, but you could have forgiven him some. He had provided everything any man reasonably could have done to take Morton into the top flight, with a team more than good enough to compete.

Rangers then strolled to a 2-0 win at Ibrox with goals by John McDonald and Ian Redford in what I described as "an insipid match played between two uninspired sides". Gers boss John Greig was glad to have secured fourth place and a spot in Europe. That an Ibrox manager could take pleasure in finishing fourth was indicative of the Light Blues' status behind Aberdeen, Celtic and Dundee United in the general scheme of things.

Still Morton were not mathematically relegated. With three games to go they were four points behind Motherwell. John McNeil was allowed to go on loan to Arsenal, giving him a second bite at football at a more rarefied level after his failure to impress at Dundee United. It said everything of Rooney's view of what qualities were needed if his men were to escape relegation by the skin of their teeth that McNeil was permitted to depart. McNeil had skill aplenty, but too often he seemed almost disinterested. I don't think any player sets out to have a quiet afternoon, but on occasions one felt John was in a wee world of his own; that it would have taken a movement of tectonic plates to enliven him.

Once more, the manager rallied himself to speak defiantly of fighting to the bitter end. There was an air of resignation, though, in Greenock and district. At least five points out of six would be needed in the last three fixtures if salvation were to be achieved.

The crunch was to come at Cappielow on 30th April, 1983, with the visit of Dundee United. They were leading the Premier table on 50 points, one ahead of Celtic, each having played 33 games. Aberdeen were on 48 points from 32 games.

It was a moment for contemplation. Here were United and Morton, two roughly comparable clubs in terms of theoretical support. In a matter of a few short seasons one had taken the high road to league challengers and very creditable European competitors, the other the low road back towards whence they came.

Despite their success, and the aesthetic appeal of their footballing style, United still could not guarantee a sizeable audience. With that in mind they took the unique step of literally paying for their support to accompany them to Cappielow for what they saw as a must-win match in their title quest. Each club had everything to play for. The stage was set for a dramatic afternoon. In a crowd of 6,820, there were 4,100 'Arabs' in the Sinclair Street ground. One veteran press man remarked that it was a wondrous state of affairs when a title-chasing team had to bribe its fans to turn out. Another west coast scribe retorted that had it been Aberdeen in opposition, with the same free entry offer, the gates would have been closed and the ground full at two o'clock.

United's rent-a-crowd were in full voice, but Morton competed strongly. That was until the 31st minute when Jim Duffy took Richard Gough late in a tackle outside the box and to the left of goal. Eamonn Bannon bent the free kick round the right side of the defensive wall and off the left post. It then bounced across the goalmouth where Davie Dodds followed up to net his 25th goal of the season.

There was still tension among the visiting Tangerine horde but seven minutes after the interval they erupted in joy when a Dodds head flick sent Dave Narey through the middle and he finished perfectly. When Ralph Milne outpaced Joe McLaughlin to add a third the game as a contest was over. Hamish McAlpine, who had sustained a leg knock, was replaced in goal by Paul Hegarty and a fourth strike came towards the end when Paul Sturrock broke past Jim Duffy on the left, crossed and Davie Dodds ran in at the back post. His shot struck the upright but he bundled the rebound home to send United into raptures.

Morton, in contrast, were deflated. Down and out. There was one of these lulls in which you could hear a silk handkerchief drop on a feather mattress, interrupted by an exasperated Mark Ritchie who was sitting in the stand with mum Rena. "Dad," he implored, "do your tricky things on them!"

"It would," I commented, "have required all of dad's considerable repertoire of tricky things, with some assistance from the Wizard of Oz, to retrieve the situation now."

As the final whistle blew Morton officially were relegated. United were jubilant and could now see the league championship becoming a reality. I wrote: "The Tangerines look set for the big prize; and good luck to them. Their whole approach is based on the purist McLean's total football philosophy. If they succeed they will have done so against the odds and with one of the best disciplinary records of any league winning side. I hope they triumph: I like their style." They went on to win the championship.

On Saturday 7th May Celtic read the last rites at Parkhead in a 2-0 win which their manager, Billy McNeill, described as their worst performance of the season. Goalscorers were Roy Aitken and Charlie Nicholas, the audacious Charles hitting his 49th goal of a remarkable personal season. Morton had finished ninth and accompanied Kilmarnock into the First Division.

CHAPTER TWELVE

Rooney pays the price

On the Monday 9th May, 1983, the Morton board met to discuss the consequences of relegation.

I telephoned on Tuesday morning expecting a statement relating to plans for the forthcoming First Division campaign. I did not anticipate the stunning news that followed – the announcement of the sacking of manager Benny Rooney and his assistant Mike Jackson. Not, in fact, 'sacking', I was told, but 'redundancy'.

The club said that as they were losing £4,250 per week they were left with no alternative but to dispense with the managerial pairing. It was startling news given the success Rooney had brought to Cappielow.

That afternoon, in the pub that he co-owned with Allan McGraw in Greenock, a shattered Rooney told me: "Morton have told me they are unable to honour my contract which still has 11 months to run. They have offered me a settlement which I will discuss with my lawyer tomorrow.

"My assistant Mike Jackson and reserve coach Eddie Morrison have also been placed in the same situation. I'm very disappointed it's come to this. Morton have been my life for the last seven years. I don't want to say any more. My record is there for everyone to see. I know my ability."

Chairman Hugh Currie had earlier said: "Due to the serious financial problems facing the club it has been found necessary, if we are to have any chance of survival, to drastically cut our running costs."

Mr Currie went on to pay tribute to Rooney and Jackson, saying: "They are both great guys and we are sorry it has come to this. But it is really a question of survival. Let me make it quite clear that there is no ill feeling between us: it's simply that we can't afford them.

"We certainly wish Benny and Mike every success in the future in the sincere hope that it will not be long before they find a new club, as they are two young men with an abundance of talent. It has been a very unpleasant and traumatic day. But if we carried on the way we were going, there would be no more Morton in a month's time."

Managing director Hal Stewart said, in typically descriptive style: "We have tried to live in a mansion for long enough, but we are living in a 'but and ben'."

Along with the statement came the news that there would be no reserve team next season and a squad of only 16 players. Not only were Morton relegated, they were clearly in a state little short of melt-down. It seemed incredible that a club, having been top of the Premier League a couple of seasons previously at the halfway stage, should now be on the brink of total collapse. Crowds clearly were far less than legislated for. On that point, there wasn't the level of support from the community through the gates that one might reasonably have expected.

The questions: How much did you legislate for as an average home crowd? How much did you expect from commercial income? Was any money at all put into the club by the major shareholder beyond income received? Was full-time football ever on the agenda? These were met with a polite "no comment" by both the chairman and managing director.

One must assume that there was no 'benevolent' backing from the major shareholders, Sir William Lithgow and the holding company. The large amount of income from transfer fees was not sufficient to balance the books, even as a part-time club, on anything more than a temporary basis. Morton must have contemplated the wisdom of their decision to vote to keep home gates, thus denying themselves the benefit of a share of attendances at Ibrox and Parkhead. That in itself, of course, would not have been enough to make a telling difference.

In Benny Rooney and Allan McGraw's pub that evening the atmosphere was surreal. There was a Dunkirk spirit amidst the wreckage of the day's events. Benny Rooney told me: "We're all keeping each other going now, but it will probably hit me tomorrow morning over breakfast."

Mike Jackson always wore his emotions on his sleeve, and he was angry, but with that distress also came a sense of disbelief. No one had seen this coming. The prevailing mood of shock was totally understandable.

I wrote: "He [Rooney] inherited a side struggling to stay in the First Division. Within two seasons he had taken them into the Premier League. Two cup semi-finals followed (three if you count the Anglo-Scottish Cup) and, at one point, Morton headed the Premier League after the halfway stage of a particularly notable season. Just when the club was on the verge of making a real breakthrough key players were sold. Finances, it should be said, dictated that decision. But that was no fault of the manager's. He is not in charge of finances."

And of course he wasn't. But the man lauded by the board, even on the day he was dismissed, was out the door, along with his assistant, quicker than an Andy Ritchie free kick propelled into the top corner of any net.

Looking back, Rooney's side had done superbly to stay for five consecutive seasons in a 10-club Premier League in which two clubs were always relegated. These were also seasons in which the top 10 included not just the Old Firm, but two high quality sides in Aberdeen and Dundee United, both of whom won the league. Into the bargain the Dons won the European Cup-Winners Cup while Dundee United reached the European Cup semi-final and were later to get to the final of the UEFA Cup.

If Morton were to record five consecutive Premier finishes of seventh, sixth, eighth, seventh and ninth in the current climate – and bear in mind the competition now is considerably less severe in a 12-club league with only one team being relegated – it would be considered an astounding success; a miracle with a part-time team.

Within days, club legend Allan McGraw had organised a meeting at the Morton Supporters' Club to try and drum up support for the club among the local business community. At the same time, club secretary and director Tom Robertson intimated that Arsenal had joined the list of clubs interested in Morton centre half Joe McLaughlin.

Ten free transfers were announced amidst the general cost-cutting, including first team players Roddie Hutchison, Bernie Slaven, Ian Cochrane, Eddie Gavigan and John Marr. Slaven, as it turned out, was to become a big favourite at Middlesbrough. He was also to be capped for the Republic of Ireland. If his release seems shoddy on Morton's part, I would point out that Slaven was very much a late developer. His departure at the time raised not an eyebrow. For Hutchison, I felt sympathy. Not always a fans' favourite, he could never be faulted for any lack of heart or mettle. He gave good service to the club.

Experienced midfielder Tony Higgins offered his services to the board and was accepted as charge-hand for the final match of the season against St Mirren at Cappielow. In front of a pitiful attendance, not officially given, Morton went down to a pair of goals from Frank McDougall, their 10th home defeat of the season. That in itself told a story. Fortress Cappielow had become a recreation camp for the rest of the league. The season had come to an end not a moment too soon.

On the Friday, at the end of a dire week, Benny Rooney contacted me to say: "I've accepted a settlement, for I feel I had to come out of this thing with some dignity. But, I still can't forgive the directors for the fact that they didn't take me aside some weeks before I was dismissed and tell me of the position.

"I'm quite sure something could have been sorted out and the present situation avoided. I would have been prepared to take less wages, and so would Mike Jackson if we'd been told the situation. Instead, it was just sprung on us at the meeting." There is one immutable rule in football. The manager always will carry the can.

The following week Joe McLaughlin left to join not Arsenal, but London rivals Chelsea who also had acquired Pat Nevin from Clyde. Their Scottish assistant manager, Ian McNeill, said: "Morton have agreed a fee and Joe McLaughlin and his wife will be coming down today to discuss things and see round the place." The fee for McLaughlin (23), who signed a four-year deal, was undisclosed at the time. It later transpired it was £90,000. It was the type of bargain you would get in a closing down sale, which wasn't far off the reality of the situation. Not long ago Morton had received four times that amount for McLaughlin's defensive partner Neil Orr. The truth was that they had no negotiating leverage left. Celtic also had expressed interest in McLaughlin but it would appear the 'biscuit tin' mentality still prevailed at the time. They were later to come in for the player after he had departed for Chelsea, when David Hay was manager, when his value had soared. A £650,000 offer was laughed aside by the Stamford Bridge men.

Morton completed a mini U-turn by announcing that, after all, they would run a reserve team, of sorts, the following season. It would comprise youths and first team players unable to get a game on a Saturday.

Then, on 23rd June, the Cappielow club appointed a new gaffer. Because they had made Rooney redundant, they could not appoint a manager as such. The new man was a player-coach and he was ex-Rangers full back Alex Miller. The 34-year-old, who had been at Ibrox for 17 years, said: "It is a tremendous challenge. I am looking forward enormously to the job and working with the team."

Chairman Hugh Currie commented on the new man: "He always impressed me as a player and, having met him, he impressed me even more." One thing was sure. Miller, impressive or not, faced a very tough job indeed.

All good things, it is said, come to an end. One of Alex Miller's first tasks was to finally oversee the departure from Cappielow of Andy Ritchie. At the third time of asking Motherwell finally got their man for a fee reported to be £25,000, some £5,000 less than Benny Rooney had turned down out of hand in a previous bid by the Lanarkshire club.

It seemed odd that the 'idle idol' was going to a club of which Jock Wallace, a strict disciplinarian and fitness fanatic, was manager. Perhaps Wallace thought that he was the man to whip Andy into a hitherto unknown shape, who knows. But, at age 27, Ritchie was virtually in terminal decline. In all games for Morton he had scored 133 goals in 246 appearances. Most of them were in the spectacular category. He was to play a handful of games at Fir Park before moving on to Albion Rovers in 1985. He retired soon after. Of his transfer, Alex Miller said: "Andy wanted full-time football and I felt it was in the best interests of the club to grant his wish."

Director and secretary, Tom Robertson, commented on one of the club's greatest characters and talents: "There is no denying that his achievements at Cappielow will always be remembered with affection by the supporters."

There was no doubt about that. No one who saw Andy at his best could ever forget him. He was a genius in the true sense of the word. But at the time I don't think he ever accepted his own role in his failure to get the big move he craved. That recognition came later. He became despondent as others departed for much bigger things and believed that Morton had held him back. They hadn't. Years later Andy said to me: "He [Jock Stein] said I had the talent but I wasn't putting enough into it and, of course, he was right."

I have read elsewhere of a supposed Liverpool offer of around £1million for Ritchie being rejected by Hal Stewart. The story is a fairy-tale; a fantasy. The warnings had been there when Arsenal's Frank McLintock came, saw, admired but declined to recommend to his club a move for Ritchie. His message was mirrored by so many others. No one disputed Ritchie's extraordinary talent. But always there was the reservation that he did not work enough for the team. That he left for Motherwell for £25,000 at the age of 27, when he ought to have been at the peak of a remarkable career, was a woeful waste.

If Ritchie contributed to his own downfall, his relative failure also said something for the priorities of those within the game. Not one big club was prepared to go for this multi-talented star when he was banging in goals for fun. There are 10 outfield players in a team and Morton had shown, at their best, that Ritchie's lack of work-rate could be accommodated. No one in Scotland entertained more than he did for the first four of his years at Cappielow, and football is an entertainment, though sometimes you might struggle to comprehend that in modern Scotland. It was the end of an era for Morton and for Ritchie.

John McNeil had returned from a forlorn trial at Arsenal and scored twice in a pre-season 5-0 friendly win at Stornoway before the news broke that goalkeeper Roy Baines (33) was the latest to leave Cappielow. He had been given a free transfer and joined newly promoted St Johnstone. Alex Miller said: "I decided to give Graham Kyle a chance in goal. Roy lives in Edinburgh and doesn't train with the team and I don't think that's a good thing."

Davie Hayes, Jim Rooney and Jimmy Holmes had all put pen to paper in revised deals, but Morton were a remnant of the side who had competed at their peak in the Premier League, Tolmie, Thomson, Orr, McLaughlin, Ritchie, Baines, McLaren, Scott and Miller all having left.

The one newcomer was former Celtic, Kilmarnock and Partick centre half Frank Welsh and he, along with youngsters Andrew Clinton and Mungo McCallum, was part of the side which beat Bristol Rovers 2-0 in a Cappielow friendly, McCallum and an own goal contributing the strikes. A Renfrewshire Cup Final defeat by 2-1 against St Mirren followed before the serious business began on 20th August in Edinburgh on the wide open spaces of Meadowbank Athletics Stadium with a match against promoted Meadowbank Thistle, the former Ferranti Thistle.

On the eve of the game Alex Miller sounded a warning. "Morton have to forget that they were a Premier club," he said. "We are First Division now. Tomorrow's game is all about attitude. Meadowbank will be trying to impress that they deserve their promotion last season. We must match that. If the players are professional and have ambition their attitude will be right."

Morton showed plenty of spirit on the day, winning 4-1 with goals by Jim Rooney (2), Jim Duffy and John McNeil. The side, in 4-3-3 formation was: Kyle; Hayes, Welsh, Miller, Holmes; Rooney, Duffy, Doak; Houston, Higgins, McNeil.

Alex Ferguson's brother, Martin, formerly manager of East Stirling and Albion Rovers, was appointed as Alex Miller's assistant before a League Cup second round first leg defeat by 2-1 at Hamilton, now managed by Bertie Auld. John McNeil was the Morton scorer. By the time the teams met in the second leg at Cappielow three days later, Miller had gone into the transfer market to bring former Ranger Dougie Robertson and ex-Motherwell forward Ian Clinging to the club.

They were surprise signings on the morning of the match and it was a dream debut for Robertson, just 20, who struck a hat-trick in a 3-1 victory. I wrote: "It was Robertson who stole the show. He took his goals with an authority which suggests he can provide the answer to the Cappielow club's scoring problems.

"His shielding of the ball and linking with his new colleagues – particularly John McNeil – was also of admirable quality." That shielding of the ball was in part due to Dougie's possession of a large posterior, similar to the more illustrious Kenny Dalglish's, which on occasions he used to park to good effect in an opponent's lap before laying off a pass.

The new additions leant a buzz to a club which badly needed it, and came just in time for a big test against Premier League Motherwell, Andy Ritchie and all, at Fir Park in the first of the League Cup section matches. Also in the same group were Dundee United and Alloa. It would be strange to see Ritchie in the claret and amber of Motherwell; just as strange for him to be facing old mates such as Rooney and Holmes.

It turned out to be a 3-0 win for the host club and, of course, Andy Ritchie scored a spectacular goal. Yet, Morton were by far the better side in the first 45 minutes, only to go in at the break one goal down, scored against the run of play by ex-Celt Johannes Edvaldsson. Afterwards I wrote: "If Morton learnt a lesson it is that the most important work in any football match ultimately takes place in the penalty area."

Inevitably, Ritchie rose to the occasion against his erstwhile mates, his passing skills being displayed to the full while it was his long free kick which led to Motherwell's second goal, headed home by Gillespie. The third was pure Ritchie. I reported it thus: "Ritchie brought on his special ball with the metal centre, placed a magnet in the top left hand corner of the net, and watched the usual satisfactory result." For once Morton fans could experience that horrible, sinking feeling opposition supporters had become so used to over the past seven years. Alex Miller summed up the game when he said: "We were knocking the ball about beautifully without any penetration."

In the league it was a Miller penalty which gained a point in a 1-1 draw with Hamilton at Cappielow in a ghastly match. The player-coach commented: "We never played. We lost a terrible goal [for which Miller himself had been one of those culpable]. It was so bad it wasn't true." Among the opposition were another two Cappielow 'old boys', Roddie Hutchison and Ian Cochrane. Bertie Auld's teams were almost always founded on a basis of organisation to the point of suffocating the life out of a game, never mind the opposition, and Accies were no exception. It was something I found incongruous given Bertie's career as one of the principal playmakers in the Celtic team which won the European Cup; a side dedicated to exciting, attacking football. Perhaps it was not so much Bertie's philosophy as something dictated by circumstances.

On the Wednesday evening the visitors were Premier League champions Dundee United in the next League Cup section tie. Expectations were exceeded when Morton grabbed a point in a match which ended one apiece. United boss Jim McLean said: "Over the piece I think a draw was a fair result. Morton knocked the ball about well and tried to play football. They also worked very hard and deserved the point. I'm impressed by the way they tried to play the game."

Alex Miller was pleased, saying: "I thought we played a lot of good football in the first half. In the second half we fell away a wee bit as they began to push players forward."

Both goals had some luck attached to them, United's coming from an own goal by Houston and Morton's being netted by Dougie Robertson after, first, a rare Narey mistake and then another by goalkeeper Hamish McAlpine.

Jim Duffy, who had been struggling with flu, played and gave a typically committed display.

Successive league defeats followed, however, at Brechin (3-1) and at home to Ayr (3-2).

Goalkeeper Graham Kyle was having a nightmare season and his uncertainty was having an unsettling influence upon those in front of him. Jim Duffy too was being played in midfield rather than his usual central defensive role, and that did not help matters.

A week before Christmas the problems seemed to be solved. Duffy was restored to his customary position, while Miller moved to bring goalkeeper Murray McDermott to Cappielow after he had been freed by Berwick Rangers. He went on to have a tremendous season. The immediate effect was a 2-0 win at Brockville against Falkirk, goals by McNeil and Robertson providing the crucial end result.

John McNeil then gave an imperious display at Stark's Park to net a hat-trick against Raith Rovers in a 3-1 win. "If McNeil was the player who took the eye most with his expert turns, subtle feints and explosive shooting, there wasn't a failure elsewhere," I wrote. His third strike, a wonderful curling effort which left the goalkeeper helpless, even caused excitement in the hen coop that served as a press box at Kirkcaldy. It was as good a display as ever I saw from McNeil. It was as exasperating as it was entertaining in that it showed only too well of what he was capable.

Rooney, Miller and Doak won all the important tackles in the middle of the park. One player, though, felt his contribution to be crucial. Tony Higgins had replaced Ian Clinging in the final minute of play. He didn't actually touch the ball but commented afterwards that just by appearing he had 'turned the game'.

Higgins had a rich sense of humour. On a trip to Aberdeen while in the Premier League the team stopped for lunch at a Stonehaven hotel, managed by Denis Law's brother. As the players filed back out through the lobby to get back on the bus, Tony stopped to chat to an elderly couple, clearly of his acquaintance. "How are you?" he gushed. "It's so nice to see you after all these years. My, you haven't changed a bit." And so the conversation continued for some time, the couple unable to get a word in edgeways as Higgins charmed them. Once back on the coach, one of his teammates enquired: "Who was that, Tony?"

"Haven't a clue," came the reply.

It was impossible not to like Higgins. On another occasion in Edinburgh, the team had dined at a hotel on the outskirts of the city and were waiting to re-board the bus. The players were sitting passing the time in a conference room in which a lectern was positioned. From there Tony decided to deliver a sermon, every bit as droll as the Reverend I.M. Jolly. He was going down every bit as well as the Reverend Jolly too when the manager and his assistant entered the room. Quite unfazed, Higgins glanced up, beamed and said: "Ah, brothers Rooney and Jackson, please be seated, my friends." And so he continued. I was just surprised he didn't have us all singing Abide With Me.

Morton were beginning to look like the makings of a team and when they met league leaders Partick at Cappielow they were fifth top in the 14-club First Division. Thistle it was, however, who maintained their 100% record with a 2-1 win. They went ahead by two goals before going down to nine men when McDonald and Jardine were sent off. Despite reducing the gap Morton, who had ex-Hibs goalkeeper Jim McArthur on trial between the sticks in place of the injured McDermott, continued their poor home record.

It was a different story away from Cappielow, and at Broomfield on the following Saturday goals by Eddie McNab and Dougie Robertson (2) proved too much for Airdrie.

Then suddenly, on Tuesday 4th October, 1983, came the shock news that St Mirren wanted Alex Miller as their new manager, after the departure from Love Street of Ricky McFarlane.

CHAPTER THIRTEEN

Another manager goes

By the next day the news had been confirmed: Miller was on his way. Morton chairman Hugh Currie described it as a body blow, having just appointed Miller on 23rd June.

Miller had been 'tapped' by Saints, despite Hugh Currie's refusal to allow the St Mirren board permission to speak to him. I commented: "It is not the proper way to go about things, though in fairness to St Mirren they are hardly the first to do so and they certainly won't be the last either."

Morton announced that they would advertise for a new man and that meanwhile reserve manager Eddie Morrison would take over the reins. Miller's last game was on Wednesday 5th October when the team lost 4-2 at home to Alloa in another League Cup section tie. Miller scored one of the Ton goals, from the penalty spot. At the final whistle there was some dark humour from the stand when one Morton fan shouted: "Miller must go!" as the teams trooped off the park.

His exit so soon after arrival was regrettable. In the short time he had been at Cappielow, he had brought in three more than useful players in Dougie Robertson, Ian Clinging and Murray McDermott, had begun to organise and encourage and had shown that he wanted to play a passing game. He was an avid football man, serious and a keen thinker and student of the game. Almost obsessed.

Eddie Morrison was a different kettle of fish. His answer to life invariably came in the form of a big, cheery grin. He oversaw the side's next match in which they drew 2-2 with Dumbarton at Cappielow, Robertson and Clinging getting the goals. His second game in charge was at Clydebank where another draw was gained, this time 3-3. "How did Forfar get on?" he asked me after the game was over.

"I don't know," I answered, somewhat bemused.

"You see," explained Eddie, beaming, "if Forfar lost I'm the only unbeaten manager in Britain."

Playing for Morton that afternoon was Danny Docherty, freed at the end of the previous season, but surplus to requirement at Clyde and now back in the fold. His return was marked by the last of Morton's goals.

Morrison's march continued with league wins over Alloa at Cappielow, 1-0, and Clyde away (3-2). In between came an almost inevitable League Cup section defeat at Tannadice where Dundee United's superior skills produced a comfortable 3-0 win. But Morton now were just two points behind second placed teams Falkirk and Kilmarnock. With no outstanding team in the First Division they were suddenly in 'danger' of going straight back up to the top 10. I say 'danger' because it was only too well appreciated that Morton were not financially able to go up with the type of team capable of staying up.

In a 2-2 draw with Kilmarnock at Cappielow, Morton fought back from being two down with just over five minutes left for play. Jim Duffy scored a rare goal in both senses of the word, skelping a drive home from 30 yards, while a lovely John McNeil turn and shot provided a share of the points.

Three days' later former Aberdeen and Celtic star Dom Sullivan (32) signed. He had returned to Scotland after a failed re-union with his old Celtic boss Billy McNeill at Manchester City. Partick and Kilmarnock had both been keen on acquiring Sullivan but Morton, to their credit, had stolen a march on their First Division rivals. Also on the way to Cappielow was ex-St Mirren centre back Phil McAveety.

That same evening was the return meeting in League Cup Section One with Motherwell at Cappielow. The Fir Park club were in some turmoil after growing speculation – soon to be proved correct – that boss Jock Wallace was on his way back to Ibrox. Motherwell were outplayed on the night, Sullivan adding a touch of class to the hosts' centre midfield. I reported: "It was significant that when he tired later in the second half, Morton lost a good deal of their effectiveness."

Morton went three up through Dougie Robertson, John McNeil and Sullivan himself with an excellent 25-yard drive. Andy Ritchie pegged one back via the penalty spot before a second goal from Sullivan with a deflected shot. The Motherwell fans had been singing "Wallace must stay" at the start of play. After the fourth Morton goal they were singing "Wallace for Rangers".

In a fiery match at Somerset Park Morton drew 2-2 with Ayr, Danny Docherty and John McNeil (with his 12th goal of the season) counting for the visitors, and when they beat Falkirk at Cappielow 3-1 they had moved up to third spot in the table. McNeil grabbed another two goals against the Bairns who had lost manager Alex Totten on the eve of the game after he joined Jock Wallace as his assistant at Rangers.

Eddie Morrison had now guided the team through seven league games unbeaten when it was announced that Tommy McLean would be the next manager at Cappielow. McLean had been John Greig's assistant at Ibrox and had been temporarily in charge there when Greig was sacked prior to Jock Wallace's return. He would watch Morrison's final match in charge, against Dumbarton at Boghead, before taking over officially on the Monday. Chairman Hugh Currie said: "We are sure that our cautious approach in filling Alex Miller's position will be proved to be right for the club."

Mr Currie also was fulsome in his praise of caretaker boss Eddie Morrison, saying: "I would like to take this opportunity of publicly thanking Eddie Morrison. He has done a magnificent job and we all thank him very sincerely indeed."

Morton ground out another draw at Boghead in a lacklustre 1-1 match which Eddie Morrison said "was our worst display since I took over. We didn't play."

The game was marred also by derogatory chanting from some Morton fans aimed at new man Tommy McLean who was sitting in the stand. They believed Morrison should have got the manager's job. It took no account of the fact that Eddie had stated he did not want the position. He had a good job outside football. Robertson was Morton's scorer, although the outstanding man on the field was Ton goalkeeper Murray McDermott.

Tommy McLean was emphatic that his aim was "to try and get up to the Premier League". I asked him if he felt it was possible for a part-time club to survive now in the Premier Division. He answered: "That is a very difficult question," before going on to admit that the gap between the top 10 and the rest was bigger than ever. "There are only nine full-time clubs in Scotland," he said, "and all are in the Premier League."

McLean's first game in charge was the relatively meaningless League Cup section tie against Alloa which was lost 1-0 at Recreation Park.

There followed a league clash with Airdrie at Cappielow on the Saturday. In a stirring contest, Morton won 3-2 with goals by man-of-the-match Bobby Houston (2) and Dom Sullivan. They were now second top of the First Division, three points behind leaders Partick Thistle. For Tommy McLean the win was welcome, but with reservations. "It must have been entertaining and exciting to watch," he commented, "but I was disappointed we tossed away a two-goal lead due to carelessness."

By the time they met Raith in their next game, again at Cappielow, McLean's old Ibrox buddy Tom Forsyth had been appointed as his assistant. The match against Rovers was a dismal 90 minutes and the Morton manager said: "We didn't play or create chances during the entire 90 minutes." Morton's side was McDermott; Houston, Welsh, Duffy, Holmes; Rooney, Sullivan, Docherty (Doak); Clinging (McNab), Robertson and McNeil.

On Saturday 17th December, Morton had the chance to give their fans an early Christmas present when they met league leaders Partick at Firhill. But it was the Jags who injected some zip into the festive atmosphere with a 3-1 win, thus ending Morton's unbeaten 10-match league run.

I commented: "Thistle exposed once again all the weaknesses of a defence which has played its way precariously through the league programme." Tommy McLean was more brutal. "We've only got one player in that side who can tackle and that's Jim Duffy," he lamented. Morton had slipped to fourth place, albeit they were only four points behind Partick in pole position.

On Boxing Day they picked up a home point in a scoreless draw with Brechin City, but a shot in the arm was given to their prospects when manager McLean moved to sign ex-Motherwell, Dundee United and Hearts striker Willie Pettigrew on loan until the end of the season. The 30-year-old former Scotland striker had been unable to hold down a regular place at Tynecastle.

A 1-1 draw at Hamilton was followed up with a convincing 4-0 home win against Meadowbank, Willie Pettigrew notching a debut goal with other strikes coming from Ian

Clinging, John McNeil and Dougie Robertson. Phil McAveety also made an appearance as a substitute after returning to fitness. When Morton beat Alloa 3-1 at Recreation Park with goals from McNeil, Duffy and Pettigrew, they consolidated third spot in the table on 29 points, one behind Dumbarton and two adrift of leaders Partick Thistle. Tommy McLean, nevertheless, was not entirely content, saying: "I was happy with the two points, but I was not impressed by the performance. It is no good us going up if that is how we are going to play. We would just disappoint a lot of people."

My own comment was: "It confirms my view that there is not one team in the First Division which looks capable on present ability of staying in the top 10 should it get there."

Despite having lost so many star players in the past couple of seasons, Morton still had assets others coveted. On Thursday 19th January,1984, stories broke of Hibernian's interest in Jim Holmes and Jim Rooney, two key members of the team which had taken Morton into the Premier League six seasons ago. Hibs boss Pat Stanton was quoted as saying: "We have been in touch with Morton about the possibility of signing Jim Holmes and Jim Rooney, but our first approach has been turned down." Morton rigorously denied that any such discussion had taken place. Manager Tommy McLean was angry, complaining that he was trying to build a team, not sell one, and that no one had spoken to him about either player.

When I contacted Hibs for clarification I was told that there would be no further comment. Morton remained adamant that no approach had been made. Football transfers and speculation are littered with such adversarial comment. It was up to the bystander to believe what he or she wished. What was not in doubt was that Hibs were interested in both players. It was unsettling for them.

Meanwhile, I spoke to veteran midfielder Dom Sullivan who had played under three excellent managers in his time at Aberdeen – Ally McLeod, Billy McNeill and Alex Ferguson. I wanted to know his view on their qualities. "McLeod," he said, "was a motivator of men without comparison. Billy McNeill mixed motivation with tactics and stressed each individual's contribution, while Alex Ferguson was probably the best tactically. What Ally McLeod began, Billy McNeill continued and Alex Ferguson perfected."

No one can be in any doubt about Ferguson's qualities as a manager. There is a definite case to be put forward for saying he is the best ever, but he had his share of luck at times. He took over at St Mirren when they had an excellent crop of players such as Tony Fitzpatrick, Peter Weir, Billy Stark, Frank McGarvey, Lex Richardson and Iain Munro. Then, when he went to Aberdeen, he inherited a fine squad, with a mix of top young talent and good experience who were beginning to achieve things under Ally McLeod and then Billy McNeill. And, of course, when he went to Manchester United it was said he was one game away from the sack when he guided the team to the FA Cup four years after his appointment. But Ferguson's record shows that at each club he managed he left it in a better position than when he arrived. His record tells all. Too many managers are sacked after ludicrously short periods of tenure when they have been asked to achieve the impossible. They are often fall guys to appease a dissatisfied customer base.

Dom Sullivan, who had played under some of the best in the business, had become a vital component in the Morton surge for promotion, his experience and composure on the ball inestimable factors. Shortly after I spoke to him, the news broke of the death of another of Scotland's major football characters, Hal Stewart. The man who became synonymous with Morton during the 60s died suddenly on Thursday 2nd February, 1984. His funeral was held at Linn Crematorium in Glasgow where some 400 people turned out to pay their respects, including such luminaries of the game as Jock Stein, Jock Wallace and Willie Waddell. There were representatives from the SFA, the League and the clubs of Scotland as well as a large contingent from Morton FC. Benny Rooney, Mike Jackson and Alex Miller also attended. Tommy McLean said: "His death is a big, big blow. He was a tremendous enthusiast and a first class worker for the club."

Hal, of course, had transformed Morton in the early 60s. He also began the Scandinavian football invasion of Scotland. Capitalising on Denmark's amateur status, he brought such superb players to Greenock as Erik Sorensen, Kaj Johansen, Jorn Sorensen, Preben Arentoft, Leif Nielsen and John Madsen. He was a true showman and probably the first on the managerial side to appreciate that football was not just a game or a business, it was first and foremost an entertainment industry. Hal always sought to add a bit of magic to football. In his heyday no one succeeded more than he in achieving that. He could have sold snow to the Eskimos, sand to the nomadic tribes of the Sahara, rain to the council in Greenock and made them all believe they were getting a bargain.

Hal was perfectly described by Allan McGraw as a "likeable rogue". He prevented McGraw, as a player, from getting the sort of top transfer players dream about. While doing his national service, McGraw had been part of an excellent British Army of the Rhine team and a Scottish Command team which included fellow Scots Jim Baxter and John White. Tottenham Hotspur wanted him to sign for them after he had gone down south on trial at White Hart Lane. This was the great Spurs side under Bill Nicholson including Dave Mackay, Jimmy Greaves, John White, Danny Blanchflower and Cliff Jones. McGraw told Nicholson he would go to them when his army service ended. Hal Stewart, by this time running Morton, got to hear about this. Allan's father had worked in the same company in which Hal was in management. When McGraw's dad died, Hal shamelessly exploited the situation, promising Allan a free flight home from Germany every weekend to see his mother if he would sign for Morton. For understandable reasons Allan agreed, giving up a possible top career with the best club side in Britain at the time.

Hal also later turned down a bid by Tommy Docherty's great Chelsea side, including Peter Osgood and Charlie Cook, to take McGraw to Stamford Bridge. The 'Doc' had met Allan and agreed individual terms. But Hal Stewart turned down an improved Chelsea offer of £22,500, sticking out for £30,000, and Tommy Docherty walked away. Instead of more than doubling his wages and receiving a signing-on 'fee' of £4,500, sufficient to buy a smart new bungalow in these days, Allan, whose wife Jean was pregnant at the time, had to make do with a pram and a three-piece suite from Hal.

Another move to Wolves similarly fell through. Yet there was no bitterness on Allan's part. He always had a ready smile when he spoke of Hal Stewart. When I later asked if he had any regrets over not getting one of those big moves south, Allan smiled and said: "No, not really. I might not have made it anyway." Allan's glass was always half full.

February continued with a 2-0 Scottish Cup third round win over East Stirlingshire at Cappielow, Sullivan and Robertson netting, before a 1-1 league draw at Meadowbank where Willie Pettigrew proved his worth with Morton's counter. In the next round of the cup, promotion rivals Dumbarton were dumped 2-1 at Cappielow, setting up an enticing quarter-final against St Mirren at Love Street. In the Sons' tie, Dom Sullivan ran the game from midfield while Willie Pettigrew was at his opportunist best with two predatory strikes. "A cracking game," was Tommy McLean's verdict.

Morton were coming to the boil and, when they beat Clyde 2-1 at Cappielow with goals by Jim Rooney and Pettigrew, they moved up to second place in the First Division table, one point behind pacesetters Partick Thistle.

Next up were the Jags themselves at Cappielow. The Ton support was given a pre-match boost when it was announced that Willie Pettigrew's loan from Hearts had become a permanent transfer at the cost of some £10,000. The icing on the cake came on the Saturday when the league leaders were swept off their top perch 4-2, prompting Tommy McLean to say: "A great game with great goals and a great result!"

Martin Doak, John McNeil, Dom Sullivan and Dougie Robertson were on the scoresheet and McLean continued: "We are now in a position to decide our own fate." There were still 12 games to go and Morton were only on top on goal difference, but they had made a big statement.

Nothing, of course, is ever that simple. Clydebank, with their own promotion hopes, came to Cappielow and spiked Morton's guns with a 2-1 victory, goals by Larnach and Ferguson cancelling out one by Frank Welsh. McLean was realistic in his comments when he said: "The players have done marvellously for me but we are short-staffed and it showed. I have been looking about for players but in our financial position it's difficult."

Morton bounced back with a 2-0 victory at Stark's Park against Raith Rovers, with goals by Dougie Robertson and Danny Docherty, to stay top on goal difference over Dumbarton who had leapfrogged Partick.

Next up was the Scottish Cup quarter-final against county adversaries St Mirren in Paisley. No motivation is ever required for a derby clash and the atmosphere built as the week progressed towards the Saturday. An estimated 3,000 travelled to Love Street to cheer on Morton, who had signed young Tommy Turner on the eve of the game from Glentyan Thistle. Injuries meant he was included in the squad for this eagerly anticipated tie. In the event Premier Saints squeezed through 4-3, ex-Cappielow boss Alex Miller saying: "I'm delighted to be through," while admitting that a missed penalty, when Morton were 2-1 ahead, was crucial to the outcome. Dom Sullivan had taken the spot kick only to see it strike a post and rebound to safety.

A Dougie Robertson double had negated an early strike by Saints' Frank McAvennie, then came the penalty miss. St Mirren took full advantage to go 4-2 ahead with goals by Tony Fitzpatrick and Ian Scanlon (2) before Willie Pettigrew snatched what proved to be a consolation goal.

Tommy McLean praised his side, but it was tempered by a comment which might have been made by his perfectionist brother Jim at Dundee United when he said: "I set my sights higher than that performance." The attendance was a healthy 7,933 and, of his own team's supporters, McLean commented: "They were absolutely magnificent."

The pain of defeat was exacerbated when Clyde roared to a three-goal lead at Shawfield before goals by Robertson and Rooney made defeat respectable. The loss, however, saw Morton tumble to third place, three points behind new leaders Dumbarton and two adrift of Thistle, although they did have a game in hand over both these clubs.

A goalless draw was next at home to Hamilton before Airdrie were beaten 2-1 in a very important game at the Sinclair Street ground, as much psychologically as anything else. Jim Rooney was the game's top player by a country mile, scoring the first goal and generally standing out in the sodden wet conditions. Greenock had provided the type of downpour only surpassed at the foot of the Niagara Falls. Airdrie's appropriately named John Flood hit an equaliser before Willie Pettigrew weighed in with the winner. The crowd of just 1,512 was disappointing, though the conditions clearly had an impact.

Drama and Morton were becoming well acquainted bed-fellows and on the following Thursday Ton gaffer Tommy McLean announced that John McNeil had been placed on the transfer list. He said: "The player has forced my hand. He works shifts for IBM and I have been at him to report for training during the day at Cappielow. He has been failing to appear. I spoke to him about it but it has had no effect. There has to be discipline and I have to be fair to other players."

Such public pronouncements are usually made reluctantly by managers, and only after all other avenues have been explored and exhausted. McNeil, still aged just 25, had a definite ability, to the extent that he had been on loan and trial with Dundee United and Arsenal, but always there was a question mark over his sense of desire.

Further in-house talks, however, took place and 'Peanut' finally turned up for training the day before the next match, away to Ayr United. "He appears to have a better attitude," Tommy McLean said simply. But McNeil, like Ritchie before him, was to be a player who never fully capitalised on the talents he possessed.

An invaluable brace of goals by Willie Pettigrew, back to his very best form, carried Morton to a 2-1 win over Ayr and second place in the table, one point behind Dumbarton. The platform was now set for the run-in to the end of the season. It promised to be a thrilling denouement.

Morton's momentum continued at Brechin where they won 2-1 to maintain second spot, one point behind Dumbarton but now three ahead of Partick who continued to falter. Goalkeeper Murray McDermott continued his inspired form, producing a brilliant save from a superb Ken Eadie volley with the game goalless in 67 minutes. Eight minutes later Jim Rooney sent Willie Pettigrew scampering through the middle. He accelerated past Hay and coolly placed the ball past the goalkeeper for the opener. It was his 12th strike in 16 games. Top scorer Dougie Robertson added a second, his 22nd of the season.

Pettigrew was proving his worth, although he wasn't always universally popular among the Morton fans. I commented: "Rather like a starving version of Andy Ritchie, Pettigrew can wander about, as if in a dwam, not appearing to take a great deal of interest in proceedings. Just as suddenly, however, he can explode upon a match with dramatic impact. As his manager pointed out 'no matter whether or not the fans like Willie, he is one of those players they will talk about'."

Everything was building up to the big meeting the following Saturday at Cappielow between the top two, when ex-Ranger Davie Wilson's Dumbarton would make the short trip across the Erskine Bridge for the match of the day.

Morton were looking to their top strike trio of Dougie Robertson, John McNeil and Willie Pettigrew to gun down a Sons side who had been showing commendable tenacity. Among them, these three had scored 51 goals and Robertson said: "When I was freed by Rangers I was very low, but if my goals can help take Morton back up I'll be delighted. I've got a point to prove in the Premier Division, not so much to Rangers but to myself."

An attendance of 3,800 turned out to watch the clash. Jim Rooney headed in the crucial opening goal after excellent leading up play by John McNeil. Murray McDermott produced a quite magnificent save to thwart Dumbarton's Joe Coyle as the visitors pushed on in the second half, but a Martin Doak header sealed the issue against the run of play. Manager Tommy McLean was effusive in his praise of McDermott who had produced some fine stops, saying: "We reckon Murray's been worth about 12 points to us this season."

CHAPTER FOURTEEN

A tale of two McLeans

Morton were so near their goal now, and promotion was finally secured the next Saturday at Brockville where they beat their hosts with the only goal of the game, scored by Dom Sullivan. Partick had fallen at Broomfield against Airdrie and, with three games remaining, Tommy McLean's side were back up after just a season.

The manager commented: "It's the players who have taken Morton up. No one could have asked for more than they have given me. They've worked hard and they've got their reward."

A season which had begun with the hangover of relegation, the dismissal of management duo Benny Rooney and Mike Jackson, the intention to operate with just a 16-man pool and no reserve team, had been transformed into an unlikely triumph. In fact, McLean operated with a 25-man squad and the reserve team had been saved.

It was all the more remarkable in that three men had managed the team over the course of the campaign – Alex Miller, Eddie Morrison and Tommy McLean. Miller had laid the basis of the success, bringing in Dougie Robertson, Ian Clinging and Murray McDermott before departing for St Mirren, Eddie Morrison had continued the good work by going eight games undefeated and then Tommy McLean had arrived to carry the process forward.

In an excellent team success, four men had stood out for me over the whole season – Murray McDermott, Jim Duffy, Dom Sullivan and Dougie Robertson. They provided an excellent spine to the team, though everyone played his part, not least the two 'veterans' Jim Rooney and Jim Holmes, and Willie Pettigrew. Rooney had recovered from, by his standards, a mediocre start to the season to become his normal strong force.

Morton's target was now the championship. Dougie Robertson grabbed his 23rd goal of the season in a 1-1 draw at Clydebank, in which McDermott again excelled, before Alloa were thrashed 3-0 at Cappielow, McNeil, Houston and Clinging scoring. With Dumbarton winning at Airdrie, it was now all down to the final Saturday of the season.

Kilmarnock were the visitors and, before they arrived, Murray McDermott had been voted by the fans as their Player of the Year. Tommy McLean said: "The award is thoroughly merited and I am delighted for Murray."

McDermott had to pinch himself to make sure he wasn't dreaming. He told me: "I had gone back to junior football after being freed by Berwick. I got a phone call [from Alex

Miller] out of the blue asking me to report to Cappielow. Since then things have gone so well I can't believe it. Being voted Player of the Year just adds to a wonderful season."

Meanwhile Jim Rooney and Dougie Robertson had been selected for a semi-professional Scottish team to take part in a tournament in the summer in Italy against England and the host nation.

There was a tremendous atmosphere on Saturday 12th May at Cappielow as a crowd of almost 5,000 turned out for the final match of the season against Kilmarnock. It was shirt-sleeves rolled up as some lovely spring weather added to the sense of occasion. Within 90 seconds Morton took the lead when Dougie Robertson pounced to set Killie back on their heels.

McDermott, inevitably by this time, brought off a magnificent save to deny Clark an equaliser. That was the score at half-time but, immediately after the interval, Robertson pounced again for his 25th goal of the season and the party began. The news filtered through to the crowd that Dumbarton were losing at home to Clyde. "We're going to win the league," the fans sang lustily. John McNeil made it 3-0 with a penalty and late consolation strikes by Gallagher and McKenna failed to burst the Cappielow bubble.

It was celebration time and Tommy McLean and trainer Willie Gray were flung into the bath by the jubilant players. "They threw me in!" spluttered a drookit Willie as he escaped the home dressing room. "At least they let you back out again," I replied to one of the club's most faithful servants.

Also enjoying the occasion was wee Tommy McLean's assistant, big Tam Forsyth. Unsurprisingly, no one had dared try to throw him in the bath. Forsyth was, as ever, munching on a 'Wagonwheel', one of his favourite nibbles. I wrote later: "I have discovered why large Tom Forsyth was nicknamed 'Jaws' during his playing days at Ibrox. At the time we all laboured under the misapprehension that it referred to his no-prisoners style of play. Having seen his approach to food I now know the truth. If they were to make a film of Desperate Dan, Forsyth ought to get the lead role. No cow pie would be safe within a mile of him."

Morton had won the title by three clear points, Dumbarton joining them in the step up to the top 10.

Bobby Houston, the winger converted to full back in place of the injured Davie Hayes, then announced his retiral at the premature age of 32, but it was a happy throng who left the old stadium on a lovely evening.

Morton were back among the big boys, but it was a different scenario from the one of 1977-88 when Benny Rooney had taken a team up which included several top quality players. In order to stay up, the Cappielow club would have to strengthen considerably, and that was the big concern now. No team during the First Division campaign had looked nearly strong enough to survive among Scotland's elite. The gap between the leagues was wider than ever and both Morton and Dumbarton were part-time outfits.

Tommy McLean recognised this as well as anyone when he said: "We will have to strengthen the playing staff with a view to competing meaningfully in the top 10."

The close season always brings its manoeuvrings and its posturing and Morton's first problem occurred when Dougie Robertson declared his unhappiness at the terms offered to him for the new season to come. The 21-year-old striker had struck 25 goals and felt he was worth more than Morton were prepared to pay. Tommy McLean could not have been more clear in his response: "All the first team players have been offered increased terms for next season. If he [Robertson] can do better elsewhere he can go," he stated starkly.

Worse was to follow for the fans when it soon became clear that Motherwell, relegated from the Premier League, were out to pinch Tommy McLean himself as their next manager. On 8th June, 1984, they secured their man, leaving Morton once again managerless. McLean said: "I'm a wee bit sorry to be going. I've had a magnificent time at Greenock and have received tremendous backing from the directors, players and the supporters. But a key factor for me was the locality of Motherwell." McLean lived near Fir Park. He gave another reason, and probably a more pertinent one, when he commented: "The club is continuing full-time and that is another big factor." McLean knew full well that, while Motherwell had dropped out of the top 10, they had a greater potential than the Morton side he had taken up to replace them. A cynic might say he got out when the going was as good as it could get. Few could blame him.

Cappielow director Tom Robertson commented: "He [McLean] obviously thought long and hard about it and I think an influencing factor was that Motherwell is next door to him. We made every effort to keep him and there is no doubt he is leaving us on the best of personal terms. We wish him well and are sorry that he was here for such a short time."

This time Morton moved quickly to fill the void, though they remained within the same gene pool. Five days after Tommy McLean left Cappielow, brother Willie was appointed as his successor.

Willie McLean had been managing Cypriot club Pezeporikos in Larnaca, taking them to that country's cup final. Morton chairman Hugh Currie said: "We feel we have got a good man who comes from a good footballing family. When we lost Tommy it felt like losing a son. But we asked him about his brother who was managing a club in Cyprus. Contact was made and we took it from there. I'm quite sure he'll be at Cappielow for some time."

Willie himself made all the right noises when he told me. "Consolidation in the Premier League must be the aim for next season; that and concentration upon the youth aspect. Players like Joe McLaughlin and Neil Orr don't come along every year, but we must turn over every stone in our efforts to find good young players. We need a minimum of 26 players for the Premier League."

McLean, who, like his brother, had also managed Motherwell, had left Scotland and Ayr United for the sunny climes of Cyprus. His return, as it transpired, was akin to a full-blown depression sweeping in to engulf Greenock. It was to be a quite ghastly season for the club and all concerned.

To be fair, anyone coming to manage Morton at that time was going to have a nigh impossible task to preserve their newly acquired Premier status. The club did not have a Premier quality playing staff and they had no money to improve it. Willie McLean had excellent credentials as a coach, but what Morton needed was an inspirational character. The elder McLean did not fit that mould.

His first task was to try and add meaningfully to the squad. Five players came in – centre backs Andy Dunlop from Partick and John Boag from Aberdeen, goalkeeper Colin Kelly from Dundee, full back John McClurg from Kilmarnock and ex-Morton midfielder Jim Wilkie from Queen of the South. Boag, from Port Glasgow, was a youngster who had failed to break into the highly successful Dons' team, Wilkie had already been found wanting at both Cappielow and Dumfries, as had Kelly, McClurg and Dunlop at their clubs. None could be said to enhance the Morton pool for their forthcoming task. Alex O'Hara, the ex-Rangers and Partick striker, was involved in talks and he at least would add experience.

Against that, Morton lost a player of proven quality when midfielder Jim Rooney (28) went to St Mirren for a fee reported to be £40,000. As Willie McLean said: "He is not a player I would have chosen to sell, but St Mirren made a good offer and the deal went through."

Yet another quality player had left Cappielow. Throw in the departure to Queen of the South of full back Davie Hayes, freed by Tommy McLean at the tail end of a splendid Cappielow career, and the squad which Benny Rooney had first assembled for the top 10 had been all but decimated. Only Jim Holmes and John McNeil remained. Before the campaign began the writing was on the wall.

Pre-season friendlies against English Second and First Division clubs, Middlesbrough and Watford, produced results which flattered to deceive. Dougie Robertson and Dom Sullivan scored goals in a 2-1 win over the former, and also were on the scoresheet in a 3-2 defeat by Watford whose goals came from a Mo Johnston double and John Barnes.

This false sense of relative well-being extended into the first two Premier Division outings. Dumbarton, part-time like Morton and who had accompanied them into the top flight, were beaten 2-1 at Cappielow, John McNeil grabbing both goals, the first from the penalty spot and the second with an excellent 25-yard drive. The team, in 4-3-3 formation, was McDermott; McClurg, Dunlop, Duffy, Holmes; Docherty, Sullivan and Doak; Robertson, O'Hara and McNeil.

Next up were Hearts at Tynecastle, for whom Craig Levein and Willie Johnston were best. Former Jambo Willie Pettigrew was fit again, but on the bench, for a game in which Morton again emerged triumphant 2-1, this time O'Hara and Robertson getting the goals.

Meanwhile Jim Fleeting had been appointed as an assistant coach, though he was also registered as a player in case of emergencies, while ex-Motherwell striker Jim Gillespie was signed on trial for a month.

Morton had four points out of four, but it was a false dawn. Reality was about to kick in. First Meadowbank bundled Morton out of the second round of the Skol Cup 2-1 in Edinburgh. Then it was derby time, St Mirren arriving at Cappielow on Saturday 25th August, 1984. The Saints' midfield of Jim Rooney, Tony Fitzpatrick and Billy Abercromby ran the show as the visitors handed out a 4-0 spanking, Frank McAvennie grabbing a double, Abercromby and, as if by script, Rooney adding the others. What the selfless Rooney, a true players' player, brought to Morton over the years could be seen all too readily by his display that afternoon.

The following Saturday Morton were at Parkhead. This time it was 5-0. I wrote afterwards: "Quite simply Morton were out of their depth. The Glasgow club, like St Mirren the previous week, did as they pleased in midfield where the elegant McStay and the competitive Grant were prominent."

Brian McClair hit a brace, as did the outstanding Frank McGarvey, while Peter Grant scored the remaining goal. Willie McLean commented: "The problem is in midfield where we didn't compete."

I wrote: "One is tempted to say that a further problem is that Morton have too many First Division players playing Premier League football."

It was back to Cappielow next to face league leaders Aberdeen. Fergie's side had been forced to part with Mark McGhee, to Hamburg, and Gordon Strachan, to Manchester United, but were still a formidable force. They eased to a 3-0 win at a ground where they would have been delighted to gain a point in past seasons. Billy Stark, Willie Falconer and Eric Black were the scorers.

I reported: "The Dons played the Liverpool way, with pace, power and simplicity of passing. It is difficult to find meaningful words of encouragement for Morton. In their last three fixtures they simply have been outclassed. Twelve goals have been conceded without reply."

When Dundee United, with eight Scottish caps in their line-up, inflicted another 3-0 home defeat with a Dodds double and one by Hegarty, it was becoming embarrassing for the hosts. The attendance was 2,219. It was going to be a long haul to the end of the season.

Young John Boag came in to face Rangers at Ibrox to help shore up the defence. He played alongside Dunlop, with Jim Duffy playing behind as a sweeper. That at least restricted the Light Blues to a 2-0 win, Ally McCoist and Cammy Fraser being on target.

On the last Saturday of September Morton travelled to Leith to tackle Hibernian, the only club now below them in the table. Once more they lost, this time by 3-1. I commented: "It bodes ill for a Morton team who have conceded 20 goals in their last six appearances. The only consolation is that they scored their first goal in over nine hours of football. Quite where Willie McLean and his team go from here I wouldn't care to guess.

"It is not so much the defeats themselves, as the manner of them, that causes such concern. Jim Duffy and Jim Holmes could emerge with credit while it is hard not to sympathise with youngsters like Jim Wilson and John Boag. Otherwise Morton were a sorry lot." Even Morton's goal was fortunate, Danny Docherty's drive taking a big deflection off a defender. Dom Sullivan, a player of proven Premier ability, by now looked alarmingly past his sell-by-date due to injury problems, Willie Pettigrew seemed similarly afflicted in terms of his own motivation, and if there was cause for optimism it was beyond any perception of mine.

On the Monday former Ton boss Benny Rooney, now in charge at Partick, moved to try to take Jim Duffy to Firhill in a deal involving a swap with his midfield player Jamie Doyle, but it was turned down.

It had become only too evident that Morton were a battered haddock swimming among sharks. I remember thinking, even that early, that it would have been better had the club not been promoted. That's how bad it had become. And in these circumstances Willie McLean was not the man to have in charge. He often seemed as depressed as the fans. His talent was as a coach. Morton desperately needed a motivator. And they needed fighters in their team. One or two of the experienced campaigners didn't seem up for the battle. I commented: "In the last few games Jim Duffy and Jim Holmes have been carrying the side and the burden has proved too much."

On Monday 8th October the astonishing news broke that newspaper magnate Robert Maxwell, proprietor of the Mirror Group, had expressed an interest in acquiring Morton FC. Maxwell already had an interest in Oxford United who were fourth top of the English Second Division.

The prospect of someone possibly injecting serious cash into the Greenock club was tantalising for the Morton support. Club director Tom Robertson told me: "All we know is that enquiries have been made on behalf of Mr Maxwell and we have supplied the information requested. "We are awaiting any developments that might take place. You know as much as I do about it."

Robert Maxwell was unavailable for comment, while Morton Chairman Hugh Currie, who had just returned from holiday, knew nothing about the approach. His immediate reaction, however, was one of enthusiasm given the severe financial restrictions facing the Sinclair Street club.

The following day, however, a Maxwell spokesman issued a complete denial. He said: "There is no truth in this matter." When I put it to him that Morton had confirmed that an approach had been made, and the club had supplied the requested information to Mr Maxwell, the spokesman reiterated: "There is no truth in this. I cannot say who would be doing this." And it is said politicians are economical with the truth. In retrospect, given later revelations about Maxwell, one might feel that Morton had a lucky escape.

Halfway through October, Eddie Morrison announced that he would be joining Kilmarnock as their new manager. Having guided Morton through eight unbeaten games in the run to the First Division title, in between the appointments of Alex Miller and Tommy McLean, Morrison had ruled himself out of contention for the job at Cappielow. This was due to Eddie having a good job with the Outram organisation which owned the Glasgow Herald and Evening Citizen. Circumstances had changed, and he said: "I'm looking forward to it. It's a wrench in some ways to be leaving Morton, but I'm now 100% Kilmarnock."

He carried the best wishes of everyone at Cappielow as he sought to turn round the fortunes of a club where not that long ago he had been a goalscoring hero.

For Morton, little got better. Andy Dunlop had the dubious distinction of scoring for both clubs in a 3-1 defeat at Dumbarton in which John McNeil was sent off, then Hearts came to Cappielow to deliver another loss, this time by 3-2. Making his debut from Falkirk, on a loan period, was Alan Mackin and he must have wished he hadn't turned up. "For physically imposing centre half Alan Mackin," I wrote, "it was to be a nightmare second half."

After Jim Gillespie had put the home side ahead, Mackin failed to clear in the penalty area, panicked and handled the ball. Black netted from the spot kick. A Kidd own goal gave Morton the lead once more, but Morton's Martin Doak was ordered off, allowing Hearts to take control.

John Robertson, a promising young striker at the time, pounced to equalise before the unfortunate Mackin miskicked straight to Sandy Clark to hit the winner.

When St Mirren dumped Morton 2-1 at Love Street, the Greenock side were now three points adrift at the bottom of the table. Willie McLean did not attend the after-match press conference. I wrote: "Despite having less of the ball, St Mirren grabbed two goals with expert efficiency. It was sufficient to compensate for their deficiencies in other areas." Saints boss Alex Miller was relieved, but angry too, saying: "We were terrible, just terrible."

It could hardly get worse for Morton whose next visitors to Cappielow were Celtic, complete with latest signing Maurice Johnston from Watford. A respectable defeat was all that any home fan could hope for.

Looking ahead, a beleaguered Willie McLean said: "The players need a break. If we can get a result it will make them realise that they can win. Then I feel we can move away from the bottom."

In a whirlwind start by the Glasgow club before 10,053 fans, most of them wearing the green hoops, Mo Johnston stabbed home an early goal. The first of many we thought. However, Jim Gillespie equalised and, in a torrential downpour, Morton somehow managed to nullify Celtic's superior skills. Jim Duffy, as always, was heroic at the heart of the home defence, Danny Docherty put in a huge amount of selfless running and suddenly Gillespie struck again. Willie McLean's wildest dreams were realised as his side battled on, against all the odds, to win the points. "It was," he said, "a victory for teamwork."

Morton again showed commendable resolution at Pittodrie the next Saturday, losing to league leaders Aberdeen. They took the lead through Ian Clinging and then began to assume an unexpected measure of control. But once the Dons equalised through Frank McDougall the tide turned. Further goals followed from Willie Miller and Neil Simpson before visiting goalkeeper Murray McDermott suffered an ankle injury which was to rule him out for seven weeks.

There had, however, been encouraging signs for Ton boss Willie McLean and I suggested to him that he might like to put one over brother Jim at Tannadice the following Saturday. "That is the understatement of the year," he replied. "The players have deserved more than they have got out of the last four games."

In the battle of the brothers it was Jim who was left licking the cream. His United team chose that afternoon to give full expression to their formidable array of talents. To personalise it, seven times James put the ball into William's net without reply. "There are certain points," I said, "beyond which the scoreline matters little and it is, therefore, no consolation to Morton that they got off lightly at Tannadice on Saturday."

In place of the injured McDermott in goal was young ex-Ardeer Recreation player Craig Adams. He was blameless. "It would have been easier to stop rain falling," I wrote. United assistant Walter Smith said: "I warned the players beforehand that Morton were fighting hard and would make it difficult for us." His players certainly paid heed.

It was a complete mismatch on the field, none more so than the individual contest between the tall, unwieldy Alan Mackin at centre half for Morton, and Dundee United's quicksilver striker Paul Sturrock who hit a Premier League record of five individual goals. It was so one-sided as to be totally embarrassing for the visitors. It could easily have been double figures.

For the next game, against Rangers at Cappielow, Morton resorted to introducing coach Jim Fleeting at centre back and managed to keep the score to a relatively respectable 3-1 defeat, Jim Duffy getting the home counter against two by Ian Redford and one by Ally Dawson. There was a nice touch from Ibrox manager Jock Wallace who praised young Adams' display in the home goal.

Hibs then arrived at Cappielow for a bottom of the table clash and suddenly it was Morton who got every break going. With ex-Scotland goalkeeper Alan Rough having a shocker for the visitors, Morton won 4-0, Robertson, Fleeting, Gillespie and Sullivan hitting the target. Morton were now two points behind Hibs, Dumbarton and Dundee.

It was a key spell. Dundee were next on the agenda at Dens Park, but it was to be a disaster for the Cappielow men. Albert Kidd had given the hosts a deserved two-goal lead. I reported: "Morton, simply, were being outplayed, especially in midfield where Rafferty, Connor, Brown and Kidd were in control for the Dark Blues."

Goals can change games quite dramatically, however, and when Dougie Robertson pinched one back for Morton the hosts began to get a touch of the jitters. On the sidelines Dundee manager Archie Knox was "beginning to wave his arms like a windmill" in his agitation, but disaster befell young Adams who dropped the ball to allow Connor to make it 3-1. Port Glaswegian Stuart Rafferty then produced a good run and pass to put Stephen in for a fourth goal and the game was dead. McCall added a fifth.

CHAPTER FIFTEEN

Nothing but gloom

When Morton fell to another relegation threatened club, Dumbarton, 4-2 at Cappielow the portents were ominous. A Dom Sullivan double was inconsequential. The Greenock men were firmly at the bottom, two points behind Hibs.

There seemed no prospect of lasting relief for McLean's squad. If things were bad they were to get a lot worse. Morton had reached the halfway stage of the season for a return of nine points. The second half, unbelievably, was to produce just three more.

Days later Morton signed young teenage goalkeeper David Wylie from Ferguslie United, someone who was to play a key role for the club in later years. It was Murray McDermott, however, who was back between the posts for the visit to Tynecastle where the hosts won 1-0 with a controversial penalty. Morton could have thrown the towel into the Premier ring at that point and saved themselves a heap of misery.

St Mirren came to Greenock, wandered around Cappielow like tourists, and won 2-0, McAvennie and Gallagher scoring without reply. Willie McLean summed up: "Our display was a disgrace. It's time for the players to stand up and be counted."

Two successive Saturdays fell foul of frost, Morton agreeing with Aberdeen to a change of venue on the second. Centre half Frank Welsh played his first game of the season after recovering from an Achilles tendon injury, replacing the hapless Mackin who had returned to Falkirk. Aberdeen plundered the visitors to the tune of five goals, leaving Alex Ferguson in great humour. I wrote: "It's stretching the bounds of optimism to incredulous limits to expect escape from relegation now."

There was a brief respite when Morton took part in the Tennent's Sixes at Ingliston, losing in the final to Hearts, but picking up a welcome £6,000. Willie McLean commented: "It's a pity we can't play the rest of the Premier League indoors." Just the sort of remark to encourage the troops.

On Saturday 26th January, 1985, Morton were paired with Rangers at Cappielow in the third round of the Scottish Cup. The surface was hard and sprinkled with frost and the remnants of snow. Rangers, not surprisingly, tried to get the game called off, but referee Kenny Hope turned a cloth ear to their appeals. I commented: "Frankly I couldn't see how Cappielow could pass an inspection when it failed to do so on the two previous Saturdays when the pitch was in better condition."

The pitch proved a leveller and Rangers were held to a 3-3 draw, Robertson (2) and Clinging matching goals from Prytz, McDonald and McPherson. Willie McLean, for once, was delighted with the attitude of his players, paying particular mention to Jim Duffy and Dougie Robertson. He also took time to have a dig at the Ibrox men, saying they were not a patch on Alex Ferguson's Aberdeen. "They rely upon individuals," he concluded. Some Rangers fans probably felt the same as they were singing "Don't let us down again" in a second half in which Morton were the better team.

On Wednesday it was up the motorway to Govan for the replay and this time Rangers triumphed 3-1, Sullivan getting the visitors' consolation strike. Wing magician Davie Cooper was the Ibrox star, tormenting Morton down both flanks almost at will.

By coincidence Morton met the same opponents at the same venue on the Saturday, this time in the league, and once again the Light Blues came out on top with goals by John McDonald and Derek Johnstone, who had returned to Ibrox from Chelsea for a second spell. It was an undemanding, if not entirely convincing, win for the home team and I wrote: "Morton stuttered along in first gear throughout the match while Rangers, always in control, gave the impression of being an expensive limousine which needs a service."

In the press box I sat alongside Andy Ritchie, who was covering the game for a Sunday newspaper. I remarked to him that, at the age of 28, he should still be out there playing. He informed me that, after his unhappy sojourn at Albion Rovers following his departure from Motherwell, no one in Scotland had contacted him to ask if he wanted a game. Outside the stadium at the end of the match Morton director Ian McPherson approached Ritchie and asked: "Are you fit for 90 minutes?"

"Was I ever?" came the reply, quick as a flash and with a neat sense of self-deprecation. Andy was soon to head down to London to work as a security guard. His exit from football was rather like Rembrandt choosing to put down his palette and become a street sweeper.

Morton's next four games, against Hibs, Dundee, Hearts and Dumbarton, would prove decisive to their fortunes. They were at the bottom of the pile on a meagre nine points, six less than Hibs, seven less than Dumbarton and no fewer than nine behind Dundee.

Hibs administered a crushing blow by 5-1 at Easter Road, though home manager John Blackley was less than impressed. He said: "I felt Morton handed it to us. I had wanted to win this game in style but I didn't think we played all that well." It was a withering comment.

Willie McLean, not for the first time or the last, failed to attend the press conference, but on the Monday he lambasted his players through an article with me in the Greenock Telegraph. He frothed: "The players have got to stand up and take a long, hard look at themselves over the season. Those who don't pass the test have been told why and where they have failed. There has been a lack of concentration and professionalism."

McLean then said of one unnamed forward: "His contribution has been nil." Aware that he too was part of this debacle, he continued: "I can accept criticism of myself to a certain point. It is my job to prepare the players and to select them. But what I can't do is play for them."

My own comment was: "The real problem for Morton this season has been that the transfer of key players has caught up with them. You can't make a silk purse out of a sow's ear." Since Benny Rooney had taken his side up to the elite league, Morton had sold players to the value of £900,000.

Celtic then continued the increasing wretchedness of the season with a 4-0 trouncing at Parkhead, goals by McStay, McGarvey, Provan and young Paul Chalmers.

There was some respite from the despondency when it was announced that old favourite Bobby Thomson would be returning to Cappielow on loan from Hibs where he had become surplus to requirement. He had left Morton in 1981 for Middlesbrough for a then club record transfer fee of £170,000. At the age of 30 his career had ground to a virtual halt, but there were hopes he might resurrect it in Greenock.

Thomson's first game of his second spell was at Cappielow against Dundee, but his presence was not enough to prevent a 1-0 defeat. John McNeil, back after injury, missed a penalty kick. Hearts inflicted a second loss by the same scoreline at the same venue to leave Morton stranded at the foot of the table, eight points adrift of Dumbarton with nine games remaining. It was becoming academic now.

An understrength St Mirren managed to win the Renfrewshire Cup Final before Dundee United cruised to a 3-0 win at Cappielow, a double by Dodds and one by Gough being more than enough to take care of the limited home threat. The gap in ability was yawning. Yet again there was no appearance at the press conference by Willie McLean. More worrying, the crowd was a paltry 909.

There was at least recognition that the youth policy, which had been virtually non-existent since the days of the emerging Neil Orr, Joe McLaughlin and John McNeil, would have to be overhauled. To that effect Allan McGraw was put in charge of the under-18s. He was, in fact, to make massive strides in the development of young players in the years to come.

Pat McCurdy (20) came in from Hibs, Willie Pettigrew moving the other way, while young Ian Alexander also arrived from Motherwell, this following yet another defeat, by 1-0 to Dumbarton. Willie McLean continued to berate his team, saying "the front players [against Dumbarton] were an absolute disgrace."

It was becoming a trifle wearying and I wrote: "It is up to the Morton boss to instil pride in performance in his players, just as it is up to them to respond."

If only the season could have ended then. But this farce had some way to run yet. At Cappielow Martin Doak hit a double against Celtic, normally a feat to be lauded. Unfortunately Celtic swept seven goals of their own into the Morton net. Brian McClair was the hero with four, Frank McGarvey adding two and Owen Archdeacon the remaining counter. Morton were now 10 points behind Hibs and Dumbarton, not that it mattered a jot. It was like counting the number of harpoons in a dying whale.

In a match postponed on the Saturday due to snow, Morton travelled to Paisley on Tuesday 2nd April for a meeting with derby rivals St Mirren. A miniscule ray of sunshine pierced the stygian gloom when goals by Martin Doak, Ian Alexander and Bobby Thomson gave them a 3-2 win. It was their first victory since 1st December, after 13 consecutive defeats, and carried them into double figures with 11 points.

It may have had no fundamental bearing on their fate, but a derby victory was worth some encouraging comment. Not from Willie McLean who, once again, failed to appear at the press gathering. Alex Miller was left to say of his Paisley buddies' efforts: "It was a joke. We were an absolute disgrace."

Dundee United then administered the coup de grace on 6th April when they put down Morton as effectively as any vet would a wounded animal, five goals rippling the Morton net without response. Jim McLean referred to his brother's side gently: "It's always sad to see any team go down. We did it to them the last time they went down too." Well, at least this time he kept the death within the family.

In four games United had hit 18 goals past Morton for the loss of none. On this most recent occasion they were four up at half-time, adding just one more after the interval, and the after-match chat in the Tannadice changing room was volcanic. I recall waiting in the corridor outside the dressing room area along with former United full back Derek Stark who had left football to join the police force. You would have thought the Tangerines had lost, such was the seething tirade which spewed forth from the United manager. "That's a bit severe," I suggested to Stark. He smiled and shrugged, as if to say "normal procedure".

In a quieter moment I spoke to Jim McLean. I always found him to be generous in his comments of other clubs' players and he had a special word for Jim Duffy who stood out like a defiant buttress in a building that was otherwise collapsing into rubble. "He is a great example of a professional," said McLean. "He leads from the front."

Brother Willie was becoming increasingly voluble about his own side's shortcomings and after Rangers had glided along to a 3-0 Cappielow win he exclaimed: "We have conceded nearly 100 goals this season, yet our best players are in defence! Our failure has been in the middle and up front.

"Our forward players today were inept. Alexander, Turner and Robertson were powder-puff. I've got a player with the talent of John McNeil playing with the reserves. And that is where he deserves to be playing. There's no point in having ability if you're not prepared to fight."

A scoreless draw at Dens Park took Morton to 12 points, what was to be their final tally in this atrocious season. For the next match, against Hibernian at Cappielow, striker Dougie Robertson did not turn up, leading to an "indefinite suspension". It was symptomatic of the general malaise. In a 2-1 defeat Tommy Turner netted for the home side on an afternoon when Aberdeen also won the league.

Entirely deservedly, Jim Duffy was overwhelmingly voted Player of the Year by the Morton fans in the annual Telegraph poll. He was also voted Players' Player of the Year by his fellow professionals, quite an accolade given the extent of his team's demise.

The final match of the season was at home to champions Aberdeen when a Dons side, their thoughts already on sun-kissed beaches, went through the motions to win 2-1, Bobby Thomson netting the home goal in his last game before returning to Hibs.

Frank McDougall netted the Dons' 100th goal of the season and, coincidentally, it was also the 100th scored against Morton in the league; one for the quiz books.

After the match Willie McLean announced that he was resigning. "This is my last game in charge here," he said. "My contract is up in June and I will not be making any effort to have it renewed. This season has been one of disillusion and disappointment." There was, he said, no pressure from the board on him to go.

Chairman Hugh Currie was sympathetic, saying: "Mr McLean was pitch-forked into the job. He had no financial backing, because we had none to give him. We're very sorry he's leaving. He's had a rotten time but has always been a gentleman to deal with." There was also a sharp rebuke for the players. "I do not think the players gave us 100%. They let us down badly," concluded Mr Currie.

I had said at the outset of the campaign that I did not think Morton would survive. After losing Jim Rooney, and with Frank Welsh being injured from the outset, the task became Herculean. I wrote, however: "I did not expect the collapse that ensued. The players must take their share of the blame, but it is too easy and simplistic to place all the blame upon them. Several were Willie McLean's signings, and there has to be motivation and leadership from the top. Willie McLean, in turn, was a board appointment."

I have said before that McLean was quite the wrong type of man to have as a manager in the circumstances in which Morton found themselves. There was no doubting his coaching skills, but at that time Morton needed someone like Ally McLeod who could lift individuals and provide inspiration. Willie was never that type of personality. He was a very introverted individual. He was wary of, if not actually hostile to, the press. He never liked the business of press conferences and quite often he simply did not attend them. That was his prerogative, but at times it seemed counter-productive. If you want to encourage a positive press for your club or team, you have to engage with them. There are times when it is useful to have the journos onside.

Right or wrong, it is always that bit more difficult for the hacks to come down hard on a manager when he has been pleasant and helpful towards them. And the reverse applies equally. It is simply a matter of human nature.

Where Benny Rooney and Alex Miller would talk football all day, with Willie McLean the opposite was true.

I remember one instance when I was reading a magazine after a pre-match lunch at the Swallow Hotel on the outskirts of Dundee. McLean came and sat down next to me and I asked if he could tell me his team for the afternoon's match. He clammed up immediately.

Somehow the chat got round to the fact that I was thinking about building my own house. Immediately Willie became like a man transformed. He had built one or two of his own abodes and he began to talk enthusiastically of projects he had overseen. He was positively genial, giving me several hints and much welcome and clearly excellent advice. It was the longest and most amenable conversation I had with him. I was left none the wiser about football, but I knew a hell of a lot more about the pitfalls of building one's own house.

The free transfer list was then released – Jim Fleeting, Craig Adams, Andy Dunlop, John McClurg, Eddie McNab, Frank Welsh, Ian Alexander, Paul McAllister, Jim Reid, Andrew Clinton and Alistair McKechnie. There was a question mark over whether or not Dom

Sullivan would remain. He didn't, moving on to Alloa having suffered increasingly from injury problems.

Dundee then came in with a bid of £45,000 for Jim Duffy who was under freedom of contract. It was knocked back.

CHAPTER SIXTEEN

Legend McGraw takes over reins

Soon after Dundee had come in for Jim Duffy, I was able to reveal that Morton were about to appoint club legend Allan McGraw to the role of manager. This was finally confirmed on the 21st May, 1985. Chairman Hugh Currie had already said that the club hoped to bounce straight back to the top 10, but McGraw was warier.

He said: "Of course I want promotion, but first of all I have to instil motivation and pride into the players. It is important too that I get the community behind me. Everyone knows that Morton have no money to spend on new players, so it's important that we build a healthy youth policy." With four managers in a two-year period, this was something that had been neglected.

Chairman Currie said of his new appointment: "Allan offered his services to us and we were glad to accept. We cannot afford full-time players but Allan will be a full-time club manager."

McGraw, in fact, was to hold down the job for an amazing 12 years. He built one very fine team in the course of that time, but I would argue that his greatest achievement was the institution of the best youth policy the club ever had in my time covering their activities. Allan also told me that, as a chairman, Hugh Currie "was a dream". He reflected years later: "There was no interference on the football side. He would take to do with the business side and let the football people get on with their job."

McGraw knew full well how the past season had alienated many people in the community and was keen for much better links with the fans, schools and youth football organisations. "In essence," I wrote, "what McGraw is talking about is better public relations and that, frankly, was certainly not a priority last season."

Hibs were next with a bid for Jim Duffy, offering either £50,000 or £45,000 plus Bobby Thomson. Both options were rejected, but the following day Dundee finally got their man for a £75,000 fee. Allan McGraw commented: "I'm sorry to see him go, but I couldn't stand in the boy's way. He was desperate to go."

Dundee were getting a bargain for, as Allan McGraw pointed out, Duffy was a thorough professional. For Dark Blues boss Archie Knox there was no gamble whatever in bringing him to Dens Park. Duffy came with a platinum guarantee of reliability.

Gradually Allan McGraw began to make his own acquisitions. In came Jackie McNamara from Hibs as player-coach, while 31-year-old midfielder Lex Richardson, so often a target of Morton's in the past, was recruited from Dundee on a free transfer.

And back to the fold came two Cappielow 'old boys', George Anderson from Airdrie as a player but who would also act as reserve coach, and Billy 'Sugar' Osborne who would take charge of the youngsters at the club. The first seeds of renewal were being sown.

Ian Clinging was made available for transfer before the first league game of the season at Firhill where Benny Rooney's Partick awaited Morton.

The visitors struggled somewhat in midfield and up front, though in defence George Anderson was outstanding. I wrote: "He tackled as strongly as ever, read the play expertly and, as a bonus, scored the Morton goal with a fierce header from a John McNeil corner." He had good support from Jackie McNamara.

Thistle deservedly equalised when John Donnelly fired home a wonderful free kick which, as Partick assistant boss Mike Jackson said, was "reminiscent of Andy Ritchie".

Donnelly was a very talented individual, but another of those whose ability was diluted by a poor attitude at times. Some said he lacked grey matter. He had gone to Leeds United, failed, and come to Thistle for £15,000. Later, when Bertie Auld returned for a second spell at Firhill, Mike Jackson related a tale concerning Donnelly. "I had gone in to Firhill to see Bertie," said Mike. "I heard a hell of a rammy going on inside his office. I knocked on the door and Bertie shouted 'come in.' When I opened the door there was Bertie and the boy Donnelly rolling about the floor. Bertie looked up from underneath Donnelly and said: 'We're just discussing the boy's request for a wage rise.'"

The Firhill draw was a decent opening result for Allan McGraw's management career, but it simply papered over some very big cracks. Montrose came to Cappielow and won 2-1, John McNeil netting the home goal from the spot, Dunfermline administered a Skol Cup section defeat on penalties, again in Greenock, and then a point was gleaned at Methil in a 4-4 draw with East Fife. The main feature was a fine double by Lex Richardson.

St Mirren won convincingly, 4-1, in the Skol Cup and then Morton lost 2-1 at home to Dumbarton. In fairness that last result was very much against the run of play as admitted by Sons' manager Davie Wilson and his assistant Derek Whiteford, but it exposed a crisis of confidence in goalkeeper Murray McDermott. He had been the club's Player of the Year two seasons previously but the trauma of losing 100 goals in the Premier League had clearly affected him and he was badly culpable at both goals. He was never to be the same goalkeeper again.

It led to Morton signing another custodian, Robin Rae from Hibs, but in the next match they lost at Shawfield against Clyde to drop into second bottom spot in the table. Allan McGraw was ordered to the stand after dissent following the dismissal of Lex Richardson and declared that he was going to fine himself.

The following week Kilmarnock were the opposition. I observed on the Friday before the game: "It seems as if tomorrow's match at Cappielow is not so much a meeting of Morton and Kilmarnock as one between those old friends Allan McGraw and Eddie Morrison, the respective managers." By the time the dust settled, Morton had delivered a morale-boosting

3-0 victory, goals coming from Gillespie (2) and Doak. New goalkeeper Robin Rae had produced one excellent save when the score was just 1-0 which proved to be the game's defining moment.

Incidentally, Morton at that time signed young defender Jim Hunter from Glentyan Thistle, a player who was to play a key role in the seasons to come.

If the Killie result was a ray of hope, it was soon extinguished. Forfar won 3-2 at Cappielow, John McNeil getting both home goals, before Hamilton ruthlessly exposed Morton's deficiencies in a 5-0 thrashing at Douglas Park. I reported: "The Greenock men fell like lambs to the slaughter. When you look through the Cappielow ranks at the number of highly experienced players involved in that display it was hard to credit that the surrender came so easily."

Allan McGraw said: "I felt sorry for the fans who spent money travelling through to watch a performance like that."

Back at Cappielow the next Saturday Morton drew 2-2 with Ayr in a game which included six bookings and two ordering-offs. It was not an impressive display and I commented: "Up front John McNeil had his moments, not least in scoring both goals, but the over-riding impression when watching Morton these days is of a series of disjointed units. There is Morton, but there is no team."

Another draw, at Brechin, followed, Alex O'Hara scoring, before Morton brought in Jimmy Simpson and Joe Coyle from Dumbarton, Danny Docherty moving to Boghead in exchange. But at Cappielow a week later Falkirk won 3-0, Morton now being bottom of the First Division with six points from 11 games. The collapse continued at Recreation Park where Alloa also won 3-0. I wrote: "This defeat may prove to be a watershed in the affairs of the Greenock club."

Allan McGraw said bluntly: "I'm ashamed. Some of them [the players] seem to think they're too good for this club. A few have been given the chance to go. If they don't accept a free transfer they won't be in my plans." Soon after the club announced that former Port Glaswegian John Wilson, now living in Kilmacolm, would be joining the board of directors.

He was a self-made businessman and managing director of Sir J.H. Biles, Design Consultants and Naval Architects and Engineers. He had been brought in to add some business acumen to the Cappielow board. He said: "I feel that for too long Morton have been in the doldrums. It is imperative that we have a strong financial base."

I asked what he would bring to the club and he replied: "I am a new face with a fresh attitude and a fresh approach which can perhaps be a catalyst for others."

"Would he be able and willing to inject much needed finance into the club?" I enquired.

"I'm quite prepared to invest if there is something worth investing in," was his circumspect answer.

On the previous incumbent's spell in the manager's chair John Wilson was quite specific. "Willie McLean was nothing short of a disaster. That situation was allowed to continue too long before any action was taken. The policy of scouting and linking with youth, juvenile and junior football was non-existent. The present manager has inherited that."

In fact, the youth side had been neglected for some time before the arrival of Willie McLean and it was only now, under Allan McGraw, that it once more became a priority.

Meanwhile, after the showdown between McGraw and the players in the aftermath of the 3-0 Alloa defeat, forward Jim Gillespie chose to take the offer of a free transfer, but another sore defeat followed when Airdrie administered a 4-1 thrashing at Cappielow. A turning point had been the dismissal of Jackie McNamara with the game goalless. Tommy Turner, always a trier, was the scorer for the hosts.

At that point McGraw chose to throw in youngsters Jim Hunter and Danny Diver to the side, denuded as the squad was by injuries and the suspension of Martin Doak, John Boag and Jackie McNamara. Diver, tall and rather ungainly, grabbed one of the goals in a 3-2 win over Clyde while I wrote that "Hunter showed composure beyond his years. He is definitely a young player with a future". Lex Richardson and Tommy Turner were the other scorers.

That welcome two points, which saw Morton share bottom spot on eight points with Ayr, was not the start of a revival, however, as Eddie Morrison's Kilmarnock reversed the result at Cappielow early in the season, triumphing 3-0 in a match in which Morton goalkeeper Robin Rae looked badly culpable at two of the goals. That encouraged McGraw to introduce another youngster, David Wylie, and the 19-year-old never really looked back, going on to become one of the best goalkeepers in the club's recent history.

Successive defeats followed to Forfar away by 2-0, then Hamilton at home by 1-0, but Wylie at least had been a stand-out, while the man he displaced, Robin Rae, was transfer-listed having failed to turn up for training.

Morton, though, had played 17 games for just eight points. They were bottom of the table and in serious trouble. It was the nadir of the season for the manager and his players. The knives were out among the restless natives.

On Saturday 7th December, 1985, the team travelled down to Somerset Park for a bottom of the table confrontation, Allan McGraw making no bones about the importance of the meeting. One more defeat and, even at that stage in the season, one wondered if there could be a way back for the Greenock club. But Morton's young players, such as Hunter, Wylie and Turner, had added much needed enthusiasm and at last the beleaguered Greenock side got a vital win. Goals by John McNeil (2) and Dougie Robertson led to a 3-0 success in which Wylie in goal was inspirational at key moments and Turner was the top outfield player. Allan McGraw summed up the relief in the camp when he said: "At last I can enjoy a weekend."

It was the start of an excellent 11-game undefeated run.

There was misfortune for centre half Frank Welsh who had just come back to Cappielow, from Hamilton, when he tore ligaments in his second game, but by now Morton were visibly growing in confidence. In eight games they had gathered 13 points, moving up to sixth from bottom after a 2-0 home win over Alloa. Lex Richardson suffered concussion after a clash of heads with Alloa's Donaldson. "For a while after, the player thought he was on the golf course," Allan McGraw said afterwards. Perhaps that explained an under-par display.

Next up was a Scottish Cup third round clash at Tannadice against Dundee United, surely a test of the recovering Ton. Goals by Coyne (2), Redford and Bannon saw the Tangerines ease into the next round, but it was a far from disgraced Morton performance.

Good league form continued, a 2-1 win at Broomfield against Airdrie being followed by a 1-1 draw at Rugby Park against second top Killie.

A 3-2 home win over Brechin, goals from Dougie Robertson and John McNeil (2), took Morton up to sixth place in the table. The elixir of confidence was all too evident. John Boag and Jim Hunter, a total contrast in style and physique, had formed an effective central defence barrier. Boag, tall, raw-boned and unsophisticatedly rugged, was a fearsomely defiant centre half, while Hunter, small, thoughtful and calm, reminded me often of sweeper John Clark of the great Celtic team of the late 60s. David Wylie was in top form between the sticks, and the experience of Jackie McNamara and Lex Richardson was proving invaluable in midfield where Tommy Turner provided the workrate. Up front John McNeil and Dougie Robertson were rediscovering their flair and goalscoring capacity. It was as if Morton had stumbled out of the suffocating undergrowth into the warmth of the sunshine.

League reconstruction was again a topic of debate, with Morton favouring the new 12-12-14 set-up most seemed to back. Chairman Hugh Currie commented: "We think it is quite reasonable."

But there was to be another departure from Morton, this time not a player, but director Freddie Fletcher who had been tempted by Rangers to join the Ibrox board. Freddie, in fact, was to be instrumental in bringing Graeme Souness to Ibrox for the start of what was to be a massive revival for the Ibrox club who all too often had lagged behind Celtic, Aberdeen and Dundee United in recent seasons. He was leaving a club whose own fortunes were improving and manager Allan McGraw said: "There is a good atmosphere at the club now. We've worked hard behind the scenes to set a pattern for the players. We're sticking to it and we're getting results."

The Cappielow board were sufficiently satisfied to organise a five-day trip to Magaluf during which the players would play a couple of friendlies and get a welcome winter break. It was ironic that no sooner had the working holiday been arranged than Morton's fine run came to an end, Ayr upsetting the applecart 1-0 at Cappielow before a crowd of 1,856.

Draws followed in March against Montrose (1-1) at Cappielow and Partick in Maryhill where six goals were shared, supporting the old saying 'Firhill for Thrills'. Not so thrilled were former Morton management pairing Mike Jackson and Benny Rooney who had seen their team pegged back after leading 3-1. For once, youngsters David Wylie and Jim Hunter looked vulnerable, their inexperience finally catching up with them.

In the next game, against Dumbarton, Wylie fumbled a passback from John Boag, only to make amends by saving the resultant penalty. At the other end it was another goalkeeping mistake by Arthur which allowed Dougie Robertson to score the only goal of the game.

John McNeil and Dougie Robertson again showed their renewed zest by grabbing the goals in a 2-2 draw with East Fife, the match being preceded by a minute's silence in respect of one of Morton's valuable helpers behind the scenes, Jock Anderson.

Victory then followed against Airdrie, Alex O'Hara grabbing the only goal of the 90 minutes, before Morton travelled through to Brockville to meet promotion contenders Falkirk, minus John McNeil who had got married the previous day. The Greenock men took a 2-0 lead quite against the run of play as the Bairns played some fine football. Back came Falkirk to equalise, but Jimmy Simpson snatched the winner to take Morton further up the table. The distress of the previous season had been put firmly behind them.

Allan McGraw, Jackie McNamara, George Anderson et al had finally turned round a situation which had been in virtual terminal decline. I wrote: "Allan McGraw and his backroom staff, and the players themselves, have done a marvellous job this season to haul Morton back up by the scruff of the neck when they were at their lowest ebb."

The Greenock club were in mid-table comfort, neither challengers nor in danger of relegation. Their next task was to meet champions Hamilton at Douglas Park.

The hosts decided to make a Gala Day of the match. "Hamilton are to allow the female species of the population in to Douglas Park tomorrow free of charge," I said in my preview of the game. "There could well be a lot of hairy-kneed, unshaven, big raw-boned lassies in frocks two sizes too small queuing up at the turnstiles." Morton director Ian McPherson, a representative of the Scottish League, presented the trophy to the Lanarkshire club. On the day, Morton lost 2-1, their second defeat in 19 games.

The next Saturday they beat promotion contenders Forfar 2-0 at Cappielow before a crowd of 1,514, an attendance which disappointed manager McGraw. It is, of course, always much more difficult to win people back after they have become disillusioned. Another home win – 3-2 against Clyde – followed in which veteran midfield man Lex Richardson was the key player, making one goal, scoring one and generally running the game. The season ended with a 2-0 defeat at Alloa, though there followed a Renfrewshire Cup Final loss to St Mirren by 1-0, Paul Lambert scoring for the Saints. This fixture had by now become devalued, both sides choosing to field understrength teams.

Morton were rebuilding and, on 22nd July, I was able to reveal that they had made a serious bid to bring back Jim Tolmie to Cappielow. The striker, still only 25, had left Manchester City. He told me: "Morton made me a good offer and I was tempted to go there, but the Swedish deal [with Markaryd] was too good to believe. I really had no choice."

CHAPTER SEVENTEEN

Who stole the pies?

There were two new additions to the squad, however, Jimmy Boag arriving from Port Glasgow Juniors, and twenty-five-year-old Rowan Alexander from Brentford. Both were strikers.

Alexander, who had previously played for St Mirren and Queen of the South, was to play a big part in the coming seasons. More than anything, however, Allan McGraw and his colleagues had re-established morale at Cappielow; that and the beginnings of a highly credible youth policy which would serve the club well in the years to come.

Alexander made his debut in the league opener against Clyde, now managed by John Clark, at Cappielow. Morton were the bookies' tip for the First Division title and the result suggested it wasn't a daft choice as they won 3-0 with goals by Turner, Robertson and new boy Alexander who opened the scoring with an acrobatic scissors kick.

There followed a 2-2 draw with Kilmarnock at Rugby Park, Robertson and Alexander again being on target. The latter scored with a fine header from a Jim Holmes cross. For a relatively small man, Alexander had an excellent ability to time his leap to perfection, and also seemed to be able to stay up longer than others. Denis Law had been the master of the technique, so much so that it became known as the 'Law Hang'. I wrote after the game: "Alexander may turn out to be one of Morton's best signings for some time. He is not yet fully match fit, yet he has scored a goal in each of his two outings and looks very competent in everything he does."

It was all set up for the following Saturday at Cappielow when leaders Dunfermline were the visitors, but it was to be a dark day in the club's history.

Club chairman Hugh Currie (63) died suddenly on the morning of the game. He had become a director in 1969 before succeeding retiring chairman Peter Scott in 1975. Director Tom Robertson said: "Hugh Currie was keenly interested in football. First and foremost he was a devoted Morton man. During his chairmanship he steered the club through some very difficult and some very happy times. Those at Cappielow will know what I mean when I speak of the loss of his energy and single-minded enthusiasm for the club."

Manager Allan McGraw said: "When we were going through bad times at the start of last season he always encouraged me. If I asked him for anything he always gave me a straight answer, whether it be yes or no. I'll miss him."

I always found Hugh Currie to be a gentleman, with a ready smile and warm welcome. The relationship between press and football club management and directors is necessarily one which has its occasional tensions, but I never experienced a problem with Hugh Currie. He had no quibble with reasoned criticism and never held a grudge, even if he held a differing opinion. He was straight and he was honest.

The game itself that Saturday was marked by a minute's silence after which Morton fell to a 1-0 defeat. To complete a thoroughly downcast afternoon, Jimmy Simpson was stretchered off after a collision with Dunfermline goalkeeper Ian Westwater. He suffered severe ligament damage which was to end his career. Club physiotherapist Gerry McElhill described it as "the worst injury I have come across in 15 years of football."

It became clear in the week ahead that Simpson would have to retire after an operation by Peter Scott at the Victoria Infirmary in Glasgow. Allan McGraw commented: "It is very sad. Obviously we'll miss him, but the first thing is to organise something to help the boy."

Fund-raising efforts were held throughout the community for Simpson while a testimonial match was organised for mid-October against Rangers.

Morton's next match was a Skol Cup tie against Premier League Dundee at Cappielow which they were leading 2-1 with 11 minutes to go through goals by Rowan Alexander and Tommy Turner. A Harvey equaliser took the tie into extra time, however, and the Dark Blues proved too strong, running out 5-2 winners.

On the Saturday, Morton travelled to Brechin where they beat the host club 5-2, Dougie Robertson scoring four times and Ian Clinging getting the fifth. "After a week of tragic news at Cappielow, this was just the result everyone at the club needed," I commented.

Local businessman Bill Knox, a partner in builders' merchants A.F. McPherson & Co., was appointed to the board, while the following day it was announced that Morton goalkeeper David Wylie was to be included in the Scotland under-21 party to meet West Germany on 9th September.

Dumbarton ruined the renewed feel-good factor by putting three past Morton without reply at Cappielow, before another newcomer was brought on to the board at Greenock. Owner of local confectionery manufacturer Fuller's, Douglas Rae, was appointed before the East Fife match at Methil which the Fifers won 1-0.

In terms of quality that match proved to be on a par with one of McGonagall's poorer poems. Even one East Fife substitute commented: "They'll get football stopped playing like that." My own comments echoed that. "It really was a ghastly game, as witness the fact that the first note I took was in the 26th minute, and that was out of sheer desperation."

The highlight of the afternoon was the discovery at half-time that someone had, quite literally, stolen the pies. The young girl in charge of the teas was distraught, leading to the groundsman putting his arm round her shoulder and telling her: "Dinna worry, lass, it's nae your fault." The heading of my match report in Monday's paper was "Who stole the pies at Methil?" It had, after all, been the highlight of the afternoon.

Former Hibs star Ralph Callachan, freed by Newcastle, was now training at Cappielow but did not play in Morton's next match, at Firhill, where former Ranger Derek Johnstone was now player-manager in place of ex-Morton duo Benny Rooney and Mike Jackson.

Partick gave a truly miserable display as Morton strode to a 5-2 win, Rowan Alexander's brace taking him to five goals in seven outings. Martin Doak also hit the net twice with unopposed headers and Ian Clinging added the fifth.

One would normally extol the virtues of a Morton win of such proportion, but Partick were worse than culpable. I wrote: "Frankly, Thistle were awful. They would have been hard pushed to defend a granny's purse."

Even Derek Johnstone, who had subbed himself at half-time, had to concur, saying: "The only way to stop Maradona scoring goals would be if Thistle signed him." I took time to observe: "They also have a ball-boy who spent his entire afternoon reclining in a chair behind the Thistle goal." Why not, when his heroes were doing the equivalent on the park!

With Ralph Callachan making his debut, Morton then put Queen of the South to the sword by the same 5-2 margin, this time at Cappielow. Alexander hit his first hat-trick for the club, Robertson and Turner adding the other strikes. Mike Jackson was now back with Queens and managed typically to combine his frustration with humour when he commented on the sending-off of his player Shanks: "Shanks had a brainstorm, and he'll have another when he sees his wage packet."

Morton were now fifth in the division, five points behind leaders Dunfermline, and were in confident mood when Montrose came to visit a week later. The east coast men proved real party-poopers, winning 2-0. Allan McGraw was left to say: "We have an awful habit of building up people's hopes and then dashing them."

A 2-2 draw at Forfar followed. Dougie Robertson and Rowan Alexander again proved their worth with the goals, taking them to joint top of the scoring charts on nine goals and setting up a meeting at Cappielow with new league leaders Airdrie. Morton were playing in fits and starts and they badly needed an injection of consistency.

As September, 1986, drew to a close, Morton met league leaders Airdrie at Cappielow with a side which lined up as follows (1-4-3-2): R. Turner; Hunter; O'Hara, Boag, Doak, Holmes; Clinging, Richardson, T. Turner; Robertson, Alexander.

With Jim Hunter playing as sweeper behind the back four, allowing Alex O'Hara and Jim Holmes to push on up the flanks, Morton put in a tremendous first half performance. "Some of their football during that spell was delightful to watch," I wrote, "and it was especially gratifying for the supporters given that their home form has been less than inspiring so far this season."

The interval came with Morton thoroughly deserving their 2-0 lead through goals by Jim Holmes and a typical Rowan Alexander header.

Robin Turner did well in goal in place of the injured David Wylie and, despite a fightback by the Diamonds in the second half which produced a goal, Morton took the points and moved to fifth in the table, six points adrift of leaders Dunfermline. Jim Holmes was in top form, also producing two goal-line clearances and generally showing his quality.

Clyde were beaten 2-1 away from home, courtesy of a Dougie Robertson double, taking him to joint top scorer in the division on 10 goals along with team-mate Rowan Alexander. When Morton beat Kilmarnock 2-0 at Cappielow with goals from John Boag and the on-fire Alexander, they had moved to three points off pace-setters Dunfermline.

There wasn't in truth an outstanding team in the league and Morton's lack of depth was illustrated when Brechin came to Greenock and won 3-2, Rikki Ferguson playing in goal on loan from Hamilton due to injuries to Wylie and Turner. Then leaders Dunfermline arrived to take a point in a 1-1 draw in which home midfielder Lex Richardson was the man-of-the-match in an otherwise rather insipid 90 minutes.

There was a break from league duties on Sunday 19th October when a star-studded Rangers arrived under new manager Graeme Souness for a testimonial match for Jimmy Simpson whose early season injury against Dunfermline had ruled him out of football altogether. On a day of heavy showers, almost 5,000 turned out at Cappielow to put some much needed funds into Jimmy's pocket.

Rangers won 5-2 against a Morton select containing Jim Leighton, Danny McGrain, John McMaster, Gary McAllister, Jim Duffy and Andy Ritchie. Andy looked as if he'd stuffed a couple of pillows under his shirt and padded them out with a winter duvet.

In the Rangers side were English internationalists Chris Woods and Terry Butcher, and Scottish caps Ally McCoist, Ian Durrant and Davie Cooper. Souness later commented: "We were delighted to be able to help Jimmy." In his turn, Simpson said: "I'd like to thank Graeme for bringing his players here."

On the following Saturday, Morton had another new goalkeeper in place of injured pair Wylie and Rae. It wasn't just any old name, but former Leeds and Scotland custodian David Harvey, named best goalkeeper in the 1974 World Cup. Harvey was now turning out for English non-league club Harrogate Town. He was blameless as Morton lost 2-1 at Cappielow to Partick, Alexander grabbing the home goal before a crowd of 2,322.

Once again, however, they bounced back, beating Queen of the South 2-1 in Dumfries, an own goal and one by Alexander taking Morton up to third place in the table. It confirmed their excellent away form in which they had only lost once, scoring 19 goals in eight games.

Greenock was a different story where East Fife grabbed a point, Martin Doak equalising. David Harvey was in top form, at one point diving full length to touch a Blair drive round the post. It was indicative of Morton's patchy form that their best three players were all defenders – Harvey, the outstanding Holmes and Doak.

Morton were very much in the promotion race, but always at the back of the mind was the feeling that, like everyone else in the division, they were not strong enough to compete at the top level. It was not a problem that was going to be solved easily. The club had declared that they needed an average home gate of at least 3,500 to break even. In reality they were attracting little over 2,000.

On 8th November, it was second v third at Boghead where Dumbarton, under manager Alex Totten, were the hosts. Totten had moved to sign old Morton favourite Jim Rooney from St Mirren, using some of the money gained from Hearts for the sale of winger Allan Moore. Meanwhile, Morton had transferred Joe Coyle to Arbroath. David Wylie was back in goal after regaining fitness, but it was the home side who got the points in a 2-1 win.

Morton's see-saw form continued when they beat Montrose 3-0 at Links Park. Ian Clinging gave a fine display as a stand-in at right back, while Jackie McNamara came out of partial retirement to fill gaps left by injury and suspension. Both were excellent, as was Lex Richardson with two goals, one from the penalty spot. Jimmy Boag scored the third strike as Morton moved five points behind leaders Dunfermline.

Another home point was dropped in a goalless draw with Forfar before a fine 2-1 win at Broomfield kept McGraw's side in touch with the leaders. They were now four points behind Dunfermline.

As the festive season approached manager Allan McGraw issued an edict to striker Dougie Robertson: "Lose a stone in weight by New Year's Day or face a heavy fine." I don't think a pun was intended. Dougie always did carry a bit of extra padding in the nether regions, but recent expansion was threatening the material integrity of the largest pair of shorts in the club. McGraw explained that he had no complaints about the player's effort in training, saying: "Maybe we'll have to sew up his mouth."

Robertson responded to the criticism with a superb double strike in a 3-2 Cappielow victory over Clyde, his second goal being a magnificent drive from 22 yards into the roof of the net. Jim Holmes added a third with a curving, Ritchie-esque, free kick over the defensive wall. "The camel stores food in its hump as a sort of reserve energy supply," I conjectured, "and perhaps Dougie does similarly in his rump."

It also came to light that Robertson was in danger of becoming a celebrity. I explained at the time: "Douglas is now in exalted company, sharing the same tea-based diet as used by Samantha Fox. If it has the same effect on Dougie as it has had on Sam, crowds should multiply at Cappielow." It would have been stretching the imagination too far to say that Dougie and page three model Sam might even become bosom buddies.

Morton were now in third spot, three points behind Dunfermline at the top of the league. But consistency was still a problem. Killie administered a 2-0 beating at Rugby Park where both John Boag and Jackie McNamara were ordered off. With John McNeil and Dougie Robertson being booked, Morton's resources were soon going to be stretched almost as far as Dougie's shorts. McNamara's dismissal was theatrical. He and Killie's Cook had gone down in a challenge. Attempting to extricate themselves from the tangle there was some minor handbags at dawn. Jackie got up and wandered towards the dugout, later claiming he thought he was about to be subbed. The referee called him over, McNamara said: "I'm going off anyway," and the match official produced a red card to help him on his way.

George Cowie of Hearts was signed on loan to fill in at right back and scored a wonderful goal at Brechin where Morton won 3-1, John McNeil and Rowan Alexander also netting. For Alexander it was a welcome relief after an eight-game barren spell in front of goal. Christmas came and hopefully Alexander's fellow striker Robertson was allowed a turkey leg after reportedly losing 10lbs on his enforced diet.

On 27th December came a top table clash with league leaders Dunfermline at Cappielow. George Cowie was again on target, as was John McNeil, and when the dust settled the points were shared, Ian McCall and Norrie McCathie hitting the net for the Pars. The crowd was a healthy 3,420, but still below the figure that would merit a festive chuckle in the counting house of the club accountants.

Morton then crushed Dumbarton 4-1 at Cappielow in a bizarre game in which four of the five goals came from the penalty spot. John McNeil converted two before being subbed while the others came from Dougie Robertson (penalty) and Rowan Alexander, their 13th and 25th strikes of the season respectively. But still the Cappielow men couldn't string a series of results together and lost out at Methil to East Fife, also contenders, by 2-1 on a bone hard surface. Jackie McNamara skelped home the Ton counter with a 20-yard drive. Since coming into the side out of semi-retirement in October, due to injuries and suspensions, McNamara had been a key player in midfield where his experience proved invaluable. Incidentally, at this time Celtic boss Davie Hay had come in with a £650,000 offer for ex-Morton centre half Joe McLaughlin, a bid Chelsea turned down. It was ironic given that Celtic had expressed interest in McLaughlin when he had left Cappielow for just £90,000.

Morton's home form had not been as good as they would have wished but they rectified that with two top results within three days. First, Queen of the South were disposed of 2-0, Holmes and McNeil scoring, before Montrose were soundly thrashed 6-1 in front of an enthralled Cappielow crowd. I wrote: "It was the quality of their football as much as the goals which delighted the spectators."

The front three of Dougie Robertson, Rowan Alexander and John McNeil excelled with some intricate inter-play, each ending up on the scoresheet. In midfield Lex Richardson organised and controlled, while at the back Martin Doak was a solid centre half. Doak, Ian Clinging and Jimmy Boag also hit the net in the side's most impressive display of the season thus far.

In the third round of the Scottish Cup, Morton travelled to Shielfield Park to end the hopes of Berwick, John McNeil working a brilliant series of one-twos with Lex Richardson before sweeping home the first goal. Alexander produced a distinctive headed goal to finish the job. The draw could scarcely have been better, derby rivals St Mirren coming out of the hat in a tie scheduled for Cappielow.

McNeil was enjoying a purple patch as Morton gained a point at Forfar in a six-goal thriller. McNeil scored before limping off injured, Robertson and Alexander hitting their 15th and 18th strikes of the season. The latter moved on to 19 with a vital winner at Firhill against Partick, celebrating with his by now familiar forward roll. Morton were two points behind leaders Dunfermline, though having played two games more.

They had proved themselves to be the best football-playing side in the division. They were also beginning to show that they could grind out points when necessary. A new arrival, until the end of the season, was Rob Roy goalkeeper Cameron Melville, as cover for the injured Robin Turner. It was Cammy's second spell at Cappielow.

On Saturday 14th February another of the promotion hopefuls, Airdrie, came to Cappielow where a Dougie Robertson double gained the points in a 2-1 win. At last Morton were top of the league, albeit on goal difference and having played three more games than Dunfermline. But they were on a run and there was a determination about them.

This game against Airdrie was also notable for the booking of goal hero Robertson, the first and only player I have seen to be cautioned for pulling down an opponent's shorts as he skipped past him. Not an easy thing to do! O'Neill was the embarrassed Airdrieonian, displaying all four cheeks at once.

Morton's biggest crowd for quite some time packed into Cappielow, officially 8,118, as St Mirren rolled down from Paisley for the fourth round of the cup. Alex Smith was their manager now, and he had warned his Premier players against any complacency. For Morton, it was a chance to measure themselves against top opposition.

When the final whistle blew the Saints had secured their place in the draw with a narrow 3-2 victory, just deserved on the run of play. I reported: "It was a valiant effort by Morton." Two goals by Paul Chalmers and one by Ian Ferguson were enough for a Buddies' side which fought back from 2-1 down, Rowan Alexander and John McNeil getting the home goals.

Morton could see the finishing line on the horizon and on Friday 27th February they added to their squad by bringing Aberdeen's John McMaster back to his home town. The 32-year-old was surplus to the requirements of new Dons boss Ian Porterfield and came to Cappielow in a player-coach capacity. He brought a wealth of experience, having been in the Aberdeen team that beat Real Madrid to win the European Cup Winners-Cup and also the Super Cup against Hamburg. He had won titles and domestic cups under Alex Ferguson and came after stating he was impressed by Morton's aim of building a productive youth policy.

Manager Allan McGraw had meanwhile had an operation on an old knee injury sustained in the 60s while playing for Morton. It was a wonder he still had a leg at all. In one season he had over 20 cortisone injections on the knee. Two or three would be considered appropriate now. The result of these injections, and the considerable wear and tear of playing on it, was a disintegrating bone which was to cause him no little pain throughout his life. It would occasionally pop out of place and had to be forced back in; an excruciating procedure. I performed the 'service' once for Allan when he fell coming out of Broomfield. Not wishing to hurt him I was far too tentative. "Wrench it," he grimaced. Eventually brute force worked. A brief grunt and a couple of heavy duty pills was Allan's response, though an ashen face told its own story. He never complained and still doesn't. I'm ashamed to say I always tried to make sure I wasn't too near on occasions when he fell again.

McGraw was fit enough to see his side beat old chum Eddie Morrison's Kilmarnock 2-1 at Cappielow in a game in which both teams had spells of dominance. In a wonderful 20 minutes of football, Morton drew 2-0 ahead with goals from Martin Doak and Rowan Alexander, both coming from John McMaster corners. An Ian Bryson inspired comeback followed, Cuthbertson reducing the deficit, but Killie's best efforts to level came to nothing. The down side for Morton were injuries to both Richardson and McMaster.

Even without them, however, they went on to beat Brechin 1-0 in a scrappy match at Cappielow. Rowan Alexander got the winner with his 22nd goal of the season. Morton had shown that they had found the way to win even when playing well below their best.

That led perfectly to the big showdown between themselves and league leaders Dunfermline at East End Park on 21st March. There was a five-point gap between the clubs and Allan McGraw commented on the eve of play: "If we don't win tomorrow I don't think anyone will catch Dunfermline."

A crowd of 5,959 turned out, almost a thousand travelling from Greenock. Jackie McNamara led the way in midfield, flanked by the hard-working Ian Clinging and Tommy Turner. McNamara's positional sense, support, covering and sheer determination made him his side's key figure. At left back Jim Holmes was his elegant best.

Tommy Turner opened the scoring for the visitors before Norrie McCathie levelled for the hosts. By now the Pars were sensing victory but, against the run of play, Morton were awarded a penalty and John McNeil slotted home what proved to be the winner. Morton were now just three points behind the leaders, each having played 37 games.

Every game now was a cup final for the promotion contenders and third top Dumbarton were Ton's next opponents at their Boghead ground. Allan McGraw appealed to his support to turn it into a home game for Morton and they were certainly in the majority by kick-off time the following Saturday.

Rowan Alexander, by now the darling of the Morton faithful, opened the scoring with his 23rd goal of the season as the visitors asserted themselves. Gradually, however, the Sons forced their way back into the game and equalised through McCoy. It looked as if it would end level when home goalkeeper Arthur attempted to launch a kick upfield, only for the ball to hit Jimmy Boag in the penalty area and rebound 15 yards off the Morton striker into the home net. The luck was going Morton's way. With Dunfermline drawing, they had closed the gap at the top to two points with six games to go. The momentum was with McGraw's men.

East Fife, fourth in the division and still technically in the promotion hunt, arrived at Cappielow on the first Saturday of April. Big, strong and very much a route one football team, they ground out a 1-1 draw. It was, amazingly, their 21st draw of the league campaign. They were happy with the result, which to me seemed quite bewildering given that they had to win to maintain a challenge.

Morton were the masters of their failure to take both points when goalkeeper David Wylie took his eyes off a straightforward John McMaster passback to let it roll into the net. My comment was that "it was sheer farce". The home goal was scudded in from 20 yards by Jackie McNamara 20 minutes from time.

Wylie atoned for his complete lapse in concentration the following week when he brought off two or three key saves in the 3-2 defeat of Queen of the South in Dumfries. Goals by O'Hara, Robertson and ex-Queens favourite Rowan Alexander meant that, with four games to go, Morton needed five points to make sure of promotion.

All good things come to an end, and Morton's 12-match unbeaten run ground to a halt at Cappielow where Partick Thistle deserved their 2-1 success, John McNeil's goal not being sufficient before a crowd of 2,969. They were still four points clear of Dumbarton in third place, and just one behind leaders Dunfermline.

Victory at Montrose in their next match would ensure promotion given the vast numerical superiority of their goal difference and manager McGraw commented on the morning before the game: "If we win tomorrow it's finished. We would have what we want most." Morton didn't just scrape over the line, they won 4-1, Alexander (2), Richardson and an own goal proving too much for a plucky home side.

Skipper Jim Holmes summed up: "It's been a long, hard season, but it's all been worthwhile. It's nice to see the fans enjoying it too."

Manager Allan McGraw commented: "I'm delighted for everyone, especially the players who have worked so hard during the season."

I reported: "The toothless grin on the face of player-coach Jackie McNamara told all."

Two games remained and Morton were now desperately hoping to claw back Dunfermline's one-point advantage. They did so the next Saturday when they beat Forfar 3-1 at Cappielow on the same afternoon as the Fifers fell to Airdrie at Broomfield. John McNeil hit two goals in a good performance, but the star man was the veteran McNamara. I said of his performance: "McNamara is 34 going on 16, his enthusiasm for the game remaining undiminished. He has provided a perfect example of what professionalism is all about."

In the week leading up to the finale at Broomfield where a good Airdrie side awaited the Ton, Jimmy Simpson received his testimonial cheque for £18,500, being some recompense for the loss of his career in that awful, accidental clash early in the season with Dunfermline goalkeeper Ian Westwater. He said: "I would like to thank all the folk who have helped me; the public, the fans and the club. I would also like to congratulate the boys on gaining promotion. It couldn't happen to a nicer man than the manager, Allan McGraw. Of all the men I have played under he has been the fairest."

On the eve of the final match, with Morton needing a point for the title, McGraw was clear in his aim. "We can't defend. We're going to go and try to win the game. If we end up with a point I'll be delighted."

There was drama to come. A grimly determined Airdrie took a one-goal lead from a Vinnie Moore penalty and hung on. As the match entered the final few minutes news spread that Dunfermline were winning 3-1 against relegated Montrose. The Morton dugout was a shrine to disappointment. Then, suddenly, there was a huge roar from the substantial Cappielow following on the terraces and in the stand, listening in on their transistor radios. Dunfermline had lost 1-0. The title was Morton's. The battle may have been lost, but the war was won.

Skipper Jim Holmes felt a sense of anti-climax, saying to me as I spoke to him on the trackside: "It's bad winning like this."

"They don't seem to mind," I replied, gesturing to the Morton fans who had gathered on the field to cheer their heroes. The supporters then supplied a nice touch when they burst into song: "There's only one Jimmy Simpson." The players joined in. Simpson was later to receive a specially struck championship medal.

CHAPTER EIGHTEEN

Up and down again

In the week following, Rowan Alexander, who had scored 26 goals throughout the season, was voted Player of the Year by the supporters, while skipper Holmes received the votes of his fellow professionals to take the Player of the First Division title.

Both Holmes and Alexander were selected for a Scottish semi-professional side who took part in a four-nation tourney involving Holland, England and Italy.

Jackie McNamara gained his reward for a marvellous season when the Cappielow board appointed him as assistant manager to Allan McGraw.

With the gulf between Premier League and First Division ever widening, it was going to take a supreme effort for Morton to stay up among the top guns. To that end they began to make plans to strengthen. Lex Richardson left to pursue the twilight days of his career with Arbroath, McGraw replacing him with 29-year-old Albert Kidd, the ex-Dundee and Falkirk midfielder. Another to come in was old-fashioned winger Jimmy Robertson, aged 30, from Queen of the South. His transfer fee was decided by tribunal, £12,000 going to the Doonhamers.

Businessman Andy Gemmell, who had once played for Morton in the early 60s, became Morton's main sponsor through his company A.G. Alloys Ltd. He also sponsored the Broomloan Stand at Ibrox and was soon to join the board at Cappielow in what was seen as a progressive financial development.

Over the close season, significant improvements had also been made to the facilities at Cappielow in order to try and increase income through sponsorship and corporate deals.

Morton did not seem to me to be strong enough to remain in Scotland's top league but manager Allan McGraw was confident that his men could prove the doubters, such as me, wrong. Before a glamour pre-season friendly with Arsenal at Cappielow he said: "People may think our only aim this season will be survival, but we've got greater ambition than that and we've set ourselves a target of a place in Europe.

"The directors have set up a very impressive bonus scheme and I want to emphasise we're not just here to make up the numbers."

Former double winner with Arsenal in 1971 and Scottish international George Graham arrived in Greenock with a star-studded team on Saturday 25th July, 1987. Pre-season friendlies are seldom a reliable guide as to a team's forthcoming fortunes, but the hosts put up a spirited display in going down 1-0.

I wrote: "Arsenal provided the glamour, representing all that is big in terms of reputations and finance in football. Charlie Nicholas, Graham Rix, David O'Leary, Kenny Sansom and new £800,000 signing from Leicester City, Alan Smith, were all there. For Morton, whose entire side cost a tiny fraction of the transfer fee for Smith, to lose only 1-0 was a creditable result."

George Graham later commented that, on clear-cut chances, Morton were worth a draw. He continued: "I brought the team up here because I knew they would get a competitive game," this in reference he said to the fact that Scots always like to do a number on the English. Morton's team on the day was (4-3-3): Wylie; Clinging, Doak, Hunter, Holmes; Turner, Kidd, McMaster; McNeil, Alexander, J. Robertson.

Jim Hunter was a defensive rock at the back while John McMaster and new signing Albert Kidd were an impressive partnership in midfield. Arsenal's scorer was Perry Groves in front of a crowd of 4,185.

Shrewsbury were then beaten 2-0 before Morton announced the bizarre news that Albert Kidd was on his way to Australia to Hellas of Adelaide in a four-year deal. Allan McGraw said: "Before he signed for us he told us he might get an offer to go to either America or Australia and that if it came up he would have to think of his family. We had to honour his decision to leave."

I commented: "That Morton should enter into an agreement of this nature with the player in the first place might strike some as a bit unusual, but they did not have the resources to offer Kidd a signing-on fee and the player would not agree to a more permanent arrangement."

All Kidd's arrival had done was build up the fans' hopes only to see them dashed. He was never replaced and there is no doubt a player with his experience and workrate would be missed. It placed a greater onus on John McMaster who had, frankly, disappointed the fans after his arrival at the tail-end of the previous season. I wrote: "There has never been any doubting his ability, but some wondered if he was fully fit." Against Arsenal, however, McMaster had looked much sharper after getting a pre-season under his belt.

My own view, nevertheless, was that fresher legs would be needed to help out in midfield. The defence too had lost far too many goals in the successful First Division campaign and this led me to write: "I am of the view that Morton will do exceptionally well to retain their Premier place this time round."

Celtic arrived in Greenock for the first league match of the season and proceeded to underline Morton's task with a convincing 4-0 thrashing. The vulnerable home defence was fully exposed and I reported: "Confirmation of just how hard it is going to be for Morton to survive in the Premier League this season was supplied in this match before a crowd of 14,000. Those of us who feel Morton are not equipped to remain in the top division saw nothing to make us alter our view."

An Andy Walker double, plus goals from Mark McGhee and Billy Stark, saw Celts ease home. On the following Wednesday Aberdeen won 3-1 at Pittodrie, despite John McMaster giving the visitors the lead with a splendid free kick against his old mates. Strikes by Joe Miller, Neil Simpson and Davie Dodds put the new boys in their place.

Then Dundee United administered another 3-1 defeat, this time at Cappielow. Dougie Robertson was the home scorer, while Ian Redford (penalty), Paul Sturrock and Jim McInally hit the net for the Tayside team.

Worse, though, was to follow when First Division Clyde came to Cappielow in a Skol Cup tie and provided an embarrassing 5-1 humbling in front of 1,889 fans. Allan McGraw said: "It's the first time since I've been in charge that I could say I've seen them throw in the towel."

Injuries and the lack of strength in depth to the squad meant that the manager was very restricted as to making changes. He had to rely more upon a change in attitude by his players as they prepared to face Hibernian at home the following Saturday.

A crowd of 3,900, many from the capital, witnessed a thrilling 3-3 draw which carried Morton off the bottom of the table. Ian Clinging, John McMaster and Jimmy Boag were the home marksmen against a Hibs team for whom winger Micky Weir was the star.

The point was welcome but Morton's defensive capabilities were all too glaringly obvious. I reported: "Something will have to be done to tighten up at the back if Morton are not to lose a record number of goals in this league." Two season ago Willie McLean's side had set that record by conceding 100.

Moves were afoot to try and strengthen the squad, but Hearts' Andy Watson turned down a move after the clubs had agreed terms and in the next game, a derby clash at Love Street, Morton lost 2-1 to St Mirren whose scorers were Ian Ferguson and Frank McGarvey. Jimmy Boag, dubbed the 'flying postman' after his full time job, got the Morton counter. John Boag and Ian Ferguson were sent off after a clash, while John McMaster missed an early penalty.

Morton were now two points adrift at the bottom of the pile after five games and manager McGraw said: "If we keep making the same mistakes we are going to get punished. We have made enquiries for two or three players. I'm hopeful something will happen soon." It couldn't happen soon enough as Hearts, much improved under the leadership of Alex MacDonald and Sandy Jardine, came to Cappielow and won 2-1, John Colquhoun and John Robertson scoring, John McNeil netting a penalty for the home team.

The scoreline flattered Morton and Allan McGraw was frankly honest in his after-match remarks. "They were streets ahead of us," he said. "If it had been a boxing match they would have stopped it at half-time." At least the attendance of 5,143 must have given the home directors some measure of consolation, though at least half were from Edinburgh.

It was a depressing time for the home supporters. They then read about another collapsed deal when Hearts' defender Malcolm Murray turned down a move to Cappielow, his personal terms not being to his satisfaction. A beleaguered looking Allan McGraw said: "I feel a wee bit sick. That is four times we have agreed terms with clubs for players and the transfer has fallen through at the last minute." But the manager was still optimistic that his side would get it right.

Morton were bottom of the league after six games on just one point when Dundee drove into town. In an amazing match the hosts went on to record a very welcome first win of the season by 4-3.

Both defences were playing pass the parcel, but it was Morton who ended up victorious. Rowan Alexander grabbed a double, including one from the penalty spot, while Jimmy Boag and Jimmy Robertson added the others. Robertson, a constant thorn in the flesh of Dens full back Tosh McKinlay, scored a beautiful individual goal, a thoroughly deserved reward for some productive running.

The former Queen of the South winger had lovely close control and was reminiscent in many ways of former Coventry and Scotland winger Tommy Hutchison in the way he could take the ball past an opponent. After the match I strode into the manager's office where Allan McGraw was sitting, beaming in his chair. "What did I tell you?" he grinned in response to his pre-match optimism which, I confess, I had not shared. Dark Blues boss Jocky Scott was less pleased. "An absolute disgrace!" he spluttered.

Morton were still trying to add to their pool and revealed that enquiries for Alan Sneddon from Hibs and Willie Brown from St Johnstone had failed over what were considered to be grossly inflated fees. They did, however, bring in ex-Clydebank and Dundee United winger Gerry Ronald. Like Jimmy Robertson, he had good close control and individual skills, but Morton badly needed fighters and energy.

It was next off to East End Park where the side who had accompanied them into the Premier League, Dunfermline, awaited. It was not a happy afternoon for the blue and white hoops. Despite Rowan Alexander grabbing his third goal in two games, Morton fell with a thud by 4-1. I was not optimistic in my view of this Greenock side and said: "At the end of the day the game is all about players, and Morton simply don't have sufficient of Premier League quality." There was experience, but not enough running power in midfield, and always there was a defence which made too many simplistic errors. In eight matches, 24 goals had been lost. Within a few days the club made a move to try and solve at least one of the problems, ex-Celtic and Hearts centre half Roddy MacDonald arriving from Tynecastle.

MacDonald went on to do a good job for Morton, but his debut coincided with one of these days no one connected with Morton will want to recall. Graeme Souness's rebuilt Rangers awaited at Ibrox, Woods, Butcher, Roberts, Francis, McCoist, Durrant and all. Hat-tricks by Englishman Mark Falco and Ally McCoist, and an own goal by Jim Holmes, were the end product of their swaggering pomp as they swept to a 7-0 triumph.

A shell-shocked Greenock fan asked: "What will you have to say about that?"

There was not a great deal to say. The fact is that Rangers were simply a vastly superior team. Morton had too many players in their side whose best days were well behind them.

It is never a pleasant business to be an enquiring press member of a defeated manager in such circumstances. Allan McGraw said: "We've got to get our heads up and get back to work. We won't meet Rangers every week. I know it sounds silly after you've just lost 7-0, but I don't think we'll get relegated."

I wrote: "There would be few, if any, among the press who will agree, but there is none who does not wish one of the game's most likeable men well." The attendance of 35,843 was indicative of the vast renewal of faith among the supporters of the Light Blues.

The next Saturday at Cappielow, the attendance was somewhat lower, 2,554 turning out to watch Morton draw with Motherwell. It was a welcome point after the mauling in Govan, even if Motherwell were the better team on the day, former Ranger Bobby Russell being the game's stand-out performer. Jimmy Boag was the home scorer with Well's John Philliben getting his side's goal.

Making his Morton debut was 18-year-old right back Derek Collins of whom Allan McGraw said: "I have high expectations of him." Former Ton gaffer Tommy McLean commented: "I'm disappointed at the result. We missed chances and should have taken more from the game." For Morton's Roddy MacDonald the return to normal football after his debut at Ibrox must have been satisfying, and he gave a dominant display.

In their next outing Morton capitalised on their recovery with a splendid 4-1 win over fellow relegation rivals Falkirk at Cappielow. I wrote: "It was, frankly, vital for morale in the Greenock camp that both points were collected." Jimmy Boag was the hero with a brace, Roddy MacDonald produced another top display, while there were goals too from the Robertson clan of Dougie and Jimmy. Importantly, Morton had clawed their way off the bottom rung of the ladder. Of the four teams at the foot of the table, who by now were becoming isolated, Motherwell and Dunfermline were on eight points, Morton on six and Falkirk on four.

The next three games produced just one point in a goalless draw with St Mirren at Cappielow. That was sandwiched between a 3-1 loss to Celtic at Parkhead and a 3-0 defeat at Tynecastle against Hearts. Celtic careered into a three-goal lead in just 19 minutes through Whyte, McAvennie and Walker before Alex O'Hara reduced the deficit just before the interval. Thereafter Celts were content to play out time and manager Billy McNeill commented accurately: "We were three up – and it might have been six – and then I think the players did as much as they had to after that."

Allan McGraw drew comfort from a committed second half display by his players.

The Hearts match was very similar and Ton assistant manager Jackie McNamara summed up: "Hearts took their foot off the pedal when they were three up, just as Celtic did."

These were worrying times for Morton fans. There was not the same smothering cloud of depression that accompanied their last excursion into the Premier League under Willie McLean. That was due to a better club set-up and the vastly different mind-sets of the two managers involved. But once again Morton were having to work with a very limited group of players and the likely consequences were only too clear.

Dundee then won at Dens Park with the only goal of the game. That was scored by Harvey in a first half in which the hosts were very much the better side. But it was a different story in the second 45 minutes. An interested spectator was ex-Morton defender Jim Duffy who had suffered a serious knee injury, forcing him to make the decision to end his career with the Dark Blues. He summed up the second half as well as anyone when he said to Ton boss Allan McGraw: "We couldn't get out of our half. You deserved something." What you deserve and what you get in football, as in life, don't always add up.

In front of 3,593 fans, Morton then lost at home to rivals Dunfermline by 2-1, falling back down to bottom place. It was becoming a four-club fight to avoid the drop among Motherwell, Dunfermline, Morton and Falkirk. The Dunfermline goals came before half-time and were the result of two awful blunders, first by goalkeeper David Wylie whose miskick led to Smith netting, then a complete mix-up between Wylie and Hunter which allowed Watson in to score.

Morton did pull one back in the second half when Jimmy Boag ran on to score from an excellent through ball by John McMaster. It was not enough. After the game Pars boss Jim Leishman poked his head tentatively round Allan McGraw's office door to ask: "Is it safe to come in?"

Individual errors were killing Morton. But there was some relief when a no-score draw was achieved against Aberdeen. Again introduced into the team was teenage right back Derek Collins and he gave a decent performance. It was a happier manager's office after the match.

At Brockville the next Saturday, Morton went down 2-0 to a Falkirk side themselves battling to avoid the trapdoor to the First Division while, on the following Wednesday, a valuable point was collected at Easter Road against Hibs. Also collected by the team coach on the way home were about 20 grateful Morton fans whose bus had broken down.

Injuries were now beginning to pile up for the Cappielow men who suffered two consecutive home losses, 1-0 to Dundee United and then 3-0 to Rangers. With no fewer than seven players out injured, the team then lost away to Motherwell to fall three points behind the second bottom Fir Park club.

The real worry now was the failure to create chances. Celtic emphasised the growing problem when they cruised to a 4-0 victory at Cappielow, Frank McAvennie scoring all the goals. Parkhead boss Billy McNeill could appreciate his counterpart's concerns. Asked about whether or not there was added pressure as Celtic manager with the advent of the burgeoning fortunes of rivals Rangers, he replied with a nod towards Allan McGraw: "What about this man? I could have bought Morton for what I've spent on players recently. What's he supposed to do if he hasn't any money?" It was a question which needed no answer.

Ian Porterfield's Aberdeen administered another 4-0 thrashing at Pittodrie and Morton had now gone 12 games with only one goal to their credit.

There was some brighter news at Cappielow when it was announced that the club had renewed their links with Denmark, established back in the 60s, by signing three players – Thomas Jacobsen, Lars Christensen and Carsten Margaard, a forward, midfielder and central defender respectively.

Christensen and Margaard must have wondered what they were coming to when they were in the team which collapsed at home in a thoroughly distressing 7-1 loss to Dundee. I commented: "In all my years of reporting on Morton's matches, I can't remember as heavy a defeat on home soil. It was a performance verging on the juvenile."

An incredulous Allan McGraw said: "Can no one mark players? How can a sweeper play in front of his defence?" Ironically, Morton had taken the lead in just three minutes through Rowan Alexander.

Both Christensen and Margaard had not played for seven weeks and they looked well off the pace. Morton were now eight points behind fourth bottom Motherwell. With three going down, it was becoming a precarious situation.

It was then off to East End Park to meet Dunfermline. Allan McGraw had held a talk-in with his players in the week before the game and revealed: "A few things were said, and I think it was constructive on both sides. I know most people have already written us off, but we can bounce back if we buckle down and do a professional job."

The bottom end of the table told a different story – Motherwell on 17 points, Dunfermline 16, Falkirk 13 and Morton on nine. But it was a vastly improved Morton who battled out a 1-1 draw against the Pars, Carsten Margaard providing a good central defence partnership alongside Roddy MacDonald.

Christensen, a big, strapping blond-haired example of Viking manhood, showed glimpses of skill, putting through Alexander for the opening goal, but a late strike by Mark Smith saved the day for the hosts after Wylie had failed to hold the ball. For all his imposing physique, Christensen didn't look too keen on the more combative side of the game. He plummeted quicker than a double bass falling off the Empire State building under one challenge from Craig Robertson. It led Morton assistant manager Jackie McNamara to comment after the game: "I think we've found out that Lars likes to sleep with the light on."

On Boxing Day Morton managed another precious point when Hearts arrived in Greenock for what turned out to be a goalless draw. The Edinburgh club's continuing revival under Alex MacDonald was indicated by the attendance of 6,726, containing over 3,000 maroon-clad Jambos.

Another goalless draw followed against St Mirren at Love Street. Morton had tightened up defensively compared to the profligacy of the first half of the season, but by now they could hardly buy a goal. In their first 11 games they had hit the net 17 times. Only four goals had been scored in the next 17 matches. Carsten Margaard had proved a good acquisition at centre back, but the front half of the team seemed devoid of any serious threat at all.

At Ibrox the resurgent Rangers under Graeme Souness were held for 62 minutes. Then the roof fell in on the visitors, a McCoist hat-trick and two goals by Durrant leading to a 5-0 scoreline. When the dam broke the blue tide swept irresistibly forward. Tom Turner was also ordered off for dissent, having earlier been booked. Allan McGraw was angry with Turner for letting down his team-mates while Souness, for his part, commented: "We are happy to score goals; the whole thing [the title] might be settled by goals." The Ibrox manager was also pleased with the form of his recent signing, Mark Walters.

Morton were now four points behind second bottom Falkirk.

The next match, against relegation threatened Motherwell at Cappielow, was now vital. In a last throw of the dice, Morton arranged through agent Kaj Johansen, the former Morton and Rangers star, to bring two more Danes to Cappielow – striker Henrik Terkelsen and forward/midfield Carl Kristensen.

Motherwell, fourth bottom in a season in which three teams would be relegated, were determined to pull away from trouble. Their side, under manager Tommy McLean, arrived backed by a vociferous support. The Lanarkshire club had paid for a fleet of buses for their fans and it was a big-game atmosphere at Cappielow.

They triumphed 2-0 and, in so doing, put a gap of 10 points between themselves and Morton. Morton had lost with a whimper and boss McGraw lamented their attitude, saying:

"You wouldn't have thought it was important to our players."

Neither Terkelsen nor Kristensen impressed and both were to return to Denmark. Relegation had become inevitable, if not yet a statistic. That left Jacobsen, Christensen and Margaard among the Danes still in Greenock, signed as they were until the season's end. Jacobsen had not played and was very much surplus to requirements. Christensen was what I would call not so much a fair weather as a heatwave player. Margaard was the one worth keeping, but that was not going to be an option given Morton's finances.

Allan McGraw summed up: "While it is mathematically possible we will keep going."

Hibs then arrived at Cappielow, with Neil Orr in their team after returning from down south, and a 1-1 draw was achieved. Even a point, however, was no real use to Morton by now. Jimmy Boag was the scorer, while Lars Christensen went close with a powerful free kick from fully 40 yards which Andy Goram did well to parry for a corner.

While Christensen could certainly hit the ball with ferocious pace, and supply some neat touches, he was obviously uncomfortable with the physical combat of Scottish football. He had the build of a gladiator and the heart of a fieldmouse. If tackling were abolished he might have been a star.

Queen of the South were beaten 2-1 at Palmerston in the third round of the Scottish Cup, Dougie Robertson, fit again, and Rowan Alexander notching the goals. Queens' goal came from former Morton man Danny Docherty, following up his own penalty kick which was saved by Davie Wylie.

Morton's lack of punch by now was taken for granted. Dundee United won 2-0 at Tannadice, but the real killer blow was a 0-0 draw at Cappielow against Falkirk. In the 22 games Morton had played since they beat the Bairns and scored four goals in the process, the Greenock men had managed to hit the net just five more times. Relegation was not yet confirmed, but everyone knew the reality of the situation.

Goals by Sandy Clark and Gary Mackay took Hearts through to the last 16 of the Scottish Cup at Tynecastle before a crowd of 13,646 while the following Saturday league leaders Celtic scraped a 1-0 win at Parkhead with a complacent performance. Roy Aitken got the winner from a penalty hotly disputed by the visiting players.

Allan McGraw said: "I feel sorry for them [the players] because they deserved more from the game than we got."

For home boss Billy McNeill there was pleasure that his side still topped the league, but he commented: "We got away with it in the end but it was not a performance I would like to see repeated."

If there was a silver lining to the big storm clouds gathering over Greenock it was in the development of the youth policy begun by Allan McGraw. John McMaster oversaw it, with excellent help from friends of the manager such as George Gillespie, Bert Reid, John Kerr and Jake Anderson. For the latter four, it was all unpaid work and, in later years, was to prove invaluable to the Greenock club.

Already there were tentative enquiries about goalkeeper David Wylie, who would be 22 in April, and 19-year-old right back Derek Collins.

Morton were in most neutral observers' minds already relegated and, on Saturday 5th March, they went down again when Tommy Coyne's 50th goal for Dundee in his 69th appearance was sufficient to gain both points at Dens Park. Home manager Jocky Scott nevertheless was generous in his after-match comments, saying: "We were the luckiest team to get away with that."

Morton had hit woodwork twice, had a goal controversially disallowed and also saw another attempt slip just wide of the target. Morton fans took the chance to present their ex-captain Jim Duffy, forced to quit the game through injury while with Dundee, a cheque as a contribution to a testimonial arranged for him by the Dens club.

Meanwhile, Morton announced that Martin Doak would be allowed to go while a Falkirk bid for Jim Holmes was turned down.

There was a respite from the rigours of the league when Newcastle came up to Greenock for a friendly match on Thursday 10th March. In their ranks they had Brazilian international striker Mirandinha as well as a young English under-21 international by the name of Paul Gascoigne. Of the bold Gazza, still just 20, I wrote at the time: "He is a character from a bygone age. Many good judges believe him to be the most promising young player south of the border. He would also appear to have a penchant for the odd brown ale and Mars bar." An understatement, with hindsight.

In front of a modest Morton support of 2,354 it was a flash of brilliance by the young Gascoigne which won the game. I reported: "The English under-21 internationalist, already rated in the £2million class, sold a perfect dummy on halfway and accelerated straight down the middle of the park, bursting clear of the home defence. He swerved past the outcoming David Wylie who stuck out a foot and sent him tumbling in the penalty area. Up stepped 'Gazza' himself to convert the spot kick."

You knew you were watching something special that night.

"A big lad who looks as if he wouldn't be too quick over the ground, he took off like a jet-propelled Andy Ritchie to win the penalty," was how I described Gascoigne. Gazza was to move to Spurs at the end of the season for £2million, a then record fee.

In the Morton side that night was 18-year-old Archie Gourlay. He gave a quiet display, adorned by occasional glimpses of the skill his manager Allan McGraw had mentioned in recent weeks. McGraw said: "His ability is not in question but he has had to work on his stamina and physique."

A week later young Gourlay was off to join Gascoigne at St James' Park, Newcastle manager Willie McFaul being impressed enough to spend £50,000 on him. McFaul said: "I jumped in before anyone else." It was a move which would give an extra £30,000 to Morton should Gourlay make the first team. Allan McGraw commented: "Gourlay deserves to make it. He is a worker and we have never doubted his ability."

Unfortunately for Gourlay, he never did reach the heights, falling out of favour when Jim Smith took over from Willie McFaul at Newcastle.

Morton's poor season continued with a 2-0 defeat at Love Street to derby rivals St Mirren, a display Allan McGraw described as "a disgrace". Then Dunfermline arrived at Cappielow to administer a 3-0 whacking, a result which kept alive the East End club's faint hopes of staying in the top flight. In that Pars side was a future Morton manager, Davie Irons.

Verification of Morton's Premier demise came on Saturday 26th March when Hearts beat them 2-0 at Tynecastle. I reported: "Most folk accepted Morton's relegation from the Premier League to be a fact several weeks ago, but on Saturday came the statistical confirmation. They are now officially down.

"The one emerging ray of hope this season has been the solid foundation of a meaningful youth policy which, in the long run, may be the salvation of Morton and their ambitions." Derek Collins, Archie McGeachy and the recently departed Archie Gourlay had followed David Wylie and Jim Hunter into the first team.

There were, of course, those who were disgruntled at Gourlay's departure, seeing it as further evidence that the board lacked ambition. In fact Morton were not in a financial position, nor did they have the support through the turnstiles, to turn down any reasonable offer for one of their players. When Aberdeen were forced so recently into parting with players such as Mark McGhee, Neale Cooper and Eric Black, and Celtic saw Mo Johnston, Brian McClair and Murdo MacLeod depart, what hope was there for Morton? The board too, it should be remembered, took no remuneration for their services.

I wrote: "If I have any criticism of Morton it is that some on the board entertained quite unrealistic hopes for this season, but they were new to the job and I am sure they would admit it has been a learning process for them too. They remain as keen for Morton to do well as any fan on the terracing."

CHAPTER NINETEEN

McGraw banks on youth

Allan McGraw was beginning a far-sighted process based on youth, but it would take time to produce a real dividend. His aim, he stated, was to get Morton into a position in which they could dictate, as far as possible, who goes and who stays.

One who was not staying at Cappielow was veteran full back Jim Holmes. The 33-year-old was on his way to Falkirk who paid £10,000 for his services. He had been a fantastic servant to the club for 12 years, having joined them on a free transfer. Only the fact that he had a good job outside football prevented a move to a bigger, full-time club. Hibs had once tried to tempt him years ago, but failed for that very reason. But why one of the Old Firm never came in for him is a mystery to me, for he was the best full back in the country in his prime.

It was around this time that I met Andy Ritchie who was coming up to Scotland to see his old team-mates against Motherwell at Fir Park. By this time Andy was in charge of the Barbican YMCA in London, where he lived with wife Rena and sons Mark and Stephen.

He still turned out for the Barbican X1. "I'm as fit as ever," he told me with a grin. "The old pace is still there over three yards."

I had to ask: "Why did you chuck it, Andy?" this bearing in mind he was out of the game at the age of 28.

He replied with typical humour: "I'd been working too hard. I burnt myself out!"

He was, of course, disillusioned that no one had come in for him when he was in his prime at Morton; that and the fact that so many of his team-mates had gone to pastures new in big transfer deals.

Eventually there came the belated move to Motherwell at the age of 27, then soon after an ignominious slide down the ladder to Albion Rovers. "I felt I was working under a series of nutcases," Ritchie reflected of those twilight days of his career.

"I enjoyed it at first when big Jock [Wallace] took me to Motherwell. He got me as fit as I'd ever been, but he wouldn't let me play. If I spent more than a couple of seconds on the ball he would be roaring from the dugout.

"I remember him saying once 'the game's no' aboot buns and scones.' I hadn't a clue what he was talking about. He repeated it again, adding 'it's aboot passing and running.' I told him I got the second bit, but not the first."

As Andy watched, Motherwell beat Morton 1-0 in a truly uninspiring game. I don't know about buns and scones, but it was 90 minutes without any discernible passing or running of any relevance, never mind the honeyed skills Ritchie once brought to football with such élan.

Allan McGraw had been into hospital for yet another operation on his crumbling left knee when Rangers were due to visit Cappielow. The Ibrox club, emancipated under Graeme Souness and his assistant Walter Smith, had assembled a cast worth multi-millions. In their first season in charge they had won the championship and given Scottish football the most almighty shake-up. This time round they were to lose out to Celtic.

They arrived in Greenock, having met Morton three times over the season, with a 15-0 score in their favour. The result virtually was a foregone conclusion.

Horror of horrors for the men from Govan! Relegated Morton pulled off the shock of the season when they sent the Light Blues back up the motorway on the end of an implausible 3-2 defeat.

I wrote: "It was truly incredible. Morton had gone 30 league games without winning, had scored only four goals in their last 27 outings, and had failed to score in their last nine."

Allan McGraw, who had somehow talked his way out of a hospital bed, was there to see it, though his assistant Jackie McNamara was in charge on the day. McGraw stated: "I wish it was the start of the season." McNamara just couldn't stop grinning. He was like a large, smug green cat that had just stolen Rangers' blue cheese.

Derek Collins had begun an amazing afternoon when his cross-cum-shot flew over Woods, who was expecting a cross, and landed in the net. Ian Ferguson, not long transferred from St Mirren, equalised with his first goal for the Govan club, before goals by Rowan Alexander and Tommy Turner gave the hosts an unbelievable 3-1 lead. At this point the Radio Clyde reporter, sitting next to me, had to repeat the news three times before the person on the other end of the line would believe him.

Ian Durrant managed to pull back a consolation goal for Rangers, but it was Morton who went off to a standing ovation from the home support in a crowd of 10,716. Rangers, including such illustrious names as Woods, Roberts, Wilkins, Walters, McCoist, Durrant, Brown and Ferguson, disappeared quicker than sand through a sieve into the dressing room and then out of Cappielow.

An ongoing barney between the national press and Rangers meant no comment from the Ibrox manager after the game. I observed: "As has been the pattern, there was no appearance by either Graeme Souness or Walter Smith at the after-match press conference. As an outsider to the quarrel between themselves and elements of the national press, I find the whole business incredibly childish."

There were some among the press who seemed to revel in the confrontation. Souness, however, was unlikely to be the type of personality to attempt to win friends and influence people of any description, never mind the media. It had been written about him as a player that if he were chocolate he would eat himself. I never found it hard to see why. In my experience, press communication involving Rangers in those days was, dare I say it, like seeking an audience with the Pope. There was an air of attempting to converse with deity.

Of the match itself that Saturday I continued: "After so much gloom here was a performance full of commitment, passion and some good football. I wouldn't single anyone out as being man-of-the-match; there were too many who contributed notably." For the record, the Morton team that day was (4-3-3): Wylie; O'Hara, Doak, Hunter, Rogers; Collins, McMaster, Turner; Bateman, Alexander, McGeachy. Subs: Arthur, Robinson.

Aberdeen then resumed normal service the following week when an experimental young side came, saw and conquered 2-0, goals scored by Charlie Nicholas and Ian Porteous. Then it was on to Brockville and a quick reunion with Jimmy Holmes. Falkirk, needing a win in their attempt to avoid the drop, won 4-1. Holmes told me after the match: "That was my first win bonus since Morton beat Falkirk over 30 games ago." Holmes, who had not had a chance to say goodbye to the Morton fans, said: "Please tell them all how much I appreciated their support for 12 years." The feeling certainly was mutual. There has never been a more consistent player at Cappielow. At his best he was peerless among Scottish full backs. He was also a consummate professional.

On the last Saturday of April, Dundee United were the visitors to Cappielow. It was to mark the debut of another top young prospect, 16-year-old Derek McInnes. Allan McGraw commented: "He's a good passer, he controls the ball well and he takes up good positions. I have no doubt he will make it as a professional footballer." Never were truer words spoken. McInnes came on as a substitute for Martin Doak after 58 minutes in a game United won at a stroll by 4-0. Scorer of all four goals was Finnish international Mixu Paatelainen.

The fans, meanwhile, had voted Jim Hunter as their Player of the Year in the annual poll run by the Greenock Telegraph, a choice heartily endorsed by manager McGraw. Another youngster, Kevin McGoldrick, was in the Scottish under-15 side who beat their England counterparts 3-1. He also scored one of the goals. McGoldrick was, at the time, very highly thought of, but he was to become one of that great regiment of players who never make the leap from huge potential to a finished product.

The final match of the season saw Morton lose 2-0 to Hibs at Easter Road. The game was notable mainly for the first goal. Hibernian goalkeeper Andy Goram launched a huge punt downfield. Morton's young custodian David Wylie let it bounce as he came off his line. The ball bounced once again and a dismayed Wylie misjudged it and could only help it on its way into the net in his desperate attempt to save.

It was one of a few errors Wylie had made in the last few weeks of the season and Allan McGraw said: "I feel sorry for the lad because there have been times when he has saved us. If I'd a reserve keeper of quality I would have left him out a long time ago."

Falkirk and Dunfermline joined Morton in the drop down into the First Division and the Cappielow club then announced a list of 11 free transfers – Neil Armour, Jim Arthur, Alan Bateman, Brian Robinson, Jim Rogers, David Verlaque, Brian Cassidy, Willie Forrester, Gary Graham, David McQuade and Brian McShane.

John Wilson had meanwhile become the real power at Cappielow, taking over the chairmanship on virtually a permanent basis after dispensing with his business interests. He also had become the major shareholder. More changes occurred.

Assistant manager Jackie McNamara decided he wished to concentrate on his own businesses – two pubs in Edinburgh – and he explained: "I've been with only three senior clubs – Celtic, Hibs and Morton. I can honestly say I have enjoyed my time with Morton as much as any of the others."

McNamara felt he was leaving the Greenock club in a far better position than when he arrived, saying: "There's a properly established youth policy now. When I first arrived the place was a shambles. I can't take any credit for that [the youth policy], but it's encouraging to know the basics are there.

"I will always be grateful to Allan McGraw for giving me a chance. He's a man for whom I've so much time and respect. When I phoned and told him I had decided to go, I'd a lump in my throat."

The feeling was mutual, Allan McGraw commenting: "Jackie and I had a great relationship and we thought along the same lines. He'll be greatly missed here."

Player Martin Doak then announced his intention to emigrate to Australia while two directors also decided their time was over at Cappielow. Tom Robertson, who had been with the club since 1957 when he joined as treasurer, said: "There's no rift. I simply wish to reduce my personal business commitments, though I will continue to be involved with Morton through Henderson & Co. who are secretaries to the club."

Tom soon became club secretary after joining up at Cappielow in his capacity as treasurer. He was then appointed to the board in 1978. I don't think it is an exaggeration to say that in his time with Morton he was virtually the Chief Executive Officer. He was the director I always contacted if I wished to know anything about the administrative side of football, whether it be rules and regulations pertaining to the SFA and SFL, suspensions of players etc. He also happened to be a very nice man with a ready smile and welcoming manner. I felt he would be missed.

The other director to bow out was John L. McPherson, better kent as Ian, who had served a stint as chairman after Hugh Currie's death. He quit after 19 years on the board, saying: "It's a new board at Cappielow and I thought it was time for someone else to have a bash. The parting is amicable."

My first memory of Ian as a director was when I was on a train leaving Queen Street accompanying Morton to a First Division match on the east coast. He asked me to join him and other directors in a first class compartment. He brought down a case from the luggage rack above his head and said: "I have something for you in here." I was expecting an official document to be revealed, perhaps relating to some sort of story. Instead, when he opened the case, a veritable mini bar was revealed. "You'll join me in one," he beamed with an anticipatory glow. It would have been impolite to refuse. My report on the game that day was glowing.

Also departing from the club were reserve coach George Anderson and youth coach Billy Osborne. They left on less than agreeable terms, though Osborne was soon to reverse his decision. John McMaster had been put in charge of all coaching, from first team down to youth, and Anderson said: "I was left with no option but to resign. There was nothing for me to do. I have nothing against John McMaster, but I don't see how one man can be in charge of all coaching throughout the club." Anderson's beef was not with the manager, but higher up the chain of command.

Manager Allan McGraw responded: "No one wants George to leave, but I can understand his reasons for going. John McMaster is full-time and has the opportunity to work with the players every day."

As the close season continued, 20-year-old forward Michael Deeney arrived from Pollok United as did the teenage centre half Brian Reid from Renfrew Waverley. Deeney was much sought after and Morton considered themselves to be very fortunate to secure his services. Another newcomer was full back Mark Pickering from Ardeer Thistle.

Allan McGraw was expecting a very tough season ahead and commented: "It will be dog-eat-dog. This is a very competitive First Division and a place in the top half is probably a realistic aim."

A 1-1 draw with Dundee and 3-2 defeat by Aston Villa were the precursors to the start of the season when a disappointing host team lost 2-0 to Clyde. In the Skol Cup, Brechin were beaten 2-0 at Glebe Park, John McNeil and Rowan Alexander scoring, before the first league point was gleaned at Broomfield where Morton drew 1-1 through a late Tommy Turner goal. Morton lined up with David Wylie in goal, Jim Hunter sweeping, and a back four of Derek Collins, John Boag, Roddy MacDonald and Ian Clinging. Gerry Ronald, Derek McInnes and Tom Turner comprised the midfield with Paul Roberts and John McNeil up front.

Aberdeen were just too strong in the next round of the Skol Cup at Cappielow, winning 2-1, Rowan Alexander grabbing the home strike with a typical headed goal. Clydebank were then beaten 1-0 at Cappielow with a display a less than pleased manager McGraw described as "daylight robbery".

But already the vultures were beginning to descend on Cappielow and its emerging youth programme. Two English First Division clubs and one Scottish Premier side expressed interest in the precociously talented 17-year-old Derek McInnes. They were left in no doubt that there would be no bargain buy.

On the first Saturday of September Morton met Partick Thistle at Firhill in a game they ultimately won 4-1, but was remembered unfortunately for all the wrong reasons.

The 80s had become the decade of the 'casual encounter', Casuals being the self-styled name for an old problem in society – the yob culture. Young neds banded together for the sole purpose of causing trouble at football matches, attaching themselves to various clubs, wearing no team colours, and with no regard for anything other than achieving for themselves a notoriety which they misguidedly associated with 'status'. Sociologists would write books about it. Common sense was all that was required to know that they were attention-seeking morons with the collective intelligence of a lentil.

Paul Roberts and Rowan Alexander had given Morton a 2-0 lead when the idiots decided to run amok and invade the pitch, causing innocent young fans among the Partick support to seek safety on the field of play. The referee led the teams off the park and, eventually, the few police in attendance, together with stewards, restored order. Visiting manager Allan McGraw was visibly upset and rebuked one of the Casuals. He later informed me that he had asked the individual where he came from, to be told 'Greenock'.

That, of course, was no proof of identity, but verification came later through the courts where it was confirmed that the troublemakers had, indeed, come from the Greenock area. I wrote: "It was the worst example of hooliganism I have seen at a match involving Morton in all my years of reporting. They are a cowardly bunch of young thugs who do the game and the clubs to which they attach themselves no good at all."

Play eventually resumed and Morton scored further goals through Roddy MacDonald and Ian Clinging, moving up to fourth place in the table.

A Rowan Alexander goal secured a point in a home draw with St Johnstone before Morton travelled to Brockville to meet promotion prospects Falkirk, now under the charge of ex-Morton star Jim Duffy. Paul Roberts grabbed the only goal for Morton to put his side joint top of the league.

Jim Duffy summed up by saying that Morton "had won it up here", pointing to his head as he made the remark. An Alexander strike gave Morton another single goal win over bottom club Queen of the South and, when Morton won a seven-goal thriller at Rugby Park against Kilmarnock, the Greenock club had taken a two-point lead at the top of the First Division.

Rowan Alexander was the two-goal star, other strikes coming from Ian Clinging and Jimmy Robertson. The game also marked the debut of Michael Deeney as a substitute. Less fortunate was that it also proved to be another nail in the coffin of Eddie Morrison's managerial career, who was soon to leave Killie.

Morton were doing better than expected, but always there remained a lack of strength in depth. In midfield too they were very lightweight, a noticeable weakness as Raith Rovers won 1-0 at Cappielow with a Steve Simpson goal.

Ian Clinging scored the only goal of the game at Station Park against Forfar, young Derek McInnes being rested, and, when Ally McLeod's talented young Ayr side were beaten 2-0 at Cappielow, Morton had regained outright leadership of the league by two points over Falkirk and Dunfermline. Turner and Alexander were the scorers, Alex O'Hara stiffening up the centre midfield position and Gerry Ronald displaying lovely passing skills.

Next up at Cappielow were Dunfermline in the match of the day in the division. A Tommy Turner penalty proved conclusive before a crowd of just over 4,000 and prompted one fan, in front of the press benches, to utter: "If we don't watch out we could go back up to the Premier League."

The following week, again at home, an ultra-cautious Meadowbank side arrived in 5-4-1 formation, a sweeper playing behind two banks of four, leaving one loan striker upfield. In these days such negativity was almost unheard of outside of Italy, but a Boyd own goal and a strike by top scorer Rowan Alexander maintained Morton's pole position, two points clear of Falkirk with 13 games played. Less than 2,000 fans turned out.

A feature of Morton's play had been the miserliness of a defence which had leaked so badly the previous season. It was the calm before the storm. In two successive performances, away to St Johnstone and at home to Falkirk, they conceded no fewer than nine goals, losing

4-2 and 5-1 respectively. The result was a tumble into third spot. Allan McGraw commented: "We've lost nine goals in the last two games. That's as many as we have lost in the previous 13. Maybe we are not as good as we thought we were."

Jim Duffy was delighted with his Falkirk side, as was his assistant, Dom Sullivan, another old Morton veteran. Eddie Morrison, back at Cappielow having been sacked by Kilmarnock, cautioned: "Enjoy it while you can."

Morton halted the fall from grace with a 3-2 win at Dumfries against Queen of the South, goals coming from Jimmy Robertson, Rowan Alexander and Roddy MacDonald. Days later striker Dougie Robertson, unable to regain a regular place in the starting line-up after recovering from an Achilles tendon injury, asked for a transfer. His request was accepted, Allan McGraw saying: "He's not happy, but he has to work for his place like everyone else."

The manager's pre-season ambition of mid-table respectability had been an accurate reflection of his side's true standing. It was confirmed when Airdrie arrived at Cappielow under manager Gordon McQueen, the ex-Leeds, Manchester United and Scotland centre half.

McQueen was backed by multi-millionaire local businessman John Dalziel who had made his money in the baking industry and had splashed out £450,000 on players since arriving at Broomfield. In spending terms McQueen was the Graeme Souness of the First Division. Goals by MacDonald and Lawrie gave the Diamonds a merited victory and McQueen summed up: "It helps when you can spend money and get some quality in your team."

Ian McPhee and Gordon McLeod from Dundee United were among those most prominent against Morton. After the match I wrote: "If envy were tangible, you could have cut it into thick slices in Allan McGraw's office."

1988 was drawing to a close and Morton were finding their level in a league in which only one club would be promoted to the Premier League.

On 10th December they met promotion contenders Dunfermline at East End Park, a match which provided a platform for the introduction of yet another product of Allan McGraw's youth policy. Eighteen-year-old centre half Brian Reid made his debut in a game in which Alex O'Hara was sent off, Jimmy Robertson getting the visitors' goal. The star man was 17-year-old Derek McInnes, prompting McGraw's assistant, John McMaster to say: "He arrived today."

Morton were now five points off the lead. It was the start of a gradual slide down the league to a place of mid-table respectability which, in fact, had been the manager's pre-campaign realistic prediction, if not ambition.

Ally McLeod's Ayr United then defeated Morton 3-1 at Somerset Park, the Greenock club's fifth loss in six outings, midfield worker John Fowler getting the goal. I commented: "McLeod was rather like a badly poured pint of beer; frothy and overflowing, as he wound down in his office afterwards."

He had encountered the whole roller-coaster ride of football. Success at club level with Ayr and Aberdeen was followed by taking his country to the World Cup in Argentina in 1978. He captivated the nation with his optimism, so much so that people actually believed Scotland really had a chance to win the tournament. Such mild hysteria had not been entirely without foundation, if a tad over the top. Scotland had, in fact, shown some admirable form. But pride cometh before a fall. Bruce Rioch and Don Masson, key midfield men in the qualifiers, were in decline when the tourney got under way. Graeme Souness finally forced his way into the team when the damage had been done. The Willie Johnston drugs scandal, which led to the West Brom winger being sent home after taking a banned nasal spray, also led to some disastrous publicity. McLeod too had done little homework on his opponents and that proved costly. Too late, of course, Scotland beat one of the favourites, Holland, and supplied the goal of the tournament by Archie Gemmill. Holland were to lose the final to the host nation.

Ally, one of the nicest men I met in the football world, was vilified upon his return home by the same folk who had built him up to be a hero. There is nothing nastier, more mean-spirited, than a vengeful mob.

McLeod was far removed from those days on another continent in his tiny wee office at Somerset where the after-match hospitality rivalled that of Cappielow at the time. He grinned at the members of the scribbling fraternity, packed in like sardines, and declared: "You know, I believe bad luck usually lasts about 10 years. Argentina was in 1978, so maybe I've turned the corner."

A Rowan Alexander goal gained Morton a home draw against Forfar, the kick-off being preceded by a minute's silence to mark the death of Morton chief scout George Gillespie. He had played his full part in the assembly of a rich young seam of talent at Cappielow. George was a real character. He was also one of the worst drivers of a motorcar I have ever encountered. He didn't seem to know there were more than three gears in a car. The number of clutches he must have gone through. I remember Allan McGraw telling me that George was once stopped by the boys in blue going down a one-way street in the wrong direction. "This is a one-way street," he was informed with due solemnity. "That's fine," replied George, "I'm only going the one way."

A goal by Dougie Robertson won both points against Partick Thistle in Greenock before Tommy Turner's penalty secured a point at Clydebank as the season progressed, but Meadowbank Thistle disrupted the revival with a 2-1 win at Edinburgh's athletics stadium, another Turner spot-kick being Morton's contribution.

Meadowbank Stadium was the most soulless place to play football, bounded by its running track and with its sole stand adjacent to the pitch some 30 yards away. I recalled my last visit when the highlight was of "big, affable Tony Higgins jumping hurdles set up on the perimeter track, with all the grace of a giraffe with a broken leg". I felt that "a knitting bee in Battery Park would generate more atmosphere than a football game at this large, purpose-built athletics stadium". In fairness to Meadowbank's manager, Terry Christie, he had precious few resources with which to operate. He soon built a reputation as being thoroughly well organised, albeit with an emphasis on stifling the opposition.

An Ian Clinging goal gave Morton a win over Clyde at Firhill, their temporary home since moving out of Shawfield, before Raith Rovers dumped the Greenock men at Cappielow by the same 1-0 scoreline.

Then came the Scottish Cup and a tough tie against First Division promotion contenders Airdrie at Cappielow. The league's big spenders held the hosts 0-0, but in the replay at Broomfield on the Wednesday, a John Boag goal took the Ton into the fourth round, much to the delight of their travelling support. Derek McInnes once again excelled, Gerry Ronald up front and John Boag in defence also being heroes.

Another depressing trip to Meadowbank resulted in a solitary goal victory to take Morton through to the quarter-finals of the competition, Tommy Turner, the man of the season, grabbing the goal. St Johnstone awaited them in a home tie.

Before that tie, seven points were picked up against Falkirk h (2-2 Turner, McInnes), Forfar a (0-0), Kilmarnock h 2-2 (Ronald, Clinging), Partick h 1-1 (McNeil) and St Johnstone a (1-0 Deeney). In the Partick match, promising young Rangers striker John Spencer made his debut, the start of a month's loan period.

Meanwhile, two more aspiring young Morton players – Alan Mahood and Kevin McGoldrick – were included in the Scotland under-16 squad for a European tie against Finland. It was yet more recognition of the excellent work being done by the system set up by Allan McGraw and run by assistant John McMaster, backed crucially by scouts such as Bert Reid, John Kerr and Jake Anderson. Reg Scorer was also to do good work.

On Wednesday 22nd March Morton met St Johnstone at Cappielow in a tie postponed from the Saturday due to bad weather. An excellent crowd of 6,300 turned out for a thrilling tie which ended up all square at 2-2. Tommy Turner and Dougie Robertson were the home scorers, John Spencer having a penalty saved by Saints' Balavage.

Airdrie won 2-1 at Broomfield on the Saturday, Spencer getting the visitors' strike, before the St Johnstone replay on Monday 27th March, coincidentally Morton's last match at Muirton before the Perth Saints moved to McDiarmid Park. It was another gripping tie, Saints wining through to the semi-finals with goals by Maskrey (2) and Jenkins against counters by Dougie Robertson and Rowan Alexander. John McNeil missed a penalty for Morton, the fifth consecutive spot miss for the Greenock men.

On the Friday, director Bill Knox announced his resignation due to increased business commitments, leaving Morton with a board comprising chairman John Wilson and directors Douglas Rae, Kenny Woods and Andy Gemmell.

April was marked by the introduction of the Cappielow Bugle, one of a growing number of fanzine publications which were essentially the forerunners of supporters' websites on the internet, that miraculous invention yet to come with all its pluses and minuses.

Youth was by now getting its chance to shine, young Barry Strain being the latest to show what he could do. In four seasons Allan McGraw had brought through a steady stream of youngsters – David Wylie, Jim Hunter, Derek Collins, Derek McInnes, John Fowler, Mark Pickering, Michael Deeney, Archie McGeachy, Paul Roberts, Barry Strain and Brian Reid. About to break through was Alan Mahood.

Goals by Tommy Turner won both points against Clydebank and one against Queen of the South, the Dumfries draw being remarkable for Morton's seventh consecutive penalty miss. The run eventually came to an end towards the end of the season when Morton were to beat St

Mirren 5-3 on penalties in the final of the Renfrewshire Cup, a game in which young Michael Deeney suffered a fractured ankle.

As the season came towards its conclusion leaders Dunfermline won 1-0 at East End Park, David Wylie parrying a shot by Davie Irons to allow Jack to net the rebound. Next up at Cappielow were Kilmarnock, a minute's silence being a mark of respect for the dead at the Hillsborough disaster. Morton went on to win comfortably with one of their better displays of the season, Derek Collins, Ian Clinging and Rowan Alexander being on target.

Second bottom Clyde highlighted Morton's inconsistency with a 2-1 win in what was a dreich affair at Firhill. Tom Turner, who was to be voted Player of the Year by Morton fans, again got the winner.

With only one game of the season remaining, striker Dougie Robertson finally parted company with Morton after a six-year association. It was a mutually agreed separation. Still only 26, Robertson had suffered from weight problems almost throughout his time in Greenock. It was a pity. At his best, there was no deadlier goalscorer in the First Division.

Somerset Park was the venue for the closure of the season, a 1-0 win being most notable for the debut of 16-year-old Alan Mahood.

Winger Jimmy Robertson (33) and centre half Roddy MacDonald (34) joined Dougie Robertson on the way out of Cappielow, while close season attention turned to the exploits of Kevin McGoldrick who was in the Scottish under-16 team which was to reach the world under-16 final at Hampden Park against the Saudi Arabians.

Tall for his age, McGoldrick was a key member of the Scots side. His height was an advantage, but he also had good close control and grabbed two goals on the Scots' progress to the final.

There, Scotland went into a 2-0 lead through Downie and Dickov against a physically bigger Saudi side who looked suspiciously older than the 16 age limit. Brian O'Neil, fixed up by Celtic, missed a penalty when it was 2-1 to Scotland and the final eventually went into extra time after the Saudis equalised. Penalties proved decisive and poor O'Neil missed again from the spot to hand the Arabians the title. At that stage McGoldrick seemed destined for great things.

Joe Gilroy, who managed Morton for a season. He arrived at Cappielow in October, 1975.

John Goldthorp celebrates a goal on Morton's march to the First Division title in 1977-78. Also in the picture is fellow striker Eddie Morrison.

Champagne time. Morton celebrate winning the First Division in season 1977-78 after beating Airdrie 3-1 at Cappielow. Manager Benny Rooney opens a bottle of the bubbly as skipper Davie Hayes looks on with a Morton scarf draped round his neck. In the foreground is Morton managing director Hal Stewart.

Treatment time. Morton's lionhearted captain, Davie Hayes, gets medical attention from Doctor Craig Speirs, centre, and physiotherapist Gerry McElhill.

Benny Rooney, Morton's most successful manager during the author's time reporting on the club.

A young Neil Orr in a Scotland strip. He played many times for the Scotland under-18 and 21 teams.

Top team. The Morton squad which competed in the club's first season in the Premier League in 1978-79. Back row, left to right: Jim Holmes, Jim Rooney, Jimmy Miller, Roy Baines, Andy Ritchie, Cammy Melville, George Anderson, Roddy Hutchison and Ally Scott. Front row, left to right: John McNeil, Neil Orr, Joe McLaughlin, Bobby Thomson, Jim Wilkie, Billy McLaren and Jim Tolmie. Missing is skipper Davie Hayes.

Class act. Morton's cultured left back Jim Holmes receives the Sir William Lithgow Player of the Year Trophy from club chairman Hugh Currie.

Morton goalkeeper Roy Baines – one of the best.

Old friends. Mark McGhee, left, playing for Aberdeen, with Neil Orr of Morton closing him down. The two were team-mates before McGhee's move, first to Newcastle, then to Aberdeen.

Ally Scott was one of the unsung heroes of Morton's best Premier League days under Benny Rooney, his tireless running proving a great asset.

The Leith police dismisseth us. Morton boss Benny Rooney, left, can still smile after his appeal against abuse being showered on injured player John McNeil falls on the deaf ears of the Leith constabulary at Easter Road in March, 1982. Also in the picture next to Rooney is a less than amused trainer Willie Gray.

Andy Ritchie controls the ball after flicking it over Aberdeen full back Doug Considine.

Ritchie then prepares to cut inside centre half Alex McLeish…

… before shooting into the far corner of the net with both McLeish and Willie Miller beaten.

John McNeil challenges for the ball against Hearts at Cappielow.

Head boy. Morton centre half Joe McLaughlin challenges Celtic's Mike Conroy at Parkhead. Celtic skipper Roy Aitken is behind McLaughlin. McLaughlin was to gain high praise from Aberdeen boss Alex Ferguson after one notable display at Pittodrie.

Billy McLaren on the ball. His strength was a key factor in Morton's best team in their first two seasons in the Premier League.

Roddy Hutchison knocks the ball past Peter McCloy into the Rangers net at Ibrox, but the 'goal' was disallowed. Looking on are Morton's Jim Tolmie and Rangers defenders Ally Dawson and Tom Forsyth.

Bobby Thomson's dive is too late to trouble Rangers' Peter McCloy with Tom Forsyth looking on.

Bobby Thomson is thwarted at Ibrox by Rangers goalkeeper Peter McCloy. The other Rangers defenders are Gregor Steven and Sandy Jardine.

Roddy Hutchison goes for goal against Celtic at Cappielow with Roy Aitken in a spectating role.

The best day of my life. That was Hal Stewart's description of his testimonial match in May, 1980, at Cappielow. Here Hal waves to the crowd. On the left is Jock Stein, who managed the Scotland Select which lost to Hal's Morton Select. On the right is former Inverclyde Provost Jimmy Boyd.

Roddy Hutchison heads for goal against St Mirren at Cappielow with Billy Thomson beaten. Joe McLaughlin and Drew Busby look on.

American goalkeeper Dave Brcic. He had a short, but very successful, spell at Cappielow while Morton were in the Premier League.

Midfield man Bobby Thomson, right, strikes for goal with Dundee United's Paul Hegarty, left, attempting to block. In the background are United's Paul Sturrock and Morton's Jim Holmes.

The programme cover for the 1981 Morton-Rangers Scottish Cup semi-final at Parkhead. The players are Morton's Joe McLaughlin and Rangers' Colin McAdam.

Unfulfilled promise. Michael Deeney, right, is tackled by Cammy Fraser of Raith Rovers. Deeney was a highly talented player who nevertheless failed to make the grade.

King of Cappielow, Andy Ritchie, celebrates a goal with John McNeil in the background.

Lions roar. Allan McGraw enjoyed his testimonial match in 1981 when Celtic's Lisbon Lions, the first British team to win the European Cup, in 1967, turned out against a Morton Old Crocks side before the main game between Morton and Middlesbrough. Here Allan lines up with the famous Lions. Back row, left to right: Tommy Gemmell, Jimmy Johnstone, Willie Wallace, Steve Chalmers, Joe McBride, John Fallon, Allan McGraw, Billy McNeill and John Clark. Front row, left to right: Jim Craig, Bertie Auld, Bobby Lennox and Harry Hood. The only two Lions missing were Ronnie Simpson and Bobby Murdoch.

Morton players salute the fans after winning the 1994-95 Second Division Championship. Left to right are Derek McInnes, Steve McCahill, Dougie Johnstone, Alan Mahood, David Wylie and Craig McPherson.

Civic reception. Morton's 1994-95 Second Division Championship squad at a reception held in Greenock Town Hall. Seated centre is Provost Alan Robertson, flanked by Morton boss Allan McGraw, left, and director Douglas Rae.

Record man. Morton striker Derek Lilley, whose £500,000 transfer to Leeds is a club record, is beaten to the ball by Killie goalkeeper Lekovich in a crowded Cappielow goalmouth against Kilmarnock in a Scottish Cup quarter-final tie in March, 1997. Looking on, far right, is fellow striker Warren Hawke. Killie won the tie 5-2, Morton's Alan Mahood scoring a double against the club he supported as a boy.

Alan Mahood contests possession against Dundee United at Tannadice Park. Mahood formed one part of a tremendous midfield, along with Derek McInnes and Janne Lindberg, in the side which just missed out on promotion to the Premier League in 1995-96.

Derek McInnes goes up against Paul Gascoigne at Ibrox. On the left is Rangers' full back David Robertson. 'Gazza' complimented McInnes on his performance that day. McInnes was soon to join Gascoigne at Ibrox.

Cup call. Morton's Finnish international skipper, Janne Lindberg, in a photo-call with the Scottish Cup.

Morton goalkeeper Davie Wylie with the Player of the Year Trophy in May, 1994.

Joy before despair. Morton's Dougie Johnstone turns away in delight after an own goal by Craig Brewster, grounded, levels the score at 1-1 in a key promotion match against Dundee United on 6th May, 1996. Morton had to win the match to at least gain a place in the play-off for the Premier League. At the end of the day they lost out, drawing 2-2.

Tribute time. Morton's Allan McGraw was the guest of honour at a Variety Club tribute dinner in 1997, chaired by Manchester United manager Alex Ferguson. Friends and Old Firm legends Billy McNeill, left, and Jim Baxter were also in attendance.

Warren Hawke, a huge favourite with the fans, says his goodbyes with daughter Ruby on finally leaving the club after a testimonial match against a Morton side from 1995-96 season.

Derek Collins, who was a classy right back and went on to break the record for the number of appearances for Morton.

Alex Mathie, left, was a key scorer for Morton before moving to Newcastle.

Rowan Alexander became a big favourite with the Cappielow crowd, as much for the tremendous effort he always put in as his goals. Here he is in opposition to Partick Thistle.

Fans protest at club owner Hugh Scott under whose chairmanship Morton entered administration.

Chairman Douglas Rae, who rescued Morton from administration, chats to manager John McCormack who led the team out of the Third Division.

Paul Walker, whose tricky wing skills were valuable in the team which won the Third Division.

John Maisano was a skilful midfield player in John McCormack's teams.

Alex Williams on the run. There was no doubting his talent, but it was a squandered gift.

Manager Jim McInally guided Morton back to the First Division.

Morton enjoy the moment after winning the Second Division Championship. Left to right are Kevin Finlayson, Bobby Linn, Alex Walker, David McGurn, Jim McAlister, Jamie Stevenson, skipper Stewart Greacen, Chris Templeman, Scott McLaughlin, Peter Weatherson, Ryan Harding, Dean Keenan, David MacGregor, Paul McGowan, Paul Mathers and Chris Millar.

Peter Weatherson, a scorer of many valuable goals for Morton, both from attack and defence.

Morton striker Chris Templeman celebrates scoring against Premier League Kilmarnock in a notable Scottish Cup 3-1 win at Cappielow. Templeman scored a double in his best ever appearance in a Morton jersey.

Ryan Harding (hoops left) has just scored what proved to be the winner against Premier League Hibernian in Edinburgh in the Co-op Insurance Cup second round, giving First Division Morton a 4-3 win in extra time at Easter Road in August, 2008. The ecstatic Morton players wheeling away are Dominic Shimmin, Erik Paartalu and Jim McAlister.

First Division survival is assured in 2008 and Brian Wake and Kevin Finlayson, foreground, can't contain their joy.

Andy McLaren celebrates his second goal on his debut for Morton. Looking on is John Maisano.

Chris Millar, the local boy who gave excellent service to Morton before leaving to join St Johnstone.

Chris Templeman gets up to a high ball.

Stewart Greacen who was always a wholehearted captain and centre half.

Jason Walker heads for goal against Dumbarton watched by Stewart Greacen.

David MacGregor, a good defender who had bad luck with injuries.

Paul McGowan played a key role in the team which won the Second Division under Jim McInally.

Manager Davie Irons whose tenure as manager ended in disappointment.

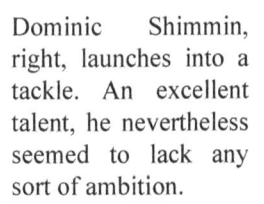

Dominic Shimmin, right, launches into a tackle. An excellent talent, he nevertheless seemed to lack any sort of ambition.

Jim McAlister at Stark's Park celebrating Morton's Second Division title success. He was transferred to Hamilton before moving on to Dundee. One of the fittest players to have covered the Cappielow turf.

Ryan McGuffie challenges Celtic's Georgios Samaras.

The irrepressible James Grady alongside Leigh Griffiths of Dundee. He went on to have a spell managing Morton after the departure of Davie Irons.

Allan McManus took over as James Grady's assistant.

Allan Jenkins. A driving presence in midfield, but so often on the injured list.

Author Roger Graham wins two bottles of wine at a reunion evening in 2009 of the Morton team which topped the Premier League in Scotland in November of 1979. Presenting them is television reporter Chic Young.

CHAPTER TWENTY

Wilson appeals for support

The 1989-90 season began with a plea by chairman and majority shareholder John Wilson for more support from the public. He said: "We were the 19th best supported club in Scotland last year. Inverclyde is one of the poorest regions in the UK and the club is suffering as a result."

Once again the chairman of the club announced that an average gate of 3,500 was required as a break even position. Given that the club had not achieved such a figure for some years one would have to assume that they were prepared to pay more than they could afford in wages in the hope of achieving higher crowds through better performances. But in my experience a succession of boards entertained overly optimistic views of potential attendances at Cappielow.

The season was also a benefit year for long-serving John McNeil, now 30, and who had been with Morton since joining from Cowal Boys' Club in 1973.

The first league game resulted in a 2-0 defeat at Stark's Park against Frank Connor's Raith Rovers team. New signing Ian McDonald from Partick Thistle, an experienced midfielder, and Derek McInnes were ruled out through injury and the side lined up as follows (4-3-3): Wylie; Collins, Reid, Boag, Pickering; Turner, O'Hara, Hunter; Ronald, Alexander, Deeney. Hunter was played in an unfamiliar left-sided midfield role due to the absence of McDonald and McInnes.

Young Michael Deeney, a talent much appreciated by manager Allan McGraw, had been told he would get at least half a dozen games in which to prove himself. Meanwhile Morton were prepared to listen to offers for 31-year-old Ian Clinging, and he was to depart for Forfar.

Queen's Park were beaten 1-0 with a Tommy Turner goal in the second round of the Skol Cup to set up an alluring tie against the might of Premier League champions Rangers, revamped by Graeme Souness. First up, however, were Clyde who came to Greenock and administered the host club's second league defeat with a solitary goal by Clarke before 1,500 fans.

On Wednesday 23rd August Cappielow was packed with 14,000 fans, over half backing the Light Blues with big-name players such as Trevor Steven, Ray Wilkins, Terry Butcher, Kevin Drinkell, Mark Walters and new signing Maurice Johnston, stolen from under the noses of would-be buyers Celtic.

Johnston was the first high-profile Catholic to pass through the portals of Ibrox. His hugely controversial signing the previous month was a commendable moral decision by manager Graeme Souness, as much as a shrewd footballing one. It was also a brave act by the player who had been a big hero of the Celtic support. Those fans were jubilant at the prospect of his return to Parkhead from French club Nantes. He had already been paraded in a Celtic strip before Souness provided the most dramatic signing coup of all time in Scottish football history by persuading him to choose the other half of the Old Firm. It was rather like Richard the Lionheart tempting Saladin to come over to the Crusaders.

On the night, Morton not only competed, but gave their illustrious opponents a fright. Rowan Alexander rose above Nisbet in the visitors' defence to head the home side in front in 14 minutes. Mark Walters equalised just before the interval and an unfortunate own goal by Mark Pickering put the Ibrox men ahead a minute after the break.

That was the way it stayed and Gers boss Graeme Souness made do with a brief three sentences after the game, saying: "It was a good game. I thoroughly enjoyed it. Their goalkeeper had a couple of good saves." Off he went before any questions could be asked.

Morton's Allan McGraw said: "We posed a lot of problems for Rangers and it was not an easy victory for them." For Morton, Jim Hunter was excellent at sweeper while teenager Brian Reid gave an authoritative display which spoke volumes of his progress at the heart of the home defence.

The league continued to frustrate, however, and two more defeats followed, 3-1 at Kilbowie Park against Clydebank, Rowan Alexander scoring, and 1-0 at home to Airdrie. The Broomfield men were continuing to splash the cash in an attempt to get up to the Premier League under manager Gordon McQueen, their latest buy being Stevie Gray from Aberdeen at a cost of £70,000. Morton were now bottom of the table.

Relief came in their next outing at Ayr where they won 3-2 with goals from Brian Reid, Jimmy Boag and Rowan Alexander. Ian McDonald, fit again, was the star man in midfield while 17-year-old Kevin McGoldrick came on as a substitute.

A 0-0 draw followed with Meadowbank before I broke the news in the Greenock Telegraph that Allan McGraw's main scouting link with the Glasgow area, wealthy businessman John Kerr, who owned Portman Motors, was threatening to sever his links with the club.

Kerr and his friend, Bert Reid, had affiliated themselves to Morton in 1986, having worked previously with Jock Wallace at Rangers, running the Ibrox youth scheme. It was an association which materialised through their friendship with Allan McGraw. They had already done a tremendous job in directing young talent to Cappielow.

Now, however, Kerr was clearly frustrated with his role. He told me that at the start of the previous season he had approached Morton chairman John Wilson with a view to buying into the club. He had wanted to create a situation in which no one person held the majority shareholding and said: "I knew Morton were in dire financial straits. I had a meeting with chairman John Wilson and told him 'you can't run it [Morton] yourself.'"

According to John Kerr, however, John Wilson would not countenance a deal which led to him relinquishing overall control. Kerr said that Wilson had offered to buy one share for every one Kerr acquired. He was unimpressed, saying: "It would have meant that my offer was virtually a donation. I shook my head and walked away from it."

Kerr was also irritated that he himself was funding the Glasgow end of Morton's youth policy, saying: "Morton never put a penny into it and my hand was never out my pocket."

Manager Allan McGraw, asked to comment, said: "It would be a disaster if John Kerr and Bert Reid left." Chairman John Wilson was unavailable for comment.

I reported the following day: "As Allan McGraw said yesterday it would cost Morton around £100 a week to run [the work done by Kerr and Reid]." That, I believed, was arguably the first expenditure which should be budgeted for given Morton's clearly stated view that their future lay in a successful youth programme. The situation regarding Kerr and Reid was further complicated by the fact that they were involved in a possible deal to take over Kilmarnock along with former player Alex Ingram.

On the field it was better news for Morton when they beat Alloa 3-2 with goals by Pickering, Deeney and Alexander. There was a special pat on the back for Deeney from manager McGraw who commented: "That was the best game he's had. He concentrated more on passing and was more of a team man."

A draw at Hamilton followed, where Andy Ritchie was now helping out with coaching, Deeney and O'Hara matching goals from Harris and Morrison. At Cappielow bottom of the table Forfar gained a point in a 1-1 draw, their scorer ironically being ex-Ton man Ian Clinging who cancelled out an Ian McDonald strike.

The following Saturday Morton travelled to Perth to meet league leaders St Johnstone. It was the Greenock men's first visit to Saints' new ground, McDiarmid Park. The novelty factor of the Perth club's new domicile led to an initial large increase in support. No fewer than 8,082 turned out for the visit of the Greenock club. Jenkins gave the hosts the lead before a great strike by Rowan Alexander led to a share of the spoils.

Andy Ritchie had meanwhile returned to Cappielow after his brief spell as a coach at Hamilton and was installed in a capacity on the commercial side prior to the visit of second top Partick Thistle on 14th October. I wrote: "I have vivid memories of those two great characters, Alan Rough of Partick and big Andy, in opposition to each other. Andy would help 'Scruff' line up his defensive wall, and then Rough would help Andy pick the ball out of the back of the net." On one occasion the two engaged in some friendly banter as Andy helped Alan assemble his defensive wall. The referee then approached Ritchie and the two conversed. It transpired afterwards in conversation with the match official that Ritchie had asked the ref if he would cut the game short by 10 minutes if he scored. The referee laughed before Andy lashed the ball into the top corner of the net past Rough.

The current hero was Rowan Alexander who scored twice as the sides shared the points. It was a result which stretched Morton's unbeaten run to seven games, leaving Morton sixth from the bottom.

A single goal defeat at Falkirk was followed by a goalless draw at home to Albion Rovers in a dire match. Meanwhile John Kerr and Alex Ingram had failed in their bid to take over Kilmarnock. Whatever issues there were between John Kerr and chairman John Wilson were clearly laid aside as the former continued to scout for Morton.

Draws against Ayr, Meadowbank and Alloa meant that Morton had shared the points in eight out of their last nine fixtures. Scoring goals was a problem and, to try and rectify it, Morton brought back Dougie Robertson from Falkirk where he had been unable to secure a first team place after his departure from Cappielow. He resumed his Cappielow career – not universally popular among the support – with a goal against Alloa. Allan McGraw's son, Mark, had made his debut in the Meadowbank goalless draw while centre half John Boag had put in a transfer request, stating he wanted full-time football.

Yet another goalless draw, against Hamilton at Cappielow, left Morton fourth bottom of the division before the relative peace was disturbed by wee winger Allan Moore of league leaders St Johnstone. He was quoted in the Sun as saying: "I've been hacked to bits by boot boys." Unfortunately the story was accompanied by a picture of Moore being tackled by Morton's Mark Pickering, the caption reading: "Morton's Mark Pickering dishes out the sort of treatment Allan Moore faces in every game he plays."

The story enraged Morton manager Allan McGraw who fumed: "It was irresponsible journalism and, if the quotes are correct, it is wrong of a professional footballer to moan about fellow pros in this way. It is a ridiculous story. It doesn't say Mark is a dirty player but the implication is there." I would imagine Moore, currently manager of Morton, advises his charges to be wary of putting themselves into situations which can lead to such sensationalism.

Morton were plodding along in the First Division, in no realistic danger of relegation yet with no prospects of climbing among the promotion contenders. The return of Tommy 'Tucker' Turner after injury at last saw them win a match when the midfielder slotted home a suspiciously offside goal to win both points against Forfar at Station Park. The victory simply preceded yet another draw, this time against league leaders St Johnstone at Cappielow.

For a goalless game, however, it was entertaining and Perth boss Alex Totten stated: "Games between us are always good because both teams like to go forward."

Allan McGraw agreed, saying: "It was a good game for a no-score draw."

The incredible number of drawn matches continued with a 1-1 result against Raith Rovers at Cappielow two days prior to Christmas, Alexander yet again being on target. It was Morton's 12th draw in 15 fixtures. The sequence was to continue, Morton gaining a point at Firhill against Clyde, Tommy Turner scoring, then Clydebank forcing a 2-2 result at Cappielow. The Clyde match was marked by the sending-off of scorer Turner, his second dismissal of the season. 'Tucker' found it hard to keep his mouth closed, and that, more than foul play, was frequently the weakness in his make-up. There was talk of him being picked on by referees, but in truth Tommy was too often the architect of his own misfortune.

The draw with the Bankies was procured after goals by top scorer Rowan Alexander and Mark McGraw, the first goal for the club by the manager's 19-year-old son who also had a good all-round performance.

Tommy Turner's disaffection after his latest ordering-off contributed to him requesting a transfer. He said: "I want away. I would love to go full-time. I've been with Morton too long."

One player returning to the fold was young Archie Gourlay who had moved to Newcastle in March, 1988, for £50,000. A change in management at St James' Park meant he was out of favour and he was loaned out to his former club for a month. Gourlay was later to leave Newcastle for Motherwell before moving on to Hartlepool, never fulfilling his early promise.

His first outing was against promotion contenders Airdrie who were too good for Morton in a 4-1 win at Broomfield under new boss Jimmy Bone. Turner scored for Morton who had John Boag and Jim Hunter sent off as the hosts went to the top of the table.

Mark McGraw was beginning to attract the scouts of other clubs and he had his best game for Morton at Firhill where Morton beat Partick Thistle 2-1. Alexander and McGraw shared the goals and I reported at the time: "McGraw had an outstanding match. He took his goal beautifully and worried the Thistle defence constantly." Another strike followed in a 1-1 draw at Clifftonhill against Albion Rovers, his third goal in four games.

Also coming back into contention for a first team place was 17-year-old Alan Mahood, recovering from injury at the start of the season. Allan McGraw commented of the youngster: "He is real quality. That boy is the jewel in the crown."

In the third round of the Scottish Cup Morton drew 2-2 at home to Raith, Alexander and O'Hara scoring. The winners of the replay could look forward to an enticing tie against Aberdeen at Pittodrie. First up were Falkirk at Cappielow where a Morton team, including six teenagers, fell 2-0 before a crowd of 2,158.

In the cup replay, Morton were in top form at Stark's Park and dumped Raith out of the competition by 3-1, goals coming from a Rowan Alexander double and one by John Fowler. Of Alexander, manager McGraw commented: "I think that was probably his best game ever for us. He was magnificent." John McNeil also made his comeback after a lengthy injury and showed up well.

Alexander was always a popular player with the supporters, as much for his inexhaustible work ethic as his goals. Had he possessed a better first touch he certainly would have played at a higher level in the game. He was also one of the best headers of a ball in the country.

The big battalions were now hovering around Cappielow, eager to run the rule over the manager's son Mark. Liverpool, Rangers and Manchester United were all on the prowl and, after Morton beat Alloa 2-0 at Cappielow with goals from O'Hara and McNeil, the young McGraw was off down south for a week's trial at Anfield. Upon his return McGraw senior said: "He [Mark] said everyone at Liverpool was brilliant. They all made him feel welcome, from the star names like Barnes and Rush, to the lady he was staying with. He was at Kenny Dalglish's for his dinner and was made to feel at home."

The young McGraw, however, was not keen on staying too far from home and when Hibs came in with an offer of £175,000 he was off to Edinburgh to join former Cappielow boss Alex Miller. None of the transfer fee would be available to Mark's dad for players, Morton chairman John Wilson saying: "Our first priority is to make Morton Football Club solvent."

It was a statement which did not go down well with the support. One critical letter to the Greenock Telegraph from James Pickett, who was later to assist in Douglas Rae's acquisition of Morton, exhorted the chairman to show "a willingness to listen to written and spoken comment: to be open about Morton's financial history and present problems". He also expressed the view that the club should not be hasty in accepting offers for young talent, referring particularly to the recent sale of Mark McGraw to Hibs for £175,000, but also more generally. Mr Wilson reiterated through the press that his first priority was to ensure the books balanced at Cappielow. He also said that he felt the money received from Hibs was a good offer.

My own view was that it was an amazing offer for a young player who had enjoyed just eight starts in senior football. Morton were being paid a big fee for potential.

Other critical views were concerned that John Wilson was being unduly cautious in not giving the manager some money from the proceeds of a transfer for which he could not possibly have budgeted. I could sympathise with that stance.

Rowan Alexander then scored the only goal of the game away to Partick and, at the same time, he was announced the First Division Player of the Month. It was 'Super Ro's' 13th strike of the season. His manager complimented him and said: "In all the years he's been with Morton he has never once been late for training." That meant something, given that Alexander had to travel twice a week from Dumfries to Greenock.

On the final Saturday of February, 1990, Morton arrived at Pittodrie to meet Aberdeen in the fourth round of the Scottish Cup.

They did more than achieve respectability, despite a 2-1 loss, and I reported: "This was a magnificent display by the First Division side against the second best team in the country. Statistically they may have lost, but they won a host of admirers for the way they went about their task."

Aberdeen manager Alex Smith was an enthusiast, saying: "They came here and played some fine football." His counterpart Allan McGraw said: "It was a shame for them [the players]. They deserved another go."

Morton had taken the lead through Tommy Turner before second half goals by Hans Gillhaus and Charlie Nicholas saw the Dons through to the quarter-finals. The large Morton support showed their appreciation by applauding their side off the park at the final whistle.

For the Greenock club, the remainder of the season was about trying to climb into a mid-table position and bring through the talented crop of youngsters at Sinclair Street. Results continued to disappoint, however. Meadowbank won 1-0 in Edinburgh then Raith beat Morton 2-1 at Stark's Park, Paul Roberts getting the Greenock side's counter. It was the club's fourth successive loss and prompted Allan McGraw to say: "Some of my players are simply not doing what they're told. Some of them seem to think that after a couple of good games they know the lot."

In March there came the return to Cappielow of a familiar and welcome face, Jackie McNamara, who had decided to help out with coaching on a part time basis.

Attendances were meanwhile plunging, 755 and then 687 turning out for successive home games against Albion Rovers and Forfar, won 3-0 and 2-0 respectively. Against Albion the unlikely scoring hero was full back Mark Pickering with a double, taking his senior career total to three, Tommy Turner getting the remaining strike. Turner and John Fowler got the goals in the win against Forfar.

The Albion match also marked the debut of another talented youngster, David Hopkin, while some much needed experience was added with the signing of former West Ham, Hearts and Dunfermline midfielder George Cowie. He had been retired from football for just over a season after a serious knee injury, but had decided to make a comeback. He had enjoyed a previous impressive spell on loan at Cappielow before joining Dunfermline and made a quiet debut against Falkirk at Brockville where Morton lost 2-0.

Another defeat followed, 1-0 to Ayr at Cappielow, before Morton announced that striker Dougie Robertson was leaving the club and football altogether. His departure caused Allan McGraw to comment: "It is ridiculous that a player of Dougie's calibre should be out of the game, but he has lost interest in football." The trouble was that Dougie, recently turned 27, had never lost his appetite for his grub.

Morton continued to struggle and were fourth bottom when Hamilton administered a 2-0 defeat at Douglas Park. Jim Hunter was their best player, but manager McGraw expressed his need for an attacker and a midfield player to augment his young squad. On 21st April they managed to beat Clydebank 1-0 at Kilbowie Park with a goal by veteran Alex O'Hara but the season was closing in ignominious fashion.

Big-spending Airdrie, still backed by John Dalziel's millions, saw their title hopes dashed at Cappielow when they could manage only a 1-1 draw, Tommy Turner once again being on the mark for the hosts, before the season ended with a 1-0 Renfrewshire Cup Final defeat at Love Street and a 3-2 home loss against Clyde, John Fowler and Rowan Alexander being on target. There were only 909 there to see a sorry end to a disappointing season.

Thirty-year-old Gerry Ronald, whose enthusiasm had seemed to wane over the course of the term, was given a free transfer while it was announced that John McNeil (31) would be awarded a testimonial match with Rangers on 17th August.

Two more old faces reappeared at Cappielow during the close season, Martin Doak re-signing for Morton having returned from Australia, and Eddie Morrison joining his old buddy Allan McGraw to help alongside John McMaster and Jackie McNamara on the coaching side.

It had been a poor season, Morton finishing fourth bottom of the table. The one real plus was that several very promising young players were either beginning or continuing their development in the senior game. Names such as Derek McInnes, Brian Reid, Alan Mahood, Jim Hunter and David Hopkin were to figure prominently in the seasons to come. And much needed income had already been garnered by the £175,000 sale of Mark McGraw to Hibs.

CHAPTER TWENTY-ONE

Ton criticised as sellers

The start of the 1990-91 season was relatively quiet for Morton. By 3rd August only utility player Derek Hamilton had been fixed up at Cappielow, the ex-St Mirren and Aberdeen man able to perform either at the back or in midfield. Five days later Wimbledon were the visitors to Greenock for a pre-season warm-up.

An interested spectator was Birmingham City boss Dave Mackay who was showing an interest in Morton's centre half John Boag. Unfortunately for Boag, he chose the occasion to have one of his poorer performances in a 3-3 draw in which home striker Rowan Alexander was the star with a hat-trick.

In the visiting team, who had been labelled in England as players of "Rottweiler football", were John Fashanu and Lawrie Sanchez. A 1-1 draw followed with Leicester City, Alexander again being on the scoresheet, before Morton met Rangers in John McNeil's testimonial match. McNeil (31) had been at Cappielow since 1973 and was the club's longest serving player.

Goals by McSwegan, Huistra and Spencer (2) gave the Gers a comfortable 4-0 victory and highlighted the need for someone to help Alexander up front. Allan McGraw had been trying to bring in former Celt Danny Crainie, but he chose to go to high-spending Airdrie instead of Cappielow.

In the first competitive outing of the season Motherwell progressed to the third round of the Skol Cup with a 4-3 win over Morton at Fir Park. Despite defeat, for David Hopkin it was a case for personal celebration as he scored twice on what was his 20th birthday. That only confirmed his promise, John Fowler getting the other strike with a penalty.

The week, however, ended with midfield star Tommy Turner (26) departing for pastures new, St Johnstone's £90,000 offer being accepted. Also on the way out was veteran Alex O'Hara (33) to Hamilton. Allan McGraw was sorry to lose both players, commenting on Turner: "He has always been one of the most skilful players in the First Division and we wish him well." Turner's Achilles heel had been his inability to keep a lid on his all too ready frustration with officialdom.

Morton badly needed some incoming movement in the transfer market, as was underlined when Airdrie, who had just missed out on promotion the previous season, thumped them

4-0 at Broomfield. For all the aspiring young talent at Cappielow, there was a real need for a couple of good, experienced campaigners. Where the balance was overloaded in favour of older heads when McGraw first took over as manager, now it was weighted the other way.

On the first Saturday of September Morton took on promotion hopefuls Dundee at Cappielow, losing out by the only goal of the game. Young Kevin McGoldrick made his first start for the club and could be satisfied with a decent performance.

Not so happy was the club's longest serving player, John McNeil (31), who had been on the receiving end of criticism from the fans. He commented: "I have been taking a lot of stick from the supporters and maybe it's time I moved on." Manager Allan McGraw defended the player, saying: "He has been a loyal servant to Morton and we don't want to see him go." McNeil ultimately chose to stay.

After two opening defeats, albeit against teams much favoured to be in the promotion race, Morton moved to strengthen their side with the acquisition of Motherwell winger John Gahagan, the 32-year-old who had been unable to hold down a regular place at Fir Park. His transfer fee was reported to be in the region of £40-50,000, a considerable sum for someone in his twilight years.

Raith Rovers then beat Morton with a goal by Gordon Dalziel at Stark's Park, a result followed by a failed Ton bid to take Falkirk striker Paul Rutherford to Cappielow. Young Michael Deeney meanwhile put in a transfer request after being disciplined for failing to turn out for a pre-season friendly against Dalry.

The bad news continued with a 2-0 loss at Hamilton and a 2-1 defeat at Falkirk, John Gahagan opening his account for the club with the consolation goal at Brockville. Gahagan's goal was also Morton's first of the season. One bright spot was the introduction of Portonian striker Dave McCabe (28), the ex-Airdrie and Motherwell forward who arrived from Fir Park for a fee of £30,000.

By the time Morton met Kilmarnock at Rugby Park, the Ayrshire side bolstered by new signings Tommy Burns and Billy Stark, they had played five and lost the lot. The gloom continued when Killie, inspired by an immaculate Burns midfield display, reminiscent of his Celtic and Scotland days, won 3-1, Morton's sole counter being a Derek McInnes penalty. Martin Doak was ordered off and the fans were beginning to make their displeasure known, both at games and in the local press.

Some much needed respite was gained when the side travelled to Firhill and recorded an excellent 4-0 victory over Partick, Dave McCabe grabbing a hat-trick and Rowan Alexander the remaining strike. The side lined up as follows (4-3-3): Wylie; Collins, Boag, Reid, Pickering; McInnes, McDonald, Hunter; Gahagan, McCabe, Alexander. At last Allan McGraw could crack a smile and he said: "This was worth waiting for."

A further 2-1 success followed at Meadowbank in the Centenary Cup for First and Second Division sides, Rowan Alexander and young Brian Reid grabbing the goals.

Director Douglas Rae then responded in the pages of the Greenock Telegraph to the criticism of both manager and club, saying that the board's overriding concern had been to reduce debt of some £400,000. That had been undertaken to a considerable degree with the selling of players, though he expected the club to be some £100,000 in arrears by the end of the season. He commended the instituted youth policy under Allan McGraw and reiterated the view that no large sums of money could be spent to strengthen the side in the transfer market.

Crowds were insufficient to pay the running costs of the club. It was the perennial problem: attendances were not going to increase until the football improved, and the football was unlikely to improve without better players. One letter writer in the Greenock Telegraph complained that Morton had earlier rejected the offer of financial help from wealthy businessman John Kerr, a friend of manager McGraw's who scouted at Cappielow. As covered earlier in this book, Kerr wished to purchase a shareholding that would have taken overall control away from chairman John Wilson, leaving no one with a majority. That had its merits, though there are those who would argue that management by committee has its own drawbacks.

Second bottom Morton then drew 3-3 at Cappielow against bottom club Brechin City, goals from McCabe (2), proving his worth, and Alexander. Just as the club appeared to have turned a corner by beating Clydebank 2-0 at home with goals by Derek McInnes and the in-form Dave McCabe, so came another awful result when Second Division Cowdenbeath bundled them out of the Centenary Cup 8-7 on penalties. The depression deepened with a 5-1 hammering at Station Park against fourth bottom Forfar. The reliable Rowan Alexander provided the only riposte as the boos of the visiting fans left no one in any doubt about their frustrations.

Given Douglas Rae's recent statement, there was not going to be any salvation through the transfer market. Improvement in the coming weeks would have to be found within the current squad, by wheeling and dealing in the market, by the judicious sale of players or by a combination of some or all of these.

With Morton lingering in third bottom position, a key meeting took place at Firhill against second bottom Clyde. At last Morton showed some form. Gahagan, Alexander and Collins scoring in a 3-1 win. The midfield organiser was the experienced Ian McDonald. Another important point was collected at Meadowbank Stadium in a 1-1 draw in which Mark Pickering scored the visitors' goal.

When Morton beat Ayr United 2-1 at Cappielow, McCabe and Gahagan on target, it was a much happier Allan McGraw who could see a growing increase in confidence among his players. Less content was visiting boss Ally McLeod. "We'd have been fourth top [if his side had won], you know," he explained dolefully in Allan McGraw's office after play was over. He looked for all the world like a big bloodhound that has just had its bone taken away. In fact, Ayr would have been joint fifth, but Ally was rarely one to let the facts get in the way of a good story.

Two big tests awaited Morton: successive games against second top Hamilton at Douglas Park, and league leaders Airdrie at Cappielow. These would determine the extent of the revival. In the first, a Dave McCabe goal secured a very decent draw, with Ian McDonald in superb form in centre midfield. His display prompted manager McGraw to say: "The wee man was magnificent. He's such a character. In the dressing room and at training he keeps the boys going. He's a comedian. If he stopped playing it would be worth his wages to keep him here for that alone.

"He's a true professional on the pitch too. He never hides, even if he is playing badly."

That was then followed up with the defeat of high-flying Airdrie at Cappielow. An early John Gahagan goal settled the home side who, despite the ordering-off of George Cowie in 30 minutes, controlled the game. It was the team's best display of the season so far and Diamonds' boss Jimmy Bone conceded: "Morton were worth their win."

Dundee upset the applecart at Dens with a one goal win, but Morton were certainly a much improved product. Twenty-year-old centre half Brian Reid was now beginning to attract attention, Norwich City joining his list of admirers.

A Dave McCabe goal gave Morton both points at Brechin against the second bottom club but, once again, growing pride came before a fall of shocking proportions when Meadowbank delivered a 3-0 beating at Cappielow in a match in which youngsters Alan Mahood and Kevin McGoldrick made appearances as substitutes. December continued with a 2-2 draw at Firhill against Partick Thistle, Martin Doak and Dave McCabe scoring. The match was marked by the welcome appearance of former Morton skipper Jim Duffy for the home side, defying medical advice to return to the game after a dreadful knee injury.

By this time it was clear that the best Morton could hope for was mid-table security. The relative glory days under Benny Rooney now seemed a distant memory. Allan McGraw had inherited a club which at the time virtually had no youth policy at all. He had turned that round significantly. There was a clutch of fine young talent at Cappielow, but there had been an inability to complement that with sufficient quality, experienced pros for a genuine promotion challenge to materialise. That grade of expertise does not come cheaply. And Morton had also discovered that, even if achieved, it was becoming increasingly more difficult to stay up. Twice – under Willie McLean and then Allan McGraw – teams had arrived in the top league only to discover they were woefully inadequate for the task ahead.

In mid-December Morton announced the signing of midfielder or full back Scott McArthur (22) from Hearts for what was described as a "modest fee". He was unable to play for some weeks due to a knee strain but his arrival coincided with one of the Greenock club's best results of the season. Kilmarnock, rebuilding under manager Jim Fleeting, were well beaten 3-0 at Cappielow, Dave McCabe scoring twice to take his total to 12 goals in 16 games since coming to Cappielow. Mark Pickering was the other man on target.

McCabe's opener, against the run of play in the 33rd minute, was typical, a burst of pace taking him clear of Killie centre half Paul Flexney before a perfect finish. He was proving well worth the investment of his transfer fee from Motherwell. Another to do well was 17-year-old Alan Mahood who showed some lovely moments of skill. Watching from the stand was father Frank. A keen Kilmarnock fan, he must have had mixed emotions. For all the rarity of his appearances, Mahood was already on the radar of some of the bigger clubs. Allan McGraw described him as "the best young player of his age I have seen in 10 years".

Morton then fell 1-0 at Somerset Park to an Ayr side which had just lost manager Ally McLeod, the victim of the latest managerial merry-go-round.

On Wednesday 2nd January, 1991, Morton vanquished Clydebank at Kilbowie Park with a 4-2 win, Dave McCabe recording his second hat-trick for the club, Rowan Alexander ending a 10-game barren spell by adding the fourth goal. Of his goal star McCabe, Allan McGraw enthused: "He has settled in well at Cappielow and his hard work has been rewarded with goals."

Liverpool and Crystal Palace were now showing interest in the young Mahood. Palace boss Steve Coppell arrived in Scotland to watch Morton playing Stirling in the third round of the Scottish Cup, hoping to run the rule over the aspiring midfielder. Unfortunately for Coppell, Mahood was left out of the side in a game decided by yet another McCabe goal, his 16th of the season. Incidentally, the match took place at Falkirk's Brockville ground as Morton had objected to playing on Stirling's newly laid synthetic surface.

Then, once again, the league set-up was changed, reverting to divisions of 12-12-14. This very same system had been rejected not that long ago as being unconducive to the welfare of Scotland's top clubs and the international team. Given that, and the fact that it was in the middle of a season, it was the usual sort of ill-conceived muddle one had come to expect of Scottish football.

The usual winter postponements were playing havoc with the fixtures, but on 2nd February Morton met league leaders Falkirk at Cappielow before a healthy attendance of 3,451. It ended up being a cagey draw, Morton coach John McMaster summing up perfectly when he said: "I think both sides showed too much respect for each other. They cancelled each other out."

Dave McCabe scored his 17th goal in 23 matches for the club in a rather disappointing 1-1 home draw against Meadowbank, Morton now being in sixth bottom position. They were safe from the threat of relegation, but with no hope of producing the sort of sustained run necessary to climb into the promotion challenging positions.

Coincidentally, Morton had been drawn at home against Meadowbank in the fourth round of the Scottish Cup. Straight off the back of their recent drawn encounter at Cappielow, Allan McGraw decided to change his normal, attacking philosophy. Terry Christie's Thistle sides were always based upon a counter-attacking strategy, encouraging teams to attack them and leave spaces to be exploited. This time McGraw opted to play them at their own game, urging his players to be patient and rely upon the pace of Dave McCabe and John Gahagan to get in behind Meadowbank's packed rearguard. It worked a treat, giving Morton a 3-0 victory with goals by McCabe, Gahagan and Alexander. The reward was a tie away to Premier Division Motherwell.

Both McCabe and Gahagan, of course, were former players at Fir Park and were eagerly looking forward to the tie in Lanarkshire. Gahagan joked: "I never know what I'm going to do with the ball, so the Motherwell defence have no chance."

Before that tie, Morton collected a point at Rugby Park, Gahagan equalising an earlier Bobby Williamson strike. Meanwhile forward Paul Roberts departed to Arbroath while John McNeil (32) was told he would be given a free transfer.

The Motherwell tie had caused a mood of expectation in Inverclyde and over 2,000 fans made the trip to Fir Park to cheer on their side. Although goalless, it was an exciting match in which rising teenage stars Brian Reid and Alan Mahood excelled. Mahood had already been selected for the Scotland under-18 side, though the replay meant he could not play against the Republic of Ireland.

Brian Reid had been a stand-out at centre half in a good all-round Morton display and manager McGraw commented: "I thought my two youngsters, Reid and Mahood, were the best players on the park." Well boss Tommy McLean was happy still to be in the competition, saying: "Morton were much more enthusiastic and determined. They deserved the replay." Only the veteran winger Davie Cooper (35) had shone for the hosts who knew they would have to up their performance level if they were to make any further progress.

Reid's reward for his form was to gain a place in the Scotland under-21 squad's European Championship tie against Bulgaria.

The Motherwell replay on Tuesday 19th March, 1991, attracted a crowd of 7,319 with an atmosphere reminiscent of the better Premier League days under Benny Rooney.

In 10 minutes a serious blow befell the hosts when left back Mark Pickering attempted to clear Davie Cooper's cross into the box. The ball smacked Tom Boyd on the head and rebounded past Wylie into the net. However, Morton recovered well, Ian McDonald's experience in midfield proving highly influential. In 64 minutes they drew level when McDonald's fierce drive was parried by Ally Maxwell, the ball falling to John Gahagan who side-footed home.

There was no more scoring and the game went into a thrilling penalty decider, the visitors finally triumphing 5-4. The unfortunate home player to miss was Mark Pickering whose clearance had led to the opening Motherwell goal. He was distraught afterwards, though he had played extremely well on the night. Allan McGraw complimented his team, saying: "I'm proud of the players. They gave me everything."

Once again Motherwell manager Tommy McLean was generous to his opponents and said: "We were fortunate to get through. We rode our luck. Any credit goes to Morton." Cappielow chairman John Wilson generously announced that the board had agreed to pay the Morton players their win bonus of £500 per man for what he decreed to be a great effort. As it turned out, Motherwell were to go on and win the Scottish Cup, wee Tommy's Steelmen getting the better of big brother Jim's Dundee United team.

Morton were about to lose more than the tie, however. Liverpool, Rangers, Notts Forest and Chelsea were among those queuing up to view the young talent in the Greenock club's ranks. Reid (20) and Mahood, soon to be 18, were the targeted twosome. On Monday 25th March Rangers' offer of £300,000 for Reid was accepted and he was whisked off to Ibrox. On the previous Saturday Mahood had travelled south with dad Frank for talks with Chelsea. The youngster's father was not keen on his son heading for the bright lights of London, which left Notts Forest and Everton in the race.

Morton then drew 1-1 with Partick at Cappielow in a flat affair, something of an anti-climax after the Motherwell ties, Derek Collins getting the goal. Another home point followed against Forfar, Morton's sixth consecutive draw. John Boag grabbed the home goal.

Finally, two days after his 18th birthday, on 28th March, Alan Mahood was on his way to Brian Clough's Nottingham Forest side, another fee of £300,000 coming Morton's way. McGraw was sorry to see such talent vanish so early, Mahood having played only 11 games for the club, but he had been promised some of the £600,000 transfer fees received for his two young starlets to bring in replacements.

Including the money paid out for his son Mark McGraw and midfielder Tommy Turner, McGraw's youth policy had gathered in some £865,000. Taking into account the £70,000 paid out for John Gahagan and Dave McCabe, it was a very tidy profit. Director Douglas Rae had earlier commented that debt at the end of the season was expected to be around £100,000. If paid off, that still left almost £500,000 as a surplus. Rae commented: "There has been a quiet revolution going on in the last six months and now we have the potential to take the club a stage further." It was explained that money would have to be set aside for ground improvements, but that the manager would have funding available to him to strengthen the depleted squad.

Allan McGraw warned against over-optimism when he counselled: "I will still have to be frugal. We are not rushing into the market. There will be no panic buying."

The season was approaching its end with Morton safely out of the relegation issue, but with little prospect of finishing higher than seventh or eighth in the table.

A Dave McCabe double against Clydebank in a 2-2 draw took him to 21 goals for the season before a pointless trip to Dens Park where Dundee won with the sole goal of the game by Keith Wright. A young Morton team containing four teenagers scrapped for a 1-1 draw at home to Ayr, the home counter being an own goal, before Hamilton administered a 4-0 walloping, something of a reality check.

Free admission to the terracings, plus £1 admission to the stand, was awarded to Cappielow fans for a postponed Raith league match which took place in midweek, young central defender Gerry Kelly scoring for the hosts in a 2-1 defeat. "It was just as well the supporters didn't have to pay," offered a less than amused manager McGraw. A crowd of 2,435 turned out. The cynical might say that the offer had been made to assuage the growing number of fans who had expressed their disquiet at Morton again being portrayed as simply a selling club, but it was a decent gesture by management.

Goals by McCabe, Gahagan and McDonald gained a 3-1 win at Brechin before Morton fell 3-0 to promotion contenders Airdrie at Broomfield, John Gahagan also being sent off for two bookable offences. Then league leaders Falkirk scratched through to a nervy 1-0 win at Cappielow with Morton looking as if they couldn't wait for the season to end.

Two league games remained. Goals by John Boag and Rowan Alexander salvaged a draw at Forfar before the curtain came down on a disappointing season with a win at Firhill against Clyde, John Fowler scoring the only goal of the game. It earned Morton ninth place in the 14-club First Division. Unfortunately top scorer Dave McCabe, whose 22 goals gained him the Player of the Year Award in the annual poll run by the Greenock Telegraph of Morton fans, broke an ankle.

On their way out of Cappielow were George Cowie as player-coach of Forres Mechanics and Derek Hamilton who had failed to gain a first team spot.

Another of Morton's youngsters, Gerry Kelly, was attracting the attention of Sheffield United, but no business was done for the central defender.

In six years, Allan McGraw had established a credible youth policy which had regained the club its solvency. He and his assistant, John McMaster, were rewarded with five-year contracts, incredible then never mind now, and the manager commented: "It means John and I will be able to carry out what we've planned, and I'm delighted at the board's decision."

McGraw had been given money to spend and his first signing was 30-year-old Stuart Rafferty, the ex-Motherwell, Dundee and Dunfermline midfielder from Port Glasgow. His fee was a club record of £60,000. Defender Graham Ogg (24) arrived from Queen's Park and then, a couple of days before the start of the league season, McGraw pounced to bring in Celtic striker Alex Mathie for another club record of £100,000.

Mathie had played 14 times for Celtic's first team and was on the wanted list of a couple of clubs, but Morton pipped newly promoted SPL club Falkirk for his signature.

Pre-season friendlies had produced losses to Hearts, 3-0, Rangers, 1-0, and Newcastle 4-1. Young Kevin McGoldrick scored the goal against the Magpies in a match which saw the introduction of yet another product of McGraw's youth system to the fray, 17-year-old striker Derek Lilley from Everton Boys' Club.

First up in the league for the 1991-92 season were Partick Thistle at Cappielow and, in an excellent display, the hosts won 2-1 with goals by Alex Mathie and John Gahagan. For Mathie, it could hardly have gone better, his goal coming just 66 seconds into his debut. Stuart Rafferty also impressed with his passing from a sitting midfield role before a crowd of 3,430, and manager McGraw declared his belief in his side's promotion credentials.

Two Martin Doak headers from two Derek McInnes crosses rescued Morton from a one-goal deficit against Stirling, then Doak was again the hero with another headed goal in a draw at Hamilton as Morton took three points from their next two matches in what was now a 12-club First Division. Unfortunately skipper Jim Hunter sustained a cruciate knee injury in a late tackle which was to rule him out for the rest of the season.

Celtic, by now under Liam Brady's managership, were too good for Allan McGraw's side in a second round Skol Cup tie at Cappielow before 9,518 fans, doubles by Charlie Nicholas and Gerry Creaney giving them a 4-1 interval advantage after Derek McInnes had given the hosts a shock two-minute lead. Graham Ogg netted a consolation goal with nine minutes to go to put a better light on the scoreline.

Morton shrugged off the disappointment with a comfortable win at Station Park against Forfar, goals coming from Alex Mathie (2), Rowan Alexander and John Gahagan.

Unbeaten in their opening four league encounters, Morton were living up to their manager's pre-season belief that they were capable of a promotion challenge. Pride cometh before a fall, however, and it was more of a nose-dive when Clydebank came to Cappielow on the last Saturday of August, 1991, and crushed the home side 7-1. Ken Eadie with a hat-trick led an embarrassing Bankies' romp, Derek McInnes getting the home strike. Allan McGraw commented: "It was a debacle. Our defence and midfield were an absolute disgrace. I have been talking about promotion, but if we produce any more performances like that we will be looking at relegation." Another to star for the visitors was teenage midfielder John Henry.

Before the next match, Morton moved to bring in Glasgow University centre half Dougie Johnstone in the face of competition from two other clubs. The 22-year-old was better known to local cricket fans as a key member of the Ayr Cricket Club 1st XI, so often rivals of Greenock Cricket Club. His inclusion in the squad was also a sign that the promise shown by Gerry Kelly had withered rather than flowered.

The next match was at Cappielow with the visit of league leaders Dundee, a test welcomed by manager McGraw after that drubbing by Clydebank. Any trepidation home fans might have felt was swept aside with a wonderful display which saw Derek Collins, Stuart Rafferty and Alex Mathie hit three unanswered goals. From despair to elation within the space of eight days. It was a much happier Morton boss who said: "Some of the football we played was magnificent." Of his players, he commented: "Their pride was badly hurt by that result [against Clydebank]."

There was particular mention once more of new midfield man Stuart Rafferty, McGraw saying: "His passing was different class."

A beautifully flighted Derek McInnes free kick was all that separated Morton and Meadowbank in Edinburgh, David Wylie having an excellent match in goal, and the Greenock men found themselves in third top spot after seven games, one point behind leaders Dundee. Arguably the best run of the day, however, was provided by physio John Tierney, almost left behind by the team bus after the match. It was like watching Chariots of Fire in slow motion as his head went back, white locks streaming behind and club anorak billowing in the night air, in a desperate, red-faced, lung-bursting sprint after the departing coach. Cheered on by the players, he made a successful lunge for the door as the driver mercifully slowed down. I believe he recovered round about Port Glasgow.

The continued success of Allan McGraw's youth policy was evidenced by 17-year-old Derek Lilley's selection for the Scottish under-18 squad in a four-nation tourney involving Italy, Holland and Belgium.

An Alex Mathie goal gave Morton a decent point at Stark's Park against Raith Rovers, though John Gahagan became the latest in a growing injury list when he suffered a knee injury which was expected to rule him out for three months.

While doing well, Morton were still at times looking vulnerable, and this was highlighted when Ayr, 3-1 down with 12 minutes to go at Cappielow, hit three goals to snatch an unlikely victory. "We were still chasing goals at 3-1 up," bemoaned manager McGraw. Morton's strikes came from Alex Mathie, Scott McArthur and an own goal. When Montrose took another home point away in a 1-1 draw, Derek McInnes netting from the spot, Morton had slumped to fifth place. I felt prompted to comment: "The stark truth is that on this showing Morton are the length of West Blackhall Street away from the sort of performance required."

Assistant manager John McMaster said: "We showed a total lack of professional attitude."

Kilmarnock simply exacerbated the problems with a single goal win at Rugby Park. It was a side under growing pressure, therefore, who arrived at Firhill in mid-October to tackle the new league leaders Partick Thistle. Making his debut was young striker Derek Lilley and, in a game punctuated by defensive errors, Morton managed to win 4-3, goals coming from Doak, Alexander, McInnes and Mathie. It was closer than it should have been as Morton were 4-1 ahead going into the last 20 minutes.

The performance left both management camps despairing at their respective rearguards. Thistle's John Lambie, who always utilised Anglo-Saxon expletives particularly effectively, summed up: "Both teams had two !!!!!!! central defenders who !!!!!!! wanted to go for the same !!!!!!! ball!"

John McMaster's response was to say: "It's good to get the two points but I'm very disappointed at the two goals we lost at the end."

Morton's side, in 4-3-3 formation, was: Wylie; Collins, Boag, Doak, Pickering; McInnes, McDonald, McArthur (Hopkin); Lilley (Rafferty), Mathie, Alexander. Three up front in those days was standard practice, 4-4-2 considered conservative and one up positively negative. It is strange in comparison with today's line-ups. That Rangers have considered it normal in recent seasons to play with one up front in domestic football would have been considered unthinkable then.

On the following Tuesday Morton beat Kilmarnock 2-1 in the second round of the B & Q Cup, an excellent Scott McArthur strike in extra time grabbing the win, while Alex Mathie hit his eighth goal of the season. On the down side, Morton added two more players to their already substantial injury list, Alexander and McDonald tweaking hamstrings.

McArthur again got on the mark when he hit the only goal of the game against Hamilton at Cappielow to take the hosts into fourth spot, four points adrift of leaders Dundee. It was a freak, if welcome, goal, coming direct from a corner, Accies keeper Ferguson completely misjudging the ball. The Morton hero, however, was Martin Doak with a solid defensive performance.

Then Raith arrived in Greenock to send their hosts packing in a B & Q Cup quarter-final, Gordon Dalziel's hat-trick overcoming strikes by Mathie and Doak.

CHAPTER TWENTY-TWO

A big talent unfulfilled

As October drew towards a close Michael Deeney announced that he wanted a transfer, a request granted by the club. The 23-year-old had been at the club for four years but had failed to deliver on the promise of a surfeit of talent.

Allan McGraw said: "Michael has tremendous skill and has been given opportunities in the past. But he seems to find it difficult to produce the goods in the first team."

In later years, Allan McGraw was to tell me that it was the one big regret of his career that he never managed to get the best out of Deeney. "Next to Andy Ritchie he was the player with the most skill in my time at Cappielow as a coach and manager," he said.

"In the reserves and at training he was tremendous, but he just didn't seem able to do it in the first team. I don't know why. He had enough chances and got all the encouragement. When we eventually let him go his own father said to me that the boy couldn't say he didn't get chances." It wasn't as if his fortunes changed when eventually he left Morton. He simply disappeared out of the game.

On the final Saturday of October Morton travelled to the east coast and a meeting with top of the table Dundee. Two points separated the clubs and at the end of the 90 minutes that gap was closed, Derek Lilley gaining the win when he sprinted onto a fine Derek Collins through pass to steer the ball home.

He was on target again, along with Martin Doak whose goals were becoming an early feature of the season, in a 2-1 win over Meadowbank. Cappielow commercial manager Eddie Morrison, a prolific goalscorer during his career, spoke glowingly of Lilley: "I think he's got great potential," he said.

An interested spectator was Blackburn Rovers manager Kenny Dalglish who was interested in right back Derek Collins. He also had been alerted about Derek Lilley. There was no move for Collins, but Allan McGraw admitted that Dalglish had been impressed by Lilley. "He's still interested in Lilley. But we don't have to sell and we want to hold on to the boy for as long as possible. He's not available at this time."

After 15 matches, Partick, Dundee and Morton were locked together on 21 points. For Allan McGraw, the key now was for the team to hang in there until his injured players started to return to the fold.

November, however, was the month when all the work of the season up to then began to unravel like a pullover caught on a barbwire fence. First, Clydebank administered a 3-1 defeat at Kilbowie, Mark Pickering scoring a consolation goal. Next came a visit from Forfar. On the eve of the game there was a scare when it was revealed that left back Pickering, a robust defender, had been run down by a forklift truck at his place of work. I broke the news to the nation thus: "The word is that Mark will make the kick-off tomorrow and the forklift truck is as well as can be expected."

Forfar continued where Clydebank had left off, winning 3-1, Derek McInnes being the home scorer. "If performances can be judged by the length of time it takes a defeated manager to emerge from the dressing room, then I think we can safely say that this ranks among Morton's worst of the season," I wrote. "After 40 minutes the press folded their tents and slipped quietly out of the park, leaving the Morton party to their inquest."

McGraw was later critical of his players, saying they were playing as individuals instead of as a team, but with typical candour he also accepted a share of blame, saying: "I think I boobed when I took off both McDonald and Rafferty. I should have left one on." Up to then the manager had occasionally rotated his midfield generals, but both had started the match. Young sweeper Gerry Kelly was also added to a lengthy injury list when he suffered a blow to his head after a collision with team-mate Pickering. He would have been better tangling with the forklift truck.

The downturn continued when Morton could manage only a point at Montrose, Alex Mathie getting their goal, then Kilmarnock, who had invested over £1,000,000 in players such as Tommy Burns, Craig Paterson, Ross Jack, Bobby Geddes, Hugh Burns and Bobby Williamson, won 1-0 at Cappielow. Manager Jim Fleeting said: "To come here and win is a great result. I like Morton. They offer so much to the game."

Allan McGraw was not in defeatist mood, despite his team falling to fifth spot, five points behind leaders Dundee. "I stick by what I've said before," he affirmed. "If we can remain in contention until the New Year we'll have experienced players like John Gahagan and Dave McCabe back and we'll be in a position to challenge."

But November had more depressing results in store. Raith Rovers won 2-0 at Cappielow in a display in which the Greenock men looked rudderless. In comparison, Raith had a strong leader on the park in player-manager Jimmy Nicholl who cajoled and encouraged. Their goals came from Gordon Dalziel and Craig Brewster, the latter with a stunning volley. When a ghastly month ended with defeat at Stirling by 2-1, Rowan Alexander grabbing the visitors' goal, Morton had slumped to seventh place, nine points behind the leaders. The one bright spot was the introduction of former Glasgow University centre half Dougie Johnstone to the team. He did well on his debut.

Meanwhile Allan McGraw's friend, John Kerr, had been appointed to the board. He and Bert Reid had been instrumental in bringing top young players to Cappielow from the Glasgow area in their five-and-a-half association with the club. Kerr believed the credit was down to the managerial team, saying: "It's due to Allan McGraw and John McMaster. You can bring good boys to the club, but what's the use if you don't play them? These two are prepared to play youngsters and give them a chance. They know a good young player when they see one. It comes from management being secure. Parents are more alert too."

Allan McGraw, however, preferred to give the praise to some unsung heroes. He said: "It's all down to the hard work of the scouts. There's no magic or secret about a successful youth policy. A lot of managers want ready-made players."

While Kerr and Reid ran the Glasgow end of Morton's youth scouting system, there were excellent local men involved in covering Inverclyde – Jake Anderson, Reggie Scorer, John McVicar and James MacDonald. Jimmy Cole covered Ayrshire, David Keiling oversaw Paisley and Lachie Campbell took care of the west of Scotland junior scene. They were all key men for Morton. They had a central role in the club's financial recovery.

It was during this downturn in Morton's fortunes on the pitch that I was in the press hall of the Greenock Telegraph as the papers thundered off the conveyor belt one lunch-time, chatting to some colleagues. A well kent and rotund news vendor, awaiting his supply of papers, spotted me. Clearly not enamoured by my scribblings in support of the manager and his youth policy, he shouted: "Hey, Graham! You know fuck all about football!"

"I beg your pardon," I retorted, "I know fuck all about lots of things!"

It was at this stage of the season that director Andy Gemmell announced that he had a vision of Morton moving to a purpose-built stadium in the waterfront which, it was hoped, would soon be developed. He foresaw the stadium incorporating a 10-pin bowling alley, health and leisure club, hotel, restaurant, multi-screen cinema, retail outlets and executive apartments. Finance, he thought, might come from an amalgam of the private sector, European Community and sports grants.

It was a highly ambitious plan. The then Greenock Telegraph editor Ken Thomson, who had been a keen advocate of a fully developed waterfront, and I had previously met with the late Hugh Currie and the current chairman, John Wilson, to discuss just such a plan. Nothing was to come of it. This was not in any way Morton's fault. I would bet on the development of the waterfront remaining a subject of much discussion, argument and disagreement long after I have taken leave of this planet.

Goals by Alex Mathie and Michael Deeney, making a, by now, rare appearance, could not prevent another defeat at the start of December, 3-2 at Ayr, virtually consigning Morton to another season of First Division football. By this time Dave McCabe, top goalscorer the previous term, was ready to make his first appearance of the season. Had the club's top striker and top defender, Jim Hunter, been available at the start of the campaign things might have turned out differently. But that's football … all ifs and buts.

Meanwhile former Cappielow star Jim Tolmie was about to return for a second spell in Greenock. The 31-year-old had returned from Swedish club Markaryd and finally put pen to paper a few days before Christmas.

Before that there was a minor upheaval when three of the club's younger players were involved in a rumpus outside an Ayrshire nightclub, resulting in two of them, Gary Stevenson and Derek Anderson, being shown the exit door. The third, David Hopkin, was fined and suspended for a couple of weeks.

John Lambie's Partick team came to Cappielow in December and delivered the final blow to any faint hope of a promotion revival with a 1-0 win, the goal scored by Davie Irons, later to become a manager at Cappielow. Lambie summed up: "It's a long time since we've won here."

Allan McGraw responded: "It's a long time since WE'VE won here."

Lambie was sympathetic towards Morton, referring to their season-long injury problems when he said: "People think you're just making excuses when you talk about injuries. But it's not excuses; it's a fact. You can't do without key players. No one can, not Rangers, Celtic or Morton."

It didn't prevent fans from voicing their protests at Morton's collapse, some of whom felt money should be made available to the manager for players. A sum of £150,000 had been spent since the start of the season. The club at that time reported that the rest of the substantial finance gleaned from the youth policy would go to ridding the club of a costly overdraft, and its high interest payments, and towards a fund for ground improvements. Chairman and majority shareholder John Wilson was adamant that the club under his stewardship would not fall deep into debt again.

On Saturday 14th December, Morton drew with league leaders Dundee in a goalless game at Cappielow which left both managers, Allan McGraw and Iain Munro, satisfied. Two weeks later Morton recovered their dash of the earlier part of the season when they thrashed Forfar 5-1 at Station Park with goals by Mathie 2, Doak, Rafferty and McInnes. Jim Tolmie played and gave a display of skill and experience while of Stuart Rafferty, who had been attracting criticism from the supporters, McGraw said: "He has been having a difficult time recently and deserves a break."

Morton's injury problems were beginning to clear and the previous season's top scorer, Dave McCabe, was now ready for a comeback. Manager McGraw commented: "I have never seen a player work as hard as McCabe." It was going to be difficult for him to force his way into the side as Alex Mathie and Jim Tolmie had both arrived at the club and were forming a decent partnership with Rowan Alexander up front. Alexander it was who notched a double in an otherwise disappointing 2-2 home draw with Montrose, before Morton took two fine points in a 1-0 win at Rugby Park against a Killie side who were now under the caretaker management of Tommy Burns. Jim Fleeting had left in January and Burns was eventually given the job on a full time basis.

Dougie Johnstone was growing in confidence with each performance and forming a good partnership with skipper Martin Doak. The Killie win prompted Allan McGraw to declare: "I still say we're in the promotion race." Morton were 11 points behind leaders Dundee and further victories followed, Clydebank, who had thrashed Morton 7-1 earlier in the season, succumbing 5-0 then Stirling going down 2-0, both games at Cappielow. Against the Bankies revenge was sweet, Mathie (2), Alexander, McInnes and Tolmie on target, while Doak and Mathie hit the net versus Stirling.

The Stirling game was notable for an injury to referee Jim McGilvray which necessitated linesman Hugh Dallas taking over. Called out of the crowd to replace Dallas on the line was

Greenock Telegraph compositor Stuart Cameron, a referee in local juvenile football. This prompted the Morton fans to start singing "The linesman's a Ton fan" much to their delight. Stuart enjoyed it as much as anyone.

Alex Mathie had now scored 18 goals for the season, while skipper Doak had hit the net eight times, a commendable strike rate for most attacking midfielders, let alone a central defender. Morton had moved up to sixth place, nine points behind the leaders.

Morton had drawn Second Division East Fife in the third round of the Scottish Cup and Mathie reached 20 goals for the season when he struck twice in a 4-2 win at Cappielow, Stuart Rafferty and Rowan Alexander adding the others. Key men were Rafferty in midfield and Tolmie up front, the latter showing delightful control and passing.

Another point was collected at Hamilton where ex-Ton player Billy McLaren was manager. He said: "I was pleased with the level of performance," while Allan McGraw agreed that a draw had been a fair result.

Raith Rovers interrupted the Greenock men's momentum with a 2-0 win at Stark's Park before Meadowbank were beaten 2-1 in Edinburgh, Doak and Alexander grabbing the goals. It was a dress rehearsal for the fourth round of the cup against the same opponents in Greenock.

A crowd of 2,755 turned out to see Morton take the lead through Alexander only for Meadowbank to hit back, scoring two of their own. Terry Christie's men were well worth their advantage as the game approached the final whistle. Right on time Morton salvaged a replay when Rowan Alexander headed in a Scott McArthur free kick. Allan McGraw commented: "We are the luckiest team in the world to be in the cup." In stark contrast Terry Christie, in his familiar fawn duffel coat, was dejected, saying: "I am desperately disappointed."

The replay took place on Wednesday 26th February. The prize for the winners was a glamour tie at Parkhead against Celtic in the quarter-finals. Poor Terry Christie was to experience a ghastly sense of déjà vu. The teams were tied together at 2-2, after Morton had fought back from two down at half-time with goals by Alex Mathie (penalty) and David Hopkin. Three minutes into injury time a cross came over and there was Alexander again to head home and send Meadowbank out of the competition.

It was a capital evening in every sense of the word for the travelling support of just over a thousand. Hero Alexander said: "I didn't think I was going to score, but I hung well, got power behind it and hit the postage stamp." It was a first class effort.

Super Ro hit his fifth goal in consecutive matches in a drab 1-1 draw at Montrose before the big cup quarter-final day all Inverclyde had been looking forward to arrived. Approximately 4,500 blue and white clad Ton fans made the trip up the M8 to Glasgow, all determined to have a great day out. As Allan McGraw commented: "The pressure is all on Celtic." Former coach Jackie McNamara wished everyone well at Cappielow and urged the players to relax and enjoy themselves. He continued: "What Allan McGraw has done at Cappielow is remarkable. The money he has brought in for youngsters in the last season or two has turned the club round."

It was Morton's biggest match since the Scottish Cup semi-final against Rangers in 1981 when Benny Rooney's team lost 2-1 at the same Parkhead venue.

Morton were true to their pre-match words and took the game to their hosts, playing some lovely football. A David Hopkin drive whistled across the area, Jim Tolmie just failing to get on the end of it at the far post, then Martin Doak's fiercely struck shot from range was tipped over the crossbar by Gordon Marshall.

This was not what the home support expected. When a chance fell to Hopkin near the six-yard box in front of goal they were seriously worried. Unfortunately 'Hoppy' was off-balance and could only toe poke the ball wide of the left post. Almost immediately Celtic broke upfield to score against the run of play, Gerry Creaney getting the final touch.

Still Morton played their share of good football, but gradually Celtic's class began to tell and further goals by Creaney and, later on, John Collins put a rather flattering gloss on what was nevertheless a deserved result.

Celtic boss Liam Brady was generous in his praise of the visitors, saying: "They caused us problems. Not many Premier League teams come here and play three up front."

Morton assistant manager John McMaster was proud of the Greenock team and said: "They [the players] never let us down. We created chances but we didn't put them away."

Allan McGraw commented: "The fact that Celtic took off a forward and put on a midfielder in the second half was a compliment to my players." The Morton team that day was (4-3-3): Wylie; Collins, Johnstone, Doak, Ogg; Hopkin, Rafferty, McArthur (Brown); Mathie, Alexander, Tolmie (Lilley 77).

Despite defeat, Morton's support stayed behind to cheer their side, appreciating their positive approach to the tie.

On the Monday after the match the news broke that Morton were attempting to bring 18-year-old Alan Mahood back to Cappielow from Brian Clough's Nottingham Forest. The midfielder, only a season before one of the most sought-after youngsters in Scottish football, had failed to settle and was keen to get back to Scotland. He was being played as an out-and-out wide player on the right side of the park for the reserves, a role in which he felt uncomfortable.

A 1-1 draw at Forfar followed, Alexander securing the point, before goals by Tolmie and Hopkin gained a midweek win over Ayr. The following day it was announced that Mahood was on his way to Greenock for a fee of £175,000, £125,000 less than Forest had stumped up the previous season. It was Morton's record signing and quite an achievement given that Motherwell, Dundee and Hibs were all keen to sign him.

The decisive factor for Mahood was that he knew he was coming back to a familiar environment in which he had prospered under Allan McGraw and John McMaster. I think there was also an element of home-sickness and he told me: "I had too much time on my hands." He was later to confide that he had felt isolated at Forest and not really part of the club. I asked him how he had found Brian Clough, to be met with a shrug. "I hardly saw him," came the reply.

Morton were to be commended for splashing out another six-figure sum so soon after the arrival of Alex Mathie and I wrote: "It is an ambitious signing. For a relatively small provincial club like Morton to spend £175,000 on a teenager is remarkable. It says a great deal for how highly they rate his potential."

Mahood watched from the stand as Morton beat Clydebank 3-2 at Kilbowie Park with goals from Tolmie, Hopkin and Doak, the latter's 10th of the season. As touched on before, it was a superb effort by Doak who played in the centre of defence. The game's top player for me, however, was the experienced Tolmie whose touch on the ball and linking play were superb.

Promotion hopes remained faint after a home goalless draw with Kilmarnock and were finally extinguished when second top Partick won 1-0 at Firhill. With six games remaining Morton were 11 points off the pace of leaders Dundee. Allan McGraw commented: "We can forget the promotion race now." But suddenly Morton could be seen to be building the basics of a side which had definite potential.

David Hopkin signed a new three-year deal and Dougie Johnstone followed suit with a two-year contract. Alan Mahood came into the team to meet Hamilton at Cappielow in a game which began dramatically when Dougie Johnstone was ordered off in just 40 seconds. He had nudged Trevor Smith off the ball in the box and was deemed to have prevented a clear goalscoring chance.

Derek Collins moved to sweeper and, with David Hopkin excelling, the team fought back well. A great pass from Jim Tolmie put Alex Mathie in for a deserved equaliser. Morton then did well to take a point from league leaders Dundee at Dens Park, Mathie and Rafferty getting the goals and Mahood giving an impressive display for half an hour after coming on as a sub.

John Boag, finding it hard to gain a regular first team place, put in a transfer request before the side beat Meadowbank 3-1 at Cappielow, Derek Lilley, David Hopkin and Scott McArthur scoring to extend the club's unbeaten home run to 11 games. Stuart Rafferty was the architect of the better passages of play.

In the final home game of the season Martin Doak was presented with the Sir William Lithgow Trophy as Player of the Year. His defensive performances were invariably enhanced by an above average strike rate for a central defender. He scored 10 goals over the course of the season, a decent enough tally for an attacking midfielder.

Meanwhile there had been a set-back in Jim Hunter's recovery from his cruciate injury, and it was to keep him out for a further lengthy spell, more surgery being required. It was a severe blow to the player who was sent out to America for what it was hoped would be a final and successful operation.

Morton's final appearance at Stirling's Annfield ground, before they moved to a new stadium, resulted in a 4-3 victory for the hosts. McInnes, Johnstone and Alexander scored for the visitors who had been two goals ahead at one stage. Allan McGraw was an unhappy manager and blasted his team. "The attitude of my players was a disgrace," he said.

I wrote that seven goals may suggest a thrilling encounter, but I did not enjoy watching football on artificial surfaces. I always felt the football was as false as the pitch on such occasions. Once again Hopkin was Morton's star player. He was attracting increasing attention from some of the bigger clubs down south.

The final match of the season saw Ayr leapfrog Morton into sixth place after a 1-0 win at Somerset Park, Dundee and Partick Thistle being the promoted pair.

David Hopkin was invited down to Bramall Lane to look at the Sheffield United set-up, but there was no subsequent offer for the midfielder.

Allan McGraw then announced his free transfer list. Young defender Gerry Kelly had not lived up to early expectations and was joined on the list by Barry Strain, Mark Quinn, Tommy Barr and Michael Deeney. Manager McGraw was aggrieved at Deeney's failure to make something of himself. "No one has ever doubted his ability," he said, "but he has failed to produce it consistently in the first team." Deeney was to drift out of the senior game altogether, signing for Shettleston Juniors.

CHAPTER TWENTY-THREE

'Hoppy' equals transfer record

Derek Collins (23) signed a three-year deal as Morton began to prepare for the 1992-93 season in which the no-passback to the goalkeeper rule was introduced. This was a positive change, intended to deny defenders the easy option of incessant time-wasting.

Stuart Rafferty and Alex Mathie hit the net in a 2-2 friendly at Cappielow against Coventry, before Rangers arrived to trounce their hosts 8-1 in an embarrassing display in which John Spencer scored four times, the other goals coming from Hateley, McCoist, Durrant and Martin.

Attempts to set up a breakaway Premier League simmered beneath the surface, Morton in the camp doggedly opposed to such moves. John Wilson issued the following statement: "The board has discussed this at great length and we will continue to work under the auspices of the Scottish Football League and the Scottish Football Association."

In their first league appearance of the season, before a home crowd of 3,274, Morton lost 2-0 to Kilmarnock. The team lined up as follows (4-3-3): Wylie; Collins, Boag, Doak, McArthur; Mahood, McInnes, Hopkin; Mathie, Lilley, Alexander. On the Tuesday the mood was lifted when Clydebank were crushed 5-1 at Cappielow, Mathie grabbing a hat-trick and Alexander and Hopkin getting the others.

Allan McGraw, always a man to play positive football, had intimated that he was going to adopt a slightly less cavalier approach away from home, and a fine 3-0 win followed in Edinburgh against Meadowbank. A delighted manager commented: "We kept our shape throughout."

With talk of a breakaway league still rumbling on, Morton as a club backed a new plan for four leagues of 10 clubs. It was ironic as they were later to criticise just such a set-up when it finally took place.

In the Skol Cup Kilmarnock again triumphed, this time 3-2 after extra time at Cappielow, Mathie and Alexander getting the home goals. Once again, however, Morton bounced back in the league when Alex Mathie scored the only goal of the game at Dumbarton.

By this time the news came that sweeper Jim Hunter would miss the entire season. He had been sorely missed and a reference was made to him by manager McGraw after a 1-0 home defeat at the hands of derby rivals St Mirren, Barry Lavety netting after goalkeeper David Wylie and centre back John Boag had collided.

Allan McGraw, however, was adamant that any side he put out would always play to win the game and reinforced his strategy when he said: "Football is a business alright, but it's an entertainment business." His philosophy seemed justified when Morton went second top of the First Division, behind Raith Rovers, Rowan Alexander returning after injury to hit the only goal of the game against Cowdenbeath at Cappielow.

There was talk of former favourite Joe McLaughlin returning to Greenock after he had been allowed to leave Watford, but too big a fee was involved and the move never took place.

On the first Saturday of September an own goal by Robertson and one by Alan Mahood saw Morton confirm their challenge at Ayr in a 2-0 win. They were now on 10 points after seven games, two behind Raith Rovers. Allan McGraw felt the promotion race was wide open and said: "I don't think there is one really outstanding team in the league. There is nothing between the top eight."

The situation was nicely set up for a clash at Stark's Park between the top two. The game did not disappoint, though the result went against the visitors as Raith held on to win 2-1 despite an excellent second half comeback by Morton. Goals by Gordon Dalziel and Craig Brewster, Rowan Alexander replying with one for McGraw's men, settled the issue for the hosts who had been the better side in the first half.

Alex Mathie missed a penalty for Morton in a second half in which Derek McInnes and Alan Mahood had run the midfield show. "It was a good, open game with good football," commented Allan McGraw.

I reported: "McInnes has come on in leaps and bounds this season, combining strength in the tackle with incisive passing and the acceptance of more responsibility. Mahood's control, positioning and distribution suggest a player far older than his teenage years. He also has a bite which belies his slight build."

By this time Chelsea, Queen's Park Rangers and Spurs were all interested watchers of Morton's top young talent. On Tuesday 15th September McInnes and Hopkin spent a day training at Stamford Bridge, though there was no move after they returned to Greenock.

Hamilton, now under the management of Iain Munro, were then beaten 2-1 at Cappielow with goals from Alexander and Mahood. I wrote: "For me the best player on the park was the 18-year-old Alan Mahood. He gave an astonishingly mature performance, capped by a magnificent goal."

Mahood began the move in his own penalty area when he collected the ball and sent a neat pass out to John Fowler. Fowler continued the move with a good pass up the line to Alex Mathie on the right wing. When he whipped in a perfect, low cross it was Mahood who was there to pass the ball into the left hand corner of the net from just inside the Hamilton penalty area. It was a classic goal, started and finished by a class player.

David Hopkin also gave a fine display, drawing admiring glances from the assembled scouts of Manchester City and Southampton, joining those from London clubs Spurs, Chelsea and QPR. It was also a game in which David Wylie saved a penalty kick by Billy Reid.

By the following Friday, Chelsea came in with a £350,000 offer for Hopkin (22) who had joined Morton in 1989 from Port Glasgow Rangers. It was announced as equalling the record transfer fee set by Neil Orr's move to West Ham, though at the time Hal Stewart claimed that Orr had gone for £400,000. It is not, of course, uncommon for clubs to be economical with the truth on the subject of fees, mindful of its propaganda value in various circumstances.

It became clear that Allan McGraw would be seeing little, if any, of the Hopkin cash. Chairman John Wilson commented: "We are setting aside a substantial amount of the transfer fee to go towards upgrading the ground in accordance with the Taylor Report."

A 1-1 draw at Stirling, in which Scott McArthur scored, saw Morton slip to fourth place, five points behind Raith, as the English battalions turned their focus on Derek McInnes. David Hopkin then contacted me to pass on his thanks to the Cappielow fans. He had not always been their favourite and he said: "I'd like to thank the fans. I had a rough time at the start, but I stuck at it and proved a lot of people wrong." There were also generous words for manager Allan McGraw and his assistant, John McMaster. "I enjoyed my time there. I learned a lot from John and the boss."

Forfar were then dumped out of the first round of the B & Q Cup when Alex Mathie hit his second hat-trick for the club, Alan Mahood and Rowan Alexander contributing a goal apiece. It took Mathie to nine goals for the season and he was now beginning to make his own impression on attendant scouts who continued to hover expectantly at Morton matches.

At last, however, there was an incoming transfer when Steve McCahill signed on a free transfer from Celtic, whom he had joined in a £100,000 deal from Dumbarton. McCahill, who was wanted by other clubs, explained his decision: "It's my home town team and they have Premier League ambitions." His arrival helped dissipate some of the irritation sections of the support were expressing at the departure of another top player.

Dunfermline then recorded a single-goal victory at Cappielow, manager Jocky Scott saying it had been "a great result for us". The game was remarkable for a second appearance of Morton fan Stuart Cameron as a stand-in linesman. Stuart, who had made his 'debut' in February, was called upon at half-time, much to the delight of his Greenock Telegraph chums with whom he had sponsored the game. Buoyed up by some much appreciated hospitality, including a few glasses of the singing ginger, they greeted every hoisting of his flag with a huge cheer, as if it were the launching of a Clydeside liner.

Allan McGraw chose that week to express his anger at Andy Roxburgh and his under-21 manager Craig Brown for not including Alan Mahood in Brown's recently announced squad. In a fine imitation of Victor Meldrew, McGraw exclaimed: "I don't believe it!"

With transfer speculation now centred on Derek McInnes, Queen's Park Rangers came in with an offer which was turned down out of hand, Allan McGraw saying: "It was nowhere near our valuation."

Morton's decline in the league table continued when they lost 3-0 at Rugby Park, Kilmarnock well worth their win. Always honest, Allan McGraw accepted the blame on this occasion. "I asked my players to do a job they're not used to," he said, referring to a change of tactics which led to Morton slipping to sixth place in the division.

I believed some on the board at Cappielow were indulging in over optimism and wrote: "Morton have stated that their priority at the moment is to upgrade their stadium. In view of the Taylor Report [which demanded all-seated grounds at Premier League grounds] and their own Premier League ambitions that is a fair enough objective, but one would hope there is a sense of realism to go with it.

"You can't sell all your best players, spend all your money on the ground, and have a promotion-winning team into the bargain."

Goals from Rafferty and Lilley gave Morton a 2-1 home win over Ayr which lifted them up to fourth place in the league, five points behind pace-setters Raith Rovers. Derek Lilley was one of the better performers and I said: "If the 18-year-old can develop the control to go with his other assets he will become some player."

There was another marvellous display too by Alan Mahood. "He is quality from the top of his head to the tips of his toes," I reported.

For the second game running it was Lilley who popped up to net the winning goal in the dying minutes, this time at Kilmarnock in the B & Q Cup. Tommy Burns had given the home team the lead only for Alex Mathie to equalise before Lilley snatched victory with five minutes to go. Morton's team that Wednesday night was in 4-4-2 formation as follows: Wylie; Collins, Johnstone, Doak, Pickering; Mahood, McInnes, Rafferty, Tolmie; Mathie, Lilley.

Craig Brown was in attendance and I sought him out after the final whistle to ask why Alan Mahood was not featuring in his under-21 squad, bearing in mind Allan McGraw's recent criticism. I wrote: "According to Brown, on the occasions they have watched Morton, Mahood has not particularly impressed." Brown said: "I've watched him once and Andy [Roxburgh] has seen him once, and we have had him watched on two or three other occasions. The message we are getting is that he is potential. I'd like to see him go forward past people more and make more forward passes."

I put it to Craig Brown, politely, that Mahood had been doing precisely that for most of the season. His goal against Hamilton was a perfect case in point. How could any midfielder be more positive than to start a move in his own penalty area and finish it in the opposition's by planting the ball in the net? Brown, equally politely, said that he took my point on board and would continue to monitor the player's development. He also said that he had been impressed by Derek Lilley and was disappointed to learn that Dougie Johnstone was over the age limit for his squad. Privately, I felt Mahood may have to learn to walk on water before he would wear the navy blue at under-21 level.

As November progressed, Morton turned down a bid of £150,000 for striker Alex Mathie from Kevin Keegan's high-flying Newcastle United while team doctor Craig Speirs was called up by Andy Roxburgh to be Scotland's medic in attendance for a World Cup qualifier at Ibrox against Italy.

Morton then announced that they would require an average attendance of between seven and eight thousand to support a Premier League team. The average in the 1978-79 season, Morton's first appearance in the top league under Benny Rooney, had been 8,079 according to the club's own figures issued in their programme. It seemed to me to be wildly optimistic to expect a return to such numbers given the continuing population decline and economic gloom in Inverclyde. It made me wonder whether promotion was ever going to be viable if that was the budgeted expectation of the potential fan base.

A statement said: "Upgrading of Cappielow is our principal priority. Transferred player replacement will come from our youth team talent which to date has never let us down."

No one reasonably could be expected to sustain indefinitely the success Morton had enjoyed in the transfer market through the sale of youth. There would be lean years, as even Jim McLean had discovered at Dundee United.

On Tuesday 24th November, Hamilton beat Morton 3-1 at Douglas Park, Derek McInnes getting the consolation goal. It was a useful psychological boost before the B & Q Cup Final between the clubs on Sunday 13th December at Love Street. Allan McGraw summed up succinctly: "They wanted it more than we did."

On the final Saturday of the month the Raith Rovers bandwagon rolled up at Cappielow. Under player-coach Jimmy Nicholl they were going from strength to strength and thoroughly deserved their top place. It was described by Allan McGraw as a "must-win match".

In a seven-goal extravaganza Rovers emerged the victors by 4-3. Gordon Dalziel, so often the executioner of Morton, struck twice, Craig Brewster and Peter Hetherston adding the others. It extended the Kirkcaldy club's unbeaten run to 26 matches. The question now was: "Who is going to be second?"

Morton had slumped to sixth place, eight points behind the leaders. Alan Mahood, presumably still not getting forward enough for Craig Brown, scored twice for the beaten hosts but had to limp off at the interval. At the time it seemed unimportant. It was to prove a fateful injury.

Kevin McGoldrick, who had shown tremendous promise in the Scotland under-15 side, was turning out to be a less than ideal prospect. Farmed out to Arthurlie Juniors, he had failed to turn up for training and was subsequently suspended by the club. How often young talent is wasted by a lack of self-discipline. Or a lack of common sense. Or both.

A 0-0 draw at Dunfermline was followed by a 2-2 home draw with Stirling, Johnstone and the returning Dave McCabe getting the home strikes.

Having dropped five points behind second top Killie, Morton's season now increasingly depended for success upon the B & Q Cup Final.

Derek Lilley missed the game due to a build-up of fluid on a knee, as a crowd of 7,391 turned up at Love Street, a comfortable majority supporting Morton. Their side lined up as follows (4-4-2): Wylie; Collins, Johnstone, Doak, Pickering; Mahood, McInnes, Rafferty, Tolmie; Mathie, Alexander.

It was Hamilton who rose to the challenge, deservedly winning 3-2. Morton never settled to any sort of pattern despite a heroic effort up front from two-goal Rowan Alexander who lacked support from an unusually out of touch Alex Mathie. Allan McGraw said: "Hamilton deserved to win. We never really got going."

Disappointing as the defeat was, the real disaster came in the form of a cruciate ligament injury to Alan Mahood. Heavily strapped as a result of that knee injury sustained in the Raith Rovers match, he tore cruciate ligaments in the same knee and was ruled out for the rest of the season. Mahood was to make a recovery after an operation in America, but there were parallels with a similar injury to Rangers' Ian Durrant. Mahood returned, becoming a fine player again, but I believe he never fulfilled his true potential. Like Durrant, instead of becoming a great player, he had to settle for being a very good one.

John Boag meanwhile was fixed up by Dumbarton, then Newcastle came in again for Alex Mathie. Their bid of £200,000 plus a further £50,000 upon the completion of a set number of matches was rejected. Celtic, from whom Morton had bought Mathie, would be due a percentage of any sell-on fee.

Mathie had scored in a 3-1 defeat at Dumbarton which resulted in the visiting support venting their wrath on the players, though some appeasement came in a fine performance to beat Kilmarnock 2-0, Alexander and Johnstone scoring.

The mood, however, was one of frustration among the support, criticism coming through the letters pages of the Greenock Telegraph and from among the crowd at games.

The New Year of 1993 was heralded by a 1-1 home draw with St Mirren before 5,170 fans. McInnes scored the home goal in a match in which Saints' goalkeeper Campbell Money suffered a leg break in a collision, and home custodian David Wylie saved the day with a penalty save from Gallagher. Of goalscorer McInnes (21), Allan McGraw commented: "Derek has done very well for us recently. He is taking more responsibility in the team and is relishing it." The manager also revealed that he had probably played McInnes too often for his own good in the early part of his career due to injuries to other players.

In the Scottish Cup, Arbroath's Sorbie left a bitter taste in Morton mouths when his hat-trick catapulted the Greenock men out at the third round stage. Allan McGraw was coruscating in his criticism of his players after the 3-0 result. "That was the worst cup performance I've seen since I became manager. It didn't seem like a cup tie to me. We only played for about 10 minutes."

Almost inevitably it was bitterly cold at Gayfield Park, situated as it is almost in the North Sea. Two female Red Lichties fans, seated behind the chittering, fleece-lined members of the press corps, provided some warmth with their commentary. While their male companions spoke glowingly of the footballing expertise of their heroes on the day, Gillian announced to all and sundry that the man-of-the-match award should go to "the guy with the best bum and legs". Her pal, Terri, at one point suggested that the two girls should embark upon a streak across the park. This struck us listeners as not so much daring as positively suicidal. To streak across Gayfield in mid-winter is possibly one of the great challenges left to mankind – Hilary and Tensing climb Everest! Terri and Gillian run naked across Gayfield in mid-winter!

Alexander, Tolmie and Lilley were out injured, Mahood was off to America for an operation, and promotion was now very much an outside bet. Also undergoing the knife, yet again, was manager Allan McGraw whose knee continued to give him considerable pain. Meanwhile Morton, in an attempt to ward off a breakaway Premier Division, had backed a new proposal of three leagues of 14-12-12. It was voted down by the bigger clubs.

David Hopkin, back up in Scotland to see his family and friends, then admitted in conversation that he very nearly missed out on a decent future in football. He said: "My football career was nearly over after the trouble in Ayrshire and I took a lot of stick for it. But in the end it did me good." This was in reference to the bother he got into along with young team-mates Gary Stevenson and Derek Anderson outside a nightclub. It resulted in Stevenson and Anderson getting the metaphorical boot while Hopkin was allowed to keep his actual ones. It was the Port lad's talent that no doubt persuaded management to fine him rather than show him the door. He was to appreciate that decision. Ach, there is nothing like a repentant sinner.

Young Craig Brown then broke a leg playing against Rangers Reserves while, on the final Saturday of January, a Scott McArthur goal gained a point at Meadowbank.

Dave McCabe had been battling back to full fitness and a fine hat-trick condemned Cowdenbeath to a 3-2 defeat at Cappielow. Assistant gaffer John McMaster described it as McCabe's "best game in a Morton jersey."

By now Alan Mahood had returned from America after a four-hour operation in the Sherman Oakes Hospital in Los Angeles to restore his knee. He was expected to be in recovery for at least nine months.

Stephen McCahill was back to full fitness following his transfer from Celtic and he gave a commanding display in a 0-0 draw at Ayr which followed a home 1-0 loss to Dunfermline. David Wylie and Dougie Johnstone were also top performers.

Morton's form was patchy, but two consecutive wins – 2-0 at home to Clydebank, goals by McArthur and Lilley, and 2-0 away to Stirling, the same players scoring the goals – revived a promotion push for the second place in the table.

The Stirling match took place in gale force winds which, I wrote: "every so often whipped up clouds of dust, sand and red blaes. Had Hal Stewart still been alive he would have turned up in the second half with half a dozen Bedouins, properly signed and registered."

There was a nice touch, unique in my reporting experience, when, after the game, referee Andrew Waddell made a point of commending the Morton players for their sporting behaviour during the match. Some light relief was also afforded by the home groundsman who, on several occasions, had to take a ladder to retrieve the ball, blown by the gale over a wall adjoining a builder's yard. Scottish football at its best! All we needed was a stray mongrel to maraud across the pitch.

Just when Morton were rallying, Hamilton arrived at Cappielow to grab the points in a 2-1 win, veteran Rowan Alexander scoring the home goal. Academicals' top performer was elusive winger Paul McDonald who was booked for kicking out at Morton left back Mark Pickering. Former Celtic centre half John Cushley, reporting in a press capacity, turned to me and uttered: "That makes it 10-1 to Pickering." Pickering was a hard wee fellow but, in fairness, he took anything dished out to him in return. He bounced back up after McDonald's well aimed boot, not favouring the dying swan act of so many of our modern day professionals.

Another trip to Stark's Park beckoned. By this time Raith were champions-elect. Awaiting Morton, as always, was Gordon Dalziel. He hit his 29th goal of a memorable season, Craig Brewster adding a second as the hosts won 2-0. I was to write: "So much about Morton these days is "ifs and buts", even looking ahead to next season; if Jim Hunter proves his fitness; if Alex Mathie and Derek McInnes are around; if Alan Mahood makes a full recovery."

Off the pitch it was announced that the diamond-patterned shirts which had divided views among the fans would be replaced by even more controversial tartan outfits next season. The mind boggled. Would it be sprigs of heather in Glengarries next?

Jim Tolmie and Martin Doak scored in a 2-2 draw at Kilmarnock, Doak, in gentlemanly fashion, managing to score for both sides. Scott McArthur and Alex Mathie hit the goals which led to a 2-0 win over Meadowbank at Cappielow.

By now the big clubs had thrown themselves behind a new league set-up of four leagues of 10. Allan McGraw was a critic and said: "The skill factor is going out of the game and this sort of system will make things worse. There are not enough youngsters being blooded and there will be even less with this sort of set-up." These are words which echo down resonantly to this day.

Lavety and Gallagher then put Morton to the sword in another derby clash, this time at Love Street, leading John McMaster to say: "The sooner some players start looking at themselves the better. There's a lack of ambition and pride, and that hurts."

Port Vale were now interested in Alex Mathie and took him south on loan for a month. It was a move which angered large numbers of the Morton support who were being told that the club were still chasing promotion. How could they, therefore, let their top striker leave for a month? It was a more than reasonable question to ask.

Defender Graham Ogg then broke a leg while training with Preston North End. It was a personal blow to the player, though by this time he had not been part of Morton's first team plans.

Amid mounting criticism about the departure of Mathie on loan, chairman John Wilson announced that there would be a £200,000 per annum loss were it not for transfer income. It was also stated that upgrading of the ground would take between five and seven years. The Premier League seemed to be fading over the horizon.

It was clear there was growing concern among the fans, and only 953 turned out for a league match at home to Dumbarton, goals by old hands Gahagan and Alexander bringing in two points in a 2-1 win. Playing for the Sons was former centre back John Boag, while watching in the stand was Blackburn boss Kenny Dalglish who was taking a keen interest in the progress of Derek Lilley.

While Dalglish was pondering on the merits of Lilley, Gerry Francis of Queen's Park Rangers was keen to bring Derek McInnes to London. The player went down to the capital to train, returning in time to take part in a 1-0 home victory over Ayr, Dougie Johnstone scoring against his home town team. It was McInnes who made the goal with a great pass on to Johnstone who had stolen in on the blind side of the visiting defence and, under pressure, shot home from the inside left channel.

McInnes then departed for a second week of training with QPR before again returning to play at Cowdenbeath where Morton won 1-0. I reported from Fife: "Central Park has all the air of a derelict building site about it. With some 300 fans scattered about its draughty environs, and a park with more bumps than Yul Brynner's dome, only the supremely optimistic had any expectations of anything approaching a classic."

Stuart Rafferty came on as a substitute to a chorus of boos from Fife fans who remembered his days at rivals Dunfermline. Some Morton fans joined in – Stuart not being flavour of the month at the time. The player had told me before the game: "I'm really going to enjoy it if I score here today." And he did, with two minutes left on the clock, silencing the home support and earning the grudging praise of sections of Morton's own following.

Raith Rovers then arrived at Cappielow as worthy champions, Morton aiming to prevent a clean sweep by the Kirkcaldy men. Gordon Dalziel had become a personal nightmare for the Greenock club, having scored four goals in three encounters already that season, to add to seven from five games the previous term. For once he had a quiet 90 minutes and Morton managed a 1-1 draw, Rowan Alexander's 10th-minute opener being cancelled out by Craig Brewster.

Hamilton then recorded a 2-1 win over the Greenock side, for whom John Gahagan hit a consolation strike, though there was a controversial moment when a Rafferty drive was deflected towards his own net by Andy Millen. The ball appeared to hit one of the stanchions at the back of the net and rebound out of the goal, but the referee saw nothing untoward and Morton dropped down to sixth place.

Alex Mathie returned from Port Vale who were keen to sign him, but not at the price Morton wanted. Mathie was now beginning to feel a touch aggrieved and said: "The Port Vale manager said he wanted to sign me but felt £300,000 was too much – and I agree with him."

Having already seen a possible move to Newcastle fall through, Mathie felt Morton were not honouring an agreement, made at the time of his move from Celtic, that he would be allowed to go if a bigger club came in for him in future. Manager McGraw said: "I know that Alex is anxious to move, but there will be no cut-price deals."

Injuries were a concern when youngsters Neil Shearer and Denis McGhee played in a home match with Clydebank, Dave McCabe grabbing both goals in a 2-2 draw, then Derek Collins was named as the season's Player of the Year after the annual vote by Greenock Telegraph readers.

The season was drawing to a close and Allan McGraw was an angry man after watching a performance which he described as the "worst ever in my managerial career" when Stirling won 3-1 at Cappielow, Alex Mathie netting the home goal. Graham Ogg, Mick Kerr, Darren Murray and John Dickson were all freed before Dunfermline's promotion hopes were shattered when Morton produced one of their better results of the season with a 2-1 victory at East End Park, Alex McEwan scoring both goals. It left the Pars in third spot, behind Kilmarnock, in the league. After the match Morton boss McGraw took the tough decision to free striker Dave McCabe who two seasons ago had finished as the club's top scorer, but who had missed much of the time since on the injured list.

By this time Morton were able to say that Alan Mahood was not expected back in action for another six to seven months.

A youth side was entered into a new eight-team league, involving most of the bigger clubs, and the close season speculation began over possible transfer deals. Allan McGraw wanted to bring back Neil Orr to Cappielow after the 34-year-old had been freed by Hibernian, but Orr opted instead for a better deal at full-time St Mirren.

Alec Grace, a Clydebank striker who had been freed by West Bromwich Albion, and former Celtic midfielder Mark Donaghy were given deals, while Stuart Rafferty was re-signed on a one-year contract.

Chairman John Wilson then announced that a sum of £70-80,000 was to be spent on the main stand, most of it unseen work beneath the structure affecting its safety. He went on to say: "We would hope to consolidate our position next season and, if possible, get ourselves into a promotion situation." He revealed that there would be no money to provide covering for either end of the ground.

CHAPTER TWENTY-FOUR

Chairman Wilson faces fans' ire as Ton go down

As July, 1993, came to a close, Alex Mathie finally got his wish when Newcastle returned with an offer of £250,000, subject to a certain number of first team games being played. It meant that Morton had taken in almost £1.5 million in approximately three years.

In an unprecedented move John Wilson revealed the exact figures relating to transfer income and outgoings. He stated that income in the last three years had amounted to £1,475,000, while player costs had amounted to £245,000, minus signing-on fees.

I could not see any realistic possibility of a promotion challenge and wrote: "Morton chairman John Wilson has gone on record as saying that ground upgrading is the priority, and it may be that local dreams of promotion will have to remain just that."

In a pre-season friendly with a Rangers side containing several fringe players, Morton won 2-0 with goals from Rowan Alexander and Ricky Thomson. Outstanding were Derek McInnes and goalkeeper David Wylie. Meanwhile old Cappielow favourite Joe Harper, who had opened a local pub, predicted a title success for Falkirk in what was going to be an intense First Division campaign. Five clubs would be relegated from the league as the divisions sorted themselves out into four groups of 10. Two new clubs would be elected into the senior leagues. Promotion hopes were fanciful, in my view. "Put at its simplest," I commented, "success this season for Morton will be to remain in the First Division."

Of the impending move to 10-club leagues Allan McGraw was scathing, saying: "It's a ridiculous and unfair system that was decided by people who don't know anything about football."

The league began ominously with a 2-1 defeat at Clyde, the old warhorse Alexander scoring for the visitors. Spirits were raised, however, when goals by Jim Tolmie and Derek Lilley saw Kilmarnock exit the League Cup on their own ground. Making his debut for Morton was midfielder Mark Donaghy.

It was a time of turmoil among the Morton fans who could see no evidence of significant ground improvement for all the players who had left Cappielow. Obscene graffiti was daubed on the walls at Cappielow, leading John Wilson to threaten to quit if there was any repetition. He said: "We have brought a club back from the brink of liquidation to a state where we no longer have to go cap in hand to the bank or anyone else."

There was no justification for the abuse he had received, but those who resorted to it were the unacceptable face of a general disquiet among many perfectly reasonable fans.

Most folk accepted that ground improvements had to be made, and that they would be costly. But there was a growing dissatisfaction with what was seen by many to be the indecent haste with which young talent was sold to the extent of impoverishing the team. In the second league match of the season Jim Jefferies' Falkirk favourites arrived in Greenock to administer a 5-1 skelping, Martin Doak's goal being scant consolation. Allan McGraw's verdict was that "Falkirk played well, but everything went for them. I can't criticise my players. They worked their tails off and played some good football. But we didn't take our chances and they did."

In an interview Neil Orr then explained why he had chosen St Mirren rather than a return to his first senior club. "It was a tough decision to make," he said. "I was tempted to come back to Morton, as I was keen to work with Allan McGraw. I also had an offer from Donald Park to go to Meadowbank as player/coach.

"Things changed when St Mirren came in for me, however. They are full-time in every sense, including money, and I was impressed with the set-up. And the fact that Morton seem to sell most of their best young players while St Mirren keep theirs for longer played its part too."

It was a revealing statement which reflected the mood in many ways of the Morton support regarding the sale of players.

In a fiery derby, St Mirren and Morton shared the honours in a 2-2 draw at Love Street in which six players were booked and one, St Mirren's Paul Lambert, was sent off. Donaghy, with his first goal for the club, and Doak were the scorers. On the following Tuesday night Premier League Partick knocked Morton out of the League Cup with a single goal victory in Greenock, though John Lambie was generous towards the vanquished, saying: "I was impressed by some of the Morton lads. Derek Lilley gave us a lot of problems." Allan McGraw felt his side had played the better football, but minus a cutting edge.

Two welcome points were taken from a home 2-1 win against Brechin City, Derek Lilley scoring both goals to give the home side three points from their opening four fixtures.

Morton then, suddenly, became Greenock Morton – officially. The explanation given was that it would identify the team more with their home town, though it irritated many traditionalists who felt everyone knew only too well where Morton came from.

Alex MacDonald's Airdrie team, third top of the league, then beat eighth-placed Morton 2-0 at Broomfield and already the warning signs were all too clear. I wrote: "Morton finished above six teams last season. This time they must stay ahead of five. They may have to add to their squad, sooner rather than later, to give themselves every reasonable chance of achieving their objective."

Clydebank then crushed the Cappielow men 3-0 at Kilbowie Park to leave the Greenock side in third bottom position. I reported: "While Morton were failing to make an impression at one end, they were gifting opportunities at the other."

Steve McCahill made a scoring return from injury in a 2-2 draw at home to Stirling, Jim Tolmie netting the other goal.

Next up were Bert Paton's Dunfermline who thrashed Morton 4-0 at East End Park. That was the catalyst for an outpouring of anger in the local press. Some relief was obtained by a 3-1 home victory over Dumbarton in which Derek Collins, Martin Doak (penalty) and Alex McEwan scored. "There is no denying Alex's skill," commented Allan McGraw, "but his attitude lets him down at times. He's a bit lazy and doesn't mark up properly."

When another point was taken from a 2-2 draw at Ayr, McEwan again being on target to complement a Scott own goal, Allan McGraw was an altogether happier manager. He said: "We are on the road back." Stuart Rafferty was the top player for the visitors and McGraw continued: "Raff gets a bit of stick from the Morton fans but he proved them wrong. His passing was superb."

Hamilton beat Morton 2-1 at Cappielow, Jim Tolmie scoring, before Clyde took a point from Greenock in a 1-1 draw, McEwan again scoring for the beleaguered hosts who had slumped to second bottom position. It was a position they stayed in after a 1-1 draw at Stirling in which Derek McInnes scored.

It was revealed that veteran striker Rowan Alexander would be given a testimonial match, but the gloom continued to descend when county rivals St Mirren sent Morton crashing out of the B & Q Cup by a 4-2 margin at Cappielow, Alexander and Tolmie scoring for the hosts. A goalless draw with Clydebank followed at Cappielow, before Allan McGraw revealed that Jim Hunter was on his way back to fitness after an absence of more than two years. Hunter, now 28, had worked valiantly to prove his fitness.

St Mirren plunged the dagger deeper into Morton's side with a 2-1 Cappielow success, none other than Neil Orr hitting the winner. Even the home goal came from St Mirren's Baker. Orr was magnanimous afterwards, saying: "It's always nice to score but I felt a draw would have been a fair result."

By this time the Morton board had acknowledged that fresh blood was required. It is never a good time to buy when you are desperate, and three bids for strikers were all unsuccessful.

Rowan Alexander then hit all three goals in a valuable win at Brechin, prompting him to say: "I feel great. It's only the third hat-trick I've scored for Morton and the first for ages." On the negative side, Derek McInnes was injured, joining Stuart Rafferty on the sidelines as the Morton crocked list mounted.

Young midfielder Steve Aitken made his debut in a goalless draw with Airdrie at Cappielow as illness compounded the Greenock club's injury catalogue. It was a match Morton had tried to have postponed. The request was dismissed by the Scottish Football League, leading to John Wilson resigning from the League's management committee. He fumed: "I believe they have impugned the integrity of our club and particularly our doctor and officials."

Out of contention were Pickering, Johnstone, Hunter, Doak, McInnes, Rafferty, Mahood, Lilley, McEwan and Brown. Of those Hunter and Mahood were, of course, long term injuries. The League's response through Peter Donald was to point out that Morton still had sufficient registered players to fulfil the fixtures, but it did little to assuage the Greenock club's ire.

Things were going from bad to worse. Hamilton knocked four past David Wylie in a 4-1 defeat on their own patch, Rowan Alexander scoring the sole visitors' effort, before the striker was sent off the following week at Cappielow in a 1-0 defeat by Ayr. Two more transfer deals fell through and November ended with a 2-0 defeat at Dumbarton. It caused me to write: "Morton plumbed the depths with this performance at Boghead. Vociferous sections of the visiting support expressed their anger – crudely at times – with chants for the removal of chairman John Wilson, his board of directors, and manager Allan McGraw."

Morton were hampered in the extreme by injuries but I wrote: "It does seem to me that Morton's stated policy last season, reaffirmed after the departure of Alex Mathie to Newcastle, that money would not be made available to the manager for incoming replacements is also backfiring on them now.

"While no one could have foreseen the present injury crisis, and that is something that can't be brushed aside, the signs were there that Morton needed an injection of fresh blood for the start of this campaign. The team, after all, finished sixth last season. They knew five teams were going down and that there would be no Hopkin, Mahood or Mathie in the ranks. Now money is available, but the right time to buy is never in the midst of a slump."

John Wilson chose to hit back at those who had abused him and his fellow directors and manager. "I will not allow these oafs," he said, "to change the way we are running the club."

I commented: "Substantial numbers of fans have lost patience with what they perceive as the steady decline of their side."

Once more Morton appealed to the League for the postponement of the forthcoming match against Dunfermline. Once more they were told to play. Manager McGraw said: "This is the worst injury situation we have ever experienced," while doctor Craig Speirs described it as "exceptional".

In the event Morton drew 0-0 with the Pars as the criticism continued from the support. It grew no less when, with five players back from injury, Stirling arrived in Greenock and won 1-0 in the run-up to Christmas.

As the voices of disapproval grew louder, John Wilson responded by revealing detailed plans of a new all-seated stand to be built at the Sinclair Street end of the ground. Phase two would entail the covering of the Wee Dublin End. That was all very well, but it was accompanied by a statement that the finance would have to come from the future sale of more players. The club's financial position was in the black, but only by £79,000 as stated by the chairman.

This effectively meant there would be no stands built in the foreseeable future. In a further statement the club said: "It is critical that Morton remain in the First Division. No way can Morton contemplate slipping down into what would be the Third Division." Such thoughts surely should have produced at least one or two signings during the close season.

Further gloom was provided when it became apparent that 22-year-old Derek McInnes was next to undergo surgery on a dislocated knee problem. Although not as severe as the damage sustained by Jim Hunter and Alan Mahood, the club could be expected to say goodbye to him for the rest of the season. December was anything but full of tidings of comfort and joy.

New Year, however, came in with some good news for a change. Making his first appearance since August, 1991, when he suffered severe cruciate ligament damage at Hamilton, was sweeper Jim Hunter. It was a hugely welcome return for a player who had become a key member of the team. It is to Morton's great credit that they had stuck by him through thick and thin in his recovery progress. As it turned out it was a splendid return to action, in an otherwise disappointing 1-1 home draw with Brechin. I reported on what became a magical comeback: "He put in two or three impressive tackles and, in fairy-tale fashion, scored his first ever goal for the club in a career spanning almost 10 years. It was a stunning drive into the bargain."

Morton badly needed a run of results to carry them up the table, but a visit to league leaders Falkirk resulted in a deflating 5-1 defeat, Ricky Thomson getting the team's sole counter. They were now nine points behind Stirling who occupied the seventh safety spot in the division.

Falkirk gaffer Jim Jefferies was sympathetic to the Greenock club's plight and said: "They have good players, but the pressure on teams like them with five clubs going down is horrendous. I feel sorry for Allan McGraw. It's a terrible situation to be in."

The travelling support was up in arms against their manager, board and team. Scarves were discarded and the police eventually moved a small band of protesters out of the ground.

Criticism was becoming constant. In a comment piece I wrote of the calls for the manager to resign: "Supporters may decry the policy of utilising the money from transfers for ground improvement rather than bolstering the team, but that is a club policy, not the manager's, whether he may or may not agree with it.

"It is not a simple argument either as to whether money be spent on ground or team. The sensible debate concerns what proportion of money should go towards necessary improvements and what constitutes 'necessary' and desirable for a club like Morton: but the priority this season should have been to remain in the First Division.

"There was understandable anger among the fans over the Alex Mathie loan deal at the end of last season to Port Vale, and I sympathise with that. But that was a deal carried out at board level in opposition to the manager's view. Neither can Allan McGraw be blamed for a horrific injury list, and it is only recently that money has been made available to him for incoming transfers.

"That is money which, injury situation or not, ought to have been on hand at the start of the season. It should not surprise anyone that quality players are now unwilling to come to Cappielow given Morton's current plight.

"Everyone is entitled to his or her opinion, and there will be frustrated fans on the terracings and well meaning men in the boardroom at Cappielow who will not agree with mine. Whatever their views, I don't believe that Morton's current problems would be made better by the removal of the manager."

The following day it was revealed that out of favour Falkirk striker Scott Sloan was the latest to turn down a move to Morton.

When you're down, nothing seems to go right. St Mirren then administered another 5-1 whacking, Alex McEwan getting the Morton goal at Love Street. Relegation was now virtually a certainty, although the club still believed the situation could be turned round. Hope was kept alive by a 1-1 draw at Cappielow against Falkirk, Martin Doak getting the home goal. It was a game in which central defender John Anderson made a competent debut on trial from Gourock YAC, Jim Hunter, David Wylie and Jim Tolmie all doing well. Anderson subsequently put pen to paper as a welcome addition to Morton's injury-hit ranks.

Morton had drawn Cowdenbeath in the third round of the Scottish Cup and they looked to be making an embarrassing exit at Cappielow when they were two down with two minutes to play. Their blushes were saved with late strikes by Alex McEwan and Derek Lilley. The fans' wrath was overheating.

Third top Airdrie were then held to a 2-2 draw at Broomfield, McEwan notching a double in a fine first half in which the visitors played some of their best football of the season, most of it inspired by Jim Tolmie. At one point the game came very close to being called off due to driving snow.

A goalless draw followed at Clydebank before Morton won their cup replay at Cowdenbeath, goals coming from John Anderson, his first for the club, and McEwan.

It gave the side some respite from the increasingly disgruntled support, and a 2-2 home draw was gained against Hamilton, John Anderson grabbing an equaliser in the fifth minute of injury time. The other goal came from Ricky Thomson, while Tolmie again was the star performer.

Then the injury jinx struck again. Martin Doak had gone into hospital for what he thought was to be a routine cartilage op, only to be told that the lining of a knee was crumbling and he would have to quit football. It was stunning news to the player. Manager McGraw said: "It's a blow to the club, but a bigger blow to the boy."

Doak had been an excellent club man. He had won the last Player of the Year Award and, for a defender, he had a remarkable strike rate, often popping up to net valuable goals. It was later arranged that he would be given a benefit game against Rangers.

He was there watching in the stand when his team-mates took on Kilmarnock in the fourth round of the cup at Cappielow the following day. Twenty-one-year-old John Anderson was outstanding. Jim Tolmie continued his fine form, playing off the front men, but a Bobby Williamson goal saw Killie through to the next round.

The following Tuesday Clyde and Morton fought out a goalless draw at the Greenock club's first visit to Broadwood Stadium, the Bully Wee's new home. It was a dire display between the third and second bottom pair. Allan McGraw summed up: "That was the worst I've seen. Fear shouldn't stop players making 10-yard passes." Had it not been for a brilliant display by goalkeeper David Wylie it would have been far worse.

Jim Tolmie was sent off for two bookable offences in a 2-1 defeat by Ayr in which Rowan Alexander scored. Second bottom Morton were now 12 points adrift of the seventh safety position in the table. Second top Dunfermline comfortably secured a 3-0 home win against the Greenock men, the one bright spot of the week being Alan Mahood's return to fitness. He played for half an hour in Martin Doak's benefit match against Rangers at Cappielow, won by an Ally McCoist goal before a crowd of 3,098. Morton were indebted to the Ibrox men for bringing down pumping gear on the day of the game to help clear water following a downpour of Biblical proportions. Playing on trial for Morton was Forfar striker David Bingham, but no business was done after the match.

On Martin Doak, Cappielow boss McGraw said: "He's been a tremendous professional for Morton. It was just a lack of pace that stopped him moving to a bigger club."

Doak had always been a reliable defender, versatile enough too to fill in when necessary in midfield, and always with the capacity to score goals.

It was then revealed that Derek McInnes faced an operation after his dislocated knee had failed to heal properly, ruling him out for at least the rest of the season.

An attendance of 1,046 watched a goalless draw at home to Dumbarton before some relief was offered by a fine 3-0 win away to Stirling in which Alan Mahood started the game. Scott McArthur (2) and Derek Lilley were on target. It was the first win since 6th November. Relegation was still a virtual certainty, but the gloom was further lifted when Mahood confirmed his comeback against Clyde at Cappielow. I reported: "Alan Mahood celebrated his 21st birthday in some style at Cappielow on Saturday, using the key to the door to unlock the Clyde defence." It was his first full 90 minutes since sustaining that severe cruciate injury in December of 1992.

Two successive victories were a great fillip, but Morton were still no better off than third bottom in a season in which five teams were to be relegated.

Falkirk won 1-0 at Brockville before a further point was secured at Clydebank in a 1-1 draw, Rowan Alexander scoring. Alexander was on target again, along with Mahood, in a 3-2 loss at Douglas Park against Hamilton. It was a defeat which preceded a stormy week for Morton.

First, director John Kerr resigned. He was unavailable for comment. Kerr, as a friend of Allan McGraw's, principally worked for Morton in a scouting capacity along with Bert Reid. These two men organised the Glasgow end of Morton's youth policy. Kerr had been outspoken over two years beforehand, claiming that he had been forced to fund the operation himself. A wealthy businessman himself, he had offered to buy shares from chairman John Wilson to the extent where no one person had full control of Morton. It was an offer which was rejected. Kerr, in co-operation with former Ayr player Alex Ingram, then made an unsuccessful bid to take over Kilmarnock before he eventually decided to accept the offer to become a director at Cappielow.

There were clearly tensions, and Allan McGraw commented on Kerr's departure: "It's always sad when someone resigns. I'd like to thank him for all the work he has put in and for the players he has brought to the club."

The following Saturday Morton were officially relegated when Ayr, still desperately trying to save themselves from the drop, grabbed two vital points at Cappielow in a 1-0 win.

Second top Dunfermline drew 2-2 at Cappielow, the home goals coming from John Anderson and Rowan Alexander. Pars boss Bert Paton added his voice to those who were critical of the forthcoming four-league set-up of 10 clubs each, saying that it would undoubtedly hamper the production of good young players.

Meanwhile criticism of Morton was growing increasingly among their own fan base, and the chairman agreed to hold a meeting with some of the aggrieved at the Morton Supporters' Club. This took place on the morning before a home 2-1 defeat by derby rivals St Mirren, the Paisley team's fourth such success of the season, in which Derek Lilley scored.

At the meeting with the fans, John Wilson announced that he was to quit as chairman of the club. He also stated that manager Allan McGraw would be sacked at the end of the following season if the team did not win promotion back to the new First Division.

The story was carried in the local paper on Monday. Mr Wilson would still be retaining his 88% shareholding in the club, but he claimed a new chairman would be appointed from the existing board, whatever that effectively meant.

It was also stated that assistant manager John McMaster would be the reserve and youth coach, with a new assistant manager being appointed, and that there would be a re-think on ground development.

Controversially, John Wilson said quite clearly that money had, in fact, been made available to manager Allan McGraw for new players after the transfer of Alex Mathie to Newcastle, a complete reversal of previous statements.

I commented: "Last season, after the transfer of David Hopkin to Chelsea and Alex Mathie to Newcastle, I asked chairman John Wilson if money would be made available to the manager for the acquisition of new players. The answer was NO on each occasion. It was made quite plain to me by Mr Wilson that replacements would come from the youth scheme.

"Upgrading of the ground was to take priority. That was the message relayed to the fans. On Saturday, however, Mr Wilson informed fans at a meeting at Morton Supporters' Club that money WAS made available to manager McGraw at the end of last season.

"Manager McGraw, on the other hand, has consistently stated money was not available. According to him, finance in any meaningful amount was put at his disposal only at the start of October of last year when Morton's injury situation and general plight made it clear something had to be done. By then Morton found it was too late. Players of quality did not want to come to a club they felt was clearly heading for the drop."

Morton's public relations was, frankly, badly lacking at this time. Chairman John Wilson's statement to the fans that money had been made available to the manager after the transfer of Alex Mathie, was frankly, something I found impossible to believe. Mathie also had spent time at Newcastle before his transfer. Yet, at the time, John Wilson vigorously denied Mathie had ever been at Newcastle. This was despite the fact that Newcastle director Freddie Fletcher, the former Rangers and Morton director, had confirmed to me that Mathie had been down to St James's Park. Someone was not telling the truth. Either that or we were expected to believe that Morton did not know their own player was at Newcastle.

I wrote: "If Morton are attempting to make a new start, and Saturday's meeting [with the fans] was helpful in many ways, then one would hope that their public relations becomes more adept."

Morton manager Allan McGraw sought a meeting the following day with John Wilson. He was furious about comments made by the chairman to the fans which appeared in the Greenock Telegraph. The manager said: "Money wasn't available for players [after the transfer of Mathie] and it's nonsense to say it was.

"If I had money I would have signed a player. No manager holds onto money when he can buy a player."

McGraw was also critical of the board's decision to make John McMaster reserve and youth coach for the next season, effectively downgrading him. He continued: "I don't want to say too much at this stage, but I'm not going to be a patsy for anyone."

It was strong stuff. At the meeting with the fans, John Wilson also had stated that "if there is a white knight who wants to invest I won't stand in their way". He was, however, brief in his remarks on the resignation of fellow director John Kerr, saying only: "I received a two-line letter indicating he wished to resign. And when I got the letter I was very sad."

Mr Wilson did, however, admit that he was wrong to allow Alex Mathie to go on loan to Port Vale for a month towards the end of a season in which the club was maintaining a position that they were still aiming for promotion. He said: "Manager Allan McGraw did know about the arrangement, although he didn't agree with it."

The district was buzzing with the unfolding story and Wednesday's front page revealed the outcome of the meeting between chairman John Wilson and manager Allan McGraw. I reported: "After a meeting with chairman John Wilson at Cappielow yesterday, Morton boss Allan McGraw emerged claiming he had an assurance it had been wrong of the chairman to say money was available to him for players at the time when Alex Mathie was transferred to Newcastle in July. McGraw was angry at the statement made by John Wilson at the official supporters' club on Saturday."

Allan McGraw summed up: "That is it as far as I am concerned. The matter is over."

John Wilson refused to comment, saying he would send a statement by fax explaining his position. Meanwhile former Morton star Joe Harper threw his hat into the ring by saying he wished to apply for the vacant assistant manager's position.

John Wilson's statement arrived by fax at the Telegraph office that afternoon, confirming what Allan McGraw had said to the newspaper. In it there was a strange comment when he said that "The Telegraph should firstly refer in future to the club chairman for verification of any 'story' from Cappielow".

This beggared belief. I replied: "Morton denied that Alex Mathie had been at Newcastle despite the fact that I informed John Wilson that Newcastle director Freddie Fletcher had confirmed to me that Mathie was at Newcastle. That was an attempt at 'verification' as Mr Wilson has asked. It didn't get me very far, Mr Wilson reiterating that Mathie had not been at Newcastle." It was a bizarre situation, given that everyone, including the chairman, accepted now that Mathie had in fact been at Newcastle; that the club had not told the truth when they said he had NOT been there.

There was more to unravel, though on the field Morton managed a welcome 2-1 win at Brechin where Alexander and Lilley hit the net.

Wednesday's Telegraph front page carried the exclusive news that three local businessmen were prepared to make Morton chairman John Wilson an offer for his 88% shareholding in the Cappielow club.

I reported: "Fronted by Mr Robert McLeod, owner of Ambassador Financial Services in Brougham Street, Greenock, the consortium sent a letter to Mr Wilson on Tuesday 3rd May requesting a meeting."

Robert McLeod said: "It is to Mr Wilson's credit that the club is now in the black, but there is a need for more vision now. Fundamental mistakes have been made and there is a need for a more open regime."

Asked for his comments Mr Wilson, who had just returned from a business meeting, said: "I don't want to say anything until I've read it [the letter from McLeod]."

The following day a critical letter was printed in the Telegraph from a former scout at Morton, John McVicar. In it he said: "The resignation of John Kerr came as no great surprise to me. I attended a few scout meetings at which John [Kerr] put forward his options and ideas. He was a very straightforward person who said exactly what he thought, and I always wondered how long he would suffer one-sided opinions before he would quit."

John McVicar went on to say that Kerr had given his percentage, as a scout, of Brian Reid's transfer fee to Rangers into a bank account for the Morton youth policy. He then repeated a complaint that Kerr himself had previously made about Morton's running of the youth policy, saying: "I eventually quit the youth set-up because of the expenses problem, lack of communication between age groups and, of course, Mr Wilson being totally oblivious to the problems within the youth set-up.

"On one occasion a player travelled from Dunoon. I explained to Allan [McGraw] about this, he went into his own pocket and gave me £5 to cover the costs, a great gesture, but no answer to the problem."

Mr McVicar was then highly critical of the decision to demote John McMaster to reserve and youth coach and also critical of a remark made by the chairman that McMaster had not, in fact, been assistant manager. Mr McVicar noted that John McMaster was referred to as assistant manager in Morton's own match programme, and that he was referred to as assistant manager in the Greenock Telegraph. He continued: "What planet has Mr Wilson been living on? I find Mr Wilson's treatment of John McMaster nothing short of a disgrace."

He concluded by saying: "Mr Wilson is quickly running out of scapegoats for the failings of the 93-94 season. Sadly, the judgement day is coming soon, because his conveyor belt of talent has well and truly broken down."

Such emphatic criticism coming from a former scout at the club simply added fuel to the fire of the fans' increasing ire. Key scouts, vital in the implementation of the hugely successful youth policy under manager Allan McGraw, had left the club.

On a more positive note, kit manager Willie Gray received a merit award at the 17th annual Scottish Players' Football Association's dinner. Nine free transfers were also announced – Ian McDonald, John Gahagan, Stuart Rafferty, Craig Brown, Alex McEwan, Ricky Thomson, Scott Beaton, Barry McLellan and Paul Graham.

On the field the season ended with a home 3-1 loss to Airdrie, veteran Alexander getting the solitary strike. The game had been preceded by a minute's silence in respect of the death of Labour politician John Smith which was, unfortunately, despoiled by the inane chants of a section of Airdrie fans who shouted "Seig Heil". They also broke the crossbar of one of the goals. These were actions thoroughly condemned by both clubs, and the police made arrests.

Goalkeeper David Wylie was voted Player of the Year and it was left to everyone to replenish their drained batteries over the summer. A meeting then took place between John Wilson and Robert McLeod regarding a possible takeover and Robert McLeod said: "I did speak to Mr Wilson. We had meaningful talks. I will be having discussions with my backers and we will get back to Mr Wilson later in the week."

By the Friday of that week John Wilson had received a written offer for his 88% shareholding, Robert McLeod claiming he had put up 50% of the finance with the rest coming from two unnamed local businessmen. John Wilson commented: "I will discuss it with my colleagues on the board. We will probably discuss it some time next week."

Meanwhile Mr McLeod stated that he wished a quick reply, saying: "I have told Mr Wilson to accept or reject the offer by Monday afternoon. He wrote to us asking for another meeting, but we don't think it is necessary. We think our offer is fair."

The deadline passed and Mr McLeod then said that the deal was off. He claimed his consortium had submitted a bid of £450,000 but no reply had been received by the Monday afternoon deadline. His parting comment was to say: "The value Mr Wilson put on his shareholding is far in excess of a realistic figure, and one can draw one's own conclusions from that. Mr Wilson was very possibly the right person for the club at a particular period of the club's history and the club has a lot to be thankful to him for.

"But I am more convinced than ever that he's not the right man to take Morton forward. There will always be a Morton as long as Mr Wilson is in charge, but one must ask what level of football they will be playing at."

John Wilson explained his reason for not taking the offer further and said: "I was not prepared to discuss something where there are two unnamed persons involved because I don't know whether these two people have the best interests of Morton at heart."

Meanwhile director Douglas Rae said that interviews would be held for the assistant manager's post and that manager Allan McGraw would "not be present at the interview stage but would be consulted about applicants." Those interviews were to be held by employment consultant Ernest Barnard. Rae explained: "Mr Barnard is an employee of mine at Buchanan's Toffees. He was called in because of his skill as an interviewer. He doesn't have a background in football, but he is a keen football person."

John Wilson was set to stand down as chairman on 30th June and a new man appointed from the board.

CHAPTER TWENTY-FIVE

Policy U-turn precedes promotion

By July a new assistant manager had been appointed, former Hibs, Liverpool, Notts Forest and Scotland midfielder Peter Cormack, almost 48. Douglas Rae said that Cormack would be responsible for fitness, training, coaching and tactics, leaving Allan McGraw in charge of selection and transfer market dealings.

John McMaster was to become the youth coach, Rae saying: "John McMaster will be concentrating on the younger players and it's very important for the club."

Cormack, who had been a team-mate of McGraw's in the late 60s at Hibs, had been in Cyprus coaching for three years prior to coming to Cappielow. At this stage it was hard not to see Allan McGraw's role as being marginalised within the club. In the event he very much remained in charge of the side, whatever statements had been made.

Derek McInnes and Jim Tolmie were to miss the start of the season, while Peter Cormack's son, also Peter, was signed after being freed by Newcastle. The 21-year-old could play either in midfield or at full back.

Morton lost a pre-season friendly 3-1 to Hearts at Cappielow, the home goal coming from young Paddy Flannery, before the first league match of the season which resulted in a 1-1 home draw with Berwick Rangers, old favourite Rowan Alexander getting the goal.

Two days later John Wilson announced a complete U-turn over his position as chairman, saying: "I really do not think that I, and to a degree the board, got anything wrong last season other than perhaps we did not act timeously enough in respect for a replacement for Alex Mathie." He was then re-elected to his post at the annual general meeting on the following Friday night.

The only changes, therefore, were at the football management level. It seemed all too clear where the blame for a poor season was being placed. At least there was some partial recognition that money ought to have been made available to the manager at the start of the previous season. But there was no mention in the chairman's statement that he had wrongly told supporters that money had been made available to McGraw after Alex Mathie's transfer, something he later retracted. There was no reiteration of his previous admission that he had been wrong to allow the club's top striker, Alex Mathie, to go on loan to Port Vale in the run-in to the season when the message coming out from the club was that they were still going for promotion; no mention, as the chairman had also admitted, that this was in opposition to the manager's wishes. There was no mention of the criticism coming from scouts that they, and not the club, had to pay expenses; no mention that at least two scouts had resigned, one of whom was a director. It appeared that the buck did not stop at the top.

In the Coca-Cola Cup Morton lost on penalties to Airdrie after being held to a 1-1 draw at Cappielow, Derek Lilley getting the home goal. On the Saturday another Lilley strike was enough to dump Meadowbank in Edinburgh. With three points now being awarded for a win, Morton had four points from their opening two games.

At Dumbarton the following week, despite going ahead in 75 seconds with another Lilley goal, Morton fell 2-1 to two late Sons' strikes, young winger Paul Blair fracturing his collarbone. Forfar striker David Bingham then turned down a move to Cappielow, and when Morton lost 2-0 at Forthbank against Stirling, the visiting fans' irritation began to surface once more.

Goals by Scott McArthur and Rowan Alexander secured both points at Cappielow against Brechin to take Morton to fourth place before it was announced that moves were being made to re-open the Scandinavian connection to Cappielow. Initially they involved three Swedish and two Finnish players, but no further detail was given.

Lilley and Alexander were on target to beat East Fife 2-1 at Bayview before Morton dismissed St Johnstone after extra time in a seven-goal B & Q Cup clash at Cappielow. Lilley (2), Alexander and McEwan were the scorers. It broke a run of seven games in which Morton had lost ties in extra time, and the star man on a rain-lashed night was Derek Lilley.

John Anderson and Rowan Alexander were on the mark in a defeat of Stenhousemuir which took Morton to third spot in the Second Division before the club suffered yet another injury blow, Jim Tolmie having to quit football at the age of 33 after a knee operation. Allan McGraw summed up when he said: "There are very few players of his quality around these days." Short on stature, Tolmie was big on ability and his second spell at the club had been marked by his subtle skills, notably his penchant for bringing others into play. He had been a top servant to Morton.

A John Anderson goal was not enough to prevent Dundee knocking Morton out of the B & Q Cup at Dens by a 2-1 margin and then Clyde came to Cappielow to administer a 1-0 defeat in the league. Former Gourock Amateur player Craig McPherson (22), a left-sided midfielder or full back, made his debut. It was turning into another patchy season, and it wasn't helped when Queen of the South won 3-0 in Dumfries, though Allan McGraw was confident that his team would improve once his injured stars returned to the squad.

Just when the gloom was beginning to descend again, Finnish internationalists Janne Lindberg (28) and Marko Rajamaki (26) arrived from MyPa on Wednesday 19th October, 1994. Lindberg had been in the Finnish side which had gone down 2-0 to Scotland in Helsinki in September. He was a quality midfield player, while Rajamaki played on the left either as a winger or wide midfielder.

Initially they were on a three-match trial period, their first appearance being in a 2-1 defeat to league leaders Berwick at Shielfield Park. Lilley got the visitors' goal while the two for

Berwick came from striker Warren Hawke, an Englishman who was soon to make his own impact at Cappielow.

Derek McInnes was now back in full training, though there was a minor set-back for Alan Mahood who needed a clean-up operation on some small pieces of floating bone in a knee.

Alexander's winner over Dumbarton at Cappielow took Morton to fifth spot in the table. The goal was made in Finland and it was a match in which Lindberg's ability stood out. I reported: "Janne Lindberg, on this showing an accomplished all-round midfielder, began the move with a beautifully struck pass up the left to compatriot Marko Rajamaki. He strode on and hit an inch-perfect cross on the run to Alexander who timed his downward header perfectly past Burridge and inside the left post."

Derek Collins was outstanding as Morton began to look much more like a team. I wrote that there would be "no gamble in signing Lindberg".

Both Finns by this time were keen to stay in Greenock, but Scotland boss Craig Brown warned that Bolton's manager Bruce Rioch was also keen on taking Lindberg to Wanderers. Brown said of Lindberg: "He is a brilliant player and if Morton have an opportunity to sign him, they should."

Inspired by their Scandinavian imports, Morton beat Meadowbank 4-0 at Cappielow, Rajamaki and Lilley each scoring twice. They were now joint second and looking a much better proposition than in the opening few games. Asked if the Finns could understand the shouts of their team-mates, Lindberg replied with a quiet smile: "It is maybe better if we don't understand everything."

On Friday 11th November, Morton moved to sign the Finns for a record £250,000 combined package. The deal had come about through yet another contact of manager Allan McGraw's, Jimmy Pearson, and I wrote: "It may well turn out to be one of the best pieces of business McGraw will carry out as manager." Pearson, who played for Morton in the 50s, had been in Finland and had met John Craig, formerly of Uddingston, and now marketing manager of Finnish club MyPa. He passed the information back to Allan McGraw that the players may be available.

Allan McGraw commented: "We have the quality in our squad now." Also coming back were other quality players, Derek McInnes and Alan Mahood, and the side were impressive in a 3-1 victory at Brechin, goals coming from Lindberg, Alexander and McCahill. The mood of the support now was in stark contrast to the frustration of just a few weeks ago.

I wrote: "Chairman John Wilson and his board, criticised for not giving money to the manager at the start of the season, have dipped into the coffers to the tune of around £250,000. That is a sizeable amount for a small provincial club, and Mr Wilson deserves credit where it is due.

"If John Wilson deserves a pat on the back for making the deal possible, manager Allan McGraw has shown that there is no substitute for good contacts and an eye for a player."

MyPa's John Craig praised Morton for the honesty, speed and conciseness of the negotiations and said: "I would like to thank Allan McGraw and everyone at Cappielow for their hospitality. One of the main things that clinched the deal was that the boys wanted to come to a family club."

Director Douglas Rae commented: "These signings will give the town a lift. There has already been a buzz about the place." This massive reversal of club policy was hugely welcomed, the extensive ground renovations basically being placed in cold storage.

On Friday 18th November the death of former club chairman Ian McPherson was announced and former colleague Tom Robertson said: "Ian was a very generous man who got on with people easily and related to them. He was a big asset at Morton."

Both Lindberg and Rajamaki played for Finland in a 5-0 win over the Faroes before an Alexander goal gave Morton a home point against Stirling. Goals by Rajamaki (2) and Anderson in a 3-0 win against East Fife at Cappielow took Morton to second top place, two points behind leaders Berwick, then a goalless draw followed at Stenhousemuir. Alan Mahood was back on the bench as Morton began to look a much stronger proposition.

Another goalless draw away to Clyde on Boxing Day garnered a point and Morton were now just one adrift of new leaders Stenhousemuir.

Striker Alan Blaikie was signed from Greenock Juniors, and suddenly Morton were a side very much looking forward to the New Year.

A Marko Rajamaki strike gained a slightly disappointing home Hogmanay point at Cappielow, Morton having enjoyed the bulk of the play against the Queen of the South side managed by ex-Morton man Billy McLaren. When Queens' late equaliser went into the net a press colleague asked who had scored it. "Dick Turpin," I replied. Morton were now in fourth place, three points behind pacesetters Stenhousemuir, managed by Terry Christie.

The Scottish Cup interrupted the league programme, and amateur Queen's Park forced a 2-2 draw at Hampden in the second round, after Morton had gone two up through Rowan Alexander and John Anderson.

For all their neat football, Morton were lacking a killer touch in the final third of the park and they almost suffered for it when plucky Berwick Rangers, maintaining their own promotion pursuit, were leading at Cappielow well into the second half. Derek McInnes had been ordered off with 26 minutes to go after a second booking and things did not look good. However, Marko Rajamaki equalised with seven minutes remaining. Four minutes later the hosts were awarded a very soft penalty when Paul Blair went down in the box. Derek Lilley made his usual clinical finish from the penalty spot for a key two points.

Next up was the cup replay against the Spiders. Once again they wove a stifling web after taking an early lead. Rajamaki again pounced with a goal in 73 minutes to level the scores before Derek Lilley provided an extra time winner. Since the departure of Jim Tolmie, Morton had lacked a front man who could hold the ball and bring others into play. I wrote: "Had they, for example, Berwick's Hawke in their line-up, who can fulfil that function as well as being a genuine predator, they would be very near the finished article."

Two successive defeats merely underlined the problem of failing to transfer possession into goals, Meadowbank winning 1-0 in Edinburgh before Dumbarton took both points at Boghead in a 2-1 victory, Rajamaki getting the visitors' consolation effort.

Niggling doubts regarding league form were placed on the back burner as the side looked forward to a third round Scottish Cup clash with Premier League Kilmarnock, now under Alex

Totten, at Rugby Park. Totten, like Allan McGraw a man who favoured positive, attacking football, had taken over from Tommy Burns after his switch to Celtic, carrying on the good work.

A crowd of 8,271 turned out, 1,401 of whom had travelled from Greenock. The tie ended goalless with the visitors taking most of the plaudits against their opponents from two divisions higher. Alex Totten summed up: "I don't think we deserved to win, but we're still in the cup and that's the main thing."

One Killie fan lightened the home mood when he commented on Morton's tartan strip. "It would be terrible to lose to a bunch of travelling rugs."

In the replay the following Tuesday night at Cappielow, Morton took a first half lead through John Anderson and played well. An inspired substitution by Alex Totten, however, snatched victory from the jaws of defeat, Steve Maskrey equalising in 75 minutes before grabbing an extra time winner. Alan Mahood was sent off for a very unfortunate second booking when he encroached within 10 yards at a free kick when the scores were level. It had been a brave effort before a crowd of 6,533. Allan McGraw said: "We had enough chances to bury them. I can't fault the players for effort and their football, but it's all about putting the ball in the net." That was something with which Morton had been struggling all season.

Bottom of the table Brechin City were dispatched 1-0 with a goal by Rowan Alexander, now 34 and in his testimonial year, before Morton's best team display of the season saw Stirling Albion comprehensively beaten 3-0 at Forthbank. I reported: "Morton gave almost the complete performance in this dissection of one of their promotion rivals at Forthbank. So often this season Morton have played good football but with a tendency to flatter to deceive. This time they put together the complete package and Stirling simply had no answer." The Morton team was (4-3-3): Wylie; Collins, Anderson, Johnstone, McArthur; Mahood, McInnes, Lindberg; Lilley, Alexander, Rajamaki.

Morton were now third top, a point behind leaders Stenhousemuir.

Blackburn and Manchester City were hovering on the periphery, maintaining their interest in Derek Lilley. Fears that he might be sold grew with the arrival on a free transfer from Dunfermline of 21-year-old striker Derek Laing. Ton chairman John Wilson, however, was emphatic that no one would be sold in the near future, at least "until such time as we are sure we are getting out of this division."

Young Peter Cormack meanwhile broke his leg in a reserve match on the eve of the Second Division match-of-the-day against Stenhousemuir, putting him out for the rest of the season. Again Marko Rajamaki was the saviour for the hosts with the only goal of the game against Stenhousemuir, a side typically well organised by manager Terry Christie. Morton were now breathing down Stenny's necks, one point adrift, and they went to the top on goal difference after a 1-1 draw with East Fife at Bayview, the visitors getting the rub of the green with an own goal.

Postponements led to Stenhousemuir and Dumbarton leapfrogging them before Queen of the South inflicted a 1-0 defeat in Dumfries. Visitors' goalkeeper David Wylie was the star man, preventing embarrassment, while the only outfield player to get pass marks was veteran

Rowan Alexander. He later said that he wanted to end his career with Morton. "I've been at a few clubs," he said, "but Morton are way ahead of the rest as far as I am concerned."

Derek Lilley grabbed a double, Derek McInnes and Marko Rajamaki weighing in with a goal apiece, as Clyde were whipped 4-1 at Cappielow, before Rajamaki hit the net in a mediocre 1-1 draw at Brechin. Another draw followed, 2-2 against Stirling at Cappielow, Rajamaki maintaining his strike rate with both home counters as the contenders geared themselves for the final run-in.

Next up were promotion contenders Stenhousemuir. The game at Ochilview resulted in a third consecutive draw, 1-1, Derek Lilley netting. It also resulted in a two-week suspension and fine for full back Mark Pickering. He had not been in the first team plans for a while and chose to skip training and travel to Dublin to attend a wedding. With Derek Collins injured, manager Allan McGraw had to select centre back Dougie Johnstone at right back. The manager commented: "It hurts me that he [Pickering] should do this. He's one that I would have said you could rely on in a tight situation." Pickering had played his last game for Morton as he was freed at the end of the season. It was a sad way to end what had been a decent career at Morton.

Every game now was like a cup tie for Morton who were second top, four points behind Dumbarton.

On 8th April, 1995, they comfortably disposed of East Fife 4-1 in Greenock, goals coming from John Anderson, Steve McCahill, Derek Lilley and Derek Laing. Marko Rajamaki was sent off for two bookable offences, the first diving and the second touching the ball into goal with his hand. The gap was now down to one point and Morton's next match was at Broadwood against Clyde, also in the race for promotion.

Led by an inspired skipper Derek McInnes, who had been enjoying an excellent season, the Bully Wee were beaten 3-1, Scott McArthur, Derek McInnes and Derek Laing scoring. McInnes's display resulted in manager McGraw saying: "As an all-round midfield player Derek is outstanding."

Queen of the South then travelled to Cappielow. They had been Morton's bogey team that season, and the jinx continued with the visitors gaining a scoreless draw. Their top player was a familiar face in Greenock, Neil Orr. He controlled the Queens' defence from sweeper, much to the delight of his manager Billy McLaren who had played alongside him in Benny Rooney's excellent Morton team.

With three games remaining, Morton were a point behind Dumbarton. At last they edged ahead when the Sons lost and Morton beat Berwick Rangers 4-3 at Shielfield Park. Warren Hawke struck a hat-trick and put the hosts two up in the early stages. Derek Lilley hit two of his own to level the scores, one from the penalty spot after home goalkeeper Young had fouled Laing. The goalie was sent off and Morton went on to win 4-3.

That set up a massive meeting the following week at Cappielow with Dumbarton, now one point behind. A crowd of 6,242 turned out, just over 5,500 being home supporters. The atmosphere was tingling and the hosts did not disappoint, goals by Derek Lilley and Marko Rajamaki gaining a 2-0 victory. I reported: "Morton, urged on by a superb support of over six thousand, crossed the finishing line with a flourish at Cappielow on Saturday to secure promotion and almost certainly the championship too.

"Dumbarton, for so long pace-setters, now face the prospect of missing out altogether on promotion. Stirling Albion's win against Clyde now puts them into second place, a point ahead of the Sons whom they meet at Forthbank next Saturday."

Derek McInnes again had given a superb performance, almost willing his men to victory. For his manager it had been a fraught 90 minutes, full of nerves, and he said: "That's the worst I've felt. I enjoyed it after the final whistle, but it was as much relief as anything else.

"The players deserve full credit. They have done it when we needed it most. The support was tremendous and I'm just glad we gave them the two goals."

Another hero was goalkeeper David Wylie who brought off a sensational save at close range from McKinnon early in the game when there was no scoring.

In the week that followed, Greenock Telegraph readers voted Derek McInnes as Player of the Year. I spoke to him and he told me: "This time last year I didn't know if I was going to play again." This was in reference to a very troublesome knee injury. "I feel physically and mentally stronger now," he continued. "I've also been helped by the fact that the team is playing well. Janne Lindberg's arrival was a big boost too. Sometimes a fault of mine was trying to do other people's jobs. Now I am trying to set a standard for myself, and I am probably playing the best football of my career."

I wrote: "This triumph has been about teamwork. Chairman John Wilson deserves credit for making the money available to the manager to bring the Finns to Cappielow. From him down to the groundstaff and backroom staff it has been a commendable effort."

McInnes was presented with the Sir William Lithgow Trophy by celebrity fan Arthur Montford before the final match of the season at home to Meadowbank.

Derek Lilley scored the only goal of the game, his 20th of the season, leading to him being joint-top scorer in the division along with Berwick's Warren Hawke. Marko Rajamaki had weighed in with 15 goals, while veteran Rowan Alexander had added another 11.

Dumbarton managed to beat Stirling at Forthbank to deservedly take second place in the table, two points behind Morton.

Derek McInnes added the Second Division Player of the Year Award to that of the fans while Allan McGraw was manager of the year for the Second Division.

Mark Pickering, Neil Shearer and Brian Sexton were given free transfers while the inevitable round of transfer speculation began. There was talk of Mark McGraw returning to Cappielow after being given a free transfer by Hibs, while Derek McInnes was now out of contract with a lengthy queue of prospective buyers lining up.

Allan McGraw was then given Honorary Presidentship of Morton Supporters' Club while Provost Allan Robertson announced that the club were to be given a Civic Reception. Gourock councillor Ross Finnie also singled out the manager, saying: "Allan McGraw has made a tremendous contribution to this community in his playing days and as Morton manager."

CHAPTER TWENTY-SIX

Agonising end to season for quality team

Allan McGraw had stated that additions would be needed for the squad for the 1995-96 season, especially if skipper McInnes were to depart. One area in which it had been acknowledged throughout the season that Morton were lacking was up front.

Too often good football was not always rewarded with goals and to that end they made their move, sooner rather than later. Allan McGraw announced that the club were engaging in talks with Berwick Rangers for the acquisition of their top goalscorer Warren Hawke. The sum bandied about was £100,000, a figure at which the Cappielow club initially baulked. Eventually, however, on 20th July, they did the business for a fee Berwick boss Tom Hendrie later confirmed was around £80,000.

Hawke told me: "I loved the games against Morton last season [and so he should have, having scored five times]. The Morton fans made the atmosphere great and it brought the best out in me." Hawke went on to say he also had been impressed by the Morton players and the way in which they played their football.

I commented: "Hawke and the two Finns have cost Morton a combined total of around £330,000, a considerable sum. This is now undoubtedly the best squad of players Morton have had since their first sojourn into the Premier League in season 1978-79 under Benny Rooney's management."

The news became even better when it was announced that Morton had persuaded Derek McInnes to sign a new one-year deal. There was little doubt he would still go if someone came in for him; indeed the deal was almost certainly done on that basis, but at least Morton would ensure they were in a stronger bargaining position. Both Finns also signed new two-year deals.

The Cappielow board were now engaged in a complete reversal of their previous policy of ground improvement being the overriding priority. That had been taken to an extreme in which it was severely impairing team building; indeed it had led to relegation to the Second Division. The board had not actually come out and said "We got it wrong" but that mattered little if the policy that had led to relegation had been abandoned. There was an almost tangible improvement in the spirits of those who followed the club as a result.

Morton replaced their tartan regalia with new, Argentina-style, vertical blue and white stripes.

Ex-Falkirk goalkeeper Willie Lamont played on trial during the pre-season tour of Northern Ireland, covering for the unavailable David Wylie. Upon the team's return they met Premier League Falkirk at Cappielow in a testimonial match for Rowan Alexander, now in his 10th season at Greenock since joining from Brentford. He played for 50 minutes in a match won by the game's only goal, scored by Marko Rajamaki.

That set up a tough league opener, away to title favourites Dundee United. After an opener by Craig Brewster, the match's best move provided a spectacular equaliser from Alan Mahood. A six-pass move resulted in Mahood smashing a 30-yard drive into the net. Morton's side that afternoon lined up as follows (4-3-3): Wylie; Johnstone, Anderson, McCahill, Collins; Mahood, McInnes, Lindberg; Lilley, Hawke, Rajamaki.

It had been an even contest and home gaffer Billy Kirkwood said: "Morton are a good team and knock the ball about well."

Ton boss Allan McGraw, accepting the result, commented: "In the end we could have got the win, but so could they."

On 19th August it was on to Ibrox for a second round Coca-Cola Cup tie against Rangers and their highly-priced stars. Only Brian Laudrup was missing from their strongest selection and, in front of 42,941 fans, the hosts won comfortably by 3-0. Scorers were Mark Hateley, Paul Gascoigne and Ally McCoist, the latter with his 300th strike for the Ibrox club.

Morton competed well, with skipper Derek McInnes outstanding, but Rangers simply had too much class in the final third of the pitch. Allan McGraw said: "Derek McInnes showed today that he is a quality player, and Janne Lindberg looked comfortable at that level."

Of his midfield tussle with 'Gazza', McInnes said: "He's a good player. He talks a lot and he tries to wind people up, but he also encourages. He told me I was doing well and to keep going."

Morton's sizeable support, filling the bottom section of the Broomloan Stand, appreciated their side's effort and applauded them off the pitch. The highlight of the game, however, was a delightful piece of skill by Gascoigne who wrong-footed Derek Collins, Steve McCahill and John Anderson before slipping a neat 12-yard shot past David Wylie.

On the following Wednesday Morton succumbed 1-0 to Livingston away from home to make an early exit from the Challenge Cup.

Their second league game of the season was at home to Dumbarton, but the complexion of the match was dramatically altered when John Anderson was sent off early on for an instinctive hand-ball on the line. Chic Charnley also netted with a superb lob from fully 45 yards, one of the best goals I have ever seen, Derek Lilley grabbing a consolation strike for the hosts. Despite having played almost all the football, it was literally a pointless exercise for the home team.

Sons manager Jim Fallon commented: "Morton played most of the football but our spirit and workmanship took us through." That was press speak. He later poked his head into Allan McGraw's room and said: "You ran all over us."

Cameroon goalkeeper Andre Boe then arrived at Cappielow as a trialist. Capped 60 times by his country, he was later to sign on until the end of the season as cover for David Wylie.

If all goalkeepers are a bit mad to begin with, Boe took eccentricity to a fine art, sometimes dribbling the ball out of his area or coming off his line to punch extravagantly.

On the first Saturday of September Morton got back on track with a 2-0 win at St Johnstone, ironically having played less impressively than against Dumbarton, while Janne Lindberg took time off from Morton to play for his country in a 1-0 defeat by Scotland at Hampden. He showed up well in a deep-lying midfield role.

Another brace by Derek Lilley earned a home point in a 2-2 draw with Jim Duffy's Dundee for whom young Port Glasgow boy Neil McCann was making a name for himself on the left wing. Before the match Neil had told the Greenock Telegraph: "I'm expecting a bit of stick from the Morton fans. And some of that will be from members of my own family. I've got a couple of uncles who are Morton fans and they say they'll be letting me know they're around."

Dundee took a two-goal lead before Morton's football paid off with two Lilley penalties. Dougie Johnstone was sent off for cawing the feet from young McCann late in the game near the halfway line. After what I had described as "an enthralling contest" Dens boss Jim Duffy said of Morton: "They play superb football and are always going to give teams problems. If they have a fault it's maybe that at times they concentrate too much on going forward. They got caught with two sucker punches today."

Allan McGraw commented: "The players never give up. We showed again that we can compete with anyone."

Duffy's comment, however, had hit the nail on the head in the early stages of the campaign, as was highlighted in a 3-2 defeat away to Airdrie, played at Broadwood Stadium as the Lanarkshire side were building a new ground. Warren Hawke did extremely well, scoring twice to get off the mark for his new club, but profligacy in defence cost the visitors dear. Allan McGraw summed up: "Our central defence is killing us. We can't keep giving goals away."

Airdrie's Alex MacDonald was the latest manager to compliment Morton on their football, but there was a lack of ruthlessness in the rearguard. On Saturday 23rd September unbeaten league leaders Dunfermline arrived in Greenock for an acid test for the host club. By quarter to five their record had gone, blasted away by goals from Derek McInnes and Warren Hawke. Not only was it an impressive 2-0 win, it was a majestic performance. I reported: "There are victories and victories, but this match produced not just a result which smashed Dunfermline's 100% record but also football of a stunning quality from the home side. On this form Morton simply play the best football of anyone in the league."

On Derek McInnes I wrote: "The Morton skipper was inspirational, scoring an excellent goal and producing a superb all-round performance. Alan Mahood and Janne Lindberg supported magnificently on either side of him." These three had formed by far the best midfield unit in the division, their overall quality allowing Morton to play an adventurous 4-3-3. The win carried Morton up to fifth in the table, seven points behind the Pars. But it was the display which offered so much encouragement for the rest of the programme.

This feel-good factor was carried over into the derby against St Mirren at Love Street. In a crowd of 5,464, the visiting section of 2,275 roared on their heroes to an emphatic 4-1 victory, another Hawke double and goals by Lilley and Rajamaki proving too much for the Saints.

It was, however, a bad-tempered game in which five home players were booked, one was sent off, and three visiting players were also cautioned.

There was also an unsavoury incident when departing visiting fans tore up around 50 seats from the new stand at Love Street. It prompted Morton chairman John Wilson to say: "The joy of winning the game was almost wiped out by the actions of a minority of hooligans." It was hard not to agree. It was mindless vandalism by a truly stupid minority of morons.

On the pitch, Allan McGraw spoke of there being "too much passion" on display and not enough football. I wrote: "Referees come in for much criticism, but on Saturday it was the players who should carry the can."

Morton were now up to third place after seven games, seven points behind Dunfermline and two adrift of Dundee United. What they needed was a consistent run, but in their next match Clydebank triumphed with the only goal of the match at Kilbowie. It was a strangely insipid display and I wrote: "Morton's performance dropped like a dead leaf from a tree, twisting and spiralling at first and then falling limply to the ground."

Recovery came in the next game when goals by Alan Mahood and Warren Hawke produced a 2-0 home win over Hamilton.

At this point Dundee United came in with a bid for Derek McInnes, somewhere near the £300,000 mark. They had money to spend after selling Billy McKinlay, but the offer was rejected, Allan McGraw saying: "The board turned down United's offer and we don't want, or need, to sell any of our players at the moment."

Derek McInnes said: "I'm flattered by United's interest, but the board have made their decision and I have to accept that. I can understand Morton's position." A second United bid was turned down as interest grew in the Morton captain, two English clubs and Rangers joining the race to capture his signature.

By this time the 'Bosman' ruling had come into play. McInnes was out of contract at the end of the season and Morton knew they would have to cash in while they could. In persuading their captain to sign a new one-year deal at the start of the season they had attempted to protect that financial interest. Four bids were now on the table, according to the Greenock club. It was clear McInnes was on his way. Allan McGraw, acknowledging that, said of this latest of his fine young crop of players to come under the transfer spotlight: "He's the best of all of them. I'm sure he'll do well wherever he goes."

On the Saturday Morton, again showing their class, whipped St Johnstone 4-1, Warren Hawke scoring his first hat-trick for the club, adding to John Anderson's goal.

I reported: "The team swept imperiously to victory, but the afternoon was tinged with sadness as fans waved farewell to skipper Derek McInnes in what was almost certainly his last appearance for Morton.

"Star of the show was striker Warren Hawke who gained his first hat-trick in Morton colours. It was an exquisite trio from the English forward and rich reward for an afternoon of endeavour and ability." Alan Mahood also excelled before a crowd of 3,313, visiting centre half Jim Weir being ordered off with the score 2-1.

Morton were third, two points behind Dundee United and seven behind Dunfermline.

By now Rangers were the principal players in the McInnes transfer story. But they too had an offer knocked back, Allan McGraw saying: "The offer Rangers made was about the same as the one made by Dundee United and it has been turned down by the board. We didn't think it was enough. And an offer from an English club was also rejected. Rangers may come back with another bid. It is up to them."

Derek McInnes was becoming anxious and said: "I'm fed up waiting. Everything was set up for a move after last Saturday. The Morton fans were brilliant to me but now it's dragging on. I just want a conclusion to it all; to know whether I'm going or staying."

McInnes was left out of the side to meet Dumbarton at Boghead, and Morton won 2-0 with another double from red-hot striker Hawke, giving him five goals in two games. Allan McGraw explained that he felt McInnes was not in the right frame of mind to play and introduced Paul Blair to the side, switching to a 4-4-2 set-up with Blair wide right and Rajamaki wide left.

It was then revealed that the hold-up in a deal being done for McInnes was due to a clause which had been inserted in the one-year contract negotiated with Derek McInnes's agent Bill McMurdo. McMurdo had stipulated that if a specific offer, believed to be a figure between £250,000 and £300,000, were received for McInnes then, once five days had elapsed, the player would be free to go. That time had passed. Morton chairman John Wilson was angry and said: "We do not consider the actions of the adviser or advisers of our player, Derek McInnes, to be appropriate in that they appear to have abused confidential contractual information." Clearly John Wilson believed the transfer fee stipulated in the contract as a minimum acceptable to Morton had been leaked deliberately to interested parties. Proving that would be almost impossible.

In fact Morton were on a hiding to nothing. If the bid received matched the figure in the contract – and it appeared it did – then there was little they could do. The wrangle over the problem continued for several days, but it was clear that McInnes would soon be on his way.

It was a blow to Morton's promotion hopes but not, I felt, insurmountable. They were four points behind leaders Dunfermline and, in Mahood and Lindberg, they still possessed two quality midfield players. Striker Warren Hawke was in sensational form, having scored 11 goals in seven games. The issue was whether or not money would be available to the manager for a replacement for his skipper when he finally departed, and whether or not Morton could avoid injuries to key players in what was a very tight squad.

McInnes was back in the side for the home match against Airdrie, Morton winning 2-1 through strikes by Marko Rajamaki and Alan Mahood. The crowd was a healthy 3,856. While the points kept Morton third top, just two points behind Dunfermline and Dundee United, the performance had dipped and Allan McGraw summed up: "Airdrie were the better team over the 90 minutes. The situation with Derek McInnes is affecting the team."

By the following Saturday the issue had virtually been resolved. I wrote on the morning of the match against Dundee at Dens Park: "Morton skipper Derek McInnes will play his last game for the club at Dens Park today before signing next week for Rangers. After a complicated contractual wrangle, both clubs have at last agreed a deal for an undisclosed fee believed to be between £300,000 and £400,000." The fee was almost certainly much nearer the £300,000 mark.

The player himself said: "I'm glad it's all over. I just have to agree personal terms and that shouldn't be a problem. At the moment I'm just trying to get my head on the game today."

At the end of a goalless afternoon in Dundee, Morton's large travelling support gave their departing captain a standing ovation. McInnes was clearly moved by the fans' reaction while Allan McGraw said: "I think he will do very well at Rangers."

He may have been only one player in the squad, but McInnes was a key man in a very restricted pool. I felt the side would particularly miss his tremendous energy and ability to win back possession. At full strength Morton would still be a proposition, but if money were available from his transfer fee, it had to be spent soon.

A week later Morton met derby rivals St Mirren at Cappielow. Several changes were made to accommodate the absence of McInnes, and a reshuffling of the back four appeared to unsettle the side who went down 3-0 to goals by Yardley (2) and Lavety. Manager McGraw commented: "In the second half they seemed to want it more than us."

By the time the next challenge came, at East End Park against leaders Dunfermline, Morton had reverted to their more normal back four, bringing in Craig McPherson in midfield as a simple replacement for McInnes. He played on the left of a midfield three, new skipper Janne Lindberg in the centre and Alan Mahood on the right.

McPherson (24) had been a late developer, coming into the senior ranks from Gourock Youth Athletic Club as a 22-year-old. A lovely passer of the ball – hence his nickname 'Hagi' after the Romanian international with the cultured left foot – he was a quite different type of midfielder from the man he was replacing. He lacked the drive and huge energy of McInnes and had to work at his game defensively.

For the second time that season, Morton gave the Pars a football lesson, in the process reducing the gap between themselves and the leaders to just one point. Goals by Derek Lilley and Warren Hawke settled the contest, while Janne Lindberg imposed his authority in the centre of midfield from the kick-off.

He got top support from Alan Mahood and Craig McPherson while I wrote that, at the back, Dougie Johnstone "had surely his best game for Morton, immense in everything he did". Alongside him John Anderson was rock solid while goalkeeper David Wylie was in command of his area.

The game, however, was overshadowed by an illness to manager Allan McGraw, necessitating him being taken to hospital in Dunfermline after half-time with a suspected heart attack. Both home boss Bert Paton and McGraw's assistant, Peter Cormack, were more concerned about that after play than they were about the result.

Paton did compliment Morton, though, saying: "We were well beaten by a good team. That's the second time this season they've given us a doing."

Cormack commented on his side's chances of promotion: "We don't have the pool of others, such as Dundee United, but we have a bit of quality if we can hold onto it."

By the Monday Allan McGraw was back at Cappielow, tests appearing to suggest his illness was related to an on-going ulcer. He said: "The doctors have given me the all-clear, so there shouldn't be a problem."

Progress continued on the field with a fine 3-0 home win over Clydebank, goals from Lilley and Rajamaki (2). Another top display came from David Wylie, who brought off two excellent saves in what was his 400th game for the club.

On the following Tuesday the news broke that Morton boss Allan McGraw had been taken to Inverclyde Royal, having suffered a heart attack. His condition was said to be stable. Club doctor Craig Speirs commented: "After the first scare two weeks ago Allan said he didn't feel particular stress, but I tend not to agree with that." The doctor went on to say that colleagues would have to accept more of the workload in future. Well-wishers swamped Cappielow with telephone calls and messages of support for a very popular man, not just in Inverlcyde, but Scottish football as a whole.

Peter Cormack assumed command and, in his first game in charge, he led Morton to a 3-2 win at Firhill where Hamilton were playing while a new ground was built. Goals came from Collins, Lilley and Anderson. Warren Hawke sustained a heavy knock on his back, but Morton remained second top, just one point behind Dunfermline. Rightly or wrongly, I felt that Hawke was never quite the same player after that injury.

Allan McGraw was allowed home from hospital on Monday 11th December, but under strict instructions to take things easy. This was no doubt as difficult for him as it would have been for an elephant and a hippopotamus, each with two bags of bulky groceries and an accordion, to get into a phone box.

In the First Division match-of-the-day at Cappielow, Dundee United arrived to meet a home side minus the injured Hawke. The lack of depth to the home squad was illustrated by the appearance of teenager Barry Mason and two defenders on the bench. Before a good home crowd of 4,660, United stole a march on Morton with a 2-1 win, Derek Lilley grabbing the home goal. Morton had slipped to third in the table.

Peter Cormack was meanwhile playing things very low key. He commented: "We've had a lot of good write-ups and recognition because of the football we're playing, and that's been good. Realistically, a place in the top four would be an excellent achievement. If we were to go up it might be too soon for us. We have probably five, maybe six, players who need experience at this level."

A freeze ruled out play over the festive period and it was 9th January before Morton played their next game, against the vastly improving St Johnstone team. The result was a shocker, the Perth team rattling six goals past their visitors who managed a consolation goal from skipper Lindberg. George O'Boyle was the home hero with a hat-trick. Peter Cormack said: "It was a drubbing. We were overwhelmed."

Opposing boss Paul Sturrock commented: "It was our best performance of the season by far, against good opposition. Morton will give a lot of teams a lot of trouble this season."

It was then announced that veteran striker Rowan Alexander (34) would be leaving Cappielow to take up a post as player-coach at Queen of the South, his home town team. Allan McGraw praised the player, in his testimonial season, saying: "We're sorry to see

Rowan go as he's been a great servant to Morton, but if he's as a good a coach as a player, he'll do well."

By the time Morton met Dundee, a point ahead of them in third place, a win was vital to regain momentum after that thrashing by the Perth Saints. A John Anderson goal was all that separated the teams at Cappielow, Allan McGraw back in a spectating capacity. Peter Cormack once again was downbeat about Morton's promotion prospects, saying: "The best squads are at Dundee United and Dunfermline and we have to recognise that. But if we are still there with three or four games left, who knows?"

The following week a goal by Warren Hawke gave Morton three points at Clydebank, a result which saw them back to third spot in the table. It also brought a comment from Peter Cormack that was to rebound on him. He said after the game: "We are kidding ourselves if we think we can go up with the squad we have. The players have done magnificently to get us into this position, but we are not thinking about promotion. Obviously if we are still up there with three games to go we will have a right good chance, but a top four place for us this season will be a success."

It was actually a view with which I had sympathy, as I had previously written, and on the Monday I said: "On the principal of nothing ventured, nothing gained, this is the time one feels Morton ought to be supplementing the ranks with one, preferably two, experienced players. If there is any money in the Cappielow coffers at all, and I appreciate that is a big 'if', now is the time to take the plunge."

No sooner had the paper come out, however, than I received a telephone call from Peter Cormack. He was, he said, angry at press comment, both in the Greenock Telegraph and national newspapers, in which he claimed he had been misquoted. This was specifically with regard to the remark "We are kidding ourselves if we think we can go up with the squad we have". I suspected – no, I was sure – he was under pressure from a person or persons on the board at Cappielow who felt his comments were defeatist. I also thought he, or they, were listening in to the telephone conversation. I asked Peter if he wished to come along to the Telegraph and listen to a replay of the tape containing his remarks, the same comments that had appeared in several different papers. The offer was not taken up. I have always been scrupulously careful not to misquote, nor to selectively quote out of context. It is why I always used a tape recorder as back-up to my notes.

When Morton beat Airdrie away from home by 2-0, Lilley and Lindberg being on the mark, Morton had risen to second in the table, four points behind new leaders Dundee United. Importantly, the Greenock men were back to playing with some real style. I wrote: "Promotion is certainly not beyond the realms of possibility. The onus is now very much on those who hold the purse strings at Cappielow. How keenly do they want to go up and can, and will, they provide the cash to bring in the couple of experienced players that would give the squad the impetus needed in the run-in to the season?"

It was not an easy dilemma. If Morton did go up they would still need to strengthen their squad, but I continued: "It would be better to go some way towards that now. If the gamble doesn't come off then players would have to go. But it would be a crying shame if Morton were to miss out on promotion by a whisker believing that they can go up with the present pool." Little did I realise how prophetic these remarks were to be.

There was some speculation that Morton may try to bring veteran centre back Joe McLaughlin back to Greenock from Falkirk, but manager McGraw said: "Joe would be a good acquisition for any club, but our priority is a midfield player."

Three more key points were collected at Love Street in another derby clash, and Morton were now one point behind leaders Dundee United with a game in hand. Young Cormack, so often the recipient of abuse from a section of Morton fans, got the goal, manager McGraw saying: "The boy had a nightmare, but he hit a great goal." McGraw went on to qualify that comment by saying that Cormack had been played out of position in midfield and that he could never be faulted for any lack of effort.

Alan Mahood had missed the game and the manager, talking of the depletion of his much vaunted midfield trio of Mahood, McInnes and Lindberg, continued: "We have missed McInnes and we can't afford to be without two of them."

There was then an upset when Montrose dumped Morton out of the Scottish Cup, a 1-1 draw (scorer Rajamaki) at Cappielow being followed up with a 3-2 defeat in the replay, goals from Cormack and Lilley. Morton had been two up at Links Park only for goalkeeper David Wylie to be ordered off after handball outside the area. In some ways it was a bonus not to have the distraction of the cup given Morton's minimal squad.

Andre Boe came in to replace the suspended Wylie for the next game, against Dumbarton at home. It was won 2-0 with goals by Lilley and Mahood and, finally, Morton found themselves top of the pile, a point clear of Dundee United and three in front of Dunfermline.

On a midweek late in February it was off to Tayside to meet Dundee United. A point would be a great result but, in the event, United blitzed Morton with four first half goals. Allan McGraw said: "We can't afford to give players like they have the freedom of the park."

Another big defeat followed when Dunfermline atoned for being outplayed twice by the Greenock men by beating them 4-1 at East End Park, Rajamaki getting the sole visiting counter. Worse still was a torn medial ligament suffered by skipper Janne Lindberg which was to rule him out for the rest of the season. Suddenly Morton's challenge seemed to be evaporating. Losing McInnes had been bad enough. To lose replacement skipper Lindberg, the captain of Finland, was a massive blow.

Lifelong Morton fan Arthur Montford, of STV sports commentary fame, was meanwhile co-opted onto the Morton board. Apart from his expertise as a commentator, Arthur was renowned for a colourful taste in sports-jackets. Were his jackets paintings, they would almost certainly be found in the Modern Art Gallery in Glasgow.

There was now growing speculation concerning the return to Cappielow of former centre half Brian Reid whose £300,000 departure to Ibrox in March, 1991, had turned sour after a serious knee injury. Manager McGraw admitted enquiries had been made, though it later became clear that this was a move by the board and not the manager. Morton's pressing requirement was for at least one experienced midfielder.

Assuming Reid were to arrive, I asked Allan McGraw if money nevertheless would be made available for a midfield player. His reply was: "We'll just need to wait and see." Sometimes what is left out of an answer tells you more than anything.

Morton's spirit had never deserted them and goals by Johnstone, Rajamaki, Cormack and Laing secured a fine 4-1 win over Hamilton. Soon after, the club revealed that Brian Reid would be returning to Morton for a fee of £100,000. I did not doubt Reid's ability, but I found it incredible that a fourth centre half was a priority given the decimation of the club's superb midfield section.

Reid was delighted to be rejoining his first senior club and said: "I'm glad to be back at Cappielow again and, in a way, it feels as though I'm coming home."

Allan McGraw diplomatically explained that Reid was a "long-term signing" and that he still wanted a midfielder as a priority. He never got one. In the end a transfer made above the manager's head almost certainly cost Morton a place in the Premier League. That is no disrespect to Reid, but the priority for strengthening was clearly elsewhere in the side.

St Mirren then beat Morton 2-1 at Cappielow in a match in which Derek Laing was sent off after a clash with Norrie McWhirter, Marko Rajamaki once again getting on the scoresheet.

Into March, Morton were going to have to rely more upon grit than any other attribute, and they had that in abundance in a 1-1 home draw with Dunfermline, now back on top of the table. The game was notable for a clash after the final whistle involving Pars players and home star Derek Collins.

With Dunfermline leading 1-0 going into the last minute, visiting defender Marc Millar went down injured and one of his team-mates kicked the ball out of play. Collins took the throw, electing not to return it to Dunfermline. With almost the last kick of the game, not as a direct result of that throw-in, Morton equalised through Marko Rajamaki. Dunfermline were incensed and some of their players were all too keen to get physically involved with Collins as he left the field.

Pars boss Bert Paton described it afterwards as "something about nothing", stressing his club's excellent relationship with Morton. He knew the score. Some further common sense came in remarks made by Derek McInnes, out of action at Rangers due to injury and watching from the stand, when he said: "I back Derek [Collins] to the hilt. If it had been a Morton player who had been injured it would have been different."

Indeed it would. It was hard not to see Millar's injury and the concession of a throw by a team-mate so late in the match as being a time-wasting exercise by Dunfermline. I have never been an advocate of this unwritten rule of sportsmanship in which players kick the ball out of play if someone is injured, for whichever side. It is open to blatant exploitation. The referee should stop play if he believes someone is seriously hurt.

Draws followed against Dundee, 1-1 (Lilley), and Clydebank 0-0. The latter was not the finest footballing spectacle and drew the evocative remark from Allan McGraw "I've had better days with the toothache." It also marked yet another severe blow to Morton's promotion aspirations, Alan Mahood sustaining a knee injury that would rule him out for the remaining four games of the season. The best midfield in the division was now no more.

Next up were Hamilton at Firhill and Morton were forced to field a completely makeshift midfield of Collins, Anderson and McPherson. The fighting spirit was undiminished, but the quality was notably absent by now. Allan McGraw summed up when he said: "We are going to have to battle. We need to bite, scratch and fight for the points." Metaphorically, Morton did all of these things.

Marko Rajamaki once more scored a key goal – his sixth in eight outings – the only one of the game as Morton took three precious points. Dundee United were top on 63 points, Dunfermline second on 62, St Johnstone on 61 and Morton on 60. From these four teams one would be automatically promoted and one more would go into a play-off.

A delighted Dougie Johnstone then stepped up to notch the only goal of the game against St Johnstone at Cappielow, a superb win in the circumstances. Even in their ravaged state, Morton managed to play some fine football, the goal coming in the 20th minute when Johnstone stole in at the back post to direct a Rajamaki cross into the net.

I reported: "They [Morton] didn't just fight and scratch their way to the points. They were the better team over the 90 minutes and fully deserved their reward, a point Saints boss Paul Sturrock magnanimously conceded."

The crowd was a very healthy 5,808. Dougie Johnstone later confirmed that the goal came from a training ground move. A student teacher studying mathematics and computing, Johnstone grinned: "We've got to get some brains in there," nodding to the home dressing room.

The injured Janne Lindberg was then voted Player of the Year in the annual poll of Telegraph readers before the penultimate game of the season at Boghead against relegated Dumbarton. A John Anderson goal was all that separated the teams in a vital win for the visitors. Sons' boss Jim Fallon said: "Good luck to Morton. I didn't think they would do as well as they have done." Pure strength of will was sustaining Morton.

Dunfermline were now on 68 points, Dundee United and Morton on 66, with United enjoying the superior goal difference. It was simple: Morton had to win to ensure at least second place and a play-off against Partick Thistle. The title itself now was not beyond Morton, and manager Allan McGraw said of Airdrie's meeting with Dunfermline the following Saturday: "I will be giving Alex MacDonald a call to see if he can do us a favour by beating Dunfermline. If he does I'll buy him a new budgie," this in reference to MacDonald's fondness for the feathered fraternity.

It was pay as you come to Cappielow for the decisive final Saturday against Dundee United, something which caused a problem on the day. The police ordered the gates to be closed with some 12,500 inside Cappielow. Some fans with season tickets found they couldn't get in, an allocation of briefs having been set aside for the stand.

Morton's dogged determination was just not enough on the day, United securing a 2-2 draw, having twice been ahead. Marko Rajamaki's equaliser in the 83rd minute came just too late on an afternoon of heartache for the hosts.

An exciting season had gone right down to the wire. Morton had begun the campaign with the best midfield unit in the league by some distance and had ended it with a makeshift trio. Their fortitude and grit simply were not enough against a quality United team.

The ensuing week brought recriminations over the decision not to make the game all-ticket. Season ticket holders were especially incensed when they discovered some tickets had been sold for part of the stand, leading to their exclusion. Chairman John Wilson said: "I can only say that I am deeply sorry to the fans who never got in. Our goalkeeper David Wylie's mother did not get in and how do you think that makes me feel?" He went on to say that season ticket holders would be reimbursed.

Morton's failure in some ways had been glorious. The players deserved enormous credit for taking it to the last game of the season, given the limitation of their squad; so too did manager Allan McGraw and his assistant Peter Cormack. One could only surmise what might have happened had the £100,000 it took to purchase Brian Reid been made available to the manager when Derek McInnes left for Rangers in November. Fine player though Reid was, he simply wasn't what Morton needed at that time.

Derek Laing was the only first team man freed at the end of the term. By the end of May, Morton had begun the process of recruiting when 18-year-old midfielder Ross Matheson was acquired after being given a free transfer from Rangers.

During July it became clear that newly promoted Dunfermline were interested in taking Ton striker Derek Lilley to East End Park, but their idea of a fee wasn't in line with Morton's valuation of the player.

CHAPTER TWENTY-SEVEN

Half-million pound departure of Lilley as Ton decline

Derek Collins, who had taken over the captaincy when Janne Lindberg got injured in the run-in to the end of the previous season, signed a new deal tying him to the club until 2000. At 27 he hadn't given up his own hopes of progressing in the game, but he was happy meantime to remain at Cappielow.

Allan McGraw then declared an interest in versatile ex-Rangers forward John Morrow who had been freed, but others were chasing him and it seemed unlikely that he would come to Greenock.

Morton undertook a pre-season tour of Finland, recording draws against MyPa, the former club of Marko Rajamaki and Janne Lindberg, 0-0, and FinnPa 1-1 (Derek Lilley). They also beat Turku 2-1 with goals by Warren Hawke and Brian Reid. For Hawke it ended a 16-match spell without scoring.

An understrength Rangers side then beat Morton 3-2 in Greenock, the home goals coming from Lilley and Rajamaki. In the Ibrox ranks was ex-Ton skipper Derek McInnes. Another strike by Lilley was enough to beat Preston North End. The star player was new signing Ross Matheson, prompting assistant manager Peter Cormack to say that Morton may well have got a bargain. "He looks like one who's slipped through the net," was how he put it.

A day later, the 4th August, 1996, tragedy struck when manager Allan McGraw's wife Jean died after a long and brave battle with cancer. It was a distressing blow for what was a very tight family unit.

On 10th August the season proper began with a Challenge Cup tie at Station Park against Third Division Forfar. Morton were on a hiding to nothing, but they fronted up well and eased through by 4-0, a Lilley double being accompanied by goals from Rajamaki and young Paddy Flannery, back at Cappielow after a loan spell at Irish club Ards.

A cup double was achieved the following Tuesday at Cappielow in the Coca-Cola Cup when Second Division Hamilton were knocked out on penalties after a 1-1 draw at full time, Peter Cormack getting the home goal.

Allan McGraw was still seeking a midfield player saying that, while delighted to have got Matheson, the player was not so much a genuine midfielder as someone who liked to operate in behind the front men.

The league programme, with Morton now playing in their familiar blue and white hoops, albeit broader stripes than traditional, began with a home match against Clydebank, won 3-0 with goals by Lilley (2) and Flannery who came on as a sub. Unfortunately Janne Lindberg was injured and missed the next match at Dens Park where Dundee won 2-1, Lilley again being on the mark. The injury jinx struck again, Alan Mahood requiring seven stitches in a leg wound sustained after a reckless tackle by Chic Charnley.

Dundee had lost several players, including wing star Neil McCann to Hearts, from the previous term, but manager Jim Duffy had managed to assemble a more than decent squad. While admiring Morton, who had done so well the previous season, Duffy did, however, offer words of caution when he pointed out that this time they would be no unknown quantity. It was a prescient warning.

Warren Hawke, who had gone 21 competitive games without scoring, was dropped as Morton beat Queen of the South, coached by old Cappielow star Rowan Alexander, 2-1 at Cappielow, goals by Lilley and Anderson. On the last Saturday of the month the Greenock side then went to the top of the division with a 1-0 home win over Falkirk, for whom manager Allan McGraw's son Mark was playing.

Minus Janne Lindberg, the goal was scored by his fellow Finn Mark Rajamaki, but it was Alan Mahood who was the top home player in a mediocre match.

There then followed a thrilling Coca-Cola Cup tie at Cappielow against Aberdeen which went into extra time after Roy Aitken's side equalised with a minute of normal time to go to make it 3-3. Derek Lilley (2) and John Anderson were the home scorers. In an astonishing period of extra time, the Dons smacked four goals past David Wylie who, despite the eventual scoreline, had an excellent game. The crowd was 6,324.

Derek Lilley, with eight goals in seven games, was carrying the main scoring burden, once again attracting the attention of would-be buyers. Allan McGraw was voted manager of the month and everything seemed to be running well.

East Fife held the Greenock side to a goalless draw at Cappielow before Morton knocked Partick Thistle out of the Challenge Cup 2-1 at home with goals by youngsters Ross Matheson and Paddy Flannery.

A 2-1 league win followed at Broadwood, the temporary home of Airdrie, goals by Rajamaki and Lindberg, though at a cost as centre half Brian Reid sprained his ankle. When Stirling were beaten 3-1 at Forthbank, Flannery, Lilley and Lindberg scoring, Morton were back at the top. Manager McGraw had described it as a must-win contest, his pre-match warning to his players being that failure would be met by them "all getting tickets for the next Sydney Devine concert." It ranks up there with the best motivational comments.

Morton had not yet really shown the quality of play which had marked their previous season. There was reason to assume, as September drew to a close, that things were going better than expected. Top of the league and yet to find their best form.

It was a false dawn. From that high point the season began to come apart. First derby rivals St Mirren administered a 3-1 defeat at Cappielow. Flannery was sent off after just 20 minutes, his manager saying: "All I've got to say is that he will be severely disciplined." The only silver lining was a goal at last by Warren Hawke, his first in 28 competitive games.

Stranraer then provided a shock in the Challenge Cup semi-final with a 3-0 win at Stair Park, prompting Allan McGraw to ponder: "After a display like that I have to question the bottle of my players."

Young midfielder Steve Aitken came in for the next match, against Partick at home, which was won with a goal by Brian Reid, and Morton had rallied to climb to second place, one point behind leaders Dundee. Aitken, in fact, was one of the team's better players, his trademark determination being a feature.

Injuries, which had been all too prominent in the last couple of seasons, again came to the fore. Janne Lindberg damaged ligaments in an ankle in a 3-2 defeat of Finland by Switzerland, ruling him out for three weeks, while Alan Mahood too was a doubt for the forthcoming game against promotion candidates St Johnstone at Perth. The situation was exacerbated by a motorway pile-up which led to Morton arriving five minutes after kick-off time at McDiarmid Park. With only time for a very brief warm-up, the visitors looked well off the pace at the start and were eventually beaten 1-0.

Clydebank then won 2-1 at Boghead, Kilbowie Park having been sold, Derek Lilley getting the sole Morton counter, and the Greenock men were now down in fourth place. The performance rather than the result dismayed Allan McGraw who said: "We were a disgrace. They just quit and I won't accept quitters. I know players don't deliberately go out to play badly and I know everyone can have a bad game, but I can't accept that and the players had better not accept it." Only Derek Collins and Steve Aitken were absolved.

I wrote: "Last season's performances, which led to them being pipped for second place on goal difference by Dundee United, set a standard." It was a standard Morton were falling well short of, even if allowing for the absence of transferred Derek McInnes and injury problems affecting key men such as Lilley, Lindberg and Mahood.

Rumours then began to circulate about Celtic taking an interest in Lindberg. The Finnish captain's contract expired at the end of the season. He was clearly playing at a level below his ability and he told the Greenock Telegraph: "If Morton do not win promotion I will have to think about my future again for my family's sake. I am now 30-years-old and if I do not get a good offer here I may have to think about something else in Europe or back home."

A 1-1 draw followed at home to Airdrie, Derek Lilley again being on target, but it was less than impressive after the visitors' goalkeeper was ordered off after 22 minutes.

By this time Lindberg was out injured again, this time a foot problem omitting him for a fortnight, though on the plus side Alan Mahood was back in action. St Mirren then inflicted defeat by 1-0 at Love Street and Morton had now taken just five points from a possible 21 in their last seven league appearances. Peter Cormack was sent off, leading to a four-match ban, and Morton had fallen to seventh place in the table.

Derek Lilley's first hat-trick for the club at home to Stirling in a 3-2 win stabilised things, but it was a disjointed display and offered little more comfort than the points themselves.

With Brian Reid and Steve McCahill now the first choice centre backs, Dougie Johnstone had expressed a desire to leave Morton, and the month of November ended with a drab goalless draw at Firhill against Partick.

Gates were falling, the home average of 4,074 of the previous season declining towards the 3,000-mark, not helped when St Johnstone came to Greenock and won 2-0. There was some respite when East Fife were cruelly exposed in a 3-0 victory at Bayview, Rajamaki, Anderson and Lilley getting on the scoresheet, restoring Morton to fifth place in the table.

A point was taken from a dour, goalless encounter at Falkirk before the year ended with a 2-2 draw at Cappielow against Clydebank, Lilley and Anderson getting on target. Extraordinarily, Warren Hawke had now gone 40 games with only one goal to his credit. For someone who had taken Cappielow by storm on his transfer at the start of the previous season it was an astonishing transformation. I have said before that I felt a back injury sustained at Firhill the previous term against Hamilton was a turning point in Hawke's Cappielow career. But, whatever the reason, a player who looked such a natural goalscorer when he arrived in Greenock was never quite the same force after those early months at Morton. He always, however, remained a firm favourite with the fans.

By now Rangers had joined the list of English and Scottish clubs interested in Morton striker Derek Lilley who enhanced his ambitions for a move with a fine strike in a 4-3 defeat by Stirling at Forthbank, Blair and Anderson getting the other goals. Cormack and Flannery then scored in a 2-0 win at Cappielow over East Fife, skipper Janne Lindberg limping off. It was turning into a very frustrating season for the Finn who had been subject to a series of injuries.

Airdrie inflicted a 1-0 defeat followed by a Partick victory by 3-1 at Cappielow, the sole redeeming factor being a goal by Warren Hawke, his second strike in 42 games. Morton were fourth bottom, a considerable disappointment after just failing to gain a play-off place the previous term. Injuries and loss of form by key players were largely to blame, plus a continuing lack of depth to the squad.

Effectively the league season was over in any meaningful way. A spirited Arbroath side held Morton to a 2-2 Scottish Cup third round draw at Gayfield, Rajamaki and Hawke scoring for the visitors. In the replay the following Tuesday, Morton brushed aside the east coast club's challenge, goals by Lilley, Blair, Hawke and Cormack being unanswered. That set up a fourth round tie against Dundee at Cappielow.

League leaders St Johnstone, making big strides towards promotion, won 1-0 at McDiarmid Park, only an inspired display by Morton goalkeeper David Wylie preventing a heavier loss, before a welcome derby win over St Mirren by 2-0 at Cappielow. The goals came from Mahood and Lilley and provided Morton with their first home league win over their Paisley rivals for 14 years. Most welcome was the return to form of Alan Mahood after a lacklustre season.

Janne Lindberg meanwhile spoke of his disenchantment with the Greenock club at the lack of fresh faces, believing staleness had crept in following the exertions of the previous season. His contract was due to run out at the end of the term and it seemed unlikely that he would be keen to stay. He wanted to play at a higher level and, despite the injury problems which had bedevilled him, he was more than capable of playing in the top flight in Scotland.

A crowd of 4,195 turned out at Cappielow for the fourth round Scottish Cup tie with Dundee, a late equaliser by the Dens men securing a 2-2 draw. Lilley and Hawke were the home scorers and it was on to Tayside on the Tuesday for the replay. In dramatic style it took a late winner from 20-year-old Barry Mason in extra time to grab an unexpected victory, David Wylie having been the earlier hero with a penalty save. The reward was a home quarter-final tie with Premier League Kilmarnock.

Morton were stumbling along in the league, a Mahood goal gaining the three points against Stirling at Cappielow, before a 2-0 home loss to Falkirk. Morton fielded virtually a reserve team with the cup clash against Killie in mind a few days later. The precaution served little purpose as the Ayrshire men triumphed 5-2 despite an Alan Mahood double. A frustrated home centre back Steve McCahill was sent off for a scything tackle on Paul Wright before a Cappielow crowd of 8,834.

The season was over for Morton in a competitive sense and in mid-March Janne Lindberg served further notice of his growing disaffection with the club when contract talks broke down. Lindberg told me: "My agent told Mr Wilson [Morton chairman John Wilson] what terms I was looking for and he [Mr Wilson] said 'no way'. He then said he would help me to find a new club. What annoys me is that they haven't offered me anything." John Wilson refused to comment.

St Mirren then beat Morton 3-1 at Love Street, Warren Hawke continuing his improved form with the visitors' goal, and the atmosphere was once more one of increasing discontent among the fans. The club appeared to be slipping backwards again and the mood was not improved when, on Friday 21st March, it was announced that Morton and Dundee United, under former Cappielow boss Tommy McLean, had agreed a deal for striker Derek Lilley. For a sum of £350,000 plus ex-Rangers striker Sandy Robertson, it was a done deal. Only Robertson's terms had to be finalised but, dramatically, United placed a time limit of midnight on the transfer taking place. Morton were unable to agree terms with Robertson in the given time and the move fell through.

On the Saturday Lilley did his cause no harm with two goals in a 3-0 away win at Partick, John Anderson scoring the third. It proved to be Lilley's final appearance for Morton. Chelsea, Leeds and Crystal Palace were now in the running for his signature, much to the annoyance of Dundee United manager Tommy McLean who accused Morton of using his club's bid to up the fee. He stated: "My information is that the chairman [John Wilson] is talking to Crystal Palace and asking them to make an offer. When they get that offer he'll phone Leeds to ask them to better it. Morton work in a strange way, but that's not a criticism. I wouldn't work that way, but it's the law of the jungle and their prerogative." If Morton were trying to maximise the fee one could hardly blame them. It was then revealed that Palace had fallen out of the bidding, leaving the way open for Leeds to conclude a deal. It was later revealed by Allan McGraw, in response to Tommy McLean's criticism, that Lilley had rejected Palace after the clubs had agreed a fee.

By Friday 28th March it was announced through the Greenock Telegraph that 23-year-old Lilley was on his way to Elland Road for a new club record fee of £500,000, a further

£200,000 being on the table should he play so many first team games. Leeds' Scottish boss George Graham had got his man. The player, dubbed Vialli by Morton fans due to his shaven head, expressed his delight while Ton boss Allan McGraw said: "I know the fans will be disappointed to lose Derek but it was an offer we couldn't refuse."

And so the forward, who had joined the club as a youngster in 1991 from Everton Boys' Club, was on his way south. He had topped the scoring charts at Cappielow for the past three seasons, his total for the current term being 22. He was full of praise for Allan McGraw, saying: "He's one of the best. He's set me in good stead. He is a very straightforward man and that is the way it should be."

Good player though he was, Lilley was never quite to make it at the top level in England. He had pace, strength, and could score goals. But his one, crucial, flaw was a lack of a good enough first touch for the highest pinnacles of the game.

As a very disappointing season drew to a conclusion, with St Johnstone running away with the title, Allan McGraw declared that he needed four more players for the new term – two in midfield and two up front. That, however, was further complicated by the fact that the contracts of Finnish pair Janne Lindberg and Marko Rajamaki were up at the end of the season. Already Lindberg was making noises of departing. In the twilight years of his career he knew he had one more big pay day. Added to that was what he felt to be a lack of ambition at Cappielow after failing so narrowly to clinch a place in the Premier League the previous season.

St Johnstone recorded their fourth win of the season over Morton by the only goal of the game at Cappielow. Some cheer was restored with a resounding 4-1 away win over East Fife, Hawke (2), Mahood and Rajamaki being on the scoresheet. Before the game there was a minute's silence in respect of the deaths of former Morton defender John Boyd and Development Club worker Jim Beckett.

Meanwhile Morton revealed a blueprint for a new stand to replace the Cowshed, submitting it to the council for approval. This came at a time when there was growing criticism from varying quarters, among them former Celtic player and Gourockian Davie Provan through a newspaper column, at the state of Cappielow. Some of the comment was merited, but I felt the comparison with the new grounds that had been built for St Johnstone, Clyde, Stirling and Livingston was not at all well founded. St Johnstone had well and truly landed on their feet through Muirton Park being in a prime development area. Not only that, but a local farmer donated land for a new stadium. This was not in any way a fair comparison to the situation in Greenock. As for the other new grounds, they were all provided by the respective local authorities to whom the clubs paid a rent.

That was never in Inverclyde Council's plans, nor would it necessarily have been desirable for Morton. If you concede ownership of your ground you have no collateral if required.

Warren Hawke continued his recovery from that awful barren spell with goals against Airdrie, in a 1-1 draw at Cappielow, and the sole counter in a victory at Clydebank, his 10th of the season, before the departed Derek Lilley was voted Player of the Year by the Greenock Telegraph readers. The final game of the season resulted in a 3-0 defeat away to Scottish Cup Finalists Falkirk, leaving Morton in third bottom position of the table.

Hawke was another yet to agree terms for the new season and he reflected the unrest among some of the senior players when he said: "I would like to see the club having a bit more ambition this year." It was an echo of a previous statement by Janne Lindberg and Hawke continued: "If Janne goes it would be a big blow."

In fact Lindberg did leave, choosing to sign on with German Second Division club Saarbrucken. Also on the way out was Finnish compatriot Marko Rajamaki. On the same Friday, 28th June, as the departure of the Finns was announced, assistant manager Peter Cormack's exodus was also revealed in the Greenock Telegraph. Neither Cormack nor any of the Cappielow board was available for comment.

It became clear that the feeling of the Morton board was that the management and coaching staff were top heavy and needed to be pruned. Allan McGraw, however, was angry at the manner of the story breaking prematurely, saying: "I know this has come from someone at a high level within the club. I am ashamed of them. They didn't respect the man's wishes." This was in reference to an agreement that the Cormack news would not be announced until the Monday when the assistant manager himself would make a statement.

Once again the club's public relations had been found wanting. It also came out through Peter Cormack that he had been approached about becoming manager at Cappielow with Allan McGraw switching to a position as director of football. Allan McGraw responded: "That has never been mentioned to me. It might have been said to Peter by someone else, but it was never mentioned to me." There were clear divisions within the board. On one hand chairman John Wilson was an avowed supporter of manager Allan McGraw while Douglas Rae had been keen to see Peter Cormack have the decisive say in team matters.

With defender Jim Hunter also announcing his retirement from football, after a third cruciate ligament injury, Morton were once again making the news in a negative sense. Lindberg, Lilley and Rajamaki were all gone, along with the assistant manager. It brought a renewed clamour of discontent among the fans.

Three Austrian players – striker Christian Koell (21), midfielder Marko Felbermayr (25) and defender Marcus Sukalia (25) – had meanwhile arrived at Cappielow on a three-month loan period arranged through agent Brian Whittaker, the former Hearts and Celtic defender. None was to set the heather alight. The heather did not even smoulder.

Striker Warren Hawke then declared his frustration at the lack of progress on the renewal of his contract, as did goalkeeper David Wylie, in his testimonial year at Morton.

Once more the fans were expressing their concerns as Morton appeared to be sinking back into a state of mediocrity.

Morton director Douglas Rae, the sole shareholder of Morton FC Enterprises, a company set up with the purpose of supplying Morton with a commercial income and benefits, then expressed an interest in a possible takeover of the club. He said: "If I ever acquired ownership, I would give a public undertaking that when the time came to sell on, any monies in excess of the purchase price would be given as a donation to the club."

In the balance sheet for the year ended 15th May, 1997, there was a trading loss of £238,466, with transfer income of £525,000 offsetting that.

CHAPTER TWENTY-SEVEN

Allan McGraw resigns, Hugh Scott arrives and Greenock Telegraph is banned

That things were less than harmonious within the club was highlighted on Wednesday 23rd July, 1997, when manager Allan McGraw (58) announced his shock resignation. He stated as his reason that he was fed up over infighting among the board who had split into pro and anti-McGraw factions.

Chairman and owner John Wilson believed McGraw's resignation was partly brought about by a member or members of his board and said: "A lot of people have to look at themselves and ask what they could have done to prevent Allan's resignation – and that includes members of the board." The board at the time comprised Wilson himself, Andy Gemmell, Ken Woods, Douglas Rae and Arthur Montford, the first three all known to support McGraw. Wilson continued: "This is the saddest day I can recall in living memory. I have lost a dedicated and capable manager."

Asked what he would do about boardroom unrest, John Wilson replied: "I will do something about it. There will be changes which may include myself."

Allan McGraw explained his position, saying: "Things have been unhealthy. I think too much of the club to have it brought into disrepute. I don't want a part of it." The manager went on to say that from board level right down through the club there was too much bickering, some of which had been finding its way into the media. He expanded by saying: "If people want to criticise they should do it to your face." Also departing, in support of manager McGraw, was chief scout Jake Anderson.

The crisis was mounting. We didn't know it then, but it was to herald probably the worst period in Morton's history.

On Saturday 26th July, 1997, I was able to reveal in the Greenock Telegraph that a wealthy Kilmacolm businessman was about to take over Morton from John Wilson. By the Monday I could say that he was financier Hugh Scott who owned Scott and Company Financial Services. He had operated in offices in Largs for 15 years.

Scott had come to a verbal agreement with John Wilson on the acquisition of his majority shareholding. He was saying all the right things; just what the fans wanted to hear. He announced that he wanted a "stadium for the people of Greenock." He continued: "Our priority is to give a commitment to the people in the Cowshed."

Scott spoke of creating a family atmosphere at Cappielow and said that Allan McGraw would now be director of football. He told me that there would be a cash injection with extended ground development a priority and fresh funding for players. There would also, he said, be an end to the internal divisions which had bedevilled Morton for some time.

Rangers player Ian Durrant (30) was targeted as a possible player-coach. Allan McGraw would be his mentor. It all sounded very positive.

Hugh Scott arrived for the club AGM, held at the Tontine Hotel in Greenock at the end of July, and straight away the alarm bells began to ring. He turned up in his Bentley along with Morton director Andy Gemmell but then proceeded to behave in the most bizarre fashion when Greenock Telegraph photographer Mark Gibson attempted to take a picture of him. Gibson and reporter Roy Templeton received a verbal tongue-lashing and at one stage Scott covered his head with his own jacket. He then chased Gibson round some cars parked outside the hotel before getting back into his car and speeding off.

He soon returned to confront Mark Gibson and Roy Templeton, who were by now quite bewildered. His attacking verbal volley continued in which he said that any deal to be done with Morton depended upon Gibson handing over his film. He then asked staff members at the Tontine Hotel if anything could be done "about the riff-raff", a reference to the Greenock Telegraph representatives. The hotel staff looked as bemused as everyone else. Needless to say no film was handed over. A picture appeared of Scott, jacket over head, in the next day's Telegraph. It was an astonishing performance by the man due to take over the town's football club.

Still there was optimism among the fans, though I wrote: "Fans, real and potential, are sceptical by nature. They have heard ambitious noises many times before in the past only for their hopes to be dashed. They need to be convinced that there is a solid base to the club's ambitions. Only time will provide that answer."

Douglas Rae and Arthur Montford were to leave the board, the latter saying: "If you are not wanted there is no point in being there and, based on what we heard at the AGM, and comments made by the chief executive after the meeting, it was clear we didn't figure in his plans."

On 9th August, 1997, the deal's conclusion was announced. John Wilson commented: "The time has come for someone with new ideas to come in and I am confident Hugh Scott will have a long and lasting relationship with the Inverclyde populace."

Scott himself said: "It's not always business reasons that drive you to seize an opportunity like this and there is a degree of emotion attached to the club."

Whatever his fluctuating popularity, John Wilson's heart was in the right place and he undoubtedly left Morton Football Club in a far healthier situation than the one in which he found it when he arrived at the club. I may have experienced difficulties with his management style on occasions, but I had no reason to doubt the sincerity of his feelings of well-being towards the club.

On the field Morton had beaten Ayr United on the opening day of the season at Somerset Park 2-1 with goals by Paddy Flannery and Alan Mahood. A deal was also concluded to bring ex-Ranger and Oldham player John Morrow to Cappielow.

Airdrie were dispatched 4-1 at home in the Coca Cola Cup thanks to a Warren Hawke hat-trick and a goal by Steve Aitken, before goals by Paddy Flannery (2) and John Anderson saw Albion Rovers knocked out of the League Challenge Cup. Unfortunately new boy Morrow broke a leg in that match.

It had been a bright enough start to the new term, but successive defeats followed to Hamilton and Motherwell by 2-0 and 3-0 respectively, the latter in the third round of the Coca Cola Cup. Stirling were beaten 3-1 at Forthbank, goals by Hawke (2), back at his scoring best, and Blair, to take Morton to third top spot in the league before an Alan Blaikie double carried Ton into the League Challenge Cup quarter-finals.

Young ex-Rangers player Jaswinder 'Jazz' Juttla came in on a free transfer before a derby defeat by 2-1 at Love Street against rivals St Mirren. Paul Blair scored the Morton goal. By now the Austrian trio of players had been found wanting, all three returning to their homeland.

A Scott McArthur goal against Clydebank was enough to take Morton into the Challenge Cup semi-final before goalkeeper David Wylie gave a top display in his own testimonial match against Rangers, won 2-0 at Cappielow by the Ibrox men.

The next day it was announced that Allan McGraw's son, Mark, would be returning to Morton on a free transfer from Falkirk. Dad Allan then found himself being honoured, the Variety Club of Great Britain holding a tribute dinner for him, the proceeds going to a children's charity. Chairing the event was Manchester United manager and fellow Govan man Alex Ferguson who said: "I can't think of anyone I'd like to pay tribute to more than Allan and I had no hesitation in accepting the invitation."

Morton drew 1-1 with Airdrie, skipper Derek Collins getting a rare goal, and things seemed to be settling down again at Cappielow. It was the calm before the storm. On Wednesday 17th September the front page of the Greenock Telegraph carried a news story in which Ravi Khosla, who owned the Douglas Hotel in Arran, claimed that Hugh Scott had failed to settle a bill after the team and staff had attended a one-night golfing break in the island at the end of July.

Khosla said: "The players and staff were great, but Mr Scott won't be setting foot back in my hotel."

Scott claimed the bill eventually had been settled. The day after the story appeared, the Greenock Telegraph was banned from Cappielow and Allan McGraw was under instruction not to talk to the newspaper. That night Morton were due to play Queen of the South at home in the League Challenge Cup semi-final.

I sent our sports reporter, Scott McBride, to cover the game from the terracings which he did in light-hearted style, at the same time canvassing the views of members of the support on the Telegraph ban. There was general befuddlement and quite a lot of disquiet. Queens, as it happened, won the game 2-0.

We were now seeing a very different Hugh Scott from the one who had charmed all and sundry with his rose-tinted vision of the future. Following upon his strange behaviour in chasing our photographer round parked cars at the club's AGM, this was another first in my experience. We had never been banned from Cappielow before. The then editor of the

Greenock Telegraph, Ian Wilson, and I talked about the situation. It was discussed whether or not in future we should attempt to cover future home matches from the stand or terracings.

My view was that we should abide by the ban and that was the decision we arrived at. It was my belief that Morton would suffer more than we as a newspaper through a lack of publicity. We should not allow ourselves to be bullied. The decision was taken that we would, alternately, cover Rangers and Celtic, there being a large support for both in Greenock and district. This might upset some Morton fans, but the ban was Scott's decision, not ours. I felt most readers would understand our position. I wrote: "In future we will heed the ban. We will cover other things."

We were witnessing, even in the first few weeks of Scott's ownership of Morton, the tip of a very chilling iceberg. The new owner's words upon taking over were one thing; deeds another.

It now seemed clear that the talk of bringing Ian Durrant to Cappielow as a player-coach was nothing more than talk. Then Scott declared via the internet that plans for ground development were to be shelved "due to boo-boys" among the support.

Cappielow was in turmoil. The team travelled to Firhill to meet Partick where they lost 2-1, John Anderson scoring. At the after-match press conference Allan McGraw was asked about the situation. He admitted that off-field matters were affecting his players and responded: "He [Scott] has got to sort it out and I'm hoping that he will do it very quickly."

In the following week it became clear that Scott was trying to acquire a new manager, Billy Stark being the man in question. The ex-St Mirren, Aberdeen and Celtic player was being lined up, along with former Celtic coach Frank Connor and ex-Aberdeen and St Mirren winger Peter Weir.

On Saturday 27th September Morton were beaten 2-0 at home by league leaders Dundee. The Greenock Telegraph were still banned. I reported on the Rangers-Motherwell match at Ibrox, a 2-2 draw. It was a strange experience. The following Wednesday the new Cappielow management team was introduced to the press at Cappielow. The Telegraph ban had been rescinded.

John McMaster left the club and Allan McGraw, to put it politely, was elevated upstairs into a meaningless role. The press conference was embarrassing. I met Allan in the corridor before it began and asked what was happening to him. He didn't know. Stark, Connor and Weir were then announced as the new manager, assistant manager and youth coach. Allan McGraw was to be director/general manager. Effectively he was being pushed aside.

The following day I wrote: "There is no doubt that his removal from the football side of the club was a blow to McGraw when the announcement was made at a press conference at Cappielow yesterday morning. Prior to the meeting he wasn't sure what was to happen.

"He managed to retain his dignity, however, and commented that he would make a decision on his future by Monday."

Hugh Scott was effusive in his praise of McGraw and said he wanted him to oversee "three new, unique multi-million pound projects." The words had a very hollow ring to them. By any standard McGraw was being shamefully treated.

Billy Stark, who had been Tommy Burns' assistant at Kilmarnock Football Club and then Celtic, deserved the full backing of the support. Whatever had happened wasn't his fault. But Allan McGraw deserved a whole lot better.

Stark's first match in charge was a 3-1 home defeat against Raith Rovers, Alan Blaikie netting. There was to be no money for new players unless others left. Morton were third bottom and the attendance, for a new manager, was a modest 2,309.

McGraw chose to remain at Cappielow and make the best of his situation, a decision based on what he felt was best for the club at that time. He said: "I had to take the phone off the hook because of the number of people calling to ask me to stay."

Meanwhile Hugh Scott announced that he wanted commercial income at Cappielow to be at least £1.5 million. I, on the other hand, wanted to be a millionaire, have a yacht in the Greek islands and a castle in the Highlands. This was now dreamland.

The previous board of directors – John Wilson, Douglas Rae, Arthur Montford, Ken Woods and Andy Gemmell – were all gone. The new board comprised Hugh Scott, his wife Elizabeth and Allan McGraw. Andy Gemmell was to be reinstated as general manager of Morton Enterprises though that did not last long.

On the park things were less than bright. A 1-0 defeat by Falkirk and 1-1 home draw with Ayr, John Anderson scoring, were followed by a 1-0 defeat at Hamilton which saw Morton plunge to second bottom spot. Midfielder Stuart Gray had been brought in on a three-month loan from Celtic, then striker Peter Duffield arrived from Raith Rovers. No fee was mentioned for the 28-year-old Englishman who marked his debut against derby rivals St Mirren at Cappielow in spectacular fashion, netting twice in a 3-0 win, Warren Hawke grabbing the third strike. Ex-Scunthorpe and Hearts midfielder Mark Gavin played his only game, as a trialist, for the club in that derby clash.

On Saturday 15th November, 1997, Morton drew 3-3 away to Airdrie, goals by courtesy of skipper Derek Collins and a Warren Hawke brace. It took Morton up to eighth place and put Hawke on eight goals for the season. The team was (4-4-2): Wylie; Collins, Anderson, Reid, Cormack; Blaikie, Mahood, Gray, McPherson; Duffield, Hawke. For Alan Mahood it marked a comeback from yet another injury, this time to a cartilage.

Billy Stark was beginning to make his mark on the side, and moved to sign 31-year-old Greenockian Owen Archdeacon from Carlisle. The two had played together at Celtic and Archdeacon went straight into the team at left back to meet league leaders Dundee at Dens Park. A Hawke strike won all three points, though Morton actually dropped to seventh place in the table.

Billy Stark was remoulding the side, based upon a flat back four, and a 3-2 win followed at Cappielow against a Partick Thistle side now threatened with liquidation. Scorers were Reid, Archdeacon and Gray before a crowd of 3,384. A creditable goalless draw at Stark's Park meant Morton had gone four games undefeated for a return of 10 points.

Yet that was the precursor to Hugh Scott launching an attack against his own potential support in a national tabloid, saying: "It still annoys me that there is so much apathy from the people of Greenock towards their local club. It really is pathetic."

Quite what he expected that level of support to be, one could only imagine. Two seasons previously, when narrowly pipped for promotion to the Premier League and playing some superb football, Morton's average crowd was 4,074. They were currently seventh in the table and their last home attendance had been over 3,300. That didn't seem at all bad to me. It was as if Scott was preparing the way for failure; providing his excuses in advance.

The revival was halted with successive defeats at home to Falkirk, by 2-0, and Stirling, 3-1 (Duffield). Morton were now third bottom and, after a dreadful performance against Stirling, manager Stark commented at the press conference: "Where do we start?"

The reply from a press man was immediate: "Perhaps with the bottle in front of you."

Days later a disillusioned Allan McGraw expressed his own personal frustration when he said: "I feel like I'm picking up my wages without doing anything. I don't like that. I don't feel involved and honestly feel that I'm not needed."

Paddy Flannery was then transferred to Dumbarton and when Ayr beat Morton 2-1 at Somerset Park, Hawke netting the consolation goal, Morton had hit the bottom of the table. The feel-good factor upon the advent of the new regime was swirling steadily down a stank.

The New Year brought with it the Scottish Cup draw, and Morton were paired in the third round with Celtic at Parkhead. It was a return for Billy Stark to the home of his last managerial role, as assistant to Tommy Burns, and a trip he welcomed. For Morton, it would be their first visit to the revamped Celtic stadium.

Cappielow owner Hugh Scott also announced that work would begin on the upgrading of Cappielow. This was to take place in three phases: 1 – the refurbishment of the south stand; 2 – the covering of the west stand; 3 – construction of a north stand. These works were to be carried out by Barr Holdings Ltd. The work would begin with phase one at a cost of £250,000. The total cost was estimated at £2.5-3 million.

1998 began badly on the field with a 3-2 derby defeat against St Mirren at Love Street, Ton goals from Blair and Mahood. Alan Mahood also was sent off for a second bookable offence a minute from time.

On Saturday 10th January Allan McGraw decided enough was enough, and resigned by mutual agreement with Hugh Scott. He had been increasingly unhappy with what he felt was a meaningless role as director of football. The original intention, for him to oversee the introduction of a player-coach, had not materialised. So, an association with Morton which had begun as a player in 1961, came to an end. No one has ever given more to a football club than Allan McGraw gave to Morton. As a player he scored a club record 58 league and cup goals in season 1963-64. As a manager he came in at a time when the club badly needed financial security. He set up a much needed and highly credible youth policy, and his transfer dealings quickly turned round a critical situation.

His belief in playing attractive football was constant, typified by the side which narrowly lost out on promotion to the Premier Division in 1995-96 season. Into the bargain he was recognised by players and press men alike as being thoroughly straight and honest. He was a gentleman. McGraw's name was synonymous with Greenock Morton and his legacy will be remembered for all the right reasons. Hugh Scott will not be able to say the same.

A 2-0 loss at home to Airdrie saw Morton remain in bottom place, though there was some light on the horizon when the side drew 0-0 at home with the league leaders. For Morton it marked the debut of Kevin Twaddle, after signing from Raith Rovers, and the final game of his loan period of Celtic midfielder Stuart Gray. Also leaving the club for Hamilton was left back Scott McArthur who wanted regular first team football.

Next up was the Celtic tie and Morton at least made a respectable exit, losing 2-0 to Wim Jansen's side. Central defender Brian Reid and John Anderson were the top visiting performers in a display in which I wrote that "enterprise was always subdued by caution". The team that day was (4-4-2): Hillcoat; Collins, Reid, Anderson, Archdeacon; Blair (McGraw), Aitken, Mahood, Blaikie (McPherson); Duffield, Hawke.

Twaddle, Reid and Duffield scored in a 3-3 draw at Firhill with Partick on a day when central defender Dougie Johnstone left the club for Stranraer and goalkeeper Neil Inglis for Clydebank. Johnstone had served Morton well, and was a bit unfortunate to lose his first team spot. Another draw, this time 1-1 with Twaddle on the mark, followed at Falkirk before Peter Cormack was ruled out for a year with a cruciate knee injury sustained while training with Carlisle. Morton also had a bid for Dunfermline's experienced midfielder Harry Curran (31) turned down.

Hugh Scott's controversial ownership continued with claims by him that he had received death threats in telephone calls made to his Kilmacolm home, a matter he reported to the police. There was less controversial news on 14th February when Morton at last moved off the bottom of the table, Hamilton being beaten 3-1 at Cappielow. A John Anderson double and a goal by Alan Mahood gave them their first win in 11 games before an attendance of 1,717.

Morton were beginning to show signs of becoming a team under Stark. Collins, Mahood and Duffield continued the progress with goals in a 3-1 home win over second top Raith Rovers for whom manager Jimmy Nicholl was less than pleased. His after-match team talk lasted 45 minutes. The Northern Irishman's rant was akin to Ian Paisley at full blast and may well have been heard back in Belfast.

Duffield and Mahood scored in a 2-2 Cappielow draw with Stirling before it was time to travel north-east to meet league leaders Dundee once more. This time Billy Stark got his man, and Harry Curran lined up in the visitors' midfield. It was not enough to prevent a 2-0 defeat, but the new boss was starting to shape a side in his own mould.

Alan Mahood scored the only goal of the game against Partick at Cappielow, his fourth in five games, and Morton by this time were fourth from the bottom and beginning a recognisable ascent. Back in action in goal was veteran David Wylie in place of John Hillcoat. Another to return in the next match was John Morrow after a leg break which had sidelined him for three months, the game ending 1-1 with a goal by Peter Duffield. Morton's squad now had a much more solid look to it.

At this time Morton's country rivals St Mirren were in ownership turmoil too. Reg Brealey, a highly controversial character who had previously owned Darlington Football Club, was attempting to take over. His bid was much against the wishes of manager Tony Fitzpatrick, unsurprisingly as Brealey had been the subject of a Frontline Scotland programme which painted him in a very poor light. The programme claimed that a warrant was still out for Brealey's arrest should he ever set foot in India where he had had business dealings. Brealey's name was to crop up later regarding Morton Football Club.

At this time Hugh Scott also banned Andy Morrison from Cappielow. Morrison had been running the official Morton website and Scott accused him of spreading a rumour linking Morton in a possible merger with St Mirren. It was a charge Andy Morrison indignantly denied, but the conflict was becoming typical of Scott's dealings with anyone he perceived to be out of step with his views.

A Hawke goal gained Morton a point against Airdrie away, then Ayr, desperately fighting against relegation, took all three points with the only goal of the game at Cappielow.

Billy Stark was shaping his own side, having signed Peter Duffield, Owen Archdeacon, Kevin Twaddle, John Hillcoat and Harry Curran, allowing Paddy Flannery, Scott McArthur, Neil Inglis, Barry Mason and Mark McGraw to leave.

But always there was unrest off the pitch. Danny Goodwin, the editor of the Morton fanzine The Cappielow Bugle, was next to be banned from Cappielow, no reason being given. This ex-policeman who, like Andy Morrison, was a lifelong Morton fan and season ticket holder, said: "I do not know what is wrong with Mr Scott. He is acting outrageously." Ironically, Mr Goodwin revealed that he had supported Hugh Scott at the time of his takeover of Morton for his bright ideas and plans for the club. He was far from being alone. Scott had talked a good game.

Hugh Scott had commented at the time of Andy Morrison's ban: "Greenock Morton do not want to make any statement to the Greenock Telegraph now or at any time in the foreseeable future." He was unavailable for any further comment on this latest ban.

There was growing unease about Hugh Scott's running of Morton, though on the pitch the revival under Billy Stark continued with an emphatic 3-0 win at Hamilton, goals coming from Hawke, an own goal and one by Duffield. Morton were fifth top and they ensured that status when they won 1-0 at home to relegated Stirling in the final match of the season, Warren Hawke netting.

The club had failed to fix up Alan Mahood, however, and he departed on freedom of contract to Kilmarnock. Hugh Scott tried unsuccessfully to demand a fee from the Ayrshire club. Another blow fell when Brian Reid made it clear he too would be leaving, again under freedom of contract. The superb midfield of two seasons past comprising Alan Mahood, Derek McInnes and Janne Lindberg was now just a memory.

Billy Stark moved quickly to replace Reid with St Mirren's Paul Fenwick. Signing the 29-year-old Canadian international, on a Bosman, was a good bit of business and he was to prove a more than capable replacement for Brian Reid.

Towards the end of July, Morton, after a tour of Ireland, had a final pre-season win over Scottish Cup holders Hearts by 4-3 at Cappielow.

CHAPTER TWENTY-EIGHT

Conflict at Cappielow as morale deteriorates

Skipper Derek Collins declared that spirits were high in the squad as they prepared to face season 1998-99 and said: "We have high aims for this season. Promotion is the aim." The campaign, however, got off to a less than inspiring start. In front of an excellent home crowd of 5,647, Morton lost to a last-minute goal from Barry Lavety of Hibernian, relegated from the Premier Division but favourites to bounce straight back up.

A League Cup defeat to Third Division Ross County followed at the same venue, again by 1-0, a third 1-0 defeat following against Ayr at Somerset.

Into the squad came 20-year-old former Leeds midfielder Martin Foster while, off the pitch, former Livingston owner Bill Hunter was commissioned by Hugh Scott to look into ways of accomplishing a new stadium.

On the pitch the Greenock men continued to stumble, a Paul Fenwick goal being the sole consolation of a 2-1 Cappielow loss to Hamilton. It then came out that boss Billy Stark was interested in a swap deal between Morton and Falkirk, Peter Duffield going to Brockville and Brian Hamilton coming to Cappielow. This developed into an unseemly wrangle between the clubs. Duffield was signed on a two-year deal by Alex Totten, no fee going Morton's way despite Duffield being under contract, while Hamilton stayed put at Brockville.

Morton chairman Hugh Scott rounded on Alex Totten, a man much respected in football circles, and said: "Falkirk's attempt to link the two deals did not suit us, and we are very pleased that Duffield has now gone." Quite why he was pleased was a mystery to me. Duffield had been signed from Raith Rovers in the previous November for what the club later termed as a substantial fee and had ended up top scorer on 13 goals. He was now leaving for nothing.

Manager Billy Stark simply stated: "If you look at Peter's career he's never been with any club for a long spell. But it's not time to press the panic button." It was a peculiar statement. Why sign the player in the first place? Why the rush to get him out the door? As always there was a story behind the story. Peter Duffield had contacted me, wishing to put his side of another sorry mess. I said I would be only too pleased to do so but, at the time, his move to Falkirk was uncertain and I cautioned him to be careful on a decision to rush into print. He took my advice and I doubt if anyone was more pleased than he to gallop through the exit gate when the time came.

A 2-2 draw at home to Clydebank saw Morton collect their first point of the season, goals from Harry Curran and John Anderson, then another point was collected at Stark's Park in a 0-0 draw with Raith Rovers.

By this time Hugh Scott had abandoned phases two and three of the plan to upgrade Cappielow and was now looking to relocate the club at a new ground. Both local junior football club grounds, Woodhall and Ravenscraig, had been considered but were quickly ruled out by Inverclyde Council.

Then came more controversy when former centre back Brian Reid joined the ranks of those criticising the Cappielow club. Reid had signed under freedom of contract for English Second Division club Burnley, but he blasted his former employers, saying: "I've always had a fondness for Morton, but I was disappointed at the way it went. It was getting bitter towards the end. The offer they made to me was an insult and I thought I deserved better than that." Reid went on to say he had enjoyed working with Billy Stark. His unhappiness lay at a higher level within Cappielow.

Confidence in the running of Morton was haemorrhaging fast and kit manager Willie Gray, who had been with the club since the start of the 60s, was next to leave after an altercation with chairman Hugh Scott. Willie was as much a part of Morton as the Cowshed and, suffice it to say, words could not express what he felt at his treatment by Scott. Gray had been an excellent servant to Morton since 1961 and would be missed for his presence alone. It was becoming increasingly hard to believe any of Hugh Scott's utterances. I wrote: "Hugh Scott's early forecast of a new all-seated Cappielow has now been replaced by statements saying that unless Morton move to a new stadium by the year 2000 the club could die."

On the pitch things began to improve when a Warren Hawke strike won all three points in a controversial match at Airdrie's new Shyberry Excelsior Stadium. Three players were sent off, including Morton's Curran and Twaddle, while Airdrie boss Alex MacDonald and Morton assistant Frank Connor were sent to the stand for swapping a few choice Anglo-Saxon expletives.

On the following Friday long-serving goalkeeper David Wylie (32) was off to Clyde. He had been at the club since 1985, giving good service and becoming a fans' favourite, but he was yet another who seemed to have fallen foul of the Ton hierarchy. At that time he held the record for most appearances for the club, with 482. In his place came ex-Motherwell, Rangers and Dundee United goalkeeper Ally Maxwell (33) whose debut was in a 1-0 derby loss to St Mirren at Cappielow.

At Brockville, Morton then lost 2-1 to Falkirk, Fenwick scoring for the visitors. Warren Hawke, the sole striker at the club, was now playing in midfield and Morton remained firmly at the bottom of the table.

Some relief came with a 3-0 home win over Stranraer, Morton leapfrogging them and Raith Rovers into third bottom spot. Goals were from Twaddle, Matheson and Blaikie.

Meanwhile Hugh Scott claimed he had received several bids for Morton, including one of £6million. I would have loved to meet anyone at that time prepared to buy an ailing First

Division club with an antiquated stadium built in a low priority area of the town for such a price. Perhaps he could have been persuaded to buy my house for a similarly inflated fee.

If the fans were in a state of unrest, the air of disturbance became positively agitated when the word leaked out that the club was to discuss a change of name. That and the possibility of ground-sharing with another club were apparently on the agenda at the forthcoming AGM. The correspondence to the Greenock Telegraph was stinging in its criticism of Hugh Scott and his ownership of Morton.

Amidst the furore Ayr administered a 2-1 beating at Cappielow, Hawke netting the home goal in a game in which forward Steve McCormick made his debut on loan from Dundee.

Hugh Scott then declared, in face of a barrage of hostility, that the subject of any name change for Greenock Morton had been omitted from the AGM agenda. He said that £5million would be needed to modernise Cappielow. This was £2million more than he had claimed weeks earlier it would take to upgrade Cappielow in three phases. He said he could provide the finance to build a new 10,000 seater stadium if he could get the cooperation of Inverclyde Council in his attempts to find a suitable site. Manager Billy Stark said confidently: "I am really positive about a new stadium." I found it impossible to share that optimism.

Hibs and Clydebank then handed out 2-1 defeats, the Morton goals coming from Twaddle and Fenwick. Morton were second bottom. It is indicative of the turmoil at Cappielow at the time that results on the pitch were becoming of secondary interest to the fans.

By the end of October, 1998, Hugh Scott revealed plans for a new £7million stadium on the ground adjacent to Sinclair Street – an old railway marshalling yard – in which car parking was provided for Morton matches. Scott commented: "We are considering several offers for Cappielow but commercial confidentiality prevents me from revealing who the offers are from." Informal discussions had taken place with the council in respect of the plans and the land which it was believed belonged to Renfrewshire Enterprise.

By this time Scott's pronouncements were reminiscent of the boy who cried wolf, summed up by former manager Allan McGraw who said of the proposed £7m stadium: "I will believe it when I see it." He was far from alone in holding that view.

October ended on a high note on the pitch when Morton leapfrogged Raith Rovers into third bottom spot after a home 2-0 victory, goals from Warren Hawke, still playing in midfield, and on-loan striker Steve McCormick. Billy Stark was a happy man and commented: "It's a wee while since I've laughed and joked after a game." The attendance was 1,468.

On Wednesday 4th November, 1998, Morton submitted plans to Inverclyde Council for a new 10,000 all-seater stadium on the adjacent ground in Sinclair Street. If plans were approved, Hugh Scott asserted that work would begin in a year's time.

St Mirren then beat Morton 1-0 at Love Street, after which Morton signed ex-Hearts forward Kevin Thomas, a talented striker whose early promise at Tynecastle had been curtailed by a bad injury. The 23-year-old made his debut in a scoreless draw with Airdrie at Cappielow, partnering Kevin Twaddle up front.

There were no goals in the next game either, Morton going down 3-0 at Cappielow to Falkirk in a very disappointing performance in which their former striker Peter Duffield netted. Making his debut in that match was ex-Raith Rovers forward Keith Wright, but he limped off with a hamstring injury. Morton struggled back up to third bottom spot after a 3-2 victory in Stranraer, Fenwick, Twaddle and Anderson scoring. Paul Fenwick had proved to be a particularly good signing and was now a key part of the side.

Under Hugh Scott's leadership, controversy and Morton were by now regular bedfellows. Another mini-crisis developed when the local police expressed their concern over stewarding for the up-coming match against league leaders Hibernian at Cappielow. Rock Steady Security, to whom the stewarding had been outsourced the previous season, were told by Hugh Scott that their services were no longer required. Hugh Scott had used them to replace the existing stewards at Cappielow when he first took over.

A meeting took place between Police Chief Inspector Steve Horrocks, Morton honorary president John Wilson, the previous owner at Cappielow, and Morton secretary Gary Miller. Hugh Scott offered no comment to the Greenock Telegraph while John Wilson informed the paper that he "was not involved." Asked by a Telegraph reporter why he was at the meeting with the police, Wilson replied: "That's what you're telling me." Told that the police had said he was at the meeting, John Wilson's response was to say: "It's none of my business. I have nothing to do with it."

Meanwhile Rock Steady director Mark Hamilton told the Telegraph that Morton had wished to cut the number of stewards. He said: "I wasn't prepared to compromise on security." Hugh Scott told the Telegraph reporter that he would not discuss the stewarding with the Telegraph. He claimed that the newspaper's earlier report on the subject was "made up", but was unable to specify what was allegedly "wrong" with the report. This was by now a familiar scenario in dealings with the newspaper and Hugh Scott.

In the event, agreement was reached between Morton and the police regarding stewarding requirements and the Hibs game went ahead, the Edinburgh side winning 3-1, Fenwick again being on the mark for the home team.

Morton skipper Derek Collins had at this time been given permission to speak to Ayr United who were keen to sign him, but it was Hibernian who pipped them to the post in a deal reported to be worth £120,000. Collins (29) had been a loyal servant to the club since signing in 1987 from Renfrew Waverley and said: "I'm delighted to be going to a big club like Hibs, but I've got many happy memories at Cappielow." A stylish, football-playing full back, he had been an excellent professional for Morton and deserved his chance, albeit late in his career, of a place on a grander stage. At the same time as Collins departed, so too did director Bill Hunter.

Billy Stark fielded young Bryan Slavin (21) in Collins' place for the game at Hamilton, also playing 17-year-old Gary Tweedie in midfield, the game ending goalless, a result which left Morton in second bottom place.

Next up were fellow strugglers Raith Rovers at Stark's Park. It was clearly a very important match for both sides and a delighted Billy Stark saw his men emerge 3-1 victors, veteran midfielder Harry Curran ending up the hero with two goals in an excellent individual display, Kevin Thomas adding the other.

The football once more took a back seat when Inverclyde Council said that they required more detail from Hugh Scott on his new stadium proposals. Planning director Bryce Boyd commented: "Morton's application is to move the football stadium and also for a major store on the current site of Cappielow. We have received reports from them on how these proposals would impact on traffic and other shops, but we need more details and must have consultations with relevant bodies."

This prompted the Morton owner to challenge Inverclyde Council committee chairman Alex McGhee to state publicly whether or not he supported a Morton move to the adjacent site in Sinclair Street. Alex McGhee replied firmly: "No one has been more supportive of Mr Scott than me. I am bitterly disappointed he has taken that attitude. We have pointed him in the right direction." There was a sense of déjà vu for the onlooker.

Billy Stark, still trying to sign players, brought in experienced former Killie defender Derek Anderson, unattached, as a replacement for Derek Collins and he was in the team who took a home point against Clydebank, John Anderson netting in a 1-1 draw.

A no-score draw with St Mirren heralded the New Year of 1999 at Cappielow, leaving Morton third bottom, before a miserable attendance of 2,936 on a Tuesday night.

As ever the football took second place. Hugh Scott by now had reported former manager Allan McGraw to the SFA, along with John Morrow, discarded by now, for critical remarks made in national newspapers. Morrow had claimed he was "forced out" by Scott while Allan McGraw replied to the charge brought against him of "bringing the game into disrepute" by saying: "If you are bringing the game into disrepute by telling the truth then I'm guilty."

By this time Hugh Scott was railing against Inverclyde Council once more. On 15th January his propensity for attracting controversy involved local charitable organisation Cartsdyke Resource Centre. They had come to the Greenock Telegraph, alleging that Morton had failed to pay a five-month-old bill of £178 for printing posters relating to the first match of the season against Hibernian. The centre claimed that they had repeatedly tried to obtain a settlement. Project co-ordinator John Scott said: "Morton have now paid the bill thanks to the Telegraph's intervention."

Onfield, Morton continued to improve their position. A fine away win by 2-1 at Falkirk, goals by McPherson and Thomas, saw them jump two places in the table, up to fourth bottom. A second away win at Airdrie by 2-0 (Twaddle and own goal) left them looking forward in confident mood to the Scottish Cup third round tie against Premier Division Dundee at Cappielow.

A lighting problem at the exit gates delayed the kick-off for 35 minutes and, at the end of the afternoon, the hosts won 2-1 with goals from Archdeacon and Matheson. Only 2,823 turned out, but it was an encouraging result for Billy Stark and his side.

A meagre 1,581 turned out for a 1-0 home win over lowly Stranraer, a result which saw Morton ascend to sixth place in the league. Kevin Twaddle was the scorer and Morton had now put together an eight-match unbeaten run.

Ayr United halted the sequence with a 1-0 win at Somerset Park before Clyde arrived at Cappielow, full of confidence, for their Scottish Cup fourth round tie. In their ranks was goalkeeper David Wylie, back at Cappielow for the first time since leaving the club. Mark McGraw was also at Clyde, though injury prevented him from playing.

Morton chose to put on one of their best displays of the season, crushing the Bully Wee to the tune of 6-1. I wrote: "In the end the Song of the Clyde, sung boisterously from the visitors' terracing, became a requiem." The attendance was a much healthier 3,243, the prize a home quarter-final tie against Celtic. The team on the day was (4-4-2): Maxwell; Slavin, Fenwick, D. Anderson, Archdeacon; Hawke, J. Anderson, Curran, McPherson; Thomas, Twaddle.

A 3-0 league win over Hamilton at Cappielow followed, a Keith Wright double and goal by Harry Curran determining the outcome. The one low note was that Warren Hawke fractured his jaw, an injury that would keep him out of the cup quarter-final against Celtic.

Morton had taken 18 points from a possible 27 and were now looking a much better proposition.

Controversy was never far away, however, and as the fans became increasingly vociferous in the local press about Hugh Scott's plans for either a new ground or the redevelopment of Cappielow, the Morton owner once again banned his manager and players from talking to the Greenock Telegraph. It was a familiar scenario.

James Pickett who, as pointed out earlier in this book, was later to help Douglas Rae acquire ownership of Morton, put four questions to Scott through the pages of the Telegraph:

1 – Who might buy Cappielow and at what price and for what purpose?
2 – How much of resultant income would help fund a new ground?
3 – What extra money would be available to the manager?
4 – How much would it cost to renovate Cappielow to the satisfaction of the authorities?

Like me, he was unlikely to get a response, of course.

Meanwhile fans were infuriated that season ticket holders would have to pay for tickets for the forthcoming Scottish Cup quarter-final tie against Celtic at Cappielow. There was a limit too to the number of stand tickets on sale. Some declared they would not attend the match by way of protest.

Manager Billy Stark's priority was to prepare the team for what was their second Scottish Cup meeting with Celtic in successive seasons. The prior term the Glasgow giants had won 2-0 on their own ground without being greatly troubled. On this occasion Stark felt that his improved squad might just be able to produce a shock.

The teams met on Monday 8th March under the Cappielow floodlights and, in the event, there was to be no surprise. Celtic, with goals from the prolific Henrik Larsson and debutant Aussie striker Mark Viduka (2), eased through to the semi-finals.

Morton were not disgraced, Kevin Twaddle being especially prominent, but the match was well summed up by home skipper and ex-Celt Owen Archdeacon when he said: "We made little errors and they punished us."

A home league draw followed against Raith Rovers, Kevin Thomas scoring the home team's counter, a game in which young striker Stephen Whalen made his debut as a substitute. Another Thomas strike won the match at Stranraer, taking Morton into sixth spot in the division, before goals by John Anderson, Harry Curran and Keith Wright gathered in full points in a 3-2 win over Falkirk. By this time full back David Murie had been acquired from Hearts.

The most satisfying result of the season followed when Morton travelled to Love Street and whacked county rivals St Mirren 5-1 with a hat-trick by Thomas and two by Wright. Airdrie then halted Morton's excellent run of results with a 2-0 win at Cappielow, but Stark's men bounced back with a 2-1 win against Clydebank, John Anderson and Kevin Thomas on the mark. Morton had climbed to fifth place.

If things were progressing nicely on the park, off it they were in turmoil. There was uproar in Inverclyde when Hugh Scott announced that it was his intention to ground-share with Airdrie the following season while awaiting a decision by Inverclyde Council on planning permission for a new stadium.

League leaders Hibs, under boss Alex McLeish, won 2-1 at Easter Road, Derek Anderson scoring Morton's consolation, as once again football took a back seat to the machinations of the Greenock club's owner.

Airdrie chairman Campbell told the Telegraph on 27th April, 1999: "Hugh Scott, on behalf of Morton, contacted me 10 days ago to ask about ground-sharing and I told him that in principle it would be okay."

It seemed that the final home match of the season, against Ayr United, could be Morton's final game at Cappielow. The ground where, for all but five years of their 125-year-old history, Morton had played their football, would soon, it seemed, be history itself.

CHAPTER TWENTY-NINE

Stark sacked and McGraw tells Scott 'Go now'

Hugh Scott had been directing his anger at Inverclyde Council for what he claimed as undue delay in making a decision on Morton's application for planning permission for a new stadium and retail outlet on the combined site of Cappielow and the adjoining former railway marshalling yard on Sinclair Street, currently used as a car park for the club's games.

The council claimed, reasonably, that it was a complicated issue, dependent upon traffic impact and retail impact assessment.

Former manager Allan McGraw was firmly behind the fans' concerns. Standing as an Independent candidate for West Renfrewshire at the forthcoming Scottish parliamentary elections, he said: "I would like a guarantee from chairman Hugh Scott that he will not sell Cappielow until a new ground is found, so that we don't end up homeless like Hamilton or Clydebank."

The prevailing view among the support was one of fury, summed up by Morton Supporters' Club secretary Michael Grana who said: "He [Hugh Scott] came here with promises of renovating the existing ground but then changed his mind. The best thing for Mr Scott to do is sell his shares to Morton-minded people now and get out."

The Morton owner refused to talk to the local press, but I put four questions to him in the Greenock Telegraph. 1 – What work (apparently costing £300,000) is required to be done to furnish a new Safety Certificate for next season? 2 – Could part of the ground be closed in order to comply? 3 – Would he ensure Cappielow would not be sold until planning permission had been given for a new stadium? 4 – If the retail element of the Morton's planning application were rejected, was there a contingency plan?

Typically by now, there was no response.

In the final home game of the season Morton, clearly affected by the turbulence and confusion, went down 4-1 to Ayr. Some 600 hundred fans invaded the pitch at the end of the game amidst chants of "Scott must go" in what was a peaceful demonstration. Outside the ground Allan McGraw addressed the fans, voicing his fears for the club's future.

The football itself was now quite incidental. Hundreds of fans were still on the pitch at 6pm. The irony was that Scott did not attend the match.

On the following Tuesday Allan McGraw then announced that he was resigning as secretary of the Managers and Coaches Association. This was in order that Scott could no longer try to use the SFA to silence criticism of his running of the club from the former manager. McGraw commented: "I will not be shut up and I'm resigning so that I'm free to speak my mind."

The protest from supporters continued at the last game of the season at Firhill where goals by Thomas and Wright secured a 2-0 win over Hamilton. A season in which Billy Stark had managed to enhance the team's fortunes on the field of play, ended with complete chaos off the park; a club in disharmony, its support in revolt and a future of total uncertainty.

Almost unnoticed, Stark signed 33-year-old Andy Millen from Ayr a couple of weeks later. The manager had done a good job over the season in the prevailing circumstances, but the focus was now on the much more vital issue of the club's very existence.

The summer merry-go-round of players began with star winger Kevin Twaddle leaving Cappielow to join Motherwell, while fringe players Jazz Juttla and Maurice George found themselves on the way out. But the main news was that Hugh Scott had decided that Morton would be staying at Cappielow for the forthcoming season. This at least was well received by the fans.

But the satisfaction at that was dissipated when the Scottish Office advised Inverclyde Council to refuse Morton's planning application for a new stadium and retail outlet due to a failure "to provide sufficient information about the potential impact on the trunk road". Although Inverclyde Council were in favour of Morton's proposals in theory, they admitted that there were serious technical problems. In a statement they said that "the applicant has failed to provide all the information required to allow for a proper assessment of the road improvements needed to accommodate such a major retail development".

This caused Hugh Scott to throw a large rattle out of his pram and, in a scathing criticism in the national media, he accused Inverclyde Planning Department of being "a Mickey Mouse Planning Department making plans on the back of a postage stamp". He also claimed that Morton would die if permission were not granted.

In response, former Morton boss Allan McGraw said: "If Mr Scott can't take Morton forward he should get out and let someone in who can do the job."

The fact was that the Scottish Office, which had nothing whatsoever to do with Inverclyde, had advised refusal of the application. The onus was very much on Hugh Scott to provide the information they required regarding traffic impact. The council remained supportive, but the ball was in Morton's court.

On the football side, manager Billy Stark replaced Kevin Twaddle by adding ex-Southampton, Hamilton and Partick winger Paul McDonald (31) to his squad. It was the new arrival who set up both goals in a pre-season friendly win away to Clyde by 2-1, the strikes coming from Harry Curran and Bryan Slavin. Billy Stark also augmented his squad by adding ex-St Johnstone and Ayr striker Ian Ferguson.

Cappielow owner Hugh Scott then introduced Steve Morgon as Morton's new chief executive. Morgon was a close associate of Reg Brealey, the highly controversial former owner of Darlington FC who had tried, and failed, to buy St Mirren Football Club. At that time Scott had met Brealey amidst rumours of possible ground-sharing should Brealey take over at Love Street. When Brealey failed in his St Mirren bid it caused the Paisley club's boss Tony Fitzpatrick to expression a feeling of "great elation".

Scott had meanwhile continued his refusal to talk to the Greenock Telegraph as well as denying his management and players any contact with the local paper.

Billy Stark had gone on record as saying that he wanted his team to move forward from the previous season's mid-table consolidation to a challenging position in the First Division. A 4-2 away win in the opening league game at Brockville against one of the pre-season favourites, Falkirk, augured well, Kevin Thomas (2), John Anderson and Owen Archdeacon scoring. Outstanding was the energetic Ross Matheson in midfield in a side which lined up as follows (3-5-2): Maxwell; Fenwick, Millen, D. Anderson; Murie, Matheson, Curran, J. Anderson, Archdeacon; Thomas, Wright.

A 2-2 draw followed in the Bell's Challenge Cup at East End Park to continue the good work, Morton winning on penalties, followed by a home, goalless, league draw with Clydebank.

The bright start was a false dawn. There followed a poor 3-1 home loss to Second Division Alloa in the CIS Insurance Cup, the consolation strike being scored by Harry Curran, then star striker Kevin Thomas was sold for what was reputed to be a fee around £130,000 to St Johnstone. He had scored 14 goals since his transfer from Hearts the previous season. His departure was lamented by a support who had warmed to him.

Dunfermline won 2-1 in a league encounter at East End Park, Keith Wright scoring for Morton, before Ross County dumped the Cappielow men out of the Bell's Challenge Cup with an emphatic 3-0 home win in which Curran was also sent off. Ton assistant manager Frank Connor made vain appeals to visiting fans to show patience as they voiced disapproval of their manager.

On Saturday 28th August, 1999, Morton faced Livingston at home with Paddy Connolly in the side, signed on a month's loan from St Johnstone. He and David Murie struck in a 2-2 draw, Connolly again being on target with the Greenock men's goal in another share of the points at Inverness.

Connolly was proving to be an inspiration, scoring in a 2-0 home win over Raith Rovers along with Keith Wright.

If the win was welcome, the attendance was alarming, only 970 turning out. The 'Cowshed' was by now out of use as demolition work was to begin in preparation for its proposed upgrading to a seated stand. I wrote: "The level of attendance seems to be a reflection of off-field uncertainty rather than anything else. After several U-turns [by Hugh Scott] concerning a new or reconstructed stadium people are becoming seriously disillusioned. They are voting with their feet."

Steve Morgon had hardly warmed his director's seat when it became clear he was now serving his notice. The club's policy of no contact with the local press meant no explanation.

The storm clouds were gathering. St Mirren won a derby clash 3-2 at Love Street, Connolly grabbing both Ton goals, then Owen Archdeacon announced his retiral from football after unsuccessfully battling against a long-term ankle problem.

Through the national press, Hugh Scott revealed that work was to start on the Cowshed to make it a 3,600 all-seated stand. He expected work to be completed early in 2000, with a ground capacity of 11,000. Scepticism was rampant. I commented: "There are those who will, quite naturally, adopt a 'seeing is believing' attitude given the history of the last two years."

In a home game against Airdrie, boos accompanied a 2-0 defeat in which Paul Fenwick was red-carded. Paddy Connolly's successful loan spell, in which he had scored five times in five matches, had ended.

Goalkeeper Ally Maxwell was then ordered off in a 3-0 loss at Ayr after which Billy Stark offloaded striker Ian Ferguson, who had failed to make an impression in his short spell at the club.

Clydebank, by now ground-sharing with Morton, lost 3-1 at Cappielow, McDonald, Tweedie and Wright netting, before a crowd of 758, all of whom were accommodated in the main stand. It was a sad sight. Two solitary workers scraped rust from the skeletal, iron framework of the roofless Cowshed during the course of the match. They were like carrion crow feeding on a carcass.

With defender Paul Fenwick ruled out of action due to an injury sustained on international duty with Canada, manager Stark brought in ex-Celtic defender Graeme Morrison, a youngster who had been playing in Finland.

There was a growing air of gloom to match the stadium as the days dragged by. I wrote: "Last week the Cowshed stood roofless, a sad uninhabited iron framework, forming a poignant foreground to the desolate shipyards behind. Cappielow owner Hugh Scott has already stated that a new, seated stand will be in its place by the time Morton meet St Mirren in a fortnight's time." Such a transformation was now in the realms of Alice in Wonderland.

Falkirk won 3-2 at Cappielow before a crowd of 1,410, Curran and Hawke scoring, as Morton slumped to third bottom of the table. Talk of a promotion challenge was now conspicuous by its absence. Reality had sunk in.

When Raith Rovers beat Morton 3-1 at Stark's Park, Curran grabbing a consolation goal, Morton had fallen once again to second bottom placing. The situation was alarming. On the following Friday I summed up thus: "Morton meet St Mirren at Cappielow tomorrow in circumstances that are becoming increasingly concerning for those with the club's interests at heart.

"Crowds have fallen by almost a half since last season, the playing pool has been weakened by the enforced retiral of Owen Archdeacon through injury and the sale of Kevin Thomas to St Johnstone, and the team find themselves in second bottom place in the table.

"On top of that the new, all-seated stand to replace the Cowshed, which owner Hugh Scott stated would be in place by the time of the St Mirren game, remains well short of completion. A great many people who would normally wend their way to Cappielow on a Saturday are no longer attending.

"The man with whom the buck stops is club owner Hugh Scott. There is a limit to people's patience and that is now wearing thin."

The next day St Mirren inflicted further misery with a resounding 4-1 defeat, Curran once more grabbing the home goal. Paisley fans far outnumbered the home support in a crowd of 3,733. That was previously unheard of. It was a cruelly embarrassing afternoon for Morton fans.

Some light penetrated the gloom when Morton thrashed Inverness 5-1 at home, goals coming from Wright, Curran, Morrison, Matheson and Aitken before a meagre Friday night attendance of 812. It was a short-lived hiatus, Hearts claiming they were owed £65,000 from Morton's sale of Kevin Thomas to St Johnstone. A spokesman for the Tynecastle club said the Edinburgh team were due half of any sell-on fee for the striker they had sold to Morton.

I wrote of "a lack of confidence among the stay-away fans in the running of the club which so often seems to follow a confrontational line as the council, police, the Telegraph, various media organs, other football clubs and the football authorities have all discovered at various times".

Livingston applied further pain with a 2-1 home win in which David Murie scored the Ton counter. Morton were in a state of melt-down. "The only certainty at the moment," I wrote, "is the uncertainty which surrounds the club's future. As gates fall and the patience of the long-suffering fans is stretched to the limit, it is left to Billy Stark to soldier on."

A scoreless home draw against Ayr before 1,168 fans followed amidst rumours of Hugh Scott being prepared to listen to offers for the ailing club. But the following day he appeared on television to say that Morton were not for sale, contrary to reports in which he had been quoted in the national press. He was still imposing his ban on anyone from Morton talking to the Greenock Telegraph.

At the start of the campaign manager Stark had called for his players to provide a promotion challenge. That now seemed farcical, but I was not of a mind to blame him, saying: "There is no doubt in my mind that performances on the field have suffered in tandem with off-field controversy."

Airdrie and Dunfermline inflicted further defeats, by 1-0 and 3-0 respectively, then Billy Stark's assistant, Frank Connor, departed with no reason given, though it was almost certainly a financial necessity. He followed the road taken previously by groundsman Ian Lyle, commercial employees Joe Harper, the former goal-scoring hero, and Denny Martin, as well as chief executive Steve Morgon.

The club was clearly in crisis. There was no sign of the Cowshed being transformed into a stand, no sign of there being any likelihood of the all-seated 11,000 capacity stadium Scott had predicted by the end of March, 2000, and the team were sitting in second bottom place in the First Division table.

I commented: "There is an air of uncertainty over the very future of the club, and those shareholders who can manage to attend the AGM, set extraordinarily for 7.30pm on Hogmanay, will no doubt wish to ask some searching questions (perhaps the first on the list will be 'why have an AGM at 7.30pm on New Year's Eve?')."

Those attending, I followed up, would also welcome an explanation as to how the owner of the club could state in the national press that "we will sell [the club] if we get the right offer, and we will be keen to sell" only to say on television a week later that the club was not for sale and never had been.

There was a clear credibility problem regarding Hugh Scott's utterances. Confidence in his stewardship of Morton had been lost, the stadium was a mess, attendances were dwindling and the team was in deep relegation trouble. Any strategy Scott might have had was falling apart quicker than a house of cards.

A Craig McPherson goal was not enough to prevent a Falkirk 2-1 win at Brockville, striker Warren Hawke leaving Cappielow on the eve of the game for Queen of the South. He had become a popular player with the support in his four-and-a-half years at the club, though his appearances under Billy Stark had become restricted, and mainly in a midfield role rather than as a striker.

The year ended with some respite on the park, Raith Rovers, for whom Frank Connor was now Peter Hetherston's assistant manager, going down to the only goal of the game, scored by Harry Curran, at a dilapidated Cappielow. The seriousness of the club's position was such that match results were incidental. The ship was springing several leaks, the rudder had broken and no one knew what storm clouds lay over the horizon.

The year 2000 began for Morton with a 1-1 draw at Love Street against St Mirren. Ally Maxwell gave a top display in goal, while the visitors' strike came from an excellent free kick by Paul Hartley, the young Hibernian forward in his second game of a month's loan period.

On Saturday 8th January, 2000, Morton travelled to Inverness where the host club sent them packing after a tremendous second half display. The 6-2 result was Morton's worst defeat of the season, young Michael Hart and Harry Curran getting the Greenock club's goals. Absent were injured Keith Wright and defender Paul Fenwick who was on international duty for Canada.

It was a momentous weekend, resulting in Hugh Scott sacking manager Billy Stark. It drew a cutting comment from Allan McGraw, recovering from a triple heart bypass operation. He said: "I don't think Billy Stark had a chance. If it's not right at the top then the job's impossible. If he [Hugh Scott] wants to do anything good for Morton he should go now. He has let the people down in everything he said he would do.

"He reported me to the SFA for bringing the game into disrepute. Well, I think the SFA should charge him with bringing the game into disrepute. We used to have a good reputation at Morton and that has now gone."

Stark, in charge since October, 1997, refused to depart from a diplomatic statement in which he said: "In my time at Morton I feel satisfied that I did the best possible job that I could in the circumstances. I would like to take this opportunity to wish all the best to the club and the players for the future."

Stark's record for the season was five wins in 22 league games against a background of constant unrest off the field. In normal circumstances it might not have been surprising for Stark to come under pressure. These were far from normal circumstances.

Hugh Scott moved quickly to fix up Clydebank's Ian McCall as the new boss. McCall was stepping into a minefield and I wrote: "Since his arrival at the club two-and-a-half years ago Hugh Scott has, frankly, failed to live up to the expectations he himself prophesised for Morton. Not only has the team gone backwards, but there is no sign of the all-seated stadium he predicted would be built."

Contradictory statements in the media had reduced his credibility with the fans to an all-time low. His style of management had led to confrontation with the council, police, local press, supporters and other clubs. Crowds had dropped alarmingly.

McCall was of a mind to renew contact with the Greenock Telegraph and, through freelance journalist Bill Marwick, he made contact with me by telephone at my home. I took the opportunity to fill him in on the difficulties which accompanied life at Cappielow these days. The result was a lawyer's letter of complaint sent to the Telegraph. McCall had apparently divulged the contents of our conversation to Hugh Scott. I was not impressed. Needless to say the lawyer's letter was ignored. It had become a predictable response from Scott in his dealings with the Telegraph.

By now the fans were in virtual open revolt at the regime at Cappielow.

Ian McCall brought in ex-Hibs and Falkirk midfielder Brian Rice as his assistant and then moved to sign Cardiff City's under-21 Welsh internationalist striker Robert Earnshaw on loan. The 18-year-old endeared himself to the Morton support with a goal on his debut performance against Airdrie, a 4-0 victory, the other strikes coming from Paul McDonald with two penalties and John Anderson.

I commented on the new boy: "Earnshaw's motor is fuel-injected and at times it left Airdrie floundering in its exhaust."

John Anderson was on the mark again in a 1-1 Scottish Cup draw with lowly Brechin at Cappielow before Morton went down 3-2 to Ayr at Somerset Park, Murie and Curran scoring. In the Morton side was another loan player, left wingback Colin Pluck from Watford.

In the cup replay at Brechin, goalkeeper Ally Maxwell emerged as the Ton hero with a superb all-round display. At full time it was scoreless, Morton winning through to a lucrative fourth round home tie with Dick Advocaat's Rangers after a penalty shoot-out.

A 1-1 league draw was achieved at East End Park against Dunfermline, Earnshaw netting again, delighting the fans with his trademark mid-air somersault.

Uproar and Morton were never far apart, however. Due to the state of Cappielow, with its dilapidated Cowshed, the governing authorities declared that Morton would play their home cup tie against Rangers at Love Street, the nearest designated ground. On the day of the league game at Dunfermline, Morton vice-president Jim McCallion stated on the radio that he feared Morton fans would vandalise St Mirren's ground, a statement which stunned those of us listening in the press box at East End Park and, not unnaturally, enraged many listening Morton fans.

The furore continued with Morton appealing to the Court of Session to be permitted to take the tie to Hampden, a request which was refused.

On 19th January, 2000, Morton made the short trip to Paisley to take on the might of the Light Blues. Ian McCall had clearly set his team out in a damage limitation exercise. They lined up (5-4-1) as follows: Maxwell; Murie, Morrison, Millen, D. Anderson, Pluck; Matheson, Curran, J. Anderson (Aitken), McDonald (Wright); Earnshaw (Slavin).

Rangers (3-1-4-2) were: Klos; Vidmar, Moore, Numan; Ferguson; Kanchelskis, Tugay, Van Bronckhorst, McCann (Albertz); Wallace, Durie (Negri).

Craig Moore scored the sole strike of the match in a tie in which Morton made virtually no attempt to contribute in any positive sense. I commented: "If you don't try to win, you deserve to lose." Ian McCall nevertheless was pleased with his side.

The main feature of the tie, from a Morton point of view, was a demonstration by the Greenock club's support in which they waved red cards aimed at Morton owner and chairman Hugh Scott. On the cards was printed the message: "After a series of broken promises and confrontations with the press, police and SFA, not to mention other clubs, famous players and supporters, the club has become isolated and therefore endangered. We fear that these broken bridges can not and will not be mended while Scott still owns the club. Therefore it is time for him to sell up. We invite you to join in our peaceful protest by showing Hugh Scott the red card before Saturday's game, at half-time and after the match. C'mon the Ton."

It was then revealed that Sheriff Officers acting for the Police Board had seized Morton's share of the gate money for the Rangers tie. A statement said: "The cash, in excess of £29,000, will be frozen until settlement is reached over a disputed bill for policing matches."

Strathclyde Joint Police Board had instructed their lawyers to arrest Morton's share of gate receipts. Assistant clerk Mike Blair said: "A court action has been raised." The police said that the charges, which Hugh Scott claimed were excessive, were entirely consistent with levels required to ensure public safety.

What little shred of credibility Scott had was now in tatters. On Friday 25th February, 2000, the Greenock Telegraph announced that Hugh Scott had stepped down as chief executive of Morton and that he had said he would quit as chairman at the end of the season.

The day-to-day running of the club had passed to newly appointed director/secretary George Carson. Allan McGraw commented: "I would be over the moon if he [Hugh Scott] were to go, but somehow I have reservations."

McGraw was expressing a view many held, that Scott merely was removing himself from the firing line. February ended with Robbie Earnshaw's return to Cardiff and a John Anderson goal gaining the points in a win over Ian McCall's old team, Clydebank.

By now the football was very much a side-show to the almost constant off-field distractions and problems which affected Morton Football Club. Raith Rovers won 3-0 at Stark's Park in a match in which star defender Paul Fenwick was left out of the side on the instruction of Hugh Scott. He had been on duty with Canada at the Gold Cup in California and the Morton owner was annoyed at having to pay his wages. In fact Fenwick had done nothing wrong, irrespective of whether or not Scott was irritated, but he had played his last game for the club. Out of contract at the end of the season, he was told not to attend training any more after a meeting with board members on Wednesday 8th March, 2000.

I commented: "Paul Fenwick has become the latest person to incur the ire of Morton chairman Hugh Scott and it is now virtually certain that the Canadian international defender will leave Cappielow when the season ends.

"He will follow players such as Peter Duffield, John Morrow and Warren Hawke, all of whom left Morton following fall-outs with the majority shareholder."

Jim McArthur, the former Hibs goalie who was Fenwick's agent, said: "After a meeting with the board I was informed that Paul Fenwick would not be picked to play for the team again as they have to plan for next season. Paul was clearly upset that he was being made to look as if he was a player lacking commitment when, of course, he is a totally committed player."

It was the last straw for many supporters and there was talk of a fans' boycott which seemed to be justified when only 684 long-suffering folk turned out for a 1-0 home win over Livingston, Harry Curran once again getting a key goal for the club, his ninth of the season.

Associated supporters' clubs then held a meeting on the 15th March to address the current situation at the club. They issued a statement in which they claimed that Hugh Scott had "managed to alienate almost the whole football fraternity" during his three-year reign at Cappielow.

Prior to the derby against St Mirren at Cappielow three days later, I wrote: "Morton are now in a critical situation. Half their stadium is akin to a piece of waste ground, the team has been steadily dismantled and the fans are deserting in their droves. The crisis runs far deeper than any victory on the park can assuage."

The fans asked questions of Scott through the local paper, appealing to him to answer the points they raised. The request fell on deaf ears.

The company which had been working on the development of the Cowshed, Inverclad, had ceased work and rumours continued to abound about possible takeovers. In the midst of this I wrote that Hugh Scott had adopted a profile "lower than a mole".

"It is time," I said, "that Mr Scott delivered an unequivocal statement as to his objectives for Morton."

The fans were now clear in their desire for Scott to sell up and go. The team lost 1-0 at Livingston in a game in which ex-Rangers and Clydebank forward John Walker, on loan from Mansfield Town, made an appearance as a substitute. Only 567 turned out for the next home match, against Inverness. The visitors won 2-0 but the entire 90 minutes, with Scott absent, was dominated by protest from the home support. Banners, among them one saying "He's Scott to go", were waved throughout, highlighting their anger at the way Scott was treating their club.

"How long can this go on?" was the headline in an article I wrote, commenting on the situation.

After a 3-0 loss at Airdrie, Morton plunged to second bottom in the table and representatives of the supporters associations met directors George Carson and Jim McCallion in private. Minus Hugh Scott, it was a worthless process. I wrote: "Messrs McCallion and Carson can't give the fans any meaningful assurances for the very simple reason they don't hold the purse strings."

An attendance of 661 watched the next home match, a 2-1 defeat by Ayr in which young Stephen Whalen scored. "Scott," I said of the club owner, "has joined the ranks of that much abused bunch, the absentee landlords, and once more was not to be seen."

The car park was closed, there was no programme on sale, the club shop was closed and a bunch of kids had to bolster the available first team regulars. This was a club careering towards the abyss.

By now rumours were circulating of an impending takeover by Mike Peden, a Birmingham property developer who had been in association with Reg Brealey at Darlington Football Club. Cynicism was rife among the fans.

"Attending Cappielow these days," I wrote, "is akin to visiting an elderly, ailing relative who is not expected to survive much longer."

Manager Ian McCall then appealed through the national press for stay-away Morton fans to return to the fold and give their support, fearing that the club may go part time otherwise. He was quoted as saying: "How we do next season depends upon the finances given to me. If we have top-of-the-range finance, then we'll go and look to win the title."

This was now beyond the realms of make-believe. I responded the next day in an article headlined "You're way off the mark, Ian". I wrote: "Fantasy or what? The issue is not full or part-time football, top-of-the-range finance, and certainly not any possibility of winning next season's championship – it is the very survival of Morton.

"As for the Morton manager trying to tell the fans that an answer to the club's problems lies in their own hands – in them returning to the fold – that is naivety in the extreme. You, Ian, should be asking those fans why they are staying away. And, while you're at it, perhaps you could ask your boss what his plans are for the future of Morton."

Morton, by this time third bottom, then lost 3-0 at home to Falkirk before a crowd of 840. On the eve of the game I commented on the fast deteriorating situation: "When you are in a customer-based business and those customers desert you in their droves, you don't tell them that the solution to your problems is for them to return. You examine the reasons why they have removed their backing and rectify the faults.

"Right now Morton are getting the support their top management deserves and one wonders what that would be minus season ticket holders.

"Including tomorrow," I continued, "three more Saturdays must be endured. All those who stick it out to the bitter end deserve a medal … only they don't; they deserve to see a light at the end of what has become a long, dark tunnel."

Even the press were becoming uncomfortable watching events unfold at Cappielow. I wrote: "No one likes to see an animal in its death throes, and Morton look too close to that for comfort. One freelance journalist, who penned a book on the last Scottish senior club to take a nosedive, Third Lanark, felt compelled last Saturday to compare the Cappielow club's plight to that of the High-High in the days before closure. Another – with St Mirren leanings for goodness sake – was moved to uttering words of concern. I swear they were well meant. It would have brought a tear to a glass eye."

Gourock man and club fan Stuart Duncan then led supporters in a bid to establish a "trust fund" to raise money to buy shares in the club. It was a constructive attempt by a concerned individual to do something positive.

It was also decided to hold a fans' rally to march to Cappielow from Clyde Square on the final day of the season in protest at Hugh Scott's handling of Morton Football Club's affairs. In four seasons attendances had plunged from an average 4,074 to 1,335. And recent crowds were now in the hundreds.

Before 349 lonely souls at Cappielow, Morton at last won a game, beating Clydebank 3-0 with goals by John Anderson, Harry Curran and Ross Matheson. It was, in fact, the Bankies' home match as they were ground-sharing with Morton, but the attendance told all. Morton skipper Andy Millen was one who could no longer maintain a pretence, and he said: "I've been involved [in football] for 18 years and have never experienced this situation at a club." He admitted that players were finding it hard to motivate themselves. It would have been astonishing had it been otherwise.

CHAPTER THIRTY

Scott must go, say protesters

On 6th May, 2000, a 2000-strong crowd, led by Morton legend Allan McGraw and local MSP Duncan McNeil, marched in protest to Cappielow for the final match of the season against Dunfermline. "Scott must go" the chants resounded. Arriving at Cappielow, most chose not to go into the ground, believing they were merely lining the pockets of the man against whom they were protesting.

Morton managed to win the game 2-0 with goals by Craig McPherson and John Anderson in front of 979 fans. I commented on Scott's position: "His 'tea is oot' as far as the fans are concerned."

Eleven days later Scott admitted on radio that liquidation was possible, though he did not believe it would happen. He also stated that Ian McCall and his assistant Brian Rice were not being given new contracts after 17 games in charge. Once more he blamed a lack of support for the club's troubles.

I responded: "And so it has come to pass that manager Ian McCall and his assistant Brian Rice are the latest to find themselves heading out of the revolving door at Cappielow after four months in the hot seats."

On Scott I said: "This is the man who ridiculed comments made in these columns months ago that, not only was Morton's stature as a full time club in jeopardy, but their very future was in doubt. Now he himself expresses major misgivings over Morton's continuing existence.

"Veiled threats of closing the club if the fans don't rally to his tattered banner are bizarre coming from someone who has claimed often enough in the past to be a 'Morton fan' himself. But then Scott is no stranger to contradictory statements."

On the 23rd May the fans' associations announced that they would lobby the Scottish Parliament in their latest move to save their club. MSP Duncan McNeil said: "Morton's problems are not caused by insolvency, but because the bond of trust has been broken between the supporters and the majority shareholder."

Duncan McNeil then tabled a private member's bill in the Scottish Parliament to highlight the plight of Morton, while the SFA announced they were to launch a probe into Morton FC.

In a joint letter, two Morton fans, Jim MacLeod and Stuart McMillan, said: "The whole Morton saga has been dragged through the local press for months and well done to the Tele for doing so, but now the national press are finally catching on to the antics of the majority shareholder." This was not before time. While one or two writers in the national press – notably Bill Leckie – had cottoned on to what was happening, some appeared blinkered, particularly Gourockian Davie Provan, the ex-Celtic and Scotland winger. Swallowing the Hugh Scott version hook, line and sinker, he was to state at one point in his national newspaper column that Inverclyde did not deserve a football club because of the lack of support from the fans to Scott's Morton. Had he done any research on the matter at all – a couple of phone calls would have sufficed – he would have realised exactly what had been going on. I think Provan is a very good football commentator but this was journalism of the laziest kind and it understandably was to make him very unpopular with the Morton following.

As June came in, the Telegraph then highlighted yet another embarrassing story concerning Morton. Former manager Ian McCall and his assistant Brian Rice had arrived at Cappielow to pick up a month's pay in lieu of notice only to be to be told to leave the ground. Brian Rice said: "We came down to get our wages but Mr Scott told us to leave the premises or none of the players would get their wages.

"He then said that unless we got off the premises immediately he would call in the police." He and McCall then stood outside the ground for five hours as players came out having received their own pay.

Ian McCall commented: "I was led to believe I would receive a month's pay. Sadly this was not the case and I suffered the indignity of standing outside on the pavement."

John Anderson meanwhile left Morton to join Livingston while it became apparent that former Aston Villa and Scotland defender Allan Evans, who won a European Cup medal with Villa, would be taking over the manager's role at Sinclair Street. He was Mike Peden's man, though there remained doubt as to whether a deal had actually been done with Huge Scott for the ownership of the club.

The SFA then revealed that Morton could face expulsion from the governing body should they fail to pay an outstanding debt of £19,000 to Hearts relating to the sale of striker Kevin Thomas to St Johnstone.

The bill, amounting to £18,979, was finally paid. The police also received £32,000 owed to them, having won their case after Sheriff's Officers had seized Morton's share of the cup revenue from the Rangers tie at Love Street. The residual money went to Morton, though it came out that St Mirren were still owed £4,000 for stewarding costs for the tie.

Midfielder Craig McPherson made his escape from Cappielow to Clyde and then the SFA revealed that they had appointed auditors to probe Morton's finances.

Football's governing body also met with MSPs of all four main parties in Scotland to discuss Morton's plight. MSP Duncan McNeil said: "It was clear there is widespread concern about Hugh Scott's stewardship of the club." That the SFA had censured Allan McGraw for bringing the game into disrepute in the past for comments made about Scott now seemed laughable.

It was revealed by Morton director George Carson that a deal between Hugh Scott and Mike Peden was "very close to being completed." Peden owned English-based Chaddington Property Development Company and manager Evans was his choice.

Evans made a plea to "give peace a chance" in the Greenock Telegraph. He said: "I have heard enough to know the problems. I see on the internet that the fans have said that if they got a new start they would buy season tickets. Well, they've got that now and I want them to get behind the team and have a go.

"We all have to pull together. I've known about this for three months and, ideally, I would have liked to have been in place earlier."

On 22nd July Morton met St Mirren in a pre-season friendly at Love Street, drawing 1-1. Scorer for Morton was on-trial ex-Hearts and Hamilton winger Jose Quitongo, joined by newcomers Martyn Naylor, Darren Davies and Gerry Maloney from Telford, Barry Town and Coventry respectively.

A no-score draw with Peterborough took place at Cappielow with a barely recognisable selection which also included former Dundee centre back Robbie Raeside.

I couldn't share Allan Evans' optimistic view of a fresh start, not until we knew a lot more about the details of any deal between Hugh Scott and Mike Peden, and I wrote: "Scott's departure is to be welcomed, there is no doubt about that. Nevertheless, going by what is known of Mike Peden's previous association with football, there is room for a healthy degree of caution upon his arrival as replacement.

"At the time of Mr Peden's arrival at Darlington as chief executive, the fans were led to believe that he had acquired the majority shareholding from Reg Brealey. It later emerged that Mr Brealey, in fact, still retained those shares. This is something which has been confirmed to me by Luke Raine, personal assistant to the multi-millionaire George Reynolds who took over at Darlington from Mike Peden. He also confirmed that the club had been left £5million in debt upon Mr Peden's departure."

It was up to Peden to allay supporters' fears and I continued: "He should bear in mind, though, that the supporters have heard fine words aplenty in the last three seasons. When you have been led down a garden path once, you don't want to be dragged down another before you have had time to shake the earth from your shoes.

"At the end of the day it is actions, not words, upon which Mike Peden will be judged in the months to come."

This did not go down well in Camp Peden. Allan Evans responded: "Mr Scott is no longer at the club and I would like to make that clear. It is now a fresh start for everyone."

Peden then telephoned me and demanded a retraction of my comment that he had not owned Darlington FC. I repeated what Luke Raines had told me on behalf of current Darlington owner George Reynolds. I also informed him of my own investigation into the matter, leading to Company Register in Gibraltar.

Darlington's share capital had been owned by St Philip Limited, registered in Gibraltar, and a trail of companies there led to one proving that Brealey had been the owner of Darlington all along. Peden's tone suddenly altered when I named these companies, the final one revealing a name conclusively linking Brealey with Darlington. "We all have to work together," he said. The retraction was suddenly forgotten.

Peden then announced that he was to seek planning permission for an ambitious £4million soccer academy on the old rail marshalling yard in Sinclair Street, the same land upon which Scott had said he wanted to build a new ground with an associated retail outlet at the old Cappielow. That proposal had been refused after advice given to the council by the Scottish Office. Peden said: "It shows our commitment to Morton and it will put both Morton and Greenock back on the map." Sceptical did not come close to summing up my feelings. No proof had yet been supplied that a deal with Scott had been concluded. It was just more words.

Allan Evans then moved to fix up French footballers Karim Boukraa (24) and Parfait Medou-Otye (27) from Le Havre and Club Paris. By this time Mike Peden was passing himself off as the new owner of Morton, something I found deeply disturbing.

I wrote: "He [Peden] must be able to convince them [the Morton fans] that neither Reg Brealey nor Hugh Scott is lurking in the background. With that in mind he will have to satisfy them that he has actually bought Scott's shares – not merely signalled an intent to buy them – and is no one's front man."

The league began with a 2-0 home defeat to a Livingston side containing ex-Ton man John Anderson. Parfait Medou-Otye shone on his debut for Morton, showing good skills for a defender, while goalkeeper Matthew Boswell, who had been training with Sunderland, was impressive.

A 5-1 CIS Challenge Cup loss followed at Clyde, Derek Anderson scoring the visitors' goal, before the team again fell, this time by 1-0 at Falkirk with Boswell the top player for Morton.

Evans finally got his side off the mark in an impressive 4-0 win at Kirkcaldy over Raith Rovers in the Challenge Cup, goals from Stephen Whalen (2), Ross Matheson and Brian Kerr. Another win over Alloa, at Cappielow, followed, goals coming from Stephen Whalen and Paul McDonald. Morton's side was as follows (4-4-2): Boswell; Murie, Raeside, Medou-Otye, Anderson; McDonald, Aitken, Millen, Curran; Matheson, Whalen.

Then Clyde were beaten away from home 3-0, Whalen (2) and Matheson scoring. The points took Morton up to fourth place and also confirmed the promise of Whalen who was attracting the attention of bigger clubs. Incidentally, refereeing was former Morton goalkeeper Cameron Melville.

East Stirling, in front of their own fans, dumped Morton out of the Bell's Challenge Cup 3-2, the visitors' goals coming from Boukraa and Matheson.

Things, however, generally were progressing on the field. But still the uncertainty over the club's ownership remained. On Friday 8th September, in a front page exclusive, I cast doubt on Mike Peden's ownership of Morton. Asked about it, he replied that a "transaction had taken place between him and Hugh Scott". Asked specifically if he now owned the majority shareholding, Mr Peden replied that "the deal had been concluded in July."

Did this mean, I put it to him, that he owned the majority shareholding – yes or no? His facetious reply was "Yes or no."

I continued to press him on an answer and asked whether or not he was the majority shareholder, or a company in which he was the majority shareholder was a holding company. He replied: "That's none of your business."

I put it to him that it was very much in the Inverclyde public's interest as to who owned the local football club. At one point Peden, who claimed his lawyer was present in his office and that the conversation was being taped, said: "If you think Mr Scott was tough I can be a lot tougher."

I recall telling him that I had not come up the River Clyde on a banana boat. He may not have heard the phrase before, but I think he understood its meaning.

It became apparent that Allan Evans was Mike Peden's manager, while Ally Maxwell was virtually fulfilling the same role on behalf of Hugh Scott.

Three days later, in another front page exclusive, I revealed that Morton vice-president Jim McCallion had resigned. The local man, who had been appointed by Hugh Scott, said: "I have resigned because of the pressure I was under. I was working for two chairmen – Hugh Scott and Mike Peden. On Friday I decided – 'to hell, finished'.

"I must be fair to Peden. He didn't give me any pressure. All the pressure came from Scott. I didn't take any money for this job. I live here and my family is hearing scurrilous rumours about me.

"Scott is phoning the club every day with instructions and some of them are incredible. To tell you the truth, we never carried them all out. If I told you he was on the phone five times in a morning, I wouldn't be lying. That's true."

Jim McCallion then confirmed what my earlier stories had questioned when he said that Scott remained the majority shareholder. He expanded: "Peden has not paid him the full amount. Scott told me he's paid less than 10%."

McCallion then revealed that players were often left wondering whether or not their wages would be paid. "Every month we're scrambling to pay the wages," he said. "It's not fair to the players. Peden is paying the English and French players their wages, and Scott the others."

Kit manager Andy Bryan, who had been sacked by Scott after a disagreement on Easter Monday, only to be reinstated when Peden arrived on the scene, was then fired again, according to McCallion under the instructions of Hugh Scott. He said: "Andy Bryan was sacked and it was Scott who told me to tell the manager [Ally Maxwell] to get rid of him."

Another club insider told me: "The lid has been waiting to come off this for some time."

Mike Peden's comment on Jim McCallion's resignation was to say: "I have no idea why Jim McCallion wanted to resign. I am about to form a new board and he would probably not have featured on it."

Peden refused to comment on Scott's continuing involvement.

Ross County administered a 1-0 defeat on the field of play at Cappielow before just 1,187 fans, but the football was now virtually irrelevant. Morton Football Club was in complete disarray.

In another exclusive on the front page of the paper of Friday 15th September I was able to give confirmation of Scott's continued ownership of Morton, coming from the man himself.

He and his wife Elizabeth had come to the Telegraph office the day before to complain about my story stating he still owned the club. It was the craziest interview in which I have ever been a part. Present also was the then Greenock Telegraph assistant editor David Carnduff.

Scott began by saying that, although he had not read my articles, he had been told that "there is a sort of coarseness [which has] crept into the main theme of Roger's pieces where he doubts whether a deal has been done."

Scott then produced, as if it were a major coup, a share purchase agreement between himself and Peden. I pointed out to him that, notwithstanding the agreement, he remained the owner until Peden had paid him the money, and that Peden had not done so.

After much farcical argument, including the by now usual threats to sue me, I said to Scott: "You are still the owner until you are paid?" He replied: "Correct."

He then went on to say he was awaiting settlement from Peden and was sure he would get settlement. Scott, however, continued to argue about the "tone" of my articles. I said in response: "You haven't read these articles so you are not entitled to say anything about that. Once you read them perhaps you can comment on that."

Scott's reply was: "That's a fair point." Yet he then continued to argue about the very point he had conceded early in the meeting, that he still owned the club until he was paid.

Asked if he still took decisions that affected the running of Morton, Scott said: "Only on a financial basis." I put it to him that he had ordered the sacking of kit manager Andy Bryan. He was only prepared to discuss that off the record. I was not prepared to do that.

His declared input into the running of Morton was also at odds with that of his former vice-chairman Jim McCallion.

The interview rambled on with Scott going round in circles, saying at one point that he "was itching" to sue me. I pointed out to him that you can't sue people successfully who have neither slandered nor libelled you. At this point his wife, Elizabeth, claimed I had "demonised" her husband.

The meeting was following the all too familiar pattern of dialogue with Scott and I drew it to a close by saying: "We have now established that you are still the owner of Morton Football Club until you receive financial settlement."

"That's correct," replied Scott.

"That is the point we were making in our story which you would have discovered if you had read it," I said. It had been like trying to draw teeth.

On the pitch Morton and Ayr drew 1-1 at Cappielow, then beat Raith Rovers 1-0 away, Stephen Whalen netting both goals and enhancing his growing reputation. Airdrie provided a reality check with a 5-1 thrashing of the Greenock men at Cappielow, before the next bout of off-field ramifications emerged.

I revealed that Morton players had spoken to the Players' Union regarding a dispute over bonus payments and signing-on fees. At the same time it was exposed that Mike Peden would not now be completing settlement of his deal with Scott until the end of the month, yet another delay. Hugh Scott remained adamant that the deal would go ahead.

Inverness then whacked Morton 4-0 in the Highlands while, off the pitch, manager Allan Evans spoke of the disappointment of what he called a club "full of whispers".

There were also rumblings coming from within Morton that the fans were not supplying the support they had promised should Hugh Scott depart. I wrote: "I would remind those who might make such complaints that Hugh Scott has not yet left, although he has stated unequivocally that he wishes to depart as soon as possible."

I also remarked on the deal itself: "We have got past the point when talk of 'teething troubles' convinces."

On Thursday 12th October, the front page of the Telegraph carried yet another exclusive to the effect that Hugh Scott was now "expressing serious concern" that his deal with Mike Peden may not go through.

Scott, so recently having threatened to sue me, had requested a meeting with me. He chose to meet me in a fast food restaurant in Greenock and laid bare his fears. He said: "It is taking an inordinate amount of time. I'm not nearly as warmly confident as I have been. I'm in a very difficult position. This guy [Peden] has had talks with me for 13 months." The 'this guy' to whom Scott referred was the very man he had said was 'the right man for Morton'.

Told of Scott's fears, Peden said: "There are still bits and pieces to be sorted out but we're quite confident."

No one else was confident, not even Hugh Scott by now.

CHAPTER THIRTY-ONE

Players threaten strike as Scott-Peden deal falters

On Friday 13th October, 2000, yet another exclusive dominated the Greenock Telegraph front page in which I was able to write that the players at Morton were threatening to go on strike over unpaid money they claimed was due to them.

Morton were due to meet league leaders Livingston at Almondvale and the game was now in jeopardy.

One player, goalkeeper Matt Boswell, said: "I'm not playing tomorrow. It looks like myself and the club have reached the parting of the ways." Boswell had been an excellent player for Morton and a thoroughly likeable young man.

Several of Peden's players were at the end of monthly contracts and were now in almost open revolt. I wrote: "A player crisis, which has been simmering for weeks now, is coming to a boil." The players were threatening strike action.

Some players had asked to meet me at Almondvale an hour before the match in the car park where they would be able to say whether or not a game would be going ahead. In the event the match went ahead. In order to protect the players I did not reveal my meeting with them.

Livingston won the game 1-0, but the after-match press conference was dominated by the threatened strike. Morton boss Allan Evans spoke of his pride in the players but then launched into an attack on the press. He said: "The written press, if you like, which [sic] have continued to throw mud all over the place – particularly on a Friday – is from my point of view aggravating.

"I might have to think about what I do as regards the media because I think we're getting a raw deal."

What respect I had for Evans, as a man doing his best in an almost impossible position, went right out the window after these remarks. He had telephoned me on the Friday afternoon before the game to complain about my story in that day's paper, despite saying he had not read it. He asked why I had not contacted him to get his view.

In fact, I had telephoned Cappielow several times on the Thursday afternoon prior to the article being written. His staff, as they would have been able to confirm, had told me he was either engaged in telephone calls or meeting players. He did not return any of my calls. Evans' response was to say "I should have made a better effort" to contact him.

He then told me that it was "part of my job to help him".

I wrote on the Monday beneath my report on the match: "I am not Allan Evans' assistant. I am here to report on the affairs of Morton Football Club as honestly as I can. I am NOT here to deliver sanitised homilies to the masses as part of some propaganda exercise.

"The bottom line is that Morton Football Club is far more important to this community – from which I come – than Allan Evans, Mike Peden, Hugh Scott or any other individual.

"The players' problems are not of the making of the press, as he [Evans] well knows."

Evans was trotting out the old nonsense of blaming the messenger for bad news. It was his boss, Mike Peden, who had signally failed to deliver his part of the bargain in a takeover deal; his boss who had been involved in half-truths and outright lies at times; his boss who was upsetting the players.

The situation at Morton FC was fast becoming completely untenable.

Allan Evans then said that by the Wednesday after the Livingston match he would be in a position to make a definite statement regarding the takeover. That date passed with no deal done, yet Evans said he remained confident.

By this time I was feeling more like a war correspondent that a football writer. I wrote: "It is high time messrs Peden and Scott got their act together. The root cause of speculation and players being unsettled and discontent over financial matters lies firmly at their door. The two men, after all, have been talking about this deal for over a year."

Former Morton assistant manager Mike Jackson, now scouting for Leeds United, informed me that the Elland Road club were interested in young Ton striker Stephen Whalen. This, at least, seemed positive, in view of Morton's financial worries.

But bad news was seldom more than a free kick away from the Greenock club. On Saturday 21st October, 2000, Morton were thrashed 4-0 by Falkirk at Cappielow, leaving them third bottom of the First Division. That was bad enough, but as the media waited near the technical areas on the pitch for the standard after-match press conference, Morton midfield player Andy Brownrigg, who had not been involved in the team for several weeks, appeared out of the players' tunnel. He was clearly agitated and accused Mike Peden of failing to pay him for eight weeks.

Brownrigg had been signed for £25,000 from Kidderminster Harriers at the start of August on what he claimed was a two-year contract. His dialogue, initially with members of Morton's stadium staff, spilled over to the press. "Eight weeks' money he owes me," Brownrigg shouted to the press of his boss Mike Peden. "I've got a contract to state that. Peden's here. Let's get it out in the open. This is the first time he's been here for God knows how long. I've got letters, final demands coming through my door and he can't pay me. He doesn't even have the common decency to put money in my bank."

The player then said that the stress of the situation had led to a split between him and his girlfriend. Owen Archdeacon, involved on the youth side at Cappielow, led a distraught Brownrigg away from the astonished press and into the clubhouse. The incident was televised.

Asked about the episode, manager Allan Evans said: "I know the player you're talking about and don't think he's worth the mention." Evans confirmed that the player was on a two-year contract and said: "I'll see him on Monday. I'll find out what the situation is and then I'll take the action I need to."

Goalkeeper Matt Boswell had withdrawn his services as a result of his claims that he was owed money, several other players were upset similarly and the ground was now a monument to neglect. Morale was plummeting by the week, if not the day. Into the bargain Andy Millen and Harry Curran had been sent off against Falkirk, incurring the wrath of Allan Evans.

I telephoned Mike Peden to give him the chance to comment on Brownrigg's outburst. According to Peden, Brownrigg had signed for a month with the proviso that, if everything went all right, he would be signed for two years once Peden had finally acquired the majority shareholding of Morton.

He claimed the player had been fined earlier in the season for spitting at an opponent. Said Peden: "He then didn't turn up for training and was fined another two weeks' wages. He also admitted to Allan Evans that he had a serious personal problem."

This was put to Brownrigg who confessed to 'hitting the bottle a bit' and said he had told Evans about this. "I didn't want to go down that road," he said. He continued: "I only failed to turn up for training because I wasn't being paid."

Peden had also told me that he expected Hugh Scott to hold an EGM "this week" at which an announcement would be made on the transfer of ownership. "We're well on," he stated. "I spoke to Mr Scott on Friday and everything is going positively."

As regards the problem with goalkeeper Matt Boswell, over unpaid wages, the goalie told me: "I've said all along that if I get my money, and an assurance that I'll be paid on time in future, I'll be happy to come back."

Peden's reply to that when it was put to him was dismissive, saying of the money owed to Boswell: "It's only a few hundred quid." It was a contemptuous and revealing remark.

Meanwhile Scottish League secretary Peter Donald told me that complaints had been received from players at Cappielow regarding financial problems and that an investigation would be held into the matter.

In the midst of all this, remarks had been made by the manager and potential owner of Morton relating to a lack of professionalism by some players. If there was a lack of professionalism it began at a far higher level. It struck me that the players had done remarkably well to carry on as they had done.

The farce that Morton Football Club had become continued when Kidderminster Harriers then told me that they were owed £26,500 by Morton for Brownrigg's transfer, being a £25,000 fee plus VAT. Mike Peden was 'unavailable for comment'.

It was then revealed to me that, at a private meeting with Morton supporters, Peden had claimed he had insisted on a right of reply to Brownrigg's remarks in my story. This was a lie. I had telephoned him offering him the right of reply, which he accepted. He also claimed that the Greenock Telegraph had been told of a sponsorship deal with a Canadian firm and had chosen not to print the story; another lie. I revealed both statements as the lies they were. Mike Peden was to say that my stories were preventing him from getting loans from the bank. By this time his credibility was less than the IQ of a cabbage.

Morton then drew with Clyde 1-1 at Cappielow before a crowd of 1,051, Robbie Raeside getting the goal, before Ross County sent them to second bottom of the league with a 3-1 win in the Highlands, Ross Matheson scoring the sole Ton counter.

Kidderminster then announced through their secretary Roger Barrow that they were reporting Morton to both the Football and Scottish Football Leagues. Barrow told me he had signed the deal, relating to Brownrigg's transfer, with Peden.

Hugh Scott responded to the news by saying: "The club is in the dark about the transfer claims made by Kidderminster. It would appear that the contract was signed by a person [Mike Peden] not authorised to deal financially on behalf of Morton."

Having said that, Scott then described Peden's unauthorised dealings as a "storm in a teacup", saying that Peden's intentions had been entirely honourable. Kidderminster could not agree and insisted they had written direct to Morton Football Club.

On the football side of things, which seemed increasingly marginal, Norwich City had joined the interest in young striker Stephen Whalen, and the player spent some time training with them before returning north with no deal being done. Raith Rovers then sent Morton to the bottom of the league with a 2-1 home defeat as talk grew of renewed protest among the dwindling support.

I then discovered that Peden – the man not authorised to carry out financial dealings on behalf of Morton – had come to an agreement with Italian agency Studio Sport to sell Stephen Whalen, for which service they would receive 25% of any transfer fee. The man dealing with the matter was Studio Sport's English representative, former Wolves player Mel Eves, who confirmed his involvement.

Morton drew 1-1 at Ayr, Harry Curran netting, the team as follows (4-4-2): Carlin; S. McDonald, Raeside, Anderson, Davies; P. McDonald, Aitken, Curran, Tweedie (Boukraa); Matheson, Whalen. Subs not used – McGregor, Robb, Maxwell.

The following Wednesday Matt Boswell contacted me to say he was taking Mike Peden to court in a civil action. The player said: "I'd love him to invite me to one of the fans' forums he has held. Let the fans ask the questions. I'll give them truthful answers and let's see whether he is prepared to deny them to my face. I'm telling the truth and he's not.

"What he has done is unfair, not just to me but several people. The way he has conducted his business is totally out of order. I don't think his fundamental interest in Morton is in football. I don't think the fans deserve him. I look forward to seeing him in court." It was an unequivocal criticism from an articulate young man who had proved to be a more than decent goalkeeper for the club in his appearances. In my view he was also a decent person. That Peden had admitted the player was owed money, dismissing it as "a few hundred quid", shed him in a very poor light.

Spurs joined Leeds and Norwich in expressing an interest in Stephen Whalen before Morton at last got some points on the board with a 2-0 home win over Inverness, Anderson and Aitken scoring. It enabled them to creep back up to second bottom spot.

On Friday 1st December I delivered the news in a front page exclusive that Morton were to apply to the Court of Session in Edinburgh to go into administration.

"With players not having received their wages for November, the whole future of Morton Football Club must now be in grave doubt," I wrote.

Hugh Scott had given Mike Peden a deadline on the previous evening to come up with funds and a firm proposal of a way forward to complete his side of the deal to take over the club. Scott told me that Peden had also been informed that it was now his responsibility to pay all the players' wages. Up to now, some players had been paid by Scott and some by Peden. Scott said: "I am not knocking Mike Peden. Relations between us are as good as they have ever been."

The next day's match against Airdrie, another club in financial difficulties, at the Shyberry Stadium was now very much in doubt.

I was invited to attend a meeting that Friday afternoon at Cappielow involving Hugh Scott, the players and their union representative Tony Higgins.

Scott confirmed that, in the interim period between his ownership and the agreed takeover with Mike Peden, there were no overdraft facilities available to Morton with the bank. He also said that since chief executive George Carson had suffered a stroke at the end of August there had been no proper administration at Cappielow. "I am chairman and majority shareholder," he stated, "but can't come to the club because the fans have made it plain they don't want me here. If there were another two or three buyers waiting in the wings we could say to Mr Peden 'on your bike', but there is no other buyer."

Scott then told the assembled players: "I've let you down and your families. But I'm a quick learner and it won't happen again." He then said that he fully appreciated that the supporters wanted a Scott-free Morton. "No one wants that more than me," he said.

The players agreed to play if they were recompensed and, on the morning of the match, Hugh Scott paid out their wages. Skipper Robbie Raeside said: "It was in the balance, but once we got our wages we went out and did what we are paid to do." Asked by one national reporter whether all the players were in agreement, Raeside said: "There's no split in the dressing room."

I commented: "It has become quite clear that Mike Peden does not have the wherewithal to complete his end of an agreement signed between himself and Hugh Scott in July. He has lost any vestiges of credibility he had, and that wasn't a lot after his involvement with Darlington. His constant utterings of how he will be in charge in a "week or two" are only too reminiscent of the boy who cried wolf. No one believes him any more."

Peden's boats were burnt. He insisted he remained interested in acquiring the club, a meaningless remark given that he had no support whatsoever in the community. Nor, of course, had Hugh Scott. Morton then paid a bill of £4,000 to the SFA in order to prevent them being thrown out of the Scottish Cup.

The gloom deepened when Alloa beat Morton 2-1 at Recreation Park to send them to the bottom of the league.

CHAPTER THIRTY-TWO

Ton enter administration

On Thursday 14th December, 2000, I revealed that Morton were to apply that day to the Court of Session in Edinburgh to put the club into administration. It was a relatively new process in football in these days, little heard of. I wrote: "Administrators would, in effect, ring-fence the debts and run the club as a going concern with the aim of finding a buyer."

A specialist firm called Kroll Buchler Phillips were duly confirmed as administrators. They had previous experience of administering Millwall FC and also re-financing at Spurs. Hugh Scott's acerbic parting shot to the Morton fans was to say: "They did not want me nearly as much as I did not want them."

Administrator Graham Martin announced that the "attendance and support of the fans is crucial to the survival of the club."

He promised to look into the financial deals undertaken by Mike Peden, for which he had no authority according to Hugh Scott. These were known to be the £25,000 transfer of Andy Brownrigg to Morton from Kidderminster Harriers, a deal with Italian Sports agency Studio Sport for the future sale of striker Stephen Whalen, for which they would receive 25% of any fee worth £150,000 or more, signed by Gianni Palladini and Mike Peden, and a £40,000 sponsorship deal with a Canadian firm, Primeplay. Included in the Whalen deal was a stipulation that if Whalen were not transferred by September, 2001, Morton would owe Studio Sport £30,000.

Hugh Scott meanwhile claimed that there were no debts at the bank and that only around £75,000 was owed to creditors.

Livingston then beat Morton 2-1 at Cappielow before a lowly attendance of 890. It was clear that the stay-away fans remained sceptical. I wrote: "If Cappielow was the Alamo, Livingston were the Mexicans and Morton the few defiant Texans." A scratch team, due to injury and suspension, played with spirit but simply were not good enough on the day.

Graham Martin appealed once more for support, making it clear that Hugh Scott now had nothing more to do with the running of Morton FC. He also said that there was a three-month period in which the club had to be saved, or it would enter liquidation.

At this point Ali Witherow, chairman of the Association of Morton Travel and Supporters'

Clubs, made his own plea for fans to support the club in every way possible, emphasising that any money received would not go towards paying off any debt incurred by the club.

The fans then launched a Save the Ton fighting fund and Ali Witherow commented: "Every pound is vital." Press officer of the fund, Jim McColl, commented: "We need to show any prospective purchaser that there is a strong and loyal Morton support here."

Tony Higgins also stressed the need for a big support for the Boxing Day game against Ross County.

At a press conference held at Cappielow, I asked administrator Graham Martin: "Would an offer for the ground marginally in excess of whatever valuation you as an administrator receive from an independent valuer be one you would consider? If so, would the person making such an offer be safe in the knowledge that he would not be liable to pick up accrued debts?"

He replied: "That is an important point. My statute role is to report back to the creditors after three months and put a proposal to them. If that proposal is as you have described and is better than the asset is, then that should be in their interest. I would say the creditors should get x-pence in the pound for what they are owed. In effect the new owner will be buying a clean balance sheet. They will not be taking on liabilities. That is part of this process. That is the potential attraction for someone coming in now as opposed to, say, coming in last week."

Although young striker Stephen Whalen had come under scrutiny from Leeds, Spurs and Norwich in recent months, no one had put forward a concrete bid. Nor were they likely to with the club entering administration. As he was the only likely saleable asset in terms of players, Morton's value predominantly lay in their ground. My information, gleaned from professionals, was that the ground was unlikely to be priced at more than £300,000-£340,000. Some figures had been bandied about nearer the million mark.

A blow befell the administrators when the Boxing Day game against Ross County was postponed due to the weather, but the Save the Ton Fund still raised a sum of £1,100 at the ground. The district was beginning to gather round the football club.

National Semiconductor donated £5,000 to the cause, while St Mirren generously offered to play their derby rivals in a friendly with all proceedings going to the beleaguered Cappielow club. Clyde also said that in their forthcoming match at Broadwood £3 from all adult visiting fans would go towards Morton.

On Tuesday 6th January a young, patchwork Ton team, containing two junior trialists, lost 6-0 to Ayr before a much healthier attendance of 2,866. In addition to the gate receipts, the Save the Ton group collected a marvellous £7000. There was a big cheer for former manager Allan McGraw when he took his seat before the match, his first return since leaving Cappielow.

McGraw also raised the possibility of a share-based rescue in which 100 people might contribute £2,000 each.

Administrator Graham Martin announced that a verbal bid had been made by Kilmacolm man John Laird. It was not accepted, but suddenly there was an air of optimism that things could be turned round.

Greenock Morton Supporters' Trust, whose initial board comprised Stuart Duncan, Jim

McColl, Iain McColl, Aileen Sellar, Danny Brown, Brian Farren and Danny Goodwin, set up a membership fee of £10 while Save the Ton treasurer Stevie Withers commented: "The bank balance doesn't look too bad but we still have a long way to go."

The ordinary fan was rallying round and each was to play a huge part in the collective attempts to save the club.

Ally McCoist agreed to guest for Morton in their friendly against St Mirren while, before that game, a match between Morton fans, prepared to pay £100 for the privilege, and celebrity team Dukla Pumpherston, would take place. Graham Martin was delighted and said: "Everyone is working in the same direction."

Airdrie, themselves in financial trouble, arrived at Cappielow and won comfortably 3-0. The attendance was 2,606 and a further £4,200 was raised by collections from the excellent Save the Ton effort.

Meanwhile local businessman Robert McLeod, who had made an unsuccessful attempt to buy the club from John Wilson, expressed his interest once more while, at a Town Hall meeting set up to explain the situation to fans, it was announced that IBM had pledged a four-figure sum to the fighting fund.

The St Mirren friendly was played before a crowd of 2,558, goals by Whalen and Matheson helping Morton to a 2-1 win. Ally McCoist was injured but, in a Morton strip, he led out the host team, St Mirren being skippered by ex-Ton favourite Tommy Turner.

In the preceding match between Dukla Pumpherston and Morton fans, the celebrity team contained ex-Morton players Roy Baines, Bobby Russell, Ian McDonald, Owen Archdeacon, Jim Rooney, Davie Hayes and Roddie Hutchison. The more youthful fans won 2-1 in an abbreviated match. Managing the Dukla side was ex-Ton legend Andy Ritchie, with television star Tony Roper also in attendance.

Stevie Withers of Save the Ton presented Graham Martin with another cheque, this time for £20,000.

The good mood was dented somewhat when Morton travelled to Peterhead for a third round Scottish Cup tie and went down very disappointingly 4-1. Ross Matheson scored the sole strike, but was later sent off. It was to lead to the sacking of manager Allan Evans, the reasons given by administrator Graham Martin being both financial and result based. Evans said: "I have no bitterness towards the club or the players." He was, however, disappointed that he was not personally informed of the decision to dispense with his services by Graham Martin.

I had taken issue with Evans' stance of blaming the media for Morton's troubles rather than his own paymaster Mike Peden, but I felt sympathy for him when he departed. He had, in truth, been placed in an impossible position. Ally Maxwell and Owen Archdeacon were to take over in tandem.

On the same day as Evans' departure was announced, there was even more shocking news when Graham Martin revealed that an independent valuation of Cappielow by surveyors Gooch-Webster had put a figure of £750,000 on the ground.

At the same time he declared that football debts of £200,000 were owed by the club.

These had to be met in full and had hitherto not been mentioned. The total liabilities for any prospective buyer came to just over £1million. Martin commented: "That is the figure they must build into their calculations."

It was a massive blow to Morton fans and sympathisers. Local valuers had thought a figure for the ground more likely to be between £300,000 and £340,000. This was substantially more than that, while the football debt had never been mentioned.

Jim McColl, press officer for the Morton Supporters' Trust, summed up: "To say that the fans were shocked and stunned would be an understatement. This could be the death-knell of this club.

"We've been talking to councillor Alex McGhee and have been told that the estimated value the district valuer had put on the ground was in the region of £300,000."

Allan McGraw said: "I don't think we've got a snowball's chance in hell of buying the club now."

In the summer of 1997, then owner John Wilson had agreed to sell Morton to Hugh Scott for £575,000 for his 88.8% shareholding. I wrote: "It is believed he received £400,000 and retained 28.8% of the shares." The club at the time was healthily in the black. It seemed illogical that a new owner now would be expected to pay out £1million for a debt-ridden club with a dilapidated stadium and very few players of any quality.

The land on which Cappielow was situated was designated as being suitable for leisure and light industry. The hope was that no one would come in to purchase it for non-football related purposes. It was essential that this did not happen.

I wrote: "The £750,000 ground valuation will become relatively meaningless if there is no money to be made out of developing Cappielow for a purpose other than football. At the end of the day anything is only as valuable as someone is willing to pay for it."

Councillor McGhee commented: "Mr Martin owes it to the people of Inverclyde to explain exactly how his surveyors have come up with this figure as it is nowhere near our figures. It is definitely giving us cause for concern."

Graham Martin was vague when I asked him if anyone had signalled an intent to buy Cappielow for any reasons other than football. "I'll come back to you on that point, hopefully in a week or two." He never did, even when asked again. He did, however say: "Our primary focus is to try to secure the future of the football club."

I remember thinking that there could be a riot in Inverclyde if Cappielow ended up being sold to a non-football related business. I commented: "It would be a disgrace if industry were to march in after Morton fans and sympathisers had donated thousands to the cause."

Morton Supporters' Trust then revealed that local surveyors Fyfe, Paton and Gerrard had placed a valuation of £250,000 on Cappielow, exactly a third of that by the surveyors appointed by the administrators. Graham Martin was unavailable for comment.

Clyde then drew 1-1 with Morton at Broadwood, followed up by a 1-0 Bully Wee win at Cappielow in a league double-header, before the Save the Ton group presented Graham Martin with another cheque, this time for £14,000. Paul Farren, their press officer, said: "This money buys another four weeks' breathing space."

The group were also prepared to pay the wages of midfield player Scott Paterson, signed for a month. Secretary Russell Steele commented: "At this stage anything we can do to help the team in their fight for survival is of the greatest importance." Co-treasurer Kenni Lee praised the incredible commitment of the local community.

On the huge disparity of the valuations placed on Cappielow, administrator Graham Martin said: "Gooch-Webster were asked what the land would be worth if the football club ceased to exist." Still he would not comment on whether or not there was interest from any non-football related business. It was worrying.

On the park Inverness beat Morton 4-2, the visitors' goals coming from Paul McDonald and Ross Matheson, before another Matheson strike gained a home point against Raith Rovers.

There was then a development when the Greenock Morton Supporters' Trust met with local businessmen to discuss a possible takeover. The Trust declared that they would meet the cost of paying off the football related debt of £200,000. Spokesman Jim McColl said: "This is great news that will allow any potential investor to get on with the real job of putting the club back on track." The proposal had been put to four businessmen and their pledges were secured.

On the playing side it was announced that young Stephen Whalen had suffered an injury which would rule him out for the rest of the season, thus virtually putting an end to any hope of a transfer fee from one of several interested English clubs.

Another £17,000, including £1,700 from the Greenock Telegraph, was raised and sent to the administrators from Save the Ton as the massive effort carried on to provide much needed funds for the football club.

Celtic came down to Cappielow for a friendly to help advance the cause, winning 1-0 before a crowd of 1,552, then giant centre back Kevin James hit a double to give Ally Maxwell his first league win in a 3-1 victory over Falkirk. March ended with a 3-0 away defeat to Ayr and time drawing near when a decision on Morton's future would have to be taken. The side were bottom of the league, but the likelihood of relegation was palatable considering the alternative of oblivion.

On Friday 6th April, 2001, the administrators declared that there was now a fortnight left to save the club. This was an interesting statement, because events proved it to be quite inaccurate. The club had been in administration for almost four months.

Inverness arrived on the following afternoon in Greenock to beat Morton 3-0. The match was notable for the substitution of young goalkeeper Andy Carlin at half-time after he made an abusive gesture to Morton fans behind the goal. Those same supporters had thought nothing of giving the youngster, who had made a mistake leading to the opening goal, their own form of verbal abuse. Carlin was replaced at half-time by Stuart Webster and then released by the club. I felt he had been disgracefully treated. Promoted too soon to the first team due to circumstances, it was hardly his fault if he made mistakes. There is an unfortunate tendency among a minority of fans to believe they have a right to subject players to any amount of foul-mouthed rubbish simply because they have paid an entrance fee. To do it to a youngster finding his way in the game was despicable.

On the field there was an upturn with successive away wins at Airdrie (2-0, goals by Anderson and Kerr) and Ross County (a double by Ross Matheson).

It was then announced that a consortium for whom Professor James Pickett of Gourock was spokesman was to make a bid for Morton. Professor Pickett said: "If the bid is successful it would ensure that Morton would continue to play at Cappielow Park."

All offers for the club and/or ground were to be placed before the administrators by five o'clock on Friday 20th April, 2001. This was significant, for it later became clear that the administrators were quite happy to change their minds.

Livingston defeated Morton 2-0 to leave them still bottom of the division, and I wrote: "A game has been lost. The real battle begins in a Gourock hotel next Wednesday." It was in the Jarvis Hotel that a meeting would be held by the administrators before the creditors and shareholders to reveal the current situation.

Ross County then beat Morton 3-0 at Cappielow to virtually relegate them.

Wednesday arrived and, after a three-hour meeting, fans and creditors were, as I commented, "left as mystified as ever over the future of the 127-year-old club".

Administrator Graham Martin spoke of an unspecified number of bids, saying: "None of them is in a state today that we can accept immediately." He said further discussion would be required before the administrators would be able to place a firm proposal before the creditors and shareholders.

I asked him if he had validated all, or any, of the creditors' claims, to be told "no". Martin continued: "We haven't validated any of them." It was, he said, an ongoing process. There was no receipt either, he said, of any of the £40,000 sponsorship money from Canadian firm Primeplay for the shirts the team wore. "It's one of a number of issues we are investigating." These investigations never seemed to get anywhere.

I appeared on a Frontline Scotland television programme on the subject of the financial difficulties of Scottish football, part of which centred on the problems surrounding Morton. The irregularity of Peden's deals on behalf of Morton were highlighted, as they had been through articles I had written previously in the Greenock Telegraph, but Graham Martin could never give an answer other than to say that investigations were ongoing. As for Hugh Scott having to take Morton into administration, I commented on the programme: "The final nail in the coffin was that he had lost entirely his customer base, the fans. When they refused to turn out there was no future for Hugh Scott with Morton Football Club."

To this day I have no knowledge of Mike Peden ever being subject to action being taken against him. Graham Martin, however, was careful to say that bidders would have to satisfy the administrators that they had money in place. Referring to Mike Peden, he said: "We have to make sure we don't go down the alleyway of last year where an offer was made and they didn't come up with the money."

Former Morton manager Allan McGraw, by now a liberal councillor, commented: "There was a lot of hard questions from the creditors and he [Martin] managed to avoid a lot of them."

One recurring theme which confused interested parties was the failure of the administrators to shine a clear light on the amount of debt for which they might be liable.

Back on the football pitch, Morton were finally condemned to relegation, despite a gallant 2-1 home win over Falkirk, goals coming from Redmond and Matheson. Before the kick-off manager Ally Maxwell led the players in applause of the crowd, in appreciation of their support in paying their wages. I wrote: "There was further mutual admiration at the end of the game in which the home side showed a tremendous spirit and admirable work ethic."

On the final Saturday of the season Morton signed off with a 3-0 away win over Alloa, taking them above the Recreation Park side. Ally Maxwell said: "I'm just glad we gave the fans the sort of performance they deserved."

There was increasing vexation, however, over the failure of the administrators to provide some real clarity about what was going on. The Save the Ton group who, they claimed, had handed over £80,000 of a total of £100,000 raised to the administrators, expressed concern about donating further cash. They were worried, and I felt with very good reason, that a non-football related bid might yet prevail for the acquisition of Cappielow.

I spoke to Graham Martin and he said: "We are trying to get a deal which will enable the club to survive and play at Cappielow. Discussions are moving forward in a positive manner."

He admitted that "several" bids had been made, only one of which was intended to keep the club going. He said his job was to try to see if there was a way in which the football related offer could be made to match the highest non-football related offer.

I was led to believe that the consortium's original offer was £300,000, enhanced by Greenock Morton Football Trust's guarantee to pay off £200,000 worth of football debt. Professor Pickett then announced that the consortium had upped their offer to the point of it being "fair to the point of generosity".

He said: "In making this offer the group is aware that many of the unsecured creditors are local tradesmen who can ill-afford to lose the money Morton owes them." But he felt that most creditors and shareholders would prefer to see an offer which kept Morton as a football club.

I wrote: "If the local business consortium, chaired by Professor James Pickett, do not succeed in their improved bid to buy Morton Football Club, then certainly it won't be for the want of trying."

I could not help but remain dubious about the nature of the non-football related bids, about which we could pry nothing from the administrator, either as to who was involved or for what purpose. I said: "The sceptical among us may feel that, at best, the non-football related bids, whatever they may be, are being used to push up the football-related bid."

I believed all now rested with the success or otherwise of the consortium bid and wrote: "Professor Pickett and the businessmen he represents are the only hope of saving Morton as a realistic going concern. If there is any justice in this whole business they will succeed."

On 31st May, 2001, the administrators revealed that the entire playing staff was to be made redundant. Graham Martin stressed that this did not necessarily mean the end of the club; it was a commercial decision.

Player Steve Aitken commented: "There's only one person to blame for this though, and that's Hugh Scott. He came in with his big ideas and promises, then walked away when it all went wrong, leaving the rest of us to deal with the mess. That man has destroyed this club."

One definite bid had been made for non-football use of the land at Cappielow. It was believed to be from a property developer. Given that the land was designated for leisure and light industry use only, it seemed unlikely to prove fruitful, but by this time conspiracy theories and speculation were running rampant.

June came and, on Monday the sixth, Professor Pickett said: "One shareholder has more than 60% of the shares, so that the fate of the club is in his hands." This, of course, was Hugh Scott. He continued: "He has said that he wants Morton to survive, but that he wants to sever his ties with the club. By saying yes he can achieve both aims; by saying no he would act against his own self-interest since liquidation would do him no favours.

"His decision will not be taken in the cosy secrecy of the polling booth, but in the harsh glare of public interest. The rejection of the bid would confirm beyond doubt what many already believe – that the misfortunes of Greenock Morton have but a single author."

It was now apparent that the consortium's bid was £410,000 plus a further £100,000 to be paid over the next five years, coming from 20% of transfer income.

This was, in effect, £10,000 more than Scott had paid to John Wilson, with a further £100,000 to come over five years. It was more than fair given the depths to which the club had sunk under Scott.

On Friday 15th June the consortium revealed they had upped the ante by imposing their own timetable. They had given the administrators five days to accept the offer or they would move to put the club into liquidation and seek a thorough review of the entire business dealings of the past four years.

On the same day it came out that the consortium's original 'line-up' comprised John Kerr of Portman Motors, who had tried to buy an interest in the club from John Wilson, local financier Robert McLeod, Kilmacolm businessman John Laird, Andy Gemmell, the former Morton director, Canadian businessman Tom Thomson, who had emigrated from Inverclyde some 12 years ago and whose son, Ryan, had played for the club, and Professor Pickett.

There was a clear rift in that original grouping. John Kerr said that there was no such thing as a consortium now, claiming that only Mr Thomson and Professor Pickett remained, while Professor Pickett responded: "People have left the consortium and at least one other person, who wishes to remain anonymous at this stage, has joined."

Professor Pickett said: "The important thing is that the consortium remains capable of meeting its financial commitment to the offer and has its funding in place."

It had become rather like a high stakes poker match. The consortium increased the pressure on the administrators and Hugh Scott by stating that, with each day which passed of their five-day deadline, they would reduce the £100,000 transfer element of their offer by £20,000.

By the time the 20th of June arrived, no progress had been made and Graham Martin was unable to be contacted for comment. On Friday 22nd June, as Martin was revealing that no bid "in its present form" was acceptable, Professor James Pickett was issuing a press release saying that expert legal advice was being sought which may lead to the administrator being taken to court.

The card table had been knocked over and the players were reaching for their six-guns.

Meanwhile ex-consortium member John Kerr entered the fray once more, saying of Professor Pickett: "If he stands aside and lets other investors in then I can do a deal with Scott. There is no consortium now. The people who are taking risks are people like me, Robert McLeod, John Laird and Tom Thomson. We're the guys who were putting up the money."

Professor Pickett responded: "I don't think that there is any other credible bid that would be acceptable to the supporters and community." He also claimed that Kerr had stormed out of meetings with the consortium when he had lost votes.

Tom Thomson then contacted the Greenock Telegraph to contradict Kerr, whom he believed to be a decent man, but stubborn. The Canadian confirmed that he was still very much part of the consortium.

We were entering what Shakespeare would have termed the denouement. On Saturday 30th June, two months after the original deadline imposed by the administrators, Graham Martin said that agreement in principle had taken place to sell Morton to a private consortium led by Professor Pickett. The consortium had meanwhile removed the £100,000 additional fee to come from transfer income over a five-year period and replaced it with a straight additional £50,000. This took their total offer to £460,000. In addition the Morton Supporters' Trust would guarantee payment of the £200,000 football-related debt.

At this point I had discovered that Inverclyde Council had agreed to lend the consortium a sum believed to be between £300,000 and £350,000.

A meeting was to be held in a fortnight's time to put the proposal before the creditors and shareholders. By this time all participants surely were exhausted; I know I was, just trying to keep up with the various fluctuations and associated turmoil. But Graham Martin warned that nothing could be taken for granted. The essence of the message was "don't stop taking the valium just yet".

CHAPTER THIRTY-THREE

Douglas Rae steps in to save Morton

At the beginning of July, 2001, the end was finally in sight when the administrators announced that they were favouring the consortium bid, fronted by Professor Pickett, for recommendation to the shareholders and creditors. One potential problem remained, in that Hugh Scott was legally bound to pay John Wilson for the 26% shareholding the man from whom he had bought the club still retained.

Scott also, comically, stated that he wished assurances that the "Pedros, Dongatons, Les Miserables and Wild Bill Hickcok" would refrain from insulting him and his family on the internet, claiming that they were part of the Save the Ton group. This was once more into the realms of farce.

On Friday 20th July, it was announced in the Greenock Telegraph that the consortium had been granted management agreement by the administrators. The process of administration had lasted over seven months.

Allan McGraw's former assistant, Peter Cormack, was then appointed as manager of Morton. This was as sure a sign as any that the anonymous man who had joined the consortium was Douglas Rae. He had been a great advocate of Cormack's during Allan McGraw's management.

McGraw himself was pleased for Cormack, though he cautioned: "It will be a big job for Peter. He's starting from scratch."

Cormack moved quickly to re-sign David MacGregor, as well as Brazilian midfielder Artur Correia. Alan Reid came in from Hibs while fans helped to try and tidy up Cappielow. Contractors began work on the dilapidated Cowshed and there was a spirit of optimism about the place.

In 10 frantic days Cormack managed to assemble a team for the Second Division opener on Saturday 4th August. "It has been a minor miracle that Morton are able to field a team to meet Stenhousemuir tomorrow," I wrote. "For that great credit goes to the community as a whole together with the Save the Ton group, the Morton Football Trust, individual fans, the consortium fronted by Professor Pickett whose deal has been signed in principle by the club's administrators Kroll Buchler Phillips and, of course, manager Peter Cormack."

A crucial meeting was due to take place at the Jarvis Hotel in Gourock on the Monday after the match at which it was hoped ratification of the new ownership would be achieved. "It is going to be a long, hard road ahead for the consortium," I said. "I join the whole community in wishing them well."

On the Saturday Morton got off to the best possible start when they beat Stenhousemuir 4-1, goals scored by Bannerman (2), Reid and Miller. I reported: "A group of players plucked from a' the airts combined to provide the perfect tonic for a crowd all too eager to support."

For the record, the team that day was: Coyle; Bannerman, Bottiglieri (Kearney), Greacen, Frail, MacGregor, Moore (O'Connor), Gibson (Tweedie), Miller, Reid, Correia.

On Tuesday 7th August, 2001, I was able to report on the front page of the Telegraph that Morton had been saved. I reported: "It took until the 11th hour of prolonged negotiation, but eventually the future of Greenock Morton Football Club was secured last night at the Jarvis Hotel in Gourock.

"An agreement, signed by the lawyers representing the local consortium wishing to purchase the club and Hugh Scott, was eventually put to the creditors and shareholders at 8.45pm by Graham Martin of administrators Kroll Buchler Phillips. It was unanimously accepted to bring to an end a meeting which had begun at 10am."

It emerged that the major contributor behind the consortium was, indeed, Douglas Rae. He did not attend the meeting, but in a prepared statement he said he had been impressed by the "resilience, dedication and effort expended by so many people". He also said that, should he ever seek to sell the club, any sum received greater than he had invested would be gifted back to the club.

I wrote: "So ended one of the longest days in Morton's history and surely one of the most significant." It truly was a Scott-free zone now.

Professor Pickett deserved considerable plaudits for calmly negotiating his way through the seemingly endless task which confronted him over many long weeks. I knew only too well from experience over four years what dealings with Hugh Scott were like. It had to have been an extremely difficult task, requiring, I am sure, a combination of steadfastness, patience and resolve.

There had, also, been a late scare when the offer of a loan of some £350,000 from Inverclyde Council was withdrawn due to what Professor Pickett was to describe as a last-minute hitch. Douglas Rae stepped in at Professor Pickett's request and, in the professor's words, "gave us a very substantial loan that saved the day".

Douglas Rae's input was crucial. Whether anyone else might have stepped in to avert a crisis, we will never know. But he put his money up front when it mattered most and deserves full credit for so doing.

Everyone was delighted, relieved and, no doubt, emotionally drained. It had been a tremendous effort by all concerned.

Clyde managed to knock Morton out of the Challenge Cup at Cappielow, winning 3-1, Sean O'Connor scoring for the hosts on the evening of the club's survival, but it scarcely seemed to matter in the bigger picture.

During the week I wrote that "everyone was simply delighted still to have a football club".

For my own part it was a huge relief to be able to get back to reporting on football matches.

A new board was appointed, comprising Douglas Rae, Professor James Pickett, Arthur Montford, accountant Iain Brown and fans' representative Jim McColl, the latter having done much good work with the Morton Football Trust. Professor Pickett had turned down the offer of the chairmanship, Douglas Rae then being appointed.

On Thursday 16th August I wrote a piece which, to my surprise, was to create a minor rumpus. In it I suggested that it would be a pity if a place could not be found at the club for some of those who had previously been involved in the consortium. Some presumably had, after all, resources from which the club might benefit.

It being the start of a new era I also wrote: "Hopefully the board will be able to make a statement at some time in the not too distant future in which their plans are outlined."

I suggested there were five questions which most fans would want answers to, as follows: 1 – How is the football debt to be paid? 2 – What sort of youth policy is to be put in place? 3 – What ground development is planned? 4 – Could the club still realistically think in terms of eventually becoming a part of the SPL? 5 – How are the shares from Hugh Scott to be allocated?

I believed answers to these would lead to clarity and transparency at the start of what was a new era. I concluded by saying that the new board would enjoy a honeymoon period, commenting: "The directors will need that time to get to grips with the job in front of them which is virtually to rebuild the club. At the end of the season we will all be in a better position to judge just where Morton can set their sights."

The response from two members of the board was indignant. In a letter to the paper Douglas Rae said "Roger is demonstrating he has not lost his talent for negativity", then said I was spreading "doom and gloom" and being critical of his new board.

I replied that this was a "gross distortion of the facts" (I too can be indignant). I had, in fact, been praiseworthy of all those connected with saving the club and had made no criticism, implied or otherwise, of members of his new board. When I wrote suggesting that it was a pity if former consortium members could not be included in the new set-up, I was mindful of the fact that Douglas Rae had stated in the past that he would only ever want to take control of the club as part of a group. I was also making a fundamental financial point; the more resources the better.

Professor Pickett then joined in the fray a day later with remarks I found to be pompous and petty. He described my statement relating to the possibility of previous members of the consortium being included as being my "pet remedy". That, frankly, baffled me. I had no "pet remedy". He continued: "I know that members of the fourth estate tend to think that there should be no limits to their right to poke their noses into everybody's business." That was a sweeping generalisation with no evidence of its relevance to me whatsoever. And coming from Professor Pickett who, as can be seen earlier in this book, was not averse to criticising previous boards and putting forward his own questions to them via the "fourth estate" (with every right), it seemed hugely hypocritical.

As someone who had spent four long years highlighting the considerable problems of

Morton Football Club – very much in the interest of the Inverclyde public – I felt it to be a particularly crass remark. If I am proud of anything in my journalistic career it is the consistent effort I made during that time to highlight what was going on at Cappielow, especially during a long period prior to national press involvement. I was pleased to have "poked my nose" into the club's affairs, even if it was often a stressful and arduous business. Mike Peden paid me, quite unintentionally, what I considered to be a compliment when he said the stories I wrote were making it impossible for him to gain credit at the bank, whether that was true or not.

After reflection it struck me that I must have hit a very raw nerve with the new owner and the professor. Perhaps splits in the consortium as earlier formed had been bitter – I have little knowledge of what went on at their meetings – but the reaction to my article seemed peculiarly aggressive. I should point out that I was later to receive a generous and conciliatory letter from Douglas Rae which I accepted in the spirit in which it was intended. My relationships with other board members, Arthur Montford, Jim McColl and Iain Brown, were never less than pleasant, more often cordial.

My path never crossed Professor Pickett's thereafter. He served on the Morton board for approximately a year, as was his wish, before stepping down again to become a fan. His part in Morton's survival should not be minimised.

On the park, Morton drew 2-2 with Queen of the South, with goals by Gibson and Reid, while Warren Hawke, now playing for the Doonhamers, got a big cheer from the home fans. Peter Cormack was delighted, saying: "Performance, attitude, commitment – first class."

Derek Collins then rejoined Morton while Stephen Frail came in to take up a coaching role, though he was also registered as a player.

But, after a home 1-1 draw with Stranraer, Stevie Aitken and Dougie Johnstone being 'old boys' in the opposition line-up, there came a slump which brought everything back into perspective. Berwick, Clydebank and Airdrie, the last in the CIS Cup, all recorded wins on their own grounds, before another two defeats at Cappielow followed, against Forfar and Cowdenbeath. The initial momentum, as often happens on a wave of enthusiasm, had juddered to a halt.

Peter Cormack manfully was still trying to build a team and Englishman Sean O'Connor, on loan from Dundee United, full back Dylan Kerr, the ex-Leeds, Kilmarnock and Reading player, and Stewart Greacen from Livingston, were all fixed up until the end of the season.

The run of defeats was finally halted when Morton gained a point at Hamilton, courtesy of goals from Sean O'Connor and Allan Moore, the latter destined to become a manager at Cappielow some years later.

Goals by Tweedie, Miller and O'Connor gained a well deserved win at Stenhousemuir, although it came at the cost of a broken jaw to Stewart Greacen, while a point was collected at home to Alloa, Bottiglieri notching what was, for him, a rare goal. Morton had some decent players in their ranks by this time, but still they were second bottom.

Clydebank then came to Cappielow and won 2-0, but in the next outing Stranraer succumbed at their own home by 4-1, Bottiglieri, Tweedie and O'Connor (2), by now a big favourite with the fans, grabbing the goals.

It was proving a hard struggle, nevertheless, and further defeats were inflicted by Forfar in the league and Queen of the South in a Scottish up tie, Scott Miller and Chris Aitken grabbing consolation goals in the two games. Aitken was the younger brother of Stevie who had been forced to part company with the Cappielow club under administration. He was a fine passer of the ball and adept at free kicks, only a lack of pace preventing him from going further in the game than he eventually did.

Finn Jani Uotinen then arrived in Greenock on the recommendation of former Ton star Janne Lindberg, coming from MyPa-47, and scored on his debut against fellow strugglers Berwick at Cappielow, but it wasn't enough to prevent a 2-1 loss. Back at Cappielow for a second spell and playing in the same game was old favourite Warren Hawke. It was a brief appearance for midfielder Uotinen as he then returned to Finland for the Christmas period because of exams.

Draws, both 1-1, followed against Cowdenbeath and Hamilton as Morton found it hard to pull away from the relegation zone, and full back Dylan Kerr then had to apologise for making a gesture to fans in the Cowshed who were voicing their displeasure at him. It was clear that the realistic aim of consolidation was not going to be accomplished easily, though Peter Cormack was confident that it would be achieved.

In January of 2002 Cormack moved to bring veteran striker Paul Wright (34) to Cappielow after he had been freed by Falkirk. He made a scoring debut against league leaders Clydebank at Cappielow in a 2-1 win, Sean O'Connor getting the other goal. He also joined up with old Killie team-mate Dylan Kerr who had played with him in the same Scottish Cup winning team in 1997.

The victory seemed to confirm Cormack's view that Morton would pull away from the relegation zone, but successive draws with Stranraer and Berwick allowed others to make up ground. When Hamilton beat Morton 2-1 in Lanarkshire, Chris Aitken getting the consolation strike, Morton were in third bottom place.

Second top Alloa then recorded a resounding 4-0 win at Recreation Park, ex-Ton players Harry Curran and Stephen Whalen being in their line-up. It was Gareth Hutchison who did the damage with a hat-trick. The Greenock men were now bottom of the table, five points adrift of Stenhousemuir and three behind Cowdenbeath.

Peter Cormack commented: "If we go down then as far as I am concerned that's failure on my part."

In an astonishing match at Dumfries, played in a gale-force wind and driving rain, 11 goals were scored, Morton going down 6-5 to Queen of the South. Peter Weatherson grabbed two for the hosts while Paul Wright, Dave McPherson, Sean O'Connor, Gavin Redmond and Warren Hawke were the visitors' marksmen. Manager Peter Cormack was sent to the stand at half-time by referee and former Morton goalie Cameron Melville for protesting at the sixth Queens' goal just before the interval. The half-time score was 6-3.

A no-score draw at Stranraer, followed up by a 3-1 win against promotion contenders Clydebank, offered some hope, though striker Sean O'Connor was whisked back to Tayside as an impending move to Queen of the South beckoned.

Morton could not put a run together and when Stenhousemuir beat them 1-0 at Cappielow they were becoming stranded at the bottom of the pile. Keeping a clean sheet for Stenny was former Ton goalkeeper Andy Carlin.

CHAPTER THIRTY-FOUR

Peter Cormack resigns, then McPherson goes too

It was a defeat which led to the shock resignation of manager Peter Cormack after just eight months in the job. He said: "I gave it my best shot. I'm standing aside now so that whoever comes in has one more chance to try and save it." Player-coach Dave McPherson was to take over for the rest of the season.

Cormack had enjoyed a good reputation as a coach under Allan McGraw's management but he faced a massive task when he took over. Morton had almost gone out of business, had no players, no coaching staff and no pre-season preparation. He had two weeks to assemble a squad of some description. Perhaps the worst thing that happened was an opening 4-1 win which encouraged existing unrealistic expectations within the club.

On the subject of coaching and management I always felt that Cormack was much better suited to the former. His coaching abilities were admirable, but man management takes other attributes and I was never convinced he possessed them. Nor did I particularly like the fact that he had stated that, while Allan McGraw's assistant, a member of the board had offered him the prospect of the manager's job. The first person he should have told about that was Allan McGraw who knew nothing about it until Cormack later left the club. His task as manager, however, would have tested Alex Ferguson's capabilities.

Forfar beat Morton 2-1 in Dave McPherson's first game in charge, but then five points were gathered from the next three outings – an away win at Berwick by 3-1, and back-to-back draws against Cowdenbeath (0-0 at home and 2-2 away).

When league leaders Queen of the South arrived in Greenock on 2nd April, 2002, Sean O'Connor made a scoring return to Cappielow, this time in Queens' blue, as the visitors comfortably eased through 3-0. It did not help that recently signed Australian defensive midfielder Marco Maisano was sent off.

By this time Morton were seeking a minor miracle. Hamilton recorded a 0-0 draw at Cappielow before Forfar arrived days later to thrash the hosts 4-1. Dave McPherson summed up: "At the end of the day it's shown that we're not good enough."

Despite a 3-2 victory at Stenhousemuir, goals by Scott Bannerman, Phil Cannie and Dave McPherson, other results meant that Morton were relegated for the second successive season.

Second top Alloa drew 0-0 at Cappielow to take the point they needed for promotion, while

Queen of the South celebrated winning the championship with a stunning 4-0 win against the Greenock club on the final day of the season at Palmerston. In their ranks were three ex-Ton players, Allan Moore, Derek Anderson and Sean O'Connor.

Douglas Rae confirmed that he would be redoubling his efforts to ensure that Morton got out of the Third Division at the first time of asking. It was the end of a season which began with the club's existence being assured, but ended with the disappointment of another drop down the leagues. It was going to be a long, hard road back.

Early in May, Douglas Rae announced that Dave McPherson would be the new manager and Stephen Frail youth team coach. It was another risky and untested management appointment. McPherson quickly announced free transfers to Chris Aitken, Gavin Redmond, Paul Wright, John Gibson, Scott Miller and Gary Tweedie, awarding three-year deals to Craig Coyle, Scott Bannerman, David MacGregor, Sean Curran and Marco Maisano.

A testimonial match took place for Derek Collins (33) between Morton and St Mirren select sides, the former winning 2-1 with a line-up as follows: Wylie (Goram); Collins (Hawke), McArthur (Pickering), Anderson, MacGregor, Matheson, Mahood (Hunter), McPherson, Alexander, Cannie and Tweedie. Collins was delighted and said: "The fans were absolutely fantastic. They were brilliant."

Then Dave McPherson moved to bring in young striker Alex Williams from Stirling Albion for a fee of £50,000. He had made a reputation for himself in the Third Division.

Meanwhile Airdrie had been forced into liquidation and were attempting to return as the new club to be admitted to the Scottish Football League in the forthcoming season. Douglas Rae was less than happy with that situation and said: "If they [Airdrie] were going to honour their football debts then I would support them, but they're trying to start with no debts. It would set a terrible precedent." It was a very reasonable statement which resonates to this day.

In the event, Airdrie failed in their application, the nod going to Gretna who, ironically, were to have their own severe problems in the not too-distant future. Airdrie, as it happens, took Clydebank's place after Jim Ballantyne bought them over.

Morton were still team building and Aussie Marco Maisano's brother, John (23), arrived as an attacking midfielder, while Finnish midfielder Jani Uotinen also returned, this time on a permanent basis. Former Hamilton centre back Paul Gaughan was acquired as McPherson sought the men he felt could take the club straight back up to the Second Division. Another trio arrived soon after, former Ton utility player Stuart McDonald, defender Anton Smith and left-sided midfielder Colin Riley. Initiatives were also being taken off the pitch to increase commercial income.

The Third Division league opener at Raydale Park resulted in a 1-1 draw with Gretna, now managed by old Cappielow favourite Rowan Alexander. Warren Hawke, restored to a striking role, hit the visitors' goal in a side which lined up as follows (4-4-2): Coyle; Collins, Gaughan, MacGregor, Bottiglieri; J. Maisano, Uotinen, M. Maisano, Riley; Hawke, Williams.

There followed a Bell's Cup Challenge first round tie against Stirling Albion at Cappielow on the Tuesday night, Alex Williams hitting the net twice against his old team, Warren Hawke adding a third in a 3-2 win. By coincidence, it was Stirling who were again the visitors on the Saturday, this time in the league, and again Morton were triumphant, this time trouncing the visitors 5-1. Williams hit another double, Hawke scored again, while the other goals came from Uotinen and Gaughan.

In the second round of the Bell's competition, Morton were drawn away to First Division Queen of the South who scraped through 1-0. Morton's discipline, however, failed them, no fewer than three players being ordered off – Alex Williams, Dean Keenan, on his debut, and Colin Riley. That contributed to a 4-2 defeat away to Peterhead in which Jani Uotinen and John Maisano scored. Unfortunately Warren Hawke fractured a cheekbone.

Queen's Park were dismissed 3-0, Williams (2) and trialist Lee Duncan netting, to take Morton to fourth place in the division.

As August drew to a close Morton moved to acquire former Scotland midfielder David Hopkin who, of course, had begun his senior career at Cappielow back in 1992. He had left for Chelsea for a £350,000 fee, before moving on to Crystal Palace, Leeds and Bradford. He had been troubled by an ankle injury which cut short his career down south and, as it turned out, he was only able to play a handful of games before finally calling it a day.

A draw followed at East Stirlingshire, Williams grabbing the Morton goal, before St Mirren defeated their county rivals at Cappielow by 3-2 in the CIS Cup first round. A shock looked to be on the cards when Morton took a 2-0 first half lead through Bannerman and Hopkin, but Saints' superior experience won the day in extra time, as they squeezed through 3-2. Marco Maisano was ordered off in extra time and, when Albion Rovers scored the only goal of the game at Cappielow on the following Saturday, the Third Division favourites from Greenock had slumped to sixth place. This was not in the pre-season script.

Next up were Montrose, and Morton recovered form to win 5-2, Uotinen grabbing a double, before league leaders East Fife were beaten 2-1 at Cappielow, Uotinen, again, and Williams getting the key goals. It was ace striker Williams who again pounced to give the Greenock side full points with the only goal of the game at Elgin, taking Morton up to third spot, just one point adrift of pacesetters East Fife and Peterhead.

Consistency, however, remained elusive. Stirling won 2-0 at home, then Gretna came to Cappielow to gain a point in a 2-2 draw, Williams and Hopkin scoring the home goals.

Once more, Morton bounced back, winning 4-1 at home to East Stirlingshire, a Williams hat-trick and a strike by Phil Cannie being indicative of their superiority.

Every time it seemed that Morton were about to take the initiative in the division, however, they stumbled, and at Hampden Park amateur Queen's Park won a point in a 1-1 draw, David MacGregor scoring.

Morton were in fourth spot and still well in touch with the leaders, but the result was to herald the sacking of boss Dave McPherson. Coming so soon after Peter Cormack's demise at the helm, it was a shock. In a statement the Cappielow board explained: "In view of the sizeable investment in both players and ground renovation it was unanimously agreed that an experienced manager should be appointed to take the club forward in a playing sense." One could say that decision should have been taken at the start of the campaign.

Dave McPherson chose that well-trodden path of so many sacked managers when he commented: "Obviously there are things I can say, but not at the moment."

At the same time David Hopkin announced that he would be retiring, his 'chocolate ankle' proving too much of an encumbrance.

The new man in the hot seat, which had hardly been warmed by McPherson and Cormack, was Queen's Park boss John 'Cowboy' McCormack. He certainly knew the division and he was full of optimism. He had the misfortune to have been sacked by Dundee at a point in a First Division season during which they were leading the league. His credentials appeared worthy.

His first game in charge resulted in a 4-2 home win over Montrose, Williams (2), Hawke and an own goal securing the points. It carried Morton to third place, four points off the lead. The crowd was 1,748, fine by Third Division standards, but nowhere near what Morton with their ambitions required to sustain them indefinitely. McCormack was under no illusions about what was expected. His task was to deliver promotion, at the very least.

On the final Saturday of November four more goals were scored, this time without reply against Elgin at Cappielow, John Maisano leading the way with a double and a man-of-the-match performance. Jani Uotinen and Alex Williams weighed in with the other strikes, for Williams his 14th of the season. A 15th followed in a home 1-1 draw with McCormack's old club Queen's Park and, when Morton thrashed promotion rivals East Fife 4-1 at Methil, Williams this time grabbing a brace, Morton were in third spot, one point behind leading pair Peterhead and Albion Rovers.

Striker Williams was proving to be the key player in the division and an 18th strike gunned down league leaders Peterhead at Cappielow. Now Morton were second top, one slender point behind Albion Rovers and very much the form side. John McCormack declared it a pleasure to work with the players and, with the attendance a healthy 2,640, everything seemed to be going according to plan.

January saw Colin Riley, Anton Smith and David Carmichael leave Cappielow, young goalkeeper David McGurn extending his contract and ex-Killie defender Robbie Henderson coming in to add to the squad. Aussie defender Lee Robertson also joined the ranks and, although hardly inspiring, a 4-3 win over Deveronvale was sufficient to carry the Greenock club into the third round of the Scottish Cup.

East Fife had meanwhile leapfrogged the Cappielow men in the table due to having played two games more, but Morton responded with a valuable 2-1 win over Albion Rovers to close the gap to just two points. Williams and MacGregor were the scorers and an on-fire Williams then delivered two more goals to knock First Division Ross County out of the third round of the Scottish Cup. The quicksilver striker, who timed and angled his runs so well, was now on 24 goals from 23 appearances and could do little wrong.

"We're quietly building things here," said a satisfied McCormack who moved into the market once more to bring veteran Ayr United striker Eddie Annand to Greenock on a loan deal to the end of the season. Young midfielder John Adam joined up from Rangers, while another youthful prospect, Jim McAlister, began to force his way into the picture.

In a top-of-the-table clash at Cappielow, Morton failed to move above leaders East Fife after a 1-1 draw, Stuart MacDonald netting before a crowd of 2,893, but the momentum was maintained with a 1-0 away win at East Stirling, John Maisano getting the key goal.

A no-score draw followed at Elgin, in which Jim McAlister made his first start after four appearances as a sub, before John McCormack moved into the market again to introduce ex-Celt Chris Millar (19) to the squad.

Next up, in the fourth round of the cup, were Stranraer at Cappielow. Two divisions above Morton, the visitors, managed by former Morton man Billy McLaren, won 2-0 before a fine attendance of 3,679. On the following Tuesday a third successive league draw away to Montrose saw Morton close to four points behind leaders East Fife. These dropped points were proving costly and, when third placed Peterhead administered a 3-1 defeat at Balmoor, Morton's 10-match unbeaten league run was brought to an abrupt end.

The early boost provided by McCormack's arrival had worn off and, although Queen's Park were beaten 1-0 at Hampden, Adam scoring, a 2-2 home draw against Stirling resulted in Morton dropping down to fourth place. Eddie Annand got both home counters, but Morton were now nine points adrift of leaders East Fife, albeit with games in hand. It was concerning.

John McCormack was adamant that his men must win their home games and Annand and Bannerman began the process with goals in a 2-1 Cappielow victory over East Stirling. At the time I wrote: "Victories in any shape or form will suffice." It was at the stage of the season when only results mattered and strong nerves were needed.

Paul Gaughan headed a vital home winner in a 1-0 win over Montrose and, when Annand popped up to prove his worth with the only goal of the game at Gretna, Morton had clawed their way back to within four points of leading pair East Fife and Peterhead.

Growing pride came before a fall, however, when Albion Rovers won 2-1 at Clifftonhill in a game in which young Ton defender David MacGregor broke an ankle.

Five games remained and goals by Warren Hawke and Scott Bannerman secured the points at home to Elgin to set up a vital clash against East Fife at Methil. In the event a sole strike by veteran Hawke, further endearing himself in the hearts of the support, won the points to take Morton two behind the Fife men at the top of the table.

It was in Morton's hands with three games remaining. Everyone connected with the Greenock camp had long since abandoned the notion that the Third Division would be any form of cakewalk. Nerves were fraught.

But, just when it mattered, Morton found their best form. At Cappielow they thrashed Gretna 5-0 (Williams 2, Bottiglieri, Annand and J. Maisano the scorers), then travelled to Stirling to win 3-0 with another double by Williams and one by Uotinen. At last the Greenock men were top of the division, one point ahead of challengers Peterhead and East Fife.

It set up a massive title contest for the finale at Cappielow the following Saturday against Peterhead. A tremendous Third Division record crowd of 8,497 turned out to see Scott Bannerman decide the occasion with a winner in the 55th minute. Cappielow erupted. The first major step had been taken towards a return to a more familiar league environment.

"We peaked at the right time," exclaimed a delighted skipper Derek Collins as his side finished the season one point clear of East Fife, who overtook Peterhead on the final day to gain the second promotion place.

I commented: "Two years ago Morton faced extinction. There have been more prestigious achievements in the club's history, but none better exemplified the spirit of a club and its community in battling against the odds."

CHAPTER THIRTY-SIX

Promotion blown amid accusations of betting scandal

Strengthening began over the summer for the new 2003-04 Second Division campaign, centre back Stewart Greacen (21) arriving from Forfar, having already had a spell on loan from Livingston under Peter Cormack.

Then winger Paul Walker (25) was signed from Partick Thistle where he had been unable to gain a regular place, followed by the arrival of Queen of the South striker Peter Weatherson (23) for a fee of £30,000 on a three-year deal. Weatherson looked to be an especially good signing.

The new-look side got off to a bright start when they beat St Mirren 1-0 at Love Street on Saturday 26th July to win the Renfrewshire Cup Final, Stewart Greacen nodding in the only goal of the match.

It is fair to say that most observers believed Morton would navigate their course back to the First Division sooner rather than later.

In their first competitive outing Morton dismissed Arbroath from the Bell's Challenge Cup in a high-scoring game before a crowd of 2,227 at Cappielow. It ended 4-3, Peter Weatherson marking his debut with a hat-trick, and Warren Hawke scoring the other goal. John McCormack favoured a 3-4-3 set-up, with skipper Derek Collins as sweeper, and the team was as follows: Coyle; Henderson, Collins, MacGregor; Millar, Bannerman, J. Maisano, Bottiglieri; Walker, Weatherson, Hawke.

A delighted Peter Weatherson said: "I don't see any reason why we can't win this competition."

Skipper Derek Collins was confident about the forthcoming league programme too, but stressed the need for consistency which, he said, "is going to be crucial".

The league began against Airdrie at Cappielow on Saturday 9th August, 2003, and Morton again were triumphant, winning 3-1 with goals by John Maisano, Alex Williams and Peter Weatherson. The game was also notable for the appearance of Charles 'Chic' Kavanagh as a stand-in assistant referee, following in the footsteps of another Ton fan, Stuart Cameron. After the referee was injured the call went out over the tannoy for Chic, a qualified referee, to report to the stand. A grinning Chic popped out from the Cowshed to answer the call, resplendent in

Morton colours. This later resulted in criticism from Airdrie United Football Club, who were less than pleased. Chic, a qualified referee, had officiated at a match between Airdrie and Morton fans on the morning of the game, won 4-3 by the Lanarkshire lads at Lady Octavia Park. In the event, at Cappielow, he was not called upon to make any controversial decision, though any time he raised his flag there were boos from the visiting support and riotous cheers from the home following. The crowd was a splendid 3,806.

Airdrie again were the opponents at Cappielow three days later in the second round of the Bell's Challenge Cup, another fine attendance of 3,317 turning out. This time United gained their revenge with a 2-1 win, John Maisano notching the home counter. David MacGregor was sent off for a rash challenge, Airdrie's Allan McManus following him off the pitch after manhandling MacGregor in the aftermath of the foul.

The top striking partnership of Williams and Weatherson secured maximum points in a 2-1 win at Stenhousemuir to take Morton to the top of the league after two games. An after-match talking point was a lock-in of the Morton team bus, a steward having accidentally dropped the key for the gates behind which it was locked down a drain. One of the gate posts had to be sawn off in order to effect the bus's release.

There was a buoyant atmosphere in Greenock, with everyone believing their team could go on and secure the championship and with it promotion back to the First Division.

A crowd of 3,402 turned out for the visit of Dumbarton, Williams and Weatherson again being on target, though the Sons managed to gain a point in a 2-2 draw. Williams had given the hosts the lead from the penalty spot only for the Sons to hit back and score twice. Weatherson gave Morton a deserved late equaliser as they slipped down to second place.

Another crowd of over 3,000 saw Morton restored to the leadership when they toppled East Fife from top spot, goals by Weatherson and Bottiglieri securing a 2-1 win. Weatherson, or 'Spoonsy' as he had been nicknamed by his team-mates, was fast becoming a hero of the fans. Partner Williams was being used with increasing frequency as an impact player from the bench, something sections of the crowd were unhappy about, but manager McCormack bluntly responded: "I pick the team that I think is the best for Morton and the players are told what the situation is. If there are fans out there who want to pick the team, tell them to come along and do it."

Goals by Peter Weatherson, Marco Maisano and Paul Walker saw off Forfar by 3-2 and, despite a 1-1 draw with Hamilton at Cappielow, Williams grabbing the vital home goal, Morton were top of the pile, two points ahead of East Fife after six games.

Premier League Dundee United, for whom Derek McInnes was a key midfield man, dumped Morton out of the CIS Cup at Tannadice in midweek. The visitors had, however, competed well in a 3-1 defeat, Weatherson again being on the mark.

A dazzling league performance at Gayfield then accounted for Arbroath 4-0, a Weatherson double and goals by Greacen and Bottiglieri increasing Morton's lead to four points. The quality of football persuaded home boss John Brownlie to say that the Greenock side were clear favourites for the title. "They passed us out of the game," he summed up.

Walker's pace and trickery up front, John Maisano's intelligent midfield play, and the goals from Williams, and Weatherson in particular, were key factors in the side's early successes. Where Williams' pace and well angled runs proved troublesome to opponents, Weatherson was able to hold the ball up and bring others into play. He was also able to turn opponents and produce ferocious shooting. By the end of September the future looked as bright as Alex Williams' silver boots.

I wrote: "The Tail o' the Bank challenge grows stronger by the week, just as the football seems to become more merciless."

November, however, began with a fall back to earth, Berwick Rangers delivering a 3-1 defeat at Cappielow. For all their fine football, Morton were often profligate at the back. This was such a performance. I reported: "Too often Morton seemed caught in a web of their own making." They were still top of the league, but it was a warning that nothing should be taken for granted.

An excellent Alex Williams strike took all three points from Alloa at Recreation Park before Stenhousemuir were crushed 5-2 at Cappielow, Weatherson (2), Williams, M. Maisano and Uotinen getting the goals to re-establish a four-point advantage at the top of the table.

Then came the journey to Airdrie for a clash with the third top side. United were the only other full time club in the division and the two clubs were favourites to accompany each other to the First Division. This would be a real test. Before the game anyone from Greenock would have been glad to accept a win of any kind. On the day Morton were magnificent. Stewart Greacen (2), John Maisano (2), Alex Williams and Paul Walker turned the contest into a 6-1 rout.

I reported: "Morton, backed by the best travelling support in the Scottish Football League, could not have contemplated such a scoreline in their wildest dreams on the eve of this match against their most serious rivals for promotion."

It was the perfect culmination of all the work that John McCormack and his players had accomplished on the training field. The team that day was (3-4-3): Coyle; Greacen (Henderson), Collins (Uotinen), MacGregor; Millar, J. Maisano (Bannerman), M. Maisano, Bottiglieri; Walker, Williams, Weatherson. It gave Morton a seven-point lead over East Fife and Airdrie.

It was a special display and I said: "Not only were the t's and i's neatly crossed and dotted, but a barrowload of exclamation marks was thrown in for good measure."

Perhaps not surprisingly the next display was a flat 1-1 draw with Forfar at home, followed by another draw, goalless this time, with East Fife at Bayview. Still Morton were six points clear of the field. I reported: "In the absence of a designated scribblers' area, I found myself in among a group of staunch Tonnites, the erudition of which astounded. 'I bet you can't get the word 'crepuscular' into your report,' said one avuncular gentleman whose pipe closely rivalled the polluting power of Longannet."

I responded that I might oblige if only I knew what crepuscular meant, to be told the definition was 'pertaining to twilight.' Crepuscular appeared, in context.

In Morton's next outing the lights went out on Hamilton who were beaten 2-1 on their own midden, an Alex Williams double giving Morton an eight-point lead as December beckoned.

Of John McCormack's side I wrote: "They try to play the game the way it should be played, helped by having a superior calibre of player to most others in the division." Promotion seemed by now to be a matter of course, even allowing for the potential of complacency.

On 6th December, 2003, there was an extraordinary 10-goal thriller at Cappielow, Morton beating Arbroath 6-4. I summed up: "What a peculiar game. Rarely can one side, in this case Morton, have scored so many spectacular goals at one end of the park only to lose so many gruesome ones at the other."

John McCormack accepted his team's defensive frailties but qualified that by saying: "Some of the goals we scored were amazing."

Berwick were tumbled from second top spot when the Greenock men travelled south to administer a 3-2 defeat, John Maisano (2) and Peter Weatherson hitting the net. It was a fine contest between two teams intent on playing attacking football. "That was a great game of football," commented John McCormack in the aftermath of a result which left Morton 12 points in front of nearest challengers Hamilton. His counterpart Paul Smith concurred, even if he was disappointed not to take a point from a game in which his men had made an excellent contribution. Morton had led 2-0 at one stage, Berwick equalising before Peter Weatherson grabbed a winner.

The year drew to a close with a 4-0 win over Vale of Leithen in the second round of the Scottish Cup, Williams (2), Weatherson and Millar on target. The crowd was a very healthy 3,231 and all with Morton at heart could enjoy a more than content festive spell. It was inconceivable that this side would not now secure back-to-back promotions.

It is doubtful if you could have placed a worthwhile bet on Morton failing to win the title. But the New Year was to herald a dramatic change in fortune for the Greenock club which no one had foreseen.

On 3rd January Morton travelled across the Clyde to play Dumbarton only to suffer their first away defeat of the season, an Iain Russell goal separating the sides. It was a defeat, but hardly critical.

The following Saturday an excellent crowd of 6,613 turned out at Cappielow for a Scottish Cup third round tie against Partick Thistle who were propping up the rest of the Premier League. Morton were expected to make it tough for their opponents, despite the two-league gap, but it proved to be a chastening experience. Thistle won more comfortably than the 3-0 scoreline indicated. I reported: "Morton received a salutary lesson at rain-soaked Cappielow on Saturday."

There was a marked physical difference between the teams, Partick's superior strength being a noticeable advantage. I continued: "It is in defence that this Achilles heel was most exposed but, frankly, it ought not to come as a great surprise. It is a weakness at times in the Second Division, masked only by the fact that the Cappielow men are immeasurably better than most, if not all, of their opponents going forward."

Ton boss John McCormack commented: "The team that went through were sharper. It's a good lesson. It lets the players know the standard they have to get to."

John McCormack then moved to introduce 20-year-old Rangers centre back Chris McLeod to his squad on loan to the end of the season before Hamilton, steadily improving under Allan Maitland's guidance, arrived at Cappielow. In an excellent game of football, honours were even at two apiece, the home goals coming from an Alex Williams double. That gave him 14 for the season, two behind partner Peter Weatherson. Skipper Derek Collins was sent off for an instinctive save leading to a penalty.

When goals by Weatherson and Williams were only enough to pick up a point at Arbroath, the first real signs of frailty were apparent. A gap at the top which had at one stage been 13 points was now seven. A 2-1 defeat at Forfar, Williams again being on target, was then followed by a 1-1 draw at home to East Fife, Scott Bannerman grabbing the goal. The lead was now five points and nerves were becoming only too apparent.

Where youthful exuberance had been a feature of Morton's free-scoring football in the first half of the season, it was now a hindrance. Derek Collins was singularly alone in providing the experience that was so obviously needed to calm the situation. And stories were emerging sporadically of some players being rather too keen on an unprofessional social life. A curfew was imposed by the club at one stage.

Alloa forced a 3-3 draw at Recreation Park, Collins, Henderson and John Maisano netting. Scott Bannerman was controversially sent off and the side had gone six league games without a win.

That poor run was ended with a 1-0 win at Stenhousemuir, Chris Millar getting the vital goal, but at Cappielow in midweek Airdrie arrived to take a point in a 1-1 draw, John Maisano scoring, and cut Morton's advantage over Hamilton, the Diamonds being a further point adrift.

The Greenock side were far from the form of earlier in the campaign, but they recovered to defeat Dumbarton 3-2 at Cappielow with goals by Greacen, Millar and Williams. Another three points were collected in a 2-1 home win over Berwick, Greacen and Cannie scoring, and the rot seemed to have been firmly halted.

It was a temporary respite. East Fife inflicted a 1-0 loss at Methil and when Alloa grabbed a point at Cappielow in a 2-2 draw, home goals by Greacen and Cannie, Morton were just two points clear of the only other full-time club in the division, Airdrie, who had hit a rich vein of form at just the right time of the season. John McCormack summed up when he said: "A draw can feel like a loss at times and it certainly does today."

On Wednesday 31st March, 2004, Morton were knocked off their perch at the top when Airdrie beat East Fife in midweek and edged ahead by one point. That 13-point advantage at the beginning of the year incredibly had disappeared altogether.

A Peter Weatherson strike steadied the nerves in a win over Arbroath, on the same day as Airdrie were smashing six past Berwick, before a 1-1 midweek draw against Forfar at Cappielow, Weatherson again getting the home counter, led to a return on goal difference to the top of the division.

Airdrie were very much the form side, however, with six games to go. On Saturday 10th April Morton's increasing vulnerability was fully exposed by a ruthless Hamilton performance at New Douglas Park. Academicals whipped six goals past them, Scott Bannerman hitting a strike in response that was not even remotely a consolation.

Tactically Morton were incredibly naive on the day. Hamilton boss Allan Maitland pushed three up front on top of the Ton back three, exposing the visitors' lack of pace and taking away the advantage of a spare man at the back. By half-time the score was 3-0, Morton having totally failed to respond to the Hamilton formation. I wrote: "The Greenock club were continually caught square and found wanting in pace. As a result they were terribly exposed." The free-running McPhee, Corcoran and Carrigan were having a field day up front for the hosts.

Morton manager John McCormack said: "I'm very disappointed for the fans." His Hamilton counterpart Allan Maitland was, naturally, delighted and responded: "I thought we were magnificent today."

Airdrie were now three points out in front of Morton, with Hamilton five behind Morton. Five games remained and, if the title was now an unlikely target for Morton, promotion was still very much within their grasp. This was acknowledged by Allan Maitland who commented that, even if his men did not go up, they had at least shown signs of real promise for the future.

A home 2-1 win over Alloa propped up Morton morale, goals by Cannie and Walker. Four games remained and second-placed Morton were five points in front of Hamilton. That surely had to be defendable.

But a 2-0 loss at Berwick pitifully exposed Morton's lack of resolution. I reported: "The sharpness up front that characterised early season displays has gone, while defensively the team continues to lose the sort of goals you would expect of a side at the other end of the table. This is a nervy team lacking in self-assurance."

The situation was made infinitely worse over the course of the following week when rumours on the internet regarding Morton players betting on Airdrie to win the title made their way into the media. On the Saturday Morton travelled across the Clyde to Dumbarton and were soundly beaten 3-0. Derek Collins also found himself being sent off. The large travelling support booed both management and players from the field.

I commented: "It is hard to believe a side who played such thrilling football for much of the first half of the season have fallen so dramatically. Perhaps other sides have sussed them out – how to stop them. Or perhaps a lack of experience and physical stature has finally caught up with them; maybe a combination of all three. Who knows?"

The rumours of players placing bets which had swept the district in the days before the Dumbarton game would not have helped. Also detrimental was the fact that striker Alex Williams had been dropped and disciplined after having been found to come out of a casino in Glasgow in the early hours of the Friday morning before the game. I wrote: "He has let himself down, his manager, the chairman, fellow players and the supporters at a critical stage in the season. His strike partner Peter Weatherson also attracted the ire of the fans at Dumbarton, the decision to substitute him in the second half being cheered. It was symptomatic of a general decline in recent months in which the sharpness and all-round ability which characterised his play appears to have all but deserted him." He had been linked with the betting allegations, though no substantiation was ever offered in support of those claims. But the fans were in no mood remotely resembling tolerance.

Hamilton were now three points behind Morton with two games left. Statistically the Cappielow club were still in comfortable command of their own destiny, but in terms of morale they were in freefall. It was a remarkable transformation.

No evidence or proof of wrong-doing emerged on the betting allegations, but the damage was done. "What this episode does reveal is how much easier it is in these days of the internet for any individual to spread malicious rumours for whatever purpose. Where before such unsubstantiated gossip might have been restricted to the pub, it can now be aired by anyone with a mind to do so on the web." Or anyone with half a mind, I might have added.

Nothing was to come of the betting rumours, but it further soured the mood of a support already disillusioned by what they perceived as an inexplicable collapse. The club carried out an investigation and claimed resolutely that there was absolutely no evidence of any wrong-doing. There was certainly no police investigation, nor did any bookmaker come forward to suggest that anything suspicious had come to light. The rumours had come to the attention of the Greenock Telegraph two days before the Dumbarton match, but the paper's own investigation was unable to substantiate any of the internet claims.

Chairman Douglas Rae said: "One of the players fingered by these allegations has said to me that he would be very happy if the police were involved because he wants his name cleared, and I can understand that."

Midfield man John Maisano commented: "I think it is disgusting that someone could come up with such a claim and would love to know where it originated."

Two games remained and Morton were still three points ahead of third top Hamilton. The prize of promotion was still very much in their own hands. Also in their favour was that their penultimate match was against bottom club Stenhousemuir – already relegated – at Cappielow.

Manager John McCormack looked ahead, saying: "The bottom line is that we have a great chance to go up. The fans have been brilliant all season and we have got to reward them."

Almost the entire length of the league separated the teams as they lined up on Saturday 8th May, 2004, before a crowd of 3,456 at Cappielow. By quarter to five the scoreline read 4-1 – but it wasn't to Morton. Incredibly Stenhousemuir had further developed Morton's nightmare. It was a startling result, made worse by the fact that Hamilton's win over Berwick had taken them ahead of Morton on goal difference.

I wrote: "As the stadium emptied at Cappielow on Saturday with a stunned support still trying to make sense of the result, the lyrics of the song blaring out on the tannoy seemed like some sort of subliminal message. 'Don't worry, be happy,' the voice crooned with some irony."

Stenhousemuir, having won just six times throughout the season, had discovered that Morton's frayed psyche had suffered one trauma too many.

I continued my observations by saying: "One question kept coming to the fore. How can a team visibly fall apart so dramatically? I cannot recall any season watching Morton when two halves of a season have been in such contrast."

John McCormack hinted that he had had to keep a lid on more troubles within the camp than had been apparent during the season when he said afterwards: "I could give you every excuse under the sun, but there are lots of problems as you go along, shall we say. It's not just loss of form."

He wasn't referring to the betting rumours, which after all could have affected only the last couple of matches, and he continued: "There are various things that happen to teams and individuals as you go along and these things aren't helped in any way at all as your form dips."

I had commented during the course of the season that there were too few experienced players in the squad and a lack of physicality, but there was also a small group of players who seemed too set on enjoying themselves off the pitch in an unprofessional manner. I wrote: "Perhaps some [players] might take an honest look at themselves and ask why the club felt it necessary to impose a curfew at one stage in the season on their activities."

The final match of the season was at the Shyberry Excelsior Stadium against the champions, Airdrie. This was the same venue where earlier in the campaign Morton had won 6-1. That now seemed an aeon ago. The task was simple: victory and hope that Hamilton lost something at Forfar. There was no miracle. Airdrie won 2-0 with a large travelling support chanting defiantly at the end. In their last 10 games Morton had scored nine goals, lost 22 and collected just eight points. Airdrie had finished 11 points ahead and Hamilton, who won 4-0 at Station Park, three in front. Dumbarton had sneaked into third spot, a point clear of the Greenock team.

Blue and white hooped players were crying on the field. I felt little sympathy at the time and wrote later: "One or two players who have been all too ready to shed tears at missing the step up to Division One might reflect on their own contribution to that failure. For one player [Alex Williams] to go to a casino until the early hours of the morning near the end of a week in which the betting allegations had made the news beggars belief. He was a lucky man to be allowed to remain at the club and he is possibly not alone in that respect.

"The manager deserves better, the support deserves better and the board does too."

John McCormack commented on his players: "I hope a lot of them have learnt, because I have as well."

McCormack was later to say: "It has been well documented that there were problems at this club with regard to behaviour of players. This is the kind of thing that could cost a manager his job. But I have the full backing of the board and I can say there will be changes made here."

Football being the business it is, however, the choice of whether or not to dispense with a troublemaker often depends upon his perceived transfer value. At least two players were lucky to stay at Cappielow for that very reason.

Among the first team squad freed were Phil Cannie, Mel Bottiglieri, Paul Gaughan, Robbie Henderson and Jani Uotinen, though it should not be assumed that all of these by any means were among the 'party boys'. Most were not. In fact, the main culprits remained. There was a feeling that the manager may not have been permitted to make as many changes as he wished, perhaps because of the potential worth of some of the perceived problem boys.

The process began over the summer to bring in new faces. Centre back Stuart McCluskey arrived from St Johnstone, and was to be made captain, striker Iain Diack came in from Arbroath, left back Marc McCulloch from Brechin and 18-year-old striker Jason Walker from Dundee.

CHAPTER THIRTY-SEVEN

New training ground, then new manager

Morton then acquired a new training facility at Quarriers Village near Bridge of Weir, a major step forward as they attempted to introduce a more professional set-up. Also coming in to Cappielow was former Ton defender Joe McLaughlin, appointed as youth manager.

This was an important role as Morton's youth section had been neglected ever since Allan McGraw had left the club in the early days of the Hugh Scott era.

St Mirren were beaten 2-1 in the Renfrewshire Cup Final, goals coming from Scott Bannerman and John Maisano, before the first competitive match of the season on Saturday 31st July, 2004, against Forfar at Station Park in the Bell's Challenge Cup.

It was clear that the target was promotion, and that a second failure would be considered a major set-back.

New captain Stuart McCluskey led the team out at Forfar in the Challenge Cup. Manager McCormack departed from his favoured 3-4-3 set-up to a flat back four, but it was Forfar who won 3-1, Jason Walker getting the sole Ton goal.

With injuries to Derek Collins and Iain Diack, the team lined up as follows (4-4-2): Coyle; Millar, Greacen, McCluskey, McCulloch; P. Walker (Hawke), Bannerman, M. Maisano (Williams), McAlister (J. Maisano); J. Walker, Weatherson.

By the time the first league game came round a week later John McCormack had reverted to his usual 3-4-3 system, but it was Berwick Rangers who won 2-1 at Shielfield, Jason Walker getting on the scoresheet for the visitors from the west coast.

The following Saturday Morton beat Stranraer 3-1 at Cappielow, Jim McAlister starring in a wide right role, also contributing one of the goals. There was a special tribute before the game to groundsman Campbell Stevenson for the excellent state of the Greenock club's playing surface. New drainage and tender love and care had transformed Cappielow in recent seasons from the quagmire it had too often been in the past to one of the best pitches in the country.

Gretna were then defeated in a CIS Insurance Cup tie in Greenock, Paul Walker scoring the game's only goal, before a 3-0 win at Dumbarton – goals by Jason Walker, Peter Weatherson and Stewart Greacen – took Morton to third top spot.

Premier League Motherwell interrupted the feel-good factor with a comfortable 3-0 win in the second round of the CIS Insurance Cup, in which Derek Collins was sent off, before a Stewart Kean double gave Ayr a league victory at Somerset. Attempts to sign strikers Scott McLean of Stirling and later Gareth Hutchison of Berwick failed before Morton got back on track with a 2-1 win over Arbroath at Cappielow, Peter Weatherson's double collecting all three points.

There was dramatic news, however, on the following Friday afternoon when the club announced the sacking of manager John McCormack and his assistant Stephen Frail. Five games into the season Morton chairman Douglas Rae dispensed with the third manager since his takeover of the club, saying: "We felt the results were having an adverse affect upon the gates. I am always saddened in a situation like this when someone has worked hard. John McCormack has worked his socks off but there have been some dressing room problems.

"John was outstanding as far as his work ethic was concerned but, unfortunately, he did not get the response from the players. I can't say why that was."

I wrote, referring to that: "In other words, in football parlance, he had lost the dressing room. If that is the case then some players might like to take a look at their own role in the manager's demise and the fact that the club required at one stage last season to impose a ban on alcohol during the week."

McCormack himself was not available for comment and it was youth manager Joe McLaughlin who was tasked with taking over the reins until a new manager could be installed. I felt McCormack had been badly let down by some players. McLaughlin threw his own hat into the ring as a candidate and, in his first game in charge, Morton took a point from league leaders Stirling at Forthbank with a 1-1 draw, Chris Millar scoring. His favoured formation was similar to McCormack's, though instead of a front three he pushed an extra man into midfield, John Maisano filling the hole in behind the strikers.

The players were behind McLaughlin, but Brechin spoiled the atmosphere with a 3-0 win at Cappielow to leave Morton in sixth place. I reported: "In a system operating three at the back, the wingbacks are a specialised position. Marc McCulloch was brought in at the start of the season as a traditional full back when it appeared that John McCormack had decided to adopt a flat back four. When he then reverted to three at the back the former Arbroath player basically had to play out of position." He lacked the pace to play wingback and it left Morton looking very lopsided.

McLaughlin, however, persevered and achieved a crushing 6-1 win at Alloa, doubles by Jason Walker and Peter Weatherson, and goals from Chris Millar and John Maisano, giving the travelling support a huge boost.

A shortleet was drawn up for the vacant manager's post, including Richard Gough and Paul Gascoigne, who, bizarrely, telephoned Douglas Rae during the middle of a home match against Forfar to express interest in the position. That game was won 2-1 through Weatherson and Millar, before Stranraer imposed a 1-0 defeat at Stair Park, Peter Weatherson getting himself sent off in the process.

That defeat may have cost Joe McLaughlin his shot at the manager's job full-time, for on the following Thursday it became clear that the hot favourite was ex-Celtic, Nottingham Forest, Coventry, Dundee United and Scotland midfielder Jim McInally. He had had a brief spell as manager of Sligo Rovers before becoming youth coach at Celtic.

The 40-year-old took over on Saturday 23rd October, 2004, against Berwick Rangers at Cappielow along with assistant Martin Clark, son of Celtic Lisbon Lion John Clark. McInally and Clark had been team-mates at Nottingham. Joe McLaughlin was to be retained as youth manager.

McInally began with a 2-1 win, goals provided by Jim McAlister, once again outstanding, and John Maisano. The new boss commented: "I'm delighted with the attitude of the players." He also made it clear that, while aware of the stories of dressing room unrest and occasional indiscipline, everyone would start with a clean sheet as far as he was concerned.

McInally immediately altered Morton's system to a traditional 4-4-2, saying: "I'm just a believer in a back four and I think the personnel we've got suits it."

His line-up against Berwick was, 4-4-2: McGurn; Collins, McCluskey, Greacen, McCulloch; Millar, J. Maisano, M. Maisano, McAlister; J. Walker, Williams.

The win took Morton third top, nine points behind leaders Stranraer and five off second placed Brechin.

The honeymoon ended a week later when Ayr came to Cappielow and won 1-0, McInally stating that the performance wasn't good enough. Alex Williams missed a penalty.

Morton then travelled to Arbroath where they notched up a good 3-0 victory, strikers Peter Weatherson and Jason Walker getting on the scoresheet, an own goal completing the trio of strikes.

A second successive home crowd of over 3,000 turned out to see another 3-0 win, this time against Stirling, Paul Walker, Jason Walker and Chris Millar finishing off some good football from the hosts. Morton had moved up to third spot, ahead of Albion on goal difference.

Third Division East Stirlingshire were no match for the Greenock men in a postponed midweek Scottish Cup second round tie, Williams, Weatherson and Millar on the mark in a 3-1 win.

The mood was optimistic and improved further when 31-year-old Alan Mahood switched from St Johnstone to Greenock, adding some vital experience to the squad. It was his third time at Cappielow and he commented: "I'm just looking forward to getting back into it." His debut came at Glebe Park where Brechin nonetheless won 2-1 with a double by Chris Templeman. Mahood came on in the second half and gave a decent display.

Morton's form continued to be fragile, however, and, after a 2-2 home draw with Alloa in which Paul Walker and John Maisano scored, Jim McInally commented on his team's defensive vulnerability: "It looks like we need to score three to win a game."

On 7th December, 2004, Morton finally got the striker they had tried to sign 18 months previously, Chris Templeman arriving from Brechin for a fee believed to be around £80,000. Formerly a Recreational Officer with Fife Council where he worked with children with special needs, he was leaving part-time football behind him. The big fellow, all six feet four inches of him, had been a prolific scorer for Brechin in the past couple of seasons and said: "When you get the chance to play full-time you've got to take it."

He missed out on the Scottish Cup second round tie away to Cove Rangers, won 7-1 by his new colleagues, doubles by Peter Weatherson and Jason Walker being complemented by efforts from Chris Millar, Warren Hawke and John Adam.

Striker Alex Williams found himself dropped once more for disciplinary reasons. It was to signal the end of his Cappielow career which had too often been blighted by misdemeanour. A player of genuine talent and pace, he was proving once more that frequently in football these assets can be undermined by a flawed character. I commented: "The player must know that too often he gets himself in the news for the wrong reasons."

Boss McInally had adopted the training methods as used by Celtic, based on a science-based Scandinavian conditioning programme. The manager said: "I've already seen a difference in one or two of the lads."

Draws were proving costly to Morton, and Berwick held them 2-2 at Shielfield Park, Marco Maisano and Chris Millar being on target. The Cappielow club were now fifth in the table and already the signs were worrying for their promotion aims.

Greenockian Shaun Dillon arrived on loan from Kilmarnock in an attempt to help shore up a defence which was too often uncertain, and the left back made his debut in a pleasing 3-0 home win over Dumbarton. Weatherson, McCluskey and new boy Templeman scored. Still Morton could not put a run together, Ayr beating them 2-1 at Somerset despite Paul Walker's strike.

Another defeat followed in the next round of the cup at Almondvale against Premier League Livingston, Richard Gough's side winning 2-1 on a night of gale-force winds. Weatherson notched the visitors' goal.

Even this early into Jim McInally's reign the fans were beginning to voice their dissatisfaction, but the manager said: "I don't blame any fans who are grumbling a bit. They have suffered a lot in the past year and I have no complaints."

On Saturday 15th January, 2005, the Greenock men moved up to third spot, still nine points behind second top Stranraer, thanks to unanswered goals from Templeman and Millar against Arbroath at Cappielow.

Meanwhile Partick and Raith were registering interest in out of favour Alex Williams while full back Marc McCulloch, only signed in pre-season by John McCormack, was told he could find another club. Williams moved soon after to Queen of the South on loan until the end of the season. He was to falter there too, however, and it was the start of an irreversible slide into footballing oblivion. It was entirely self-inflicted.

A point in a 1-1 draw at Stirling, Stewart Greacen getting the goal, reduced the gap between Morton and Stranraer to eight points. At that time chairman Douglas Rae commented: "My ultimate aim is obviously the Premier League but I won't be putting a timescale on us getting there."

First there was promotion to the First Division to be achieved, and the task was made no easier when leaders Brechin arrived in Greenock to win 2-0. It proved that money and status are no guarantees of success.

Derek Collins then left the camp for Third Division Gretna, now funded by Brooks Mileson's millions, while old favourite Warren Hawke announced his intention to retire. Collins, in two spells at the club, played 534 times, still a club record. On the way in to Cappielow was Livingston's Scott McLaughlin (21), a defensive midfielder who was signed on loan until the end of the season.

Chris Templeman showed why the club had brought him to Cappielow when he hit a hat-trick in a 4-0 romp over Forfar, Peter Weatherson getting the other goal. For such a big fellow, Templeman had a delicate touch on the ball. His weakness at times was a lack of perceived fight, but when his game worked he could be a very potent force. Another to shine was young goalkeeper David McGurn.

Jim McInally was aware that the fans were desperately seeking some consistency to their side's displays and commented: "Because we are Morton and we are the big team with the big support, it doesn't guarantee you being in the First Division. We need to build a team and work to a system that can take us there, and that's not going to happen overnight."

When Dumbarton dumped Morton 3-0 his words seemed to have had a prophetic ring to them. It was vital, then, to get back on track in the match of the day on Saturday 26th February, 2005, when second top Stranraer, the club Morton had to overtake in the promotion race, arrived in Greenock. It was a fairy-tale afternoon for Dundee United and former Scotland winger Andy McLaren. Having turned down an earlier request by his old team-mate Jim McInally to come to Cappielow, he changed his mind when he couldn't force his way into United's injury-ravaged team. A phone call to McInally resulted in his surprise appearance against Stranraer. In a 2-0 victory he scored both goals to win his way into the hearts of the home support.

Jim McInally said after the game: "It was a real stroke of luck yesterday that he [McLaren] actually decided to phone me. I think when he saw he wasn't going to get a wee shout with United this weekend, when they had a few injury problems, he decided he wanted to come here."

McLaren was delighted, saying: "It was a good start and two goals were a bonus. I feel like a football player this afternoon. It's soul-destroying training all week knowing there's not going to be an end product."

Morton were now eight points behind Stranraer, and they maintained that margin after a last-minute Chris Millar goal gained them all three points at Arbroath.

Nothing was falling into Morton's lap, however, and Forfar increased the frustration when they won 2-0 at Station Park.

Centre back Ryan Harding followed Scott McLaughlin from Livingston to Cappielow, while Greenockian Stefan Gonet was added to the goalkeeping fraternity.

Due to injuries Peter Weatherson had to move into central defence and did well in a 2-1 win over Ayr, Chris Millar and John Maisano scoring. Veteran Alan Mahood was hardly featuring by now, the feeling being that his legs had finally gone, and a further win, this time by 2-0 over Stirling, courtesy of Harding and Templeman goals, meant Morton were now six points behind second top Stranraer who were fighting determinedly to maintain their challenge. What they may have lacked in quality they more than made up for by excellent organisation under manager Neil Watt.

On an evening when the wee club from the south-west finally faltered, Morton failed to make up ground appreciably after a 2-2 draw at Alloa, Weatherson and Millar goals taking them five points shy of Watt's men. By this time Stranraer had ex-Ton boss John McCormack working as an assistant to Neil Watt and he must have appreciated the irony of the situation, having been sacked five games into the season. His last two games in charge had been victories over Stranraer and Gretna.

With seven games to go, Stranraer needed 14 points to ensure promotion. There was little leeway for error now for the Cappielow club.

League leaders Brechin hosted a key fixture against McInally's men on 2nd April and at last Morton looked to be a serious proposition, winning 2-1 with goals by Jim McAlister and Andy McLaren, reducing the gap between themselves and Stranraer to just four points; this despite Peter Weatherson being set off for two yellow card offences. Brechin were comfortably on top, seven points clear of second place with five games left.

The Morton side that afternoon was as follows (4-3-1-2): McGurn; Weatherson, Harding, Greacen, Dillon; Millar, McLaughlin, McAlister; J. Maisano (Mahood); McLaren, Templeman (P. Walker).

The performance as much as the result suggested Morton were finding real form at just the right time. Ah, but this was still a side with its capacity to disappoint. A no-score draw followed at Forfar, though once more the gap was reduced to four points when goals by Paul Walker and Chris Millar were enough to beat Alloa at Cappielow.

Yet again there came a stumble when Dumbarton fought out a 0-0 draw in Greenock on 23rd April, 2005.

Morton were fated, it seemed, not to permit anything which might be confused with a killer instinct.

On the penultimate Saturday of the season they were confronted with their final opportunity. On the Friday night they travelled down to Stranraer to stay overnight prior to meeting their prime rivals at Stair Park.

Victory was essential to reduce the gap to one point with one game to go. On the day 2,111 fans made the trip to support the blue and white hoops. Their superb support appeared to be rewarded when Peter Weatherson headed the visitors in front. But minutes later Allan Jenkins struck a superb volley to equalise. Back came Morton, but all their considerable efforts could not produce a second goal and it was Stranraer who made the journey up to the First Division. It was deserved for a threadbare group of players who had shown tremendous spirit and togetherness.

Regarding the Morton squad I wrote: "Too many ultimately wrong choices have been made in the last couple of seasons and it is significant that Marc McCulloch, Iain Diack and Stuart McCluskey are now surplus to requirement.

"If proof is required that character is a crucial factor, then it is surely provided by Stranraer. They have, frankly, overachieved in a season when some on considerably higher wages at Cappielow have underachieved."

On the final day of the season Morton beat Berwick 4-2 in a meaningless encounter at Cappielow, goals coming from a John Maisano double and counters from Chris Templeman and Shaun Dillon.

Maisano, an appreciable talent but apparently unable to sustain his effort over 90 minutes, was allowed to go, as was the veteran Alan Mahood whose third term at Cappielow was one too many. The old legs had finally succumbed to wear and tear. Also exiting were Scott Bannerman, Paul Walker, and the self-imploding Alex Williams, while Shaun Dillon returned to Kilmarnock and Warren Hawke retired. Hawke, always a favourite of the fans, was given a warm send-off. Stuart McCluskey was to depart later.

CHAPTER THIRTY-EIGHT

Gretna factor and play-offs see Ton falter

Jim McInally was beginning to shape his own squad for the 2005-06 season and he moved to introduce winger Kevin Finlayson from Stranraer, 'old boy' Derek Lilley (31) joining the Livingston influx of Ryan Harding and Scott McLaughlin. Livingston had gone into administration, just as Morton had under Hugh Scott, and their players had been freed by the club.

On the acquisition of Lilley, who had left Morton for Leeds in 1997 for a record-breaking transfer fee of £500,000, Ton boss Jim McInally said: "To be honest I'm pleasantly surprised that we have got a player of Derek's quality to come to the Second Division."

Lilley explained his choice, saying: "The chairman and the manager have got a lot of ambition and that's why I'm here. There were a few offers on the table at a higher level." The deal tied Lilley to Greenock for three years.

After two failed attempts to return to the First Division it wasn't going to get any easier. Already Brooks Mileson was committed to spending big money to transform Gretna. The Third Division champions were intent on back-to-back promotions and had assembled a formidable squad, massively disproportionate to their meagre fan base.

Also dropping out of the First Division were Raith Rovers and Partick Thistle. The competition was going to be fierce. Added to that was the introduction of play-offs to the Scottish League. It was shaping up to be a highly competitive campaign. There would be no room for faint hearts and precious little for any sort of error.

McInally brought Alex Walker from Rangers, a utility player capable of playing in either the back four or in a defensive midfield role, while the mercurial Andy McLaren was eventually fixed up after being released by Dundee United.

McInally had stated his preference for a flat back four but, with no natural full backs in his squad, he lined up in 3-4-1-2 formation for the Renfrewshire Cup Final pre-season match on 23rd July, 2005. The team was: McGurn; Weatherson, Greacen, Harding; Finlayson, Millar, A. Walker (Keenan), McAlister (MacGregor); McLaren; Lilley and Templeman (J. Walker).

Goals by Lilley and McAlister gave Morton a good victory and three days later they drew with another First Division side, Falkirk, at their new stadium.

The first competitive match was an intriguing encounter against the firm pre-season title favourites, Gretna, in a Bell's Challenge Cup first round tie at Cappielow.

Gretna had the better of the match on the general run of play, but it was Morton who emerged winners by 3-2 after a period of extra time in which Gretna's Innes was sent off.

Gretna manager Rowan Alexander, the former Morton goalscoring hero, made himself rather unpopular with his erstwhile fan club when he said after the game: "I'm fed up coming here and not getting anything out of the games. Over the last few games we've played up here we've been the better side and, again, that showed in the 90 minutes until we lost Chris [Innes]."

Jim McInally, ever honest, commented: "I felt we never imposed ourselves on them individually. But, much as they scored a great goal in the second half, and had more of the ball, I don't think they created a chance."

The Gretna team that day was (4-4-2): Main; Collins, Innes, Townsley, McQuilken; Baldacchino, McGuffie, Nicholls (Boyd), Skelton; Deuchar (Graham), Bingham.

Morton may have won, but the game revealed just how formidable Gretna would be over the course of the season.

On 6th August, 2005, the league season began, but not before youth coach Joe McLaughlin launched a pre-match surprise by announcing his resignation as youth coach after a year in the job.

Known to be unhappy about not getting the manager's position after John McCormack's sacking, when he'd filled in as caretaker boss, he said: "I handed in my resignation and it was readily accepted." He did not wish to elaborate further. For his part, chairman Douglas Rae said: "I'm disappointed. He was doing a good job." The chairman went on to say that £80,000 had been spent the previous season on the youth set-up.

In the afternoon Morton beat Raith Rovers 2-0 at Cappielow with goals by Peter Weatherson, playing by now on the right of a back three, and Andy McLaren. The attendance was a healthy 3,222.

Cappielow Park was looking in lush condition under new groundsman Mark Farrell who had continued the good work of his predecessor Campbell Stevenson.

Further wins followed at Stirling – goals by McLaren and Lilley – and Forfar at Cappielow, courtesy of an own goal. In between Morton lost out to Ayr at Cappielow in the CIS Cup, Derek Lilley scoring in a 2-1 defeat, but generally the Greenock men were looking confident and in high spirits.

Andy McLaren's fragile temperament led to his dismissal due to dissent in a 1-1 draw at Dumbarton, Peter Weatherson netting a penalty, before goals from Templeman and Lilley saw further progress at Brechin's expense in the Challenge Cup.

By now midfielder Scott McLaughlin had returned to Cappielow on a permanent move from Livingston, Stuart McCluskey heading out the exit door.

Celebrity chef Gordon Ramsay then let it be known that he would quite like to own a football club and, if so, Morton would be his ideal choice. It was a remark as light as one of his pastries.

Saturday 10th September saw Morton once more engage with Gretna, this time on league business at Cappielow Park. It was very much match-of-the-day. Absent from the action was the suspended Andy McLaren who commented: "It's hard and frustrating to be sitting there not doing anything due to my own stupidity."

For all his problems during his career with drugs, alcohol and, on the park, a low boiling point, I found McLaren a likeable character. He had a self-destruct button, without doubt, but he was only too well aware of his own shortcomings. I often felt he was as much at war with himself as with anyone else. His talent was indisputable.

He watched as Gretna won 2-0 through goals by Kenny Deuchar and Ryan McGuffie to take them three points clear at the top after five games.

Gretna had altered their formation from a normal back four to a three. At the press conference afterwards I asked their manager Rowan Alexander if it had been in response to Morton's favoured 3-4-1-2. He confirmed it had been, but then embarked on some remarks which would have been better unsaid. They were to make him very unpopular in Greenock, both with Morton fans and club management. Quite unprompted, Alexander said he could not understand Morton's selection, in particular why Jason Walker had not been in the starting line-up. Breaking all the normal unwritten rules of protocol, Alexander continued to say that Chris Templeman was only getting a game for Morton because the club had paid big money for him.

When Gretna midfielder Steve Tosh then commented that "several Morton players were on bigger money than players at Gretna" in response to newspaper comment on the high salaries at Raydale Park under the Mileson regime, it caused more than a little irritation within the Morton camp. Alexander's remarks led to one Morton supporters' organisation deleting his name from their travel club. Tosh's remarks were just that…tosh.

Morton returned quickly to winning ways when they beat Stirling 2-1 at Forthbank, goals from Jason Walker and Scott McLaughlin setting up a lucrative Challenge Cup semi-final tie against county rivals St Mirren at Love Street.

Before that, further wins were recorded over Alloa at Cappielow (5-2 Weatherson, A. Walker, Templeman, Finlayson, Millar) then Ayr at Somerset Park, Jason Walker grabbing the vital winner. The side were showing great resolve and, after the Ayr game, I wrote: "Morton won because they refused to accept any other result."

Then came the Challenge Cup semi against St Mirren. Morton gave a worthy performance in a goalless 90 minutes only to lose out on penalties after extra time.

It was back to the league. Peterhead lost 2-1 at Cappielow to goals from Templeman and MacGregor which was followed by a trip to Firhill to meet another of the promotion candidates, Partick Thistle. Gretna led the league on 20 points, Morton one behind and Thistle and Raith Rovers on 13, all having played eight games. It was a key clash, even this early in the programme.

Morton carried an impressive travelling support of 1,602 but they witnessed their side's worst performance of the season in a 2-0 defeat. I reported: "They [Morton] fell well short of their own and their fans' expectations. In virtually every department they ended up second best."

Manager Jim McInally said: "We never turned up. We were outplayed, outfought."

It made the next match all the more important, against fourth top Raith Rovers at Stark's Park. Goals by Alex Walker and Stewart Greacen were enough for a 2-1 win, but it was a temporary recovery. On the following Tuesday at Cappielow, Morton went down 2-1 to bottom club Stirling in a hugely disappointing display, Peter Weatherson being the home scorer. Jim McInally commented: "I can honestly say that is the worst I've seen since I've been here. I want to apologise to the fans who came here tonight to watch that."

Days later Gretna handed out another bitter pill to swallow when they won 3-1 in front of a happy Raydale Park crowd to stretch their lead to 10 points. Partick were second, on goal difference, ahead of Morton.

This time Rowan Alexander was more circumspect in his choice of after-match words, acknowledging that there was a long way to go. He recalled Morton being 13 points clear two seasons before and went on to say: "If we make sure that we don't fall into a sense of false security and get slack or complacent then we're doing our job. We have shown a little bit of class above the rest of the league."

Morton's collapse to which Alexander referred was unlikely to be replicated by Gretna. Where that Greenock side had been inexperienced and some of their number at times undisciplined off the park, Gretna were packed with nous and players who had operated at a far higher level of the game. The Raydale Park club had more than lived up to pre-season expectations. They also had, in their pony-tailed owner Brooks Mileson – who looked more like an ageing rock star than a football club chairman – someone who could splash serious cash at any problem that might yet arise.

Already it was beginning to look like a race for second place, and for the first time that would only guarantee a play-off place.

Dumbarton were then dispatched 4-1, goals coming from a Lilley double, McLaren and Weatherson, who joined Harding in the centre of a back four. Alex Walker was now playing as a right back.

Then Alloa were beaten 3-0 at Recreation Park, McAlister, Lilley and Jason Walker being on target. Jim McAlister had been pushed up front and told to stay wide left, rather than in the left wingback position he was later to make his own. Chris Millar was outstanding in midfield, while David McGurn brought off some excellent saves as the last line. Morton were now eight points behind Gretna.

On Saturday 19th November, 2005, Morton were off to Central Park where Third Division Cowdenbeath, under the management of Mixu Paatelainen, awaited in the first round of the Scottish Cup. Banks of snow surrounded the Fifers' pitch. There was to be no upset as Andy McLaren inspired a convincing display by the visitors who won 3-0 with a Derek Lilley brace and a strike by Jason Walker.

In a key match at Cappielow, Morton then beat rivals Partick Thistle 2-1 with goals by McLaren and Lilley. Meanwhile Jim McInally had been voted Second Division manager-of-the-month, while Mark Farrell won the groundsman's award.

Morton were playing some good football and when Ayr lost 2-1 at Cappielow, Lilley and

McAlister on the mark, they were eight points behind pace-setting Gretna and seven ahead of the Jags.

There was a reverse in the second round of the Scottish Cup when Ayr took revenge for their league defeat by winning 3-2 at Somerset. Lilley and Templeman hit the goals.

It was a game full of incident. David McGurn was injured in the first half and Stefan Gonet replaced him in goal. Jason Walker was ordered off for a second yellow card offence while young Gonet was bundled aside by Ayr's Wardlaw, the ball falling behind him into the net.

Derek Lilley also found himself being sent off, while Ton boss Jim McInally was angry at the continued abuse Andy McLaren had to face from the home fans. McLaren was booked after responding to the chants from the terracings relating to his past history involving drugs and McInally said: "I'm sick fed up with the abuse McLaren takes in games from the public. I know he's no angel but he deserves a wee bit more protection."

I commented: "It's one of the great hypocrisies in football that fans believe they are entitled to deliver any amount of abuse to players, yet feign righteous indignation should they receive a critical response."

McLaren, in fact, was on the point of quitting football altogether after the match, but was persuaded not to by his manager. The player obviously had his own issues with self-control, but there were too many people, opposing players and fans alike, only too happy to try and help him down the road to mishap.

It seemed clear that Morton would now be in one of the three play-off places in the division. But the play-offs were ludicrous in my view in such small leagues. And neither had they been properly thought through. Whoever finished second would play the third club, but the choice of first venue would be decided by a ballot. The second club, therefore, could end up playing the second tie away from home, what is always considered a disadvantage.

Morton's run of form ended when Peterhead beat them 1-0 at Balmoor Stadium. Three festive victories followed, however, Chris Millar and Andy McLaren scoring in a 2-0 home win over Raith Rovers, Derek Lilley notching the sole strike of the game at Forfar, then Derek Lilley and Peter Weatherson hitting the target at Dumbarton in a 2-0 triumph.

Morton were now five points behind Gretna, albeit having played a game more. There was, nevertheless, no sign of the Borderers slipping up.

I commented on Gretna's rise: "The normal financial rules do not apply, even less so than in the customary fickle football business. Put simply, the usual financial prudence of profit and loss, of income and expenditure, didn't apply to Gretna.

"Mileson's generosity towards a club which has become, in effect, a big boy's toy, has created a false set of circumstances. It is delightful for Gretna and their followers, though it is hard to see what good it does Scottish football as a whole. Their small fan base means that they bring no appreciable income to any other clubs on their travels.

"Already I can imagine the shudders emanating from the SPL at the prospect of Gretna going all the way to the top league."

This was, in effect, no fairy-tale. It was a bought and paid for exercise with no added benefit to anyone but Gretna. The Isle of Cumbrae could have supplied a Premier side given the same financial backing, but would that be good for football?

It was Gretna who were Morton's next opponents at Cappielow on Saturday 14th January, 2006. It was a massive match between the top two, and one Morton had to win if they were to entertain serious hopes of overhauling their rivals.

A crowd of 5,131 turned out, over 5,000 supporting the hosts. In the home ranks was 21-year-old striker James McPake, signed on loan from Livingston until the end of the season.

Gretna took a 2-0 lead, the first goal being an unfortunate mistake by stand-in goalie Stefan Gonet who spilled a Deuchar header which ended up in the net. However, Morton began a doughty fightback with goals by Lilley and Weatherson. At the final whistle the points were shared.

Such were Gretna's resources that an absence of six first team regulars hardly mattered. Rowan Alexander was able to go into the transfer market pre-match and bring in midfielders Allan Jenkins from Stranraer and John O'Neil from Falkirk. Gretna now had more strength in depth than some Premier League clubs.

McPake hit the net twice against Alloa at home a week later, Weatherson and McAlister also weighing in during a 4-1 win, but on the final Saturday of January a 1-1 draw at Somerset Park against Ayr saw ground lost in the title race. Peter Weatherson, still playing at the back, was the scorer.

On the same weekend striker Chris Templeman, unable to gain a regular place in the team, requested a loan move back to First Division Brechin who had enquired as to his availability. Jim McInally wanted the big fellow to stay and fight for his place. Initially Templeman agreed, only to change his mind right on the transfer deadline. It was an attitude which disappointed his manager who nevertheless agreed to let him go. There was little point in keeping someone who didn't show a desire to be there. The loan was arranged.

Templeman had ability and physique, but he seldom matched that with any obvious fire or ambition. He was quiet and pleasant in demeanour, off and on the pitch. Some players did not seem at all bothered at the big striker's decision and manager McInally's comment that "we all need to pull together" suggested it was better Templeman was out of the picture.

A goalless draw at home to Peterhead, in which Morton switched to an orthodox 4-4-2, Peter Weatherson moving back up front, was followed by a 1-1 draw with Partick Thistle at Firhill. These three clubs were now vying for the three play-off places in the division such was Gretna's lead and depth of squad.

Andy McLaren found himself again the victim of his own lack of control in being booked against the Jags for dissent. Jim McInally substituted him in order to prevent a likely red card and then left him out of the squad to face Stirling at Forthbank, a match the hosts went on to win 3-1, Alex Walker getting the consolation strike.

Jim McInally said of the wayward McLaren, whom he had supported so often: "We're not accepting his behaviour."

There followed a reprieve in the next match, against Forfar at Cappielow, in which McLaren returned to show the good side to his enigmatic personality, being the orchestrator of a comfortable 3-0 win, scoring a goal to accompany those by Ryan Harding and Chris Millar.

Stewart Greacen was sent off for a professional foul.

Next up were the runaway leaders Gretna at Raydale. Man-of-the-match was the tireless Chris Millar who scored a double in a merited 2-1 win. It mattered little in the title race, Gretna being 11 points ahead with a game in hand, but it confirmed Morton as comfortably the best of the rest, 12 points in front of Peterhead and Partick.

Two poor results followed, however, a goalless draw at Alloa then a shocking 4-0 home defeat at the hands of Ayr. Jim McInally was moved to say: "I'm ashamed. If we don't get promoted I will not stay beyond the end of the season." The Ayr result had prompted boos from the terracings and there was a growing minority who would have been all too happy to see the back of the manager.

The fact was, however, that Morton were comfortably clear of both Peterhead and Partick. Had it not been for the Gretna factor and Brooks Mileson's millions, they would have been heading for the championship.

I sometimes felt Jim McInally was too honest for his own good, invariably carrying the can for the sake of his players, often to his own detriment. I once spoke to him about it but he was quite clear that his job was to shield the players and deflect criticism away from them. He was nothing if not honourable.

In the next match Dumbarton were beaten 4-0 at Cappielow, a Jason Walker double being complemented by goals from Jim McAlister and Peter Weatherson. With five games to go Morton were 16 points behind Gretna, but 11 ahead of Partick and 14 in front of Peterhead.

They met these two rivals in successive meetings, losing 2-1 at Peterhead, Alex Walker scoring, then beating Partick at Cappielow, Jason Walker netting the only goal of the game.

A 1-1 draw followed at Raith Rovers, Andy McLaren scoring, and the Kirkcaldy club's boss, Gordon Dalziel, put the Morton manager's accomplishments in perspective when he said: "Jim's done a fantastic job at Morton." Dalziel too mentioned the Gretna factor and its distorting effect.

In the penultimate match of the season against Stirling, at Cappielow, Stewart Greacen won the points with an acrobatic overhead kick. This was followed up by a vibrant 2-0 win at Forfar where Morton fielded a young side containing only three regular first team players. One of that trio was the experienced Derek Lilley who grabbed both goals.

Morton had finished 13 points ahead of both Peterhead and Partick Thistle and I commented: "In any other season, without the complication of the artificial situation created at Gretna, Jim McInally would have led Morton to the championship by a convincing margin."

Not only was there a Gretna factor, but the adoption of play-offs meant that there would be no automatic promotion for the second top side. In such small leagues this was, in my view, farcical. It further lacked credibility when a ballot decided who would have the choice of playing home or away in the first play-off tie. Morton, 13 points clear of third top Peterhead, found themselves having to play the second tie away from home. There was to be no advantage whatsoever to finishing second.

In front of a midweek crowd of 3,995 at Cappielow, an anxious Morton were held to a goalless draw by a compact, organised Peterhead. The visitors had their chances to win as the hosts showed little composure on the ball and I wrote: "Morton will need to show more self-belief if they are to progress to a likely final against Partick." Partick had meanwhile won their first tie against Stranraer.

On the following Saturday the Greenock men travelled north-east to Balmoor Stadium, still favourites to win through to the play-off final.

They began the game very positively and pressed Peterhead back inside their own half. But, quite against the run of play, a very soft penalty award went the hosts' way in the 24th minute when Wood went to ground after being harassed by Chris Millar in the box. Cameron converted.

Despite considerable pressure by Morton, Peterhead were to hold out. It seemed very cruel. It was all very well to say everyone knew the rules before the season began, but this had reduced league football to an absurdity. Morton assistant manager Martin Clark summed up when he said: "I feel as though a whole year's work has been wasted." His gaffer, Jim McInally, was stunned and commented: "What can you say? We didn't deserve to lose that game."

An entire season's effort had come down to one very soft penalty award. But it was clearly nonsensical that a side finishing 13 points clear of their rivals should end up in a play-off in a 10-club league. Even Peterhead manager Ian Stewart was sympathetic, saying: "I feel for Morton to be honest. They finished second and they probably deserved to go up."

Jim McInally then had to endure some wretched abuse from a small group of Morton fans as he left the ground with his wife and two daughters. At that point he must have wondered if any of it was worth it.

I wrote: "Morton were taken to the brink of the Promised Land only to be sent once more into exile. Unlike two seasons ago, the Cappielow club were the victims of circumstances rather than the architects of their own downfall."

Partick Thistle, who had beaten Stranraer over two legs in the other semi-final, went on to win on penalties over Peterhead and regain a First Division place. The team that had finished fourth gained promotion.

Jim McInally had revised his reaction to that earlier defeat by Ayr to quit if Morton did not win promotion. With the full backing of chairman Douglas Rae and the board he saw it as his task to remedy the situation. Already he had fixed up Alloa's talented young midfielder Jamie Stevenson.

But the pain lingered. "It will," I commented, "take time now for the wounds to heal, but a look at the league table will only perplex future generations."

The close season saw the mercurial Andy McLaren leave Cappielow along with young midfielder John Adam. McLaren felt another season in the Second Division was one too many at his twilight stage. Also departing was 22-year-old English striker Jason Walker who was feeling homesick and wished to return down south.

A testimonial match was arranged for Warren Hawke while young Celtic forward Paul McGowan (19) decided to come to Cappielow on loan.

There was the by now inevitable talk of league reconstruction, just as predictably coming to nothing.

CHAPTER THIRTY-NINE

Back to the First Division

The pre-season preliminaries included a variety of friendly games, Morton losing the Renfrewshire Cup Final to St Mirren after extra time, their first final loss in the fixture for four years. Jamie Stevenson had impressed in the warm-up games, catching the eye of opposition managers too, and there was an optimistic air around the Cappielow club.

Youngsters Scott McKellar, from Ross County, and Ryan Russell (Motherwell) arrived and, on Saturday 5th August, 2006, the first league game took place at Cappielow, Morton beating Raith Rovers 2-0 with goals by Chris Templeman, now back in the fold after his loan to Brechin, and an own goal.

Templeman expressed his satisfaction at being back at Cappielow, while McGowan's ability to hold the ball and bring others into play impressed.

The team, minus suspended Peter Weatherson, lined up as follows in 3-4-1-2 formation: McGurn; Harding, Greacen, MacGregor; Keenan, Millar, McLaughlin, McAlister; Stevenson (Walker); McGowan (McLean) and Templeman (Lilley).

On Tuesday 8th August, Morton travelled to Brechin where they were knocked out of the CIS Cup by their hosts, 2-1, Paul McGowan scoring the goal.

If it was a set-back, the league was very much the priority and a good 3-0 win at Stranraer followed. An own goal, one from Chris Millar and another by Jamie Stevenson kept Morton joint top of the division. There then followed a Challenge Cup first round win at Dumbarton. The Sons took the lead in extra time only for Peter Weatherson to strike twice.

Weatherson then missed a penalty against Ayr at Cappielow, but the ensuing scoreless draw was enough to take the Greenock club to the undisputed leadership of the league, Cowdenbeath losing. Chris Millar was the man of the match. Mascot at the game was Stuart Boag, son of the former Morton defender John who tragically had been found dead at home at the early age of 41.

On Saturday 26th August, it was back to Balmoor Stadium, the scene of the heart-rending end to the previous season when Morton fell 1-0 in the semi-final play-off second leg to Peterhead. This time it was to be a very different story, as the visitors raced to a 4-0 half-time lead with some marvellous, passing football.

Derek Lilley was back in the team, taking the place of Chris Templeman and forming a productive partnership with Paul McGowan who hit a double. Weatherson and Millar scored the other goals.

It was Morton's first win in seven visits to Peterhead. Manager Jim McInally said: "The first half was ruthless, right from the word go." Morton had made a statement.

Second top Cowdenbeath were then dispatched 3-2 in the second round of the Challenge Cup at Cappielow, Scott McLaughlin, Paul McGowan and Chris Millar on target. The Greenock men were highly focused and followed up with an emphatic 4-0 win over Alloa in Greenock, McGowan, Lilley, Templeman and Millar scoring. Once again McGowan was at the heart of so much good play in a victory which kept Morton at the top of the league, one point ahead of Cowdenbeath, rejuvenated under the management of Mixu Paatelainen.

It was Mixu's men next up in the match of the day in the Second Division at Central Park. One enforced change was made, Stefan Gonet coming in for David McGurn in goal. McGurn had injured a shoulder in training which would keep him sidelined for several weeks.

Gonet did well as Morton won 2-1 with goals by Stewart Greacen and Jim McAlister, who was enjoying an excellent run of form.

First Division St Johnstone, fresh from a 5-1 victory over Partick Thistle, then came to Cappielow for the Challenge Cup quarter-finals where they lost out 3-2, goals by McGowan (2) and Harding proving decisive. McGowan impressed again and the performance drew praise from Saints' boss Owen Coyle who commented: "Morton were a breath of fresh air. The supporters were tremendous for them tonight. Greenock is a footballing town and you can tell that when you come here."

Third top Stirling were next to visit Cappielow, holding their hosts to a 1-1 draw, Lilley getting the home strike. Albion provided the sort of defensive barrier Morton were by now finding familiar at home, but the Greenock club were four points clear at the top after seven games.

Then goals by Lilley, McGowan and Millar secured a 3-1 win at Forfar. This preceded the Challenge Cup semi-final at Broadwood against Clyde. On this occasion the First Division team triumphed 3-1, Morton's counter being an own goal.

Unbeaten league form continued, however, with a win at home to Brechin, Jim McAlister capping off a fine display with the only goal of the game. Morton were now seven points clear of second placed Stirling. Their team that afternoon was (4-4-2): Gonet; Weatherson, Greacen, Harding, Walker; Stevenson, Millar, McLaughlin, McAlister; McGowan, Lilley.

The Greenock side were very much everyone's favourites for the title by now, but a stiff test awaited at Stark's Park where Raith Rovers, under new manager Craig Levein, were bolstered by the signing during the week of ex-Rangers colossus Marvin Andrews. Centre back Andrews had been a team-mate of Derek Lilley's at Livingston, picking up his first major medal when Livi won the League Cup by beating Hibernian 2–0 with goals by Lilley and Jamie McAllister.

A nasty knee injury had threatened Andrews' career while at Ibrox. This deeply religious man refused to have an operation, preferring to let nature take its course, and was eventually released by Rangers. His arrival in Kirkcaldy, where he had begun his career, caused quite a stir and in the first half the initiative was firmly with a spirited Rovers.

Raith took the lead and Jim McInally later said: "I thought at half-time we were lucky to be only one down. I said to the players 'you either take part in the game and try to win it or you just be part of the side-show.' It was as though we had accepted we would get away with losing." The side-show reference related to the furore which had accompanied prodigal son Andrews' return and the lift it had given everyone at Stark's Park.

The second half provided the desired response to McInally's pep talk, Morton banging in three goals from McLaughlin, Lilley and Templeman. "Their [the players] attitude in the second half was fantastic," McInally said.

Craig Levein was disappointed but commented on Morton: "For the way they finished they deserved the points."

Back in goal was Dave McGurn, who produced four excellent saves, while Scott McLaughlin was a stand-out in his defensive midfield role, also providing the equaliser.

It seemed nothing could stop Morton's unbeaten league momentum, and a 3-0 home win against Stranraer, goals coming from Stevenson, Weatherson and McGowan, took them nine points clear of Stirling after just 11 games. Jim McAlister's form at left wingback was beginning to attract the attention of other clubs, Plymouth Argyle having him watched.

Weatherson was once more on target at Recreation Park with a brace against Allan Maitland's improving Alloa, but it was insufficient to prevent Morton's first defeat of the league season, the hosts winning 3-2.

Before the game I had written: "Sometimes it is in the sub-conscious that self-belief can become self-satisfaction. And that can be fatal." Whatever the reasons, a combination of individual mistakes and some good play by the home club conspired to end the Cappielow side's unbeaten 11-game run.

It was a short-lived setback as Peterhead were beaten 4-2 at Cappielow, goals coming from McGowan, Weatherson, McLaughlin and Finlayson. Weatherson was enjoying an excellent season, playing mainly at the back, with occasional switches to midfield or his more conventional forward role. He was the top player in the match of the day between the top two at Forthbank on the 11th November, 2006, where hosts Stirling beat Morton 2-1 to reduce the gap at the top to three points. Chris Millar was the visitors' scorer.

Sections of the Morton support were becoming more vocal in their disapproval of the manager, something which genuinely bemused Morton boss Jim McInally. From the fans' point of view this was their fourth season in the Second Division and they had become thoroughly fed up inhabiting an environment they felt was beneath their status.

To a degree it was understandable, but failure the previous season had been a totally artificial situation. Now they were leading the league, but for some their position was not emphatic enough.

A goal by substitute Chris Templeman won the game against Cowdenbeath at Cappielow before Forfar came to put men behind the ball and hold their hosts to a 1-1 draw, Millar getting the home strike. Athletic's manager George Shaw commented: "The second half was like the Alamo; we couldn't get out of our half."

Meanwhile former Peterhead assistant manager Paul Mathers (36), who had been sacked by the Blue Toon team, was fixed up as a player to add nous to the goalkeeping department. Signed as an amateur until the January transfer window due to regulations, his arrival was seen as important by Jim McInally who said: "This is no reflection on David McGurn. We felt we needed experience in that position. Paul's been brought in to help."

Annan were beaten 3-0 in the second round of the Scottish Cup to set up an intriguing tie with Premier League Kilmarnock at Cappielow. The scorers were Greacen, Weatherson and Stevenson.

Meanwhile Stirling had closed the gap on Morton to one slender point. This induced a mood of near panic among sections of the Greenock club's support. Memories of the pain of the previous season's failure to win promotion were all too fresh. There were renewed calls for McInally to go. But it was the fans this time who were 'losing their bottle', not the players.

The mini crisis was rectified by a fine 3-2 win at Brechin with goals by Templeman, Weatherson and man-of-the-match McAlister. Two days before Christmas a goal by Jamie Stevenson was enough to win at home to Raith Rovers and then Paul McGowan did the honours at Ayr in a marvellous team performance worthy of better than the 1-0 scoreline.

In the January transfer window Morton moved to sign Peterhead striker Bobby Linn (21) to augment the squad.

It was time for a break from the anxieties of the league. Jim Jefferies arrived in town on the 6th January, 2007, with a good Killie team who were proving their worth in the top flight of Scottish football. Included in their ranks were a young Stevie Naismith, Danny Invincible and Colin Nish and they were hot favourites to proceed to the next round.

By quarter to five the form book had been turned upside down. Morton won 3-1 and it was fully justified. I reported: "It might seem like hyperbole to say that Morton were magnificent. It isn't; they were. Not only did they knock their Premier League opponents out of the Scottish Cup, they did it in style."

Jim McInally was as delighted as the support in a crowd of 6,649. He commented: "That's what happens when you just give your lot in this game."

Two-goal Chris Templeman had his best game in a Morton shirt, his second a magnificent left-foot strike on the volley after an excellent first touch with his right foot. McInally said: "He's worked harder in the last six or seven games than he's done in his entire career. Perhaps the penny has dropped."

That last remark was in respect of the general feeling that the six-foot four-inch Templeman was too gentle a giant. If you had seen Templeman only in that one game, you would have wondered why he was playing at Cappielow and not gracing the game's loftier realms. I wrote: "He has to show that it's no flash in the pan."

Well though he played in games over the remainder of the season, it was, unfortunately, not a performance he would repeat consistently. He was another of those talents who too often flattered to deceive. But on that afternoon he was magnificent. Ton's other goal came from Paul McGowan.

Killie's dismay was absolute on the day. They were not just beaten. They were humbled.

Their players had to face the combined wrath of Jim Jefferies and the even more voluble Billy Brown. As the press awaited the managers at the players' tunnel, we were able to hear all too clearly the Killie players' after-match debriefing through the open windows of their dressing room. "Their ears," I wrote, "were ringing as Anglo-Saxon expletives flew through the air like angry wasps."

So often anti-climax follows a climb to the heights, but Morton ground out a 2-1 win over Alloa at Cappielow in the following league game. Appalling weather restricted the crowd to a lowly 2038. Templeman maintained his form with a goal, Weatherson notching his 10th of the campaign. During the course of the game he occupied three different roles, at full back, midfield and up front.

On 20th January second top Stirling rode into town for the top of the table showdown. It was a key game. A crowd of 3,187 turned out to see Morton take the points 2-1, goals coming from an impressive Paul McGowan and Jim McAlister. It stretched the Greenock club's lead to 12 points and throttled any possible resumption of protest from those who still felt McInally was not the man for the job.

Derek Lilley then departed to St Johnstone before the end of the transfer window accompanied by the praise of the Morton boss. He had latterly been unable to get a regular game and McInally said: "At this time in his career he needs games. It was great to have him at Morton because he was a professional the young players looked up to. He was a role model on how to live life as a footballer."

Paul McGowan's loan period had been extended to the end of the season and it was he who netted as Morton gained a point at Cowdenbeath in a 1-1 draw in which Bobby Linn came on as a sub.

That match was the prelude to Morton's next rumble in the Scottish Cup. Fir Park was the venue for another test against Premier opposition. A superb following of 4,700 took to the M8 to follow their heroes. They formed just over half of the 9,394 attendance, occupying virtually the entire new stand at the visitors' end.

Morton found the Motherwell defence a harder nut to crack than Kilmarnock's on the afternoon, and they eventually succumbed 2-0 to goals by Brian Kerr and Scott McDonald. They hadn't been disgraced, but neither had they reached the peaks of their performance against Killie.

I reported: "Motherwell were ready. Without being particularly impressive they were steady and solid, and the Killie result had given them all the warning they needed. Motherwell's sharper finishing proved the difference between the two teams."

Outstanding for Morton were Ryan Harding, who gave his best ever display for the club at the centre of the defence, and the tireless Jim McAlister. Fir Park boss Maurice Malpas, an old team-mate of Jim McInally's, confirmed that the Morton victory over Kilmarnock had been all his players had needed to ward off any feeling of superiority.

On 10th February, 2007, Morton fell to their first home defeat of the season when Brechin won 2-0. It was a peculiar afternoon, Morton being well on top but minus a ruthless edge.

It was a temporary glitch. Ayr arrived at Cappielow and lost 4-2 to an invigorated display by their hosts. Bobby Linn notched his first goal for the club, Jim McAlister added another and Chris Templeman continued a good run of form with a double.

Ayr gaffer Robert Connor praised the home club, saying: "I think they are the best team in the league. I've not had any doubts that they would win the league."

Nothing can ever be taken for granted in football, however, and Stranraer provided a timely reminder when they won 2-1 at Stair Park. Morton had taken an early lead through Chris Templeman and played some good football, but without a second strike.

That failure to kill the game off led to a late double by the hosts in the final six minutes to take all three points and leave Morton perplexed if not stunned.

Once again Jim McInally was the object of some fans' ire. I wrote: "Every time when the team drops points it seems that the vultures are waiting to pick at the Morton boss.

"Frustration can so often spill into anger. With a very small minority it is simply mindless and abusive; with others it is born of desperation. 'Surely we're not going to blow it this time' is what is running through their minds."

On the first Saturday of March Morton atoned for that slip-up with a 2-1 home win over Peterhead. Jamie Stevenson and the prolific Peter Weatherson were the scorers. Paul Mathers also brought off a key save against his old mates when the game was scoreless. Weatherson's winner came from a tremendous free kick and Jim McInally commented: "We know he could do better defensively at times, but he's such a big player for us. It was a brilliant goal."

The tension among the support was all too obvious. Weatherson, who had played most of the season as a full back, with occasional appearances in midfield, said: "The crowd got edgy and they started to get on the players' backs but, luckily, we got the result in the end. Our crowd doesn't help at times. I'm sure it's a minority but it doesn't help the boys."

A 3-0 win at Alloa followed, goals coming from Weatherson, Stevenson and Templeman. For Jamie Stevenson, who had lacked consistency since his arrival at the start of the season, it was a notable performance. Peter Weatherson's goal was the 100th of his senior career. Also outstanding, at left back, was David MacGregor.

Morton were four points clear of Allan Moore's part-time Stirling side who were pushing their rivals all the way. The two met in the match-of-the-day at Forthbank on 17th March, 2007. Paul McGowan gave Morton an early lead but it was Stirling who grabbed two late goals in the final seven minutes to reduce the gap at the top to one solitary point.

Morton had a game in hand, with seven remaining in total, but it was a loss which caused another shudder to affect the collective body of the support. Jim McInally said: "We certainly don't make it easy for ourselves."

The manager continued: "I really feel for the fans at the moment. I know it's a rough ride, but I want to make a promise. I promise them they'll have their party at the end of the season."

At times Morton were found wanting in terms of experience, but the next weekend they dug deep at Forfar, coming away with an impressive 4-0 result. Leading from the front was skipper Stewart Greacen who scored twice, missing a penalty late in the match which would have given the big defender a notable hat-trick.

Once again Peter Weatherson, this time in midfield, was a key player and McInally said:

"He's wasted playing in this league but he knows he's probably got himself to blame for that with the way he's looked after himself over the years. But, if he gets his head on, he could play for anybody."

Cowdenbeath were beaten 3-0 at Cappielow through a Paul McGowan double and a goal by Jamie Stevenson and, with five games to go, Morton were four points clear. Three days later they grabbed three more crucial points when a Stewart Greacen volley was all that separated them from Brechin at Glebe Park. Manager McInally praised his players' spirit and attitude.

It was back to Cappielow on Saturday 7th April when bottom club Forfar arrived with an injury-hit side full of youngsters. Morton were ruthless on the day, hitting nine goals with one conceded.

Peter Weatherson supplied four goals, a Jamie Stevenson double and others by Chris Millar, Bobby Linn and Chris Templeman completing a triumphant afternoon before 3,007 fans. Morton were now seven points clear with three games remaining.

A delighted Jim McInally summed up: "It was a brilliant day. For them [the players] to have the disappointment of losing at Stirling and then come back to win their next four games is absolutely brilliant."

His counterpart, Jim Moffat, said: "There's no denying the quality and ability that's in the Morton side. All credit to Jim McInally and his players for the way they're going about their business."

Even the most pessimistic Morton fan, used to seasons of disappointment, could finally look forward to a return to the First Division.

All Morton had to do was match Stirling's result on the third last afternoon of the season. Their rivals were at Ayr while Morton were away to Raith Rovers. The blue and white hordes were set to descend upon Kirkcaldy.

In the event, both promotion rivals lost, Stirling 3-2 at Somerset, and Morton 2-0 at Stark's Park, but the championship was Morton's. In a crowd of 4,327, the visiting contingent numbered 2,288 and they cared not a jot for the result of the game. They had just won the big prize – the league.

I reported on their elation: "As they bounced and sang, even the Raith fans at the other end of the ground, enjoying their own side's win, joined in the applause. It was one of those rare occasions when everyone was happy.

"A club dragged down into the murky depths under the stewardship of Hugh Scott has fought its way back up into the sunshine."

A typically reticent Jim McInally had to be persuaded to come out onto the pitch to join in the celebrations. The fans sang: "There's only one McInally", which must have been sweet music to the ears of a man who so often failed to find favour with a support all too used to failure and consequently hyper-critical. He took a quick bow, but didn't stay long, preferring to let his players have centre stage."

The team that afternoon was (3-1-4-2): Mathers; Greacen, Harding, MacGregor; McLaughlin; Finlayson (Millar), Stevenson, Weatherson, McAlister; McGowan (Russell), Templeman (Linn).

The league trophy was presented to Morton the following Saturday at Cappielow before 5,222 fans. The match against Stranraer ended 1-1, Weatherson grabbing his 18th goal of a fantastic individual season. It was a remarkable strike rate for someone who had played mainly in defence with occasional midfield appearances.

In the final match of the season at Ayr, Morton lost 1-0 in a match in which they made several changes, giving half a dozen fringe players a run-out. In the opposition ranks were two familiar old faces, Andy McLaren and Brian Reid.

CHAPTER FORTY

Morton fall down on experience

At last, after a six-season absence, Morton were back in the First Division. They had finally finished eight points clear of a doughty Stirling side who had pushed them all the way.

Jim McInally and his assistant Martin Clark were rewarded with new contracts. Now the task was to strengthen and ensure the recovery was not built on sand.

There was acknowledgement from the manager that at least three quality players would be required to compete meaningfully in the First Division, a left-sided midfielder, a striker and a strong midfielder being targeted.

Bids failed to attract ex-St Mirren striker John Sutton and midfielder Simon Mensing, out of contract at St Johnstone. Both would have been ideal signings.

The first new arrival was midfielder Kieran McAnespie who was a free agent after leaving Fulham where his career had ground to a halt. The ex-Alloa man, now 27, had enjoyed a burgeoning reputation in his younger days, but injuries had hampered his progress. He fulfilled the need for a left-sided player, being able to operate both in midfield or at full back. There remained doubts, however, over his fitness, and these were to prove only too well founded.

Young Rangers goalkeeper Lee Robinson was also brought in on a season's loan while the manager expressed interest in former Motherwell youngster Adam Coakley.

Another to attract the attention was Slovenian striker Jani Sturm, formerly of ND Gorica. He played in a trial match against Stenhousemuir, scoring two goals and looking very much the part. A deal seemed to have been done with his agent Sirisa Latkovic, only for it to fall apart at the last moment. The player moved to Dundee instead, much to the frustration of Morton chairman Douglas Rae who said: "I would say I am bitterly disappointed, particularly after agreeing terms with his agent."

Morton were also attempting to sign Paul McGowan on a permanent basis after his successful loan spell from Celtic the previous season. The £150,000 fee slapped on him by the Parkhead club was too much for Morton's liking and twice they had bids turned down, the first for £65,000 and the second upped to £80,000.

Ex-Hibernian utility player Jay Shields arrived on a short-term contract, able to play as a defensive midfielder or full back.

But by the time Morton lined up for the opening league game against Clyde, managed by Colin Hendry, at Cappielow, there was still none of the big name signings they had highlighted as a requirement.

Nevertheless, goals by Weatherson, McAlister and Stevenson gave them a 3-2 win with a side which lined up as follows (3-5-2): Robinson; Harding, Greacen, Walker; Finlayson, Millar, McAnespie, Weatherson, McAlister; Templeman, Stevenson.

Four soldiers of the Golden Lions Scottish Infantry display team provided unusual pre-match entertainment when they parachuted onto the pitch with the Second Division league flag, eliciting a big cheer when they took off their tunics to reveal Morton tops beneath.

A 2-0 CIS Cup defeat followed in midweek at Dens Park against Dundee, but on the next Saturday at East End Park a Peter Weatherson strike gained three more points at Dunfermline's expense. Jim McAlister gave an impressive display which saw Morton take a joint lead at the top of the table.

The early promise was continued when Brian Graham scored his first senior goal for the club in a Challenge Cup win over Livingston in which Jay Shields gave a typically dogged midfield display. Shields was small but he had a big heart.

I remained sceptical, however, at the lack of experience and quality in the Greenock ranks and commented: "At some point Morton will have to strengthen their squad if they are to become serious challengers in this highly competitive division. Their start has been a bonus but it would be unrealistic to expect it to continue consistently."

A no-score draw followed at Stirling before Jim McInally revealed his interest in Clyde midfielder Dougie Imrie. Enquiries were rebuffed by Clyde before league leaders Hamilton, under manager Billy Reid, arrived at Cappielow for the team's biggest test yet. It was to be an early lesson in the huge differences between Second and First Division football.

The Lanarkshire club maintained their 100% record with a 2-0 win before a crowd of 3,189. Their greater experience and strength were all too clear. Morton were outmuscled by a side Jim McInally described as being far more 'streetwise' than his own team.

The defeat again highlighted the club's own pre-season observation of the need to add experienced quality, but time was running out before the transfer deadline.

Motherwell boss Mark McGhee expressed an interest in Morton midfielder Jim McAlister but was informed that the youngster was going nowhere at the moment.

A second successive home defeat – 1-0 to Queen of the South – followed, though Morton introduced pre-match signings Iain Russell and Michael Gardyne. Striker Russell had been brought in from Brechin, while Gardyne (21) was acquired from Celtic where he was surplus to requirement. Neither fulfilled the pre-season signing expectations of the support.

The midfield looked particularly lightweight and relatively inexperienced with Millar, McAlister, Finlayson, Stevenson and now Gardyne lacking a real balance; too much of a muchness about them. As it was to turn out also, the one experienced pro, McAnespie, was all too susceptible to old injury problems.

A McAlister goal saw Morton progress in the Challenge Cup over Peterhead in a midweek tie at Balmoor but reality once more kicked in at Livingston in the league, Morton falling 4-0.

It was a strange match. Livi had taken the lead before Morton had a wonderful opportunity to equalise five minutes before the interval. New striker Iain Russell, signed from Brechin for a reported £40,000, was clean through on goal only to slip his shot wide. Within two minutes the hosts were three ahead, adding a fourth in the second half.

Morton provided some comfort to their fans when they beat East Stirling 4-0 in the Challenge Cup quarter-finals, Templeman (2), own goal and Linn being their scorers.

Owen Coyle's St Johnstone, including old Morton favourite Derek McInnes, picked up a point in a 2-2 draw at Cappielow on 22nd September, 2007. It was an entertaining 90 minutes. Morton's midfield could play some good football, but always there was that feeling that they lacked experience and a physical, driving presence. Goals came from Russell and Stevenson.

On the final Saturday of September they lost 2-1 at Dens Park to Dundee, ironically one of the home goals being scored by former target Jani Sturm. The hosts combined know-how with some excellent young quality in the shape of midfielders Kevin McDonald and Scott Robertson. The Dark Blues began the game in style, but midweek exertions in a thrilling cup tie against Celtic, took their toll. Brian Graham equalised before Sturm hit a late winner with a half-hit shot. Outstanding for the visitors was Jim McAlister in an unfamiliar centre midfield role.

It was on to the Challenge Cup against St Johnstone at Cappielow but, for the third year in a row, Morton fell at the semi-final stage. Brian Graham scored in a 3-1 defeat in which Owen Coyle's men were clearly the better side.

On the first Saturday of October, Morton beat Partick at Cappielow 4-2. Highlight of the game was a hat-trick by Peter Weatherson, restored to a striking role. Kieran McAnespie, back in the team after injury, hit the fourth. It was an all-round hat-trick from 'Spoonsy', one with the left peg, one with the right, and a header.

I reported: "For long enough Morton manager Jim McInally has felt that Peter Weatherson has lost that edge in sharpness required to play up front, but necessity caused him to relent on Saturday and how it paid off."

Weatherson himself said: "It's given me a new lease of life. My defensive qualities were getting tested to the maximum in this league."

Another Weatherson goal brought a victory over Clyde at Broadwood to take Morton up to fourth spot in the league as a precursor to a meeting with unbeaten pacesetters Hamilton at New Douglas Park.

It was to be a highly controversial match in which young James McCarthy gave the hosts an early lead. Morton battled back and, two minutes from time, appeared to have equalised. A Michael Gardyne cross was swung in from wide right, Chris Templeman lunged forward at the ball and it flew high into the net past home goalie Bryn Halliwell.

The stand side assistant referee, flag down, ran back to the halfway line, referee Craig Thomson returned to the centre circle and the Morton players celebrated before lining up for the re-start.

Meanwhile goalkeeper Halliwell ran to the stand side assistant to protest. He was joined by other Hamilton players and eventually referee Thomson came over to join the throng. The upshot was, astonishingly, the reversal of the decision to award a goal.

Jim McInally protested vehemently and was sent to the stand. In the aftermath of what turned out to be a 1-0 home win, McInally said: "I can't believe how they [the officials] came to the decision to talk to each other when they've both given a goal."

It was the worst decision I have ever reported on by officials in a football match and, as Jim McInally later said, one can only imagine what might have happened had it occurred in an Old Firm match.

Hamilton boss Billy Reid said at the after-match press conference: "I turned away because I thought it was a goal, but what happened next was incredible. If I was on Morton's side I would be raging."

Chris Templeman, asked about his view of his disallowed 'goal', said: "The ball flashed across from the right and I just threw my body at it. It went past my head and hit me on the top of my left shoulder."

Hamilton goalkeeper Halliwell claimed Templeman had handled the ball. That was, frankly, impossible. The player's hands were in front of him on the ground, supporting him as he lunged forward to meet the ball, as a series of pictures proved. Later Hamilton secretary Scott Struthers was to claim that a video proved the player had handled the ball. This video was never made available for public scrutiny. Struthers was also to say days later that the stand side assistant had put up his flag briefly before putting it back down. Remarkably no one else I spoke to at the game, including all the press who had an excellent view, saw this. I watched the assistant carefully after the ball flew into the net, believing Templeman might just have been offside. At no point did the assistant raise his flag. Struthers, incidentally, had a role on the referees' committee.

Morton appealed, but they had as much chance of winning it as I had of skiing down Mont Blanc on a breadboard while knitting a Fairisle pullover.

On the Refereeing and Disciplinary Whistleblowers section of the SFA website an incredible explanation was offered. It said: "The assistant had awarded the goal but in discussion with the referee he could not confirm that the player had not used his arm to put the ball over the goal line and did not have an uninterrupted view of the situation.

"With this uncertainty, Thomson reverted to his original interpretation of the incident and disallowed the goal for a handling offence."

This beggared belief. It would have been laughed out of any court of law. We were being asked to believe that Craig Thomson, although giving the goal, thought the player had handled. He then asked his assistant if he could confirm that the player had *not* handled. The assistant could not give this assurance, which is presumably why he gave the goal in the first place, yet Thomson then disallowed the goal.

As I wrote: "Why did Craig Thomson not give a foul immediately if he considered Chris Templeman had handled the ball? Why did he give the goal?

"Second, why reverse the decision when, some considerable time after, and following prolonged harassing of the stand side assistant by Hamilton players, he spoke to his assistant and he gave no reason to disallow the goal?"

It was a decision which was inexplicable, made even worse days later when the other assistant at the game, on the far side of the pitch, claimed that if the goal had not been disallowed he would have put his flag up to say Templeman had handled. This smacked of collusion of the worst kind. If he had seen a handling offence he ought to have put his flag up immediately. There is no doubt in my mind that if such an incident had occurred in a high profile Premier League match, particularly one which had been televised, it would have resulted in a thorough enquiry and ensuing disciplinary action being taken against the match officials.

Jim McInally's sense of injustice was wholly understandable. As expected, the SFA swept the whole issue into a big shovel and emptied it into a convenient bin.

The following Saturday at Cappielow Stirling gained a deserved 1-1 draw. Iain Russell was the home scorer, while Jamie Stevenson missed a late penalty kick which would have given all three points to the hosts.

Adam Coakley, having failed to gain a place in the first team, then left on loan to Stranraer.

Next up for the Greenock men was a trip south to Dumfries where they put on one of their best performances of the season, beating Queen of the South 3-1 with goals by Weatherson, Russell and Millar. Weatherson's strike was top quality and the win took Morton up to fourth top spot.

Buckie Thistle provided stubborn opposition in the third round of the Scottish Cup at Cappielow, Morton winning 3-2 with a goal in added-on time by Chris Templeman, adding to those by Russell and McLaughlin.

Livingston then fought out a 2-2 draw at Cappielow, home goals coming from Millar and Russell.

It was apparent that Morton's season was all about consolidation. Their next game was also at Cappielow, this time against St Johnstone who were on the verge of the promotion race, tucked in behind pacesetters Hamilton and Dundee.

Their manager, in just his second game in charge, was old favourite Derek McInnes who had taken over from Owen Coyle. "My feelings for Morton are well documented," McInnes told me. "They're a team close to my hearts. I take my wee boy to watch Morton whenever I can."

Derek was later to tell me that he would have loved to have been asked to take up a management post at Cappielow, but the offer never came.

Honours were even on the afternoon at 2-2, Morton's goals coming from an own goal and a strike by Weatherson. The Cappielow men were now in sixth place. By this time it was obvious that the one promotion spot would go to either Hamilton or Dundee who were 12 points clear of third place.

Hamilton had a good blend of experience, excellent young talent and physical presence. Their midfield typified that, Mensing, McCarthy, Neil and McArthur combining all these qualities.

It must have been disappointing to Morton that Mensing had chosen to go to New Douglas Park rather than Cappielow, given the respective supports and resources, both of which weighed in favour of the Greenock club.

In comparison to Hamilton and Dundee, Morton were a team with a preponderance of relatively inexperienced, lightweight midfielders. They had no natural full backs and, while they had ability in their squad, there was nowhere near the balance of either of the table-topping sides.

It was the Dens men who arrived next at Cappielow, winning 2-0, young Kevin McDonald displaying his class with a lovely goal. At Firhill the next week, Jim McAlister produced an excellent display, again in the centre of midfield, as the visitors gained a 1-1 draw. McAlister capped his performance with the goal.

Dean Keenan, meanwhile, had been farmed out on loan to Ayr, while the pre-transfer window rumours began to abound. Chris Millar was set to go to St Johnstone, while Morton, refusing to confirm it, were setting up an incoming move for Gretna's midfielder Ryan McGuffie.

On Boxing Day Dunfermline produced a 1-0 victory in Greenock, and three days later league leaders Hamilton provided a football lesson at Cappielow, winning 3-1 in comfort, Iain Russell netting the consolation goal for the hosts.

Morton had set their side out in an attacking 4-2-1-3 formation, but it was Hamilton who took control, sending the Greenock club down to seventh place in the division.

On Wednesday 2nd January, 2008, Morton got the New Year off to a bright start when they beat Stirling 2-1 at Forthbank, the two Ryans, Harding and McGuffie, scoring. For McGuffie, who grabbed the winner, it was a satisfying debut in the centre of midfield. He said: "At Gretna I've been used at centre half, full back, right midfield, you name it. Centre midfield's my favourite position."

Manager McInally commented on his new acquisition: "I've seen so much of Gretna over the past couple of years and if I could pick just one of their players to have it would be him every time."

Heading out of Cappielow during the transfer window were striker Bobby Linn, who had never established himself in his short time at Cappielow, and Adam Coakley. Linn was off to East Fife, soon to be joined by big money signing Chris Templeman. Joining them was young Michael Gardyne who was leaving for Ross County.

Eventually it was agreed that Chris Millar, persuaded to sign a pre-contract agreement with St Johnstone, would stay with Morton until the end of the season before heading off to Perth.

Amidst all this movement, Morton slumped to a truly awful defeat when they travelled to Livingston to be beaten 6-1. Iain Russell's goal in the 89th minute was inconsequential.

Having started brightly enough, the visitors went down to 10 men in the 16th minute. A corner had been won and cleared quickly upfield. Kevin Finlayson, as last man, was out of position and Craig took advantage to run clear. Finlayson, desperately trying to get back, brought him down in the box and was promptly ordered off.

The penalty was netted and, as Morton heads went down, the hosts took complete control. It was a woeful performance, only David MacGregor, Iain Russell and a helpless Lee Robinson in goal, emerging with any real credit. MacGregor was eventually subbed after being booked, almost certainly to avoid having him follow Finlayson off the park such was his all too apparent frustration at the way too many of his team-mates appeared to be accepting defeat.

After the match a stunned Jim McInally was asked if he could take anything from the loss. He replied: "No, it was capitulation. There are no excuses. I am totally embarrassed and I would like to apologise to the spectators.

"At the end of the day I carry the can for that. It is totally me to blame. I signed a lot of these players and it's me to blame for what happened to them."

As always with Jim McInally it was a painfully honest admission. But it didn't tell the whole story.

I wrote: "No doubt the manager has to take his share of the responsibility for what became as hopeless a display as I have seen from Morton in recent years, but once the players take the field they must assume the lion's share of the culpability.

"Frankly," I continued, "too many in Ton strips simply did not show the resilience needed in the circumstances." It wasn't down to tactics; it was a lack of character.

Some Livi players began to flaunt the sort of party tricks with a football normally reserved for training ground exhibitions. It was, to be polite, an exhibition in extracting the urine. For Morton fans it must have been distressing to watch.

Before the match against St Johnstone the previous month I had written a piece as follows on the players: "Their work ethic cannot be questioned, nor their general level of fitness, but Morton have had it confirmed for them that the squad which won promotion last season is lacking the qualities needed to entertain further ambition. They need bolstering."

It was simply a reassertion of what I had written pre-season. I continued: "This caused one or two players some agitation, I am told, and was read out to them pre-match in the dressing room by the chairman, presumably to motivate. In the light of Saturday's events it seems a ludicrously mild comment to have made."

There was a predictably angry response from the fans, both directed at certain players and the manager.

I commented: "The manager, of course, has brought in many of these players and in that respect he may be questioned. They were good enough to win promotion but the evidence so far shows that some have gone as far as they can go, perhaps further.

"Saturday may prove to be a watershed in the careers of some at Cappielow. Others have the rest of the season to prove that they have a place in Morton's future."

In the ensuing inquest chairman Douglas Rae and manager Jim McInally decided that there needed to be a re-examination of their signing policy. McInally declared: "We can't take chances on £15k or £20k players who are unproven at this level. Michael Gardyne is one such example.

"Players such as him need time to adapt and prove themselves, but we don't have that time."

The manager went on to say that Bosman signings would now be the priority. He explained: "That way we can get proven, quality players like Ryan McGuffie and, as there's no fee, we can offer more in the way of wages. We have several targets in mind."

Once again in the transfer market Morton were reacting to circumstances rather than dictating them. It was an all too familiar story. Too often unrealistic expectations had been attached to squads which simply did not merit them.

In line with the new policy, central defender Barry Smith (33) was brought in from Icelandic club Valur. Jim McInally had played with the ex-Celtic and Dundee player and knew he could be relied upon.

Morton responded in the best possible fashion to the Livingston result when they put on a spirited, determined display in their next game, a Scottish Cup fourth round tie at home to Premier League Gretna.

They were two goals down but battled back to draw 2-2 with strikes from man-of-the-match Kevin Finlayson, eager to atone for his dismissal against Livi, and Jim McAlister, always one to give everything to the cause.

Chris Millar too was in fine form and was cheered off at the end of the game. At that time it seemed clear that he would be off to St Johnstone within days but, as it transpired, a deal was done to keep him at Cappielow until the summer.

Barry Smith settled in well at sweeper, behind the central defenders in a back three.

Next on the target list for McInally were Gretna's Allan Jenkins and Colin McMenamin. On the way out was Chris Templeman, joining Bobby Linn at East Fife.

Jim McInally commented on the player: "It's disappointing that he never really established himself." It turned out to be £80,000 wasted, basically. The big fellow never seemed to me to have the sort of hunger or ambition to go with an undoubted talent. His arena was that of the big fish in the small pond.

When Morton fell 3-0 to Queen of the South in Greenock, they had slumped to eighth place in the table. Stephen Dobbie had scored an impressive hat-trick.

The club then announced the arrival of a new director, Alistair Donald, formerly with Rangers links. His role defined by chairman Douglas Rae was "almost exclusively one of overview."

On the park things were getting no better, Dunfermline winning 2-0 at East End Park. Morton were now just two points ahead of second bottom Clyde, for whom ex-Ranger John Brown was now manager.

Yet, the side rallied in the Scottish Cup fourth round replay against Gretna, switched from Fir Park, where they were sharing with Motherwell, to Palmerston Park due to flooding. A double by the recalled Peter Weatherson, plus a goal from Chris Millar, gave them a comfortable win. By this time Gretna's dramatic rise under Brooks Mileson was beginning to show signs of collapse. The funding was running out and players were leaving rather than arriving.

Another signing was made on the back of that result, hard-working striker Brian Wake (25) coming in from promotion chasing Hamilton where he could not get a regular appearance. Added to that was the arrival of 26-year-old Gretna midfielder Allan Jenkins. The latter looked a particularly good signing.

Once more, however, Queen of the South proved more than a handful for Morton, Gordon Chisholm's men recording a good 2-0 Scottish Cup win at Cappielow before a crowd of 3,506. The Morton side that afternoon was (3-5-2): McGurn; Harding, Smith, Greacen; Finlayson, Millar, McGuffie, McLaughlin, McAlister; Weatherson, Wake.

When second bottom Clyde arrived at Cappielow on 9th February, 2008, it was Morton's most important match of the season.

It was only a few short weeks since Morton had been offering the view that they did not need to enter the transfer market. Now they were involved in an all too real scrap to avoid relegation, once again, to the Second Division.

Midfielder Allan Jenkins made his debut and gave an impressive, powerful display. Chris Millar gave the host club the lead and they dominated proceedings.

The second goal didn't come, however, and the roof fell in on the home side when Clyde struck in the final minute of play. That was bad enough, but a second goal two minutes into added-on time was a crippling blow for the hosts. Morton were now in second bottom place.

I reported: "The cold February air was matched by the mood of the crowd as they drifted out of Cappielow, boos and frustration forming an atmosphere which clearly threatens the status of manager Jim McInally."

McInally, uncharacteristically, did not appear for the after-match press conference. He went into immediate confab with chairman Douglas Rae, leaving his assistant Martin Clark to face the hacks. I wrote: "Assistant Martin Clark was completely honest when he said that the principal mistake had been not bringing in players of experience and strength in the summer."

That was true. Too long had been spent trying to pursue Paul McGowan. Attempts to bring in Simon Mensing and John Sutton – exactly the type of signings required – were unsuccessful and there was no follow-up.

I continued: "That was a collective mistake, not just one which can be levelled at the manager."

The fans were calling for McInally's resignation and this time it would be difficult to withstand the pressure. I commented: "Jim McInally will not stay if he does not believe he is the right man for the job in hand. It would not surprise me if he had offered his resignation to the chairman in the immediate aftermath.

"Those calling for his head need not think he will put himself before the interests of the club. He simply isn't that sort of person."

The following day, Tuesday 12th February, 2008, Jim McInally's resignation was announced. The man himself was unavailable for comment. Chairman Douglas Rae said that his decision had been accepted "with great reluctance." He was the fourth manager to go since the chairman's acquisition of the club.

CHAPTER FORTY-ONE

Irons follows on from McInally

Jim McInally was as honest as the day is long. Had he not chosen to go, I doubt if he would have been sacked. But he felt the right thing to do was to leave in time to give someone else a chance to revive spirits and get the fans solidly behind the club in the remaining few weeks of the season.

If he was a victim in part of his own signing policy, once again there was too much unwarranted optimism from above.

The usual circus of would-be candidates and press speculation followed as to a successor. Eventually the list was narrowed down to three – Rowan Alexander, Jim Duffy and Davie Irons.

Irons was the only one in a job, having taken over as boss at Gretna from Rowan Alexander after Brooks Mileson's close relationship with his former manager had turned all too sour. Irons was thought to have been the principal coach while Alexander's assistant at Gretna, but Duffy was the choice of a majority of the fans, if not predominantly so.

The ex-Falkirk, Dundee and Hibs boss had plenty of experience and had been a great favourite as a player at Cappielow.

Martin Clark, receiving the blessing of Jim McInally, took charge of the team for their next game, at Dundee, where they went down 2-0. On the Tuesday after the match, Douglas Rae announced that the new man in charge would be Davie Irons, along with former Ton veteran Derek Collins as his assistant.

Although Duffy had been the choice of a majority of the supporters as represented by views expressed on the internet and in the media, the new arrival generally was welcomed.

His opening statement was to say: "I'm a great believer that confidence is 90% of football. When a club changes manager it is usually because the team has been struggling. We have to lift that confidence up. There is a lot of real talent here."

Irons' first game in charge resulted in a 2-1 Cappielow loss to St Johnstone, Peter Weatherson scoring the home goal. Nevertheless the new man declared he had seen enough signs to give cause for encouragement.

In his second game in charge – a key meeting with bottom club Stirling at Cappielow – goals by Allan Jenkins and Iain Russell won three vital points in a 2-1 victory. "There was no doubt we needed that result," said a relieved Irons after the match.

Morton were now two points above Clyde who had played a game less.

Davie Irons sent out his men in a cautious 4-5-1 formation for the next game, against league leaders Hamilton at New Douglas Park. It was not enough to prevent a 3-0 home win for the best side in the division.

Barry Smith had received an injury which was to require surgery and Morton entered a four-game period in which they showed signs of tightening up defensively but at the expense of a creative edge. A 1-1 draw at Clyde (own goal being the scorer), 0-0 home draw with Partick, then further shared results with Livingston at Cappielow (1-1 McAlister) and Queen of the South (0-0) led to the team falling to second bottom spot after Clyde won their game in hand.

The two teams were now level on the points, but Clyde had a superior goal difference of two.

Davie Irons had meanwhile suffered a bereavement when his father died, and he attended the funeral on the morning of the goalless draw with Queen of the South, before turning up later at the game. Derek Collins took the team for the 90 minutes, Irons later joining him in the dugout.

With four games to go, and Clyde showing superb resilience under John Brown, these were very nervous moments for the Greenock club.

Davie Irons moved to sign tall Aussie midfield player Erik Paartalu, who had been made redundant by the collapsing edifice that was now Gretna, until the end of the season.

Allan Jenkins was absent due to a groin strain and next up for Morton were second top Dundee, desperate to keep in touch with leaders Hamilton. Irons fielded a positive 3-4-3 formation, Jim McAlister moving up front on the left and opening the scoring to give the home fans a real boost.

However, the Dens men equalised and then snatched a late winner. That disappointment was compounded by the news that Clyde had won to go three points clear, and with a superior goal difference, with just three matches remaining.

When St Johnstone won 3-2 at McDiarmid Park, Morton's goals coming from substitutes Brian Wake and Iain Russell, the play-offs loomed all too large.

On Saturday 19th April, 2008, Dunfermline, comfortably in mid-table, arrived at Cappielow in a must-win encounter for the hosts. Visitors' boss Jim McIntyre spoke of how his players would not be taking anything easy.

The tension was palpable, yet Morton chose the occasion to put on one of their most impressive displays of the season. Goals by Wake, Harding and Finlayson capped an excellent performance, made all the better when the news filtered through that Clyde had lost.

Morton were now on the same points as the Bully Wee and, importantly, they had edged ahead on goal difference.

That set up the final Saturday of the season at Firhill against Partick Thistle, managed by Ian McCall. A large crowd of 4,914 turned out, at least half from Inverclyde.

The objective was clear – victory. Clyde were at home to bottom club Stirling and the assumption had to be that they would be victorious.

Brian Wake emerged as the hero, scoring twice in a 3-0 victory, giving him four goals in three outings since his recall to the team. Wake was a thoroughly honest pro. He may not have been the most talented, but he always gave everything for the cause. He also had a habit of popping up to score important goals. Kevin Finlayson added to the scoreline.

At centre back, Stewart Greacen gave a dominant display while midfielder Chris Millar, in his last appearance for the club before departing to St Johnstone, was cheered from the field by ecstatic Morton fans.

Clyde too had won, but Morton's superior goal difference meant they had avoided the play-offs. They had found form just when it mattered most.

Davie Irons was delighted, but he tempered his joy by saying: "I don't think Morton should be scraping at the bottom end of the division. We need to look higher than that.

"The players have worked their socks off. A week ago last Friday we were three points behind Clyde and four goals down, so the turnaround has been incredible."

It was clear that changes would be made and the first was to sign Erik Paartalu on a two-year deal. Outgoing players were goalkeeper David McGurn, defensive midfielder Scott McLaughlin, Deen Keenan who had enjoyed a loan spell at Ayr, Craig Black and Scott McKellar. It seemed particularly harsh on McGurn.

Chris Millar was off to St Johnstone, honouring his obligation to Derek McInnes even after an attempt by Morton to get him to change his mind. Also told they could find other clubs were in-contract players Jamie Stevenson, Kieran McAnespie and David MacGregor. Young striker Brian Graham was informed the club would try to farm him out for experience on a long term loan.

Stevenson was yet another of those young talents, much admired, who ultimately fail to make the most of their potential. Football is littered with such examples.

On the way in to Cappielow were goalkeeper Colin Stewart (28), on a two-year deal, along with St Johnstone's veteran central defender Allan McManus (33) and Clyde midfielder Stevie Masterton (23). Of Masterton, something of a free kick specialist, Irons said: "He's a player I've been looking at for a while. I wanted to get him when I was at Gretna."

Chairman Douglas Rae announced: "We are better having fewer players and a higher quality of player." The usual winds which follow managerial change were blowing.

Morton were very much at a stage when they had to assess their priorities in accordance with their ambitions. If they really wanted to make an impression in the First Division then they had to get a better balance between youthful promise and established experience. Managerially, they also needed their latest appointment to be the right one.

It was the close season, but already Morton faced injury problems. Ryan Harding, Kieran McAnespie and Allan Jenkins all faced minor operations, while Stewart Greacen was recovering from a hernia operation.

On the way in to Cappielow was striker Jon Newby from Morecambe, a pacey player who had played for a while with Liverpool. Joining also, on trial at first and later on a year's contract, was young Rangers left back Chris Smith.

Midfielder Jamie Stevenson was sent back on loan to Alloa, the club from whom Jim

McInally had acquired him, while striker Brian Graham joined Jim McInally on a season's loan at East Stirlingshire.

Criticism had often been made of chairman Douglas Rae for not permitting his managers to utilise the transfer budget as they saw fit. This time he allowed Davie Irons that privilege. The result included the re-signing of central defenders Ryan Harding and Stewart Greacen on astoundingly improved two-year deals which knocked a huge hole in the budget.

After the Renfrewshire Cup had been lost on penalties against rivals St Mirren, the league action began on Saturday 2nd August at Broadwood where Clyde, who had won their play-off to remain in the First Division, gained a home point in a 1-1 draw. Scorer on his league debut was Jon Newby.

Fellow striker Brian Wake was ordered off late in the game for a second bookable offence. With Allan McManus and Ryan Harding on the injured list, Morton lined up as follows in 3-4-3 formation: Stewart; Weatherson, Greacen, Walker; Finlayson, McGuffie, Paartalu, McAlister; Russell, Wake, Newby.

Davie Irons then moved to bring in a second goalkeeper, Kevin Cuthbert, who had been freed by St Johnstone, and ex-Arsenal and Queen's Park Rangers centre back Dominic Shimmin (20) on a two-year deal.

"He looks a real player," commented Irons on Shimmin. "He can play anywhere in the back four or even in midfield."

Shimmin had definite ability, way beyond the level of First Division. His early performances were very impressive, but in time he was to prove an unreliable character. He seldom seemed truly fit and ultimately one even wondered if he was all that interested in playing football.

Morton followed up the point at Clyde with an impressive 6-3 win in the CIS Cup second round over Stranraer, Wake and Russell each grabbing doubles, McGuffie and Paartalu contributing the other strikes.

Paartalu, who was looking impressive in a sitting midfield role, and McGuffie scored again in a home 2-2 draw with pre-season title favourites St Johnstone in which Morton had switched to a standard 4-4-2 as follows: Cuthbert; Weatherson, Shimmin, Greacen, Walker; McGuffie, Masterton, Paartalu, McAlister; Russell, Newby.

In the Alba Challenge Cup against Jim McInally's East Stirlingshire, Morton recorded a decent away 3-0 win, Masterton and McGuffie (2) scoring. Things seemed to be progressing nicely and chairman Douglas Rae revealed that the wage budget had been increased by £180,000 from the previous season.

Morton were now a much more physically imposing team, but they were cut down to size by Livingston at Cappielow, losing 2-1, Brian Wake getting the sole home counter.

I wrote: "Morton got what they deserved out of this match – nothing. Livi's Italian boss Roberto Landini's smattering of English was liberally sprinkled with an almost child-like glee. He beamed: 'We are so happy now. They [his players] play very, very good football, believe me.'" We believed you, Roberto.

It was just the sort of display Morton, trying hard to maximise attendances on the back of a greatly enhanced budget, did not need.

In a stodgy match at Dens Park Morton lost 1-0. Worryingly they had only one chance in the entire 90 minutes, and it wasn't one they created. It fell to substitute Jon Newby who ran on to a poor defensive back-header. As Dens goalkeeper Rab Douglas came off his line, Newby fired off a drive which Douglas did extremely well to save.

The result left Morton in second bottom position after four games. And there was some harsh criticism for Newby from manager Irons who said: "I said to the lads at half-time that we would get a chance to get back into the game, but Newby had to do better with it." It seemed hyper-critical of the substitute's first touch of the ball.

Already sections of the Morton support were beginning to question their team's performances.

But there was a far better display in midweek when Morton went to Premier League Hibernian's Easter Road ground and won their CIS Cup tie 4-3 in extra time. Goals came from Russell (2), Masterton and Harding and led manager Irons to comment that it had been "a real back to front team performance".

Renewed pride came before a resounding fall. On the last Saturday of August, 2008, Morton travelled to Broomfield for their fifth league match of the season and were savaged 5-0.

It was a shocking display and I reported: "It was as one-sided as it gets. No one from either side would have expected such a result. Where the Airdrie fans' amazement turned to euphoria, Morton's large travelling support was transformed into a stunned silence."

Allan McManus was also sent off near the end of the game, while salt was liberally rubbed into the wound when former Morton holding midfielder Scott McLaughlin notched a double.

Davie Irons was scathing of his players in his after-match comments, saying to the press: "I'm absolutely disgusted; hence the long wait you have had for me to come out and speak to you. That was an absolute disgrace the way they performed."

Questioned on his own change of system, from a back four to a three, he replied: "Systems don't win you games; players win you games." Peter Weatherson, who had been badly exposed on the right of the back three, was subbed and booed off the pitch. But he was the victim of a selection policy which had seen him play twice at right back, once on the right of a back three, and once on the left of a similar formation. Pace was never Weatherson's strong point, and in the First Division his defensive abilities were coming under severe scrutiny. He was a converted forward who looked just that.

Striker Jon Newby had hardly settled in when he was being offloaded on loan to Conference League side Burton Albion. It seemed there were issues between him and the manager since the criticism he had taken for missing that chance at Dundee.

However disappointing they were in the league, Morton continued to do well in cup competitions, and won 2-0 at Dumfries against Queen of the South, Wake and McGuffie on target.

The same opponents met days later in the league at Cappielow when the Doonhamers took a point in a goalless 90 minutes. It was a game in which Morton's less than jolly giants seemed to play deeper and deeper. After six games they still had to record a win and were firmly at the bottom of the division.

Continual chopping and changing of the system hardly seemed helpful and when Partick won 2-1 at Firhill, Russell grabbing the visitors' goal, the situation was becoming alarming. The team were losing poor goals and making precious few chances. I observed: "A big, physical side who pose a threat at set pieces is what most managers trot out when they talk about Morton. Any comment of them being a side who pass the ball through the team has long since gone." So too talk of Cappielow being a difficult place to come to. Since the beginning of the previous season Morton had won only four league games out of a total of 21.

In the Co-op Cup Inverness ended Morton's run with a 2-1 defeat at Cappielow, Jim McAlister getting the sole goal.

Iain Russell scored in a 1-1 home draw with Dunfermline and when Ross County completed the first quarter of the season with a comfortable 3-0 win, Morton were five points adrift of second bottom Clyde. Davie Irons said after the match: "The players have let the club down and didn't do the job asked of them."

It was Morton's longest run without a league win since the disastrous 2000-01 season.

Chairman Douglas Rae was entertaining his own doubts about the manager's position and said: "I have had belief he will turn things round. Obviously results have been pulling me in the other way. I can't believe where the team is. We were believed to be infinitely stronger than last season; it hasn't been that in reality, apart from cup games."

Commenting on the increase of £180,000 in the wage bill, Rae continued: "People have a right to expect better."

Asked if the club was in crisis, Davie Irons responded: "What's a crisis? It's a word I wouldn't use in football. There are more important things going on in the outside world. In football terms it is not particularly good. But, before Saturday, we had lost just once in five games. Obviously Saturday was a big game. The boys let us down and I am very disappointed and angry."

A tone was developing in which the players seemed always to be taking the brunt of the blame. I commented on this: "He [Davie Irons] has been quite critical in public of players, something most bosses keep in-house." I asked the manager if he felt he still had the dressing room behind him. His reply was in the affirmative, but it was clear that several players were less than happy.

The situation further deteriorated when Ross County inflicted a 4-1 defeat upon Morton in the Challenge Cup semi-final at Dingwall. Peter Weatherson was the Morton scorer. There was growing anger among the fans and chants of 'time to go' emanated from the visiting support. After the game Davie Irons said: "Ultimately the buck stops with me, but I just said to the players: look at yourselves as well."

On Friday 17th October, 2008, chairman Douglas Rae confirmed that Davie Irons had been given two games in which to show that he was providing a solution.

The following day the beleaguered manager acted to bring in yet another ex-Gretna player, veteran striker James Grady on loan from Hamilton.

It was an inspired move. Thirty-seven-year-old Grady scored the only goal of the game against Clyde at Cappielow, albeit there was more than a hint of offside about the strike. Irons rushed onto the pitch at the end to congratulate the player in a scene more fitting to a cup final. I reported: "It was a win which almost certainly kept the Ton boss in a job."

Irons said of Grady: "He's a wee star at times. I helped him at the start of his career and he's now helping me at the end of his career."

The Morton side that afternoon was (4-4-2): Cuthbert; MacGregor, Greacen, Shimmin, Smith; Finlayson, McGuffie, Masterton, McAlister; Weatherson, Grady.

Dundee were next up at Cappielow and a 2-0 victory with goals from Weatherson and McGuffie meant the Greenock men were now within one win of four other clubs. Dom Shimmin was outstanding.

Livingston then inflicted a single goal defeat on their own ground but, in the next match, against Queen of the South at Dumfries, Morton reacted in style with a 4-1 win which at last lifted them off the bottom of the table. A double from Peter Weatherson, restored by now to his true position up front, and goals by Allan Jenkins and Stewart Greacen took Morton a point ahead of Clyde.

Dominic Shimmin was voted young player of the month.

Further success came with a notable 1-0 win over second top Dunfermline at East End Park, Erik Paartalu netting with a spectacular 22-yard drive. The big Aussie didn't often feature on the score list, but when he did it was usually with an extravagant effort.

Goals by Wake and Jenkins were enough to beat Airdrie and go some way towards avenging that earlier embarrassing defeat, though Peterhead were to provide a Scottish Cup loss at Balmoor when Stevie Masterton's early strike was nullified by two second half home goals. Peter Weatherson was sent off.

A late goal by St Johnstone defender Rutkiewicz, after a Cuthbert mistake, gave all three points to leaders St Johnstone at Perth. On the final Saturday before Christmas, Masterton and Wake goals produced a 2-1 home win over Ross County. Morton were now third bottom, seven points clear of bottom club Airdrie.

On the following Saturday at New Broomfield a poor Chris Smith passback led to the concession of the only goal of the game, Kevin Cuthbert bringing down Lynch and being sent off as a result. Morton fell to second bottom place, four points clear of the victorious Lanarkshire club. For Smith there was some sympathy from manager Irons given his inexperience.

The New Year of 2009 began with Kieran McAnespie being farmed out to Dumbarton and James Grady signing until the end of the season.

A home match against Queen of the South looked to be heading disastrously wrong when the visitors took a two-goal lead, only for Peter Weatherson to retrieve the situation with a double against his old club. The equaliser came in the fourth minute of added-on time.

Referee Steven Nicholl's overt fussiness became a feature of the game, resulting in an amusing piece of terracing theatre. At a free kick given to Morton near the Queen of the South penalty area, the referee dramatically stepped out the 10-yard gap for the visitors' defensive wall, accompanied by the numerical, ironic chanting of the home support. Mr Nicholls took 11 steps much to the amusement of his audience.

The game also was remarkable for a shuddering tackle by Dominic Shimmin on Queens' striker Gary Arbuckle. Shimmin, with impeccable timing, took the ball cleanly only for his momentum to sweep Arbuckle aside. The challenge led to the Dumfries club's striker breaking his leg. At the time, no Queens player protested, nor did their manager Gordon Chisholm. No foul was given. When it later became apparent that Arbuckle had sustained a broken leg, Chisholm unfortunately lashed out verbally at Shimmin. It created a rumpus in the national press which was at best somewhat hypocritical given that no journalist at the match had offered the view that the tackle was anything but fair. Nor had any Queen of the South player.

Shimmin was fast becoming a stand-out in the First Division, and it was hard to see at that time why he wasn't playing at a higher level.

Meanwhile Jamie Stevenson was back after his loan spell at Alloa, but he was firmly out of the manager's plans. For a young man with an abundance of talent it was regrettable, but it was yet another example of ability not being matched by either the right temperament or attitude.

A goalless draw with Dundee followed at Dens Park, in which skipper Stewart Greacen was again a dominant figure at the centre of the defence, before goals by Brian Wake and Ryan McGuffie gained a point in a 2-2 draw at home to Livingston. Morton had been two ahead in 16 minutes, only to concede goals to Griffiths and Smith in the last nine minutes.

For much of the 90 minutes Morton had looked impressive, but too often over the course of the season they seemed anxious when trying to protect a lead.

On the final Saturday of January, 2009, league pacesetters St Johnstone came to Greenock. Derek McInnes expected a tough game, and his side left with a valuable point, but he felt it ought to have been more. I reported: "St Johnstone departed Cappielow on a cold winter's night believing their performance was worth all three points, and it was difficult not to have some sympathy with that view. They certainly contributed much more to the game in a positive sense, but Morton's resilience earned them a home point."

Liam Craig on the left flank, Gary Irvine on the right, and a well balanced midfield of Chris Millar, Jody Morris and Paul Sheerin gave the Perth Saints a decisive edge in the balance of play.

I summed up by saying: "I am sure we were watching the champions elect."

In a massively competitive league Morton were in sixth place, but only two points ahead of second bottom.

Ryan Harding had meanwhile been ruled out for the rest of the season with injury and two matchless Saturdays led to Morton falling to third bottom of the table, two points ahead of Clyde.

An abysmal 1-0 defeat followed at Firhill against Partick Thistle. It led me to write: "Morton's sole tactic seemed to be based on long punts upfield. Partick at least attempted to play passes and, in Greenockian Gary Harkins, had the one man on the field best able to control the ball and bring others into play."

In the match programme for the next game, against Dunfermline at Cappielow, chairman Douglas Rae penned some painful words of his side's efforts. "I hate," he said, "having to admit to the paucity of our football currently. On Saturday almost every ball was lumped up the park to the extent that our forwards were having to run about like headless chickens."

Manager Davie Irons revealed after the game that he had used the article to motivate his players. It presumably had the desired effect. I wrote of the performance against the Pars which produced a 2-1 home win, goals by Weatherson and Greacen, as follows: "Where Morton were one-dimensional, predictable and lacking any invention against Partick Thistle the previous week at Firhill, they were expansive, creative and adventurous."

Allan Jenkins was especially effective with a driving, positive midfield display, but his Cappielow career was too often punctuated by injury problems.

Second bottom Clyde were then dismissed 4-2 at Broadwood with goals by Erik Paartalu, Iain Russell, Stevie Masterton and Brian Wake. Clyde's Gibson was sent off while Allan McManus continued to play well in place of the injured Shimmin for the Greenock club.

A draw at Queen of the South, James Grady scoring, was followed up by another with Airdrie at home, goalless this time, and when Clyde were beaten 2-0 at Cappielow with goals from Jenkins and Masterton, Morton were fifth top.

Jenkins was once again prominent, while McManus was directing operations vociferously from the back in a solid partnership with Greacen.

Iain Russell's goal gave Morton a point at Ross County and, when Dundee lost 2-0 at Cappielow to a brace by man-of-the-match Peter Weatherson, the Greenock men had risen to fourth spot in the division. Making his debut in that game was young left-sided midfielder Carlo Monti, released by Celtic.

A Brian Wake double at Livingston hauled Morton up to the heady heights of third spot and I commented: "Given the traumas of the first quarter of the season when only four points were collected there was much airing of the Great God 'If Only'. That particular deity is common to all, however. What Morton have learned over the course of the season is how to manage the most competitive of all leagues."

St Johnstone were leading the division on 56 points from 32 games, Partick on 49 and Morton on 47.

Saints clearly were heading for the title. Their next game was against Morton in Perth. The visitors had gone on an eight-match unbeaten run, but a victory by the hosts would give them the championship.

Pre-match, Saints boss Derek McInnes, who had begun his senior career at Cappielow, said: "I still have a regard for Morton and the people there."

On the day it was Saints who rose splendidly to the occasion. Despite a shock opener from Ryan McGuffie after a soft penalty award, the Perth men ran out convincing 3-1 winners.

It was a great day for the town of Perth. I reported: "It was a day to savour for the former Morton men, Saints' boss Derek McInnes and local boy Chris Millar. Both deserve their success, McInnes proving himself mature beyond his years as a manager, while Millar played a key role.

"On the day Saints were more than worthy champions. Getting over the winning line is seldom easy. In the end they achieved their goal with style and panache."

Two games remained in the programme. Stewart Greacen, one of the most likeable fellows in football, was voted Player of the Year by the fans and his manager said: "He deserves it. He's been a big player for us this season."

The aim now was to finish on a high. But defeats by Dunfermline at East End Park (2-1, young Monti getting a first goal for the club) and 2-0 at home to Ross County took the edge off the recovery for Morton.

I wrote: "All the right noises had been made pre-match about the need to finish the season with a flourish but, as so often happens on these occasions, the points went to the side needing them most."

County had escaped the play-off place to finish third bottom, while Morton ended up in sixth position.

Manager Davie Irons was less than amused at four successive defeats, saying to his players: "Don't be surprised if there's someone who's taken your jersey in the pre-season, because over the piece the league table doesn't lie and it's shown that we're not good enough to win this league."

He then went on to say to the press: "If I went with the same group of players I'm kidding myself on, because they've shown that they are not good enough this year. So, why all of a sudden next year are they going to be good enough? They can't, they won't be, so I have to make sure that changes."

Already released were Kieran McAnespie, Jamie Stevenson and Jon Newby, while goalkeeper Colin Stewart had been told he could find a new club. Chris Smith was also surplus to requirement.

New deals were accepted by Brian Wake, Alex Walker, Carlo Monti and, later, by goalkeeper Kevin Cuthbert.

But if the manager wanted to offload some players, too many were on well paid deals from which they were not going to depart easily. And heavily criticising them when you may yet have to rely on them did not seem a clever tactic. Changing a squad is not always an easy matter, as the Cappielow gaffer was to find out in the close season.

CHAPTER FORTY-TWO

The end of Irons

It was made plain to manager Davie Irons by the chairman at the start of season 2009-10 that resources were very limited, a considerable increase in the wage bill having been implemented the previous season. Talk of bringing in three or four quality, experienced pros soon was reduced to perhaps one or two.

In fact, the only addition to match the description was former Hearts midfielder Neil MacFarlane who had ended his contract at Queen of the South. The 31-year-old signed on for two years.

No club had come in for goalkeeper Colin Stewart and he eventually remained, while David MacGregor was offered a one-year deal after proving his fitness. If anyone was ever unlucky with injuries it was surely MacGregor.

Still Morton had no natural full backs, while there seemed to be a plethora of midfielders, none of whom could be described as a playmaker. Davie Irons had expressed the wish to add another striker and veteran James Grady was signed on again for six months.

Yet chairman Douglas Rae commented before the action began: "I think we will do well this season, going from what I've heard from the manager Davie Irons and seeing how much work the players have put into training."

Dominic Shimmin remained under the cloud of injury problems to thigh and hamstring which seemed interminable. It was January since he had last kicked a ball.

After a pre-season trip to Austria which included a 6-1 defeat by Slovan Bratislava, Morton went down 3-1 to Romanian champions Unirea Urziceni at Cappielow.

Visiting boss Dan Petrescu expressed his admiration of Morton midfielder Jim McAlister, so much so that he was given the opportunity to play him for 25 minutes against Plymouth Argyle who were on a pre-season tour of Scotland.

Eventually McAlister, who also had a trial at Watford, declined any possible transfer to Romania, saying that if he were to move he would rather it were within the United Kingdom.

The competitive season began on Saturday 25th July, 2009, with an Alba Challenge Cup first round tie at Dumbarton in which an Allan Jenkins strike was enough to gain victory. The same player then scored in a 2-1 Renfrewshire Cup Final defeat by St Mirren at the new St Mirren Park.

It was then off to Fife for a 3-1 win over Cowdenbeath in the first round of the CIS Cup. Long-serving Peter Weatherson impressed with a double while Neil MacFarlane scored with a scorching 30-yard drive – a rare goal in both senses of the word.

The league was everything for Morton and it began against pre-season favourites Dundee who had ploughed large quantities of cash into building a side capable of a genuine challenge. At Dens Park the Greenock men lost 1-0, but it was a respectable performance.

Grumbles among the home support, however, began to surface again when Dunfermline arrived at Cappielow on Sunday 16th August and won 2-0.

Young Ryan McWilliams was in goal, after regulars Kevin Cuthbert and Colin Stewart remained absent due to a broken foot and finger respectively. Stand-in goalie Bryn Halliwell was also a late withdrawal due to injury.

McWilliams did well enough, but I described the performance thus: "Scottish Secretary for Justice Kenny MacAskill was watching this match and at the end of the 90 minutes he would have been satisfied that the correct verdict was reached on the pitch."

Morton were bottom after two games and fans were beginning to dread a repetition of the previous season's angst-ridden start.

The mood was not lifted when Ross County handed out a second round 2-1 Alba Challenge Cup defeat at Dingwall, Stevie Masterton getting the visitors' goal.

Morton badly needed a boost and they got it at Somerset Park when they beat part-time Ayr 2-0, with a brace by Peter Weatherson, to record their first league points.

Once again I could not help but feel Morton were disadvantaging themselves by constantly altering their system. I wrote: "Continuity has not been a feature of Morton and they have switched formations several times over the past season and into this one."

The Ayr success was followed in midweek by a second round 3-1 CIS Cup loss to Premier League Kilmarnock at Rugby Park. Ryan McGuffie got the Greenock goal from the penalty spot. Some credit could be taken from the performance and it was an optimistic manager and squad who made their way to Firhill on Saturday 29th August for the league encounter with Partick Thistle.

It was a footballing disaster. I reported: "Morton arrived at Firhill full of stated optimism after victory at Ayr and a decent display, albeit in defeat, against Kilmarnock in midweek. They departed with their bubble of optimism fully deflated. All the good of that win last Saturday was frittered away in a hapless display."

The side had lined up as follows (3-1-4-2): McWilliams; Greacen, McManus, Harding; MacFarlane; Finlayson, McGuffie, Jenkins, McAlister; Weatherson, Graham.

The Jags, who normally played passing football through midfield, chose on this occasion a more direct route in order to expose the lack of pace in the Morton back three, Marc Corcoran and Liam Buchanan leading them a merry dance with their tempo and movement.

It was Thistle's Ian McCall who got his game plan spot-on. I wrote: "He won the tactical battle hands down. Three times Partick played long, three times they scored in a first 45 minutes which killed the match as a contest."

Morton were five behind when skipper Stewart Greacen's frustration got the better of him and he was sent off. The Morton fans were streaming out of the ground long before the final whistle.

Davie Irons did not attend the after-match press conference. Two days later he said: "We are hurting at the moment. It was a hard one to take but we will get it right and bounce back."

Not many shared his confidence. I commented: "You can sense when the atmosphere is right at a club, and at the moment there isn't that buzz at Cappielow which accompanies a genuinely harmonious camp."

Meanwhile the continuing absence of Dominic Shimmin became increasingly perplexing. Formally he was 'injured' but the specifics of his problems remained clouded in obscurity. Attempts to contact him proved fruitless and the Morton management were extremely vague when asked about the player. It was clear that something was far from being right.

On Saturday 12th September, 2009, the gloom merely deepened when Inverness came to Cappielow and comfortably won 3-0.

Morton were bottom of the table after five games, on three points. Inverness boss Terry Butcher was delighted with his side and remarked: "We've got a big back four, but further forward it's a bit like dwarf city. But the dwarfs can play a bit."

Indeed they could. Butcher's dwarfs were way too good for Irons' giants. The Morton boss said: "Obviously I'll take the responsibility and the blame."

By now Morton's options up front were also minimised, Iain Russell being allowed to go on loan to Alloa.

The club was in real trouble and there was no doubt that by this time the manager had a definite problem providing motivation. I said: "The body language at Cappielow these days tells its own story. Just as good times provide their own momentum, so bad are accompanied by an almost physical diminution. People seem to shrink within themselves."

During the week I wrote: "Chairman Douglas Rae has spent massively, and commendably, improving the infrastructure at Morton. Cappielow is a vastly better stadium than the virtual scrapyard he inherited, and there are plans to carry on that upgrading.

"But, in football terms a considerable sum of money has also been expended in recent years, both on transfer fees and, more recently, wages, which has so far brought a disproportionately modest return. As a club Morton must ask themselves why that situation exists, why others with fewer resources and potential seem to make at least as much impact, often more, with what they have."

Whether he believed it or not, by this time Davie Irons had lost the confidence of the dressing room and sections of his staff. Press conferences by now assumed the ambience of a wake. The inevitable finale came at Stark's Park, Kirkcaldy, on the 19th September, 2009.

Raith Rovers put three goals past Morton without reply. The travelling fans were clear in their condemnation of the situation. They wanted the manager gone. As it turned out they weren't the only ones.

Serious conversations were taking place within Stark's Park among members of the visiting board. The expressions on the faces of everyone connected with Morton spoke volumes.

At the after-match press meeting Davie Irons expressed his disappointment in the players' failure to accept responsibility. But he said he was not a quitter and would not "walk away to join those criticising from the outside." I felt the manager was unable to link that criticism with the reality of the situation. He wasn't the victim of a plot. Things were fundamentally wrong. When you have lost the goodwill of those around you, there is no road ahead.

It was no surprise when the decision was made by the Morton board over the weekend to part company with the manager. Three points from six league games had proved enough.

I exclusively reported chairman Douglas Rae's announcement in Monday's paper. "The club greatly regretted the need for change but, as football is a results driven business, change was imperative." The chairman was also known to be unhappy at the way the manager had spent the budget allocated to him, especially on wages he felt were grossly inflated.

It is never pleasant to see anyone lose a job, but in football the inevitability of management is that one day you will be sacked. Once again Morton had parted company with a manager. To say they desperately needed the next incumbent of the position to be successful was by now blindingly obvious, for it had been said all too often in recent times.

Senior players James Grady and Allan McManus were asked to take training. I put it to Grady that he might want to apply for the job himself. He replied: "I'd be lying if I said I wasn't interested. I've been hoping to get into the management side. Allan [McManus] and I have been taking the 19s and we've done our coaching badges.

"There have been issues, no doubt some have been aired in the Telegraph, but our job is to concentrate on Saturday and a big game against Airdrie."

Davie Irons commented on his removal by saying: "It was a decision based on results and I accept that." But there was a barbed comment on both caretakers when he continued: "James Grady and Allan McManus will take over in the short term I believe. I have my opinions of those two but will keep them to myself.

"Some issues I had to contend with won't go away simply because I've gone. But I enjoyed it. I maybe wasn't the most popular appointment, but I appreciate the backing that I did get."

With the bulk of the first team squad out of contract at the end of the season, whoever took over the reins was going to get an excellent opportunity to quickly change the personnel to their own taste.

Already possible candidates were being bandied about – Jim Duffy, Allan Moore, Allan Maitland, Tommy McLean and Jimmy Nicholl among them. Only one of those, Allan Moore, actually applied when it came down to it, though Jimmy Nicholl was later to tell me he would have loved the chance to manage Morton. Jim Duffy too would have taken the job but, having been knocked back once before, he saw no reason to be confident of his chances second time round and did not apply.

Another who confided his definite interest was Allan Maitland, who had enjoyed an excellent record at Clyde, Hamilton and Alloa, but in the event he also did not apply.

James Grady's first match in charge was against Airdrie. Young Brian Graham snatched the only goal of the game at Cappielow and Morton leapfrogged the Diamonds to move off the foot of the league table. An interested spectator, who took time to wave to the fans at half-time, was former boss Benny Rooney.

Grady and McManus favoured a 4-4-2 formation and their team that day was: Stewart; Finlayson, Greacen, McManus, Walker; Jenkins, Paartalu, MacFarlane, McAlister; Graham, Weatherson.

The following Saturday Morton travelled down to Dumfries to play league leaders Queen of the South. This time they triumphed 3-2, after going three up. Two goals in the final two minutes flattered Queens who had been well beaten, the Ton goals coming from Graham, Jenkins and, almost inevitably, Weatherson who had such a good scoring record against his former team.

In the first week of October Stirling Albion boss Allan Moore intimated that he would be very interested in becoming the new manager at Greenock. Interviews were to be held in the week beginning 12th October. Moore was favourite as Ton chairman Douglas Rae was known to be a firm admirer.

On the field, Morton met Ross County at Cappielow and ended up losing by the only goal of the game.

This was followed during the week by an outburst in the national papers from former manager Davie Irons in which he attacked both James Grady and Allan McManus. He said: "It wasn't just the results that proved my downfall. That has been the biggest disappointment. I don't want to sound bitter but there were things being done behind my back by those who replaced me in the job that were very hard to take."

What these things were he never stipulated, but he continued: "I can't stop thinking that I wasn't given a fair crack of the whip."

Chairman Douglas Rae professed to be "very disappointed" in Irons' comments. Grady and McManus chose to maintain silence.

I wondered what Davie Irons would have considered a fair crack of the whip given some recent abysmal performances and a morale at the club which had reached rock bottom. It is never nice, though, to see anyone lose a job. He also was one of the first to phone me with his commiserations when I was made redundant not long after.

Second top Dundee then beat Morton 1-0 before an injury stricken Greenock side lost 3-1 to Dunfermline at East End Park. The visitors' goal came from Ryan McGuffie.

It was then revealed that Douglas Rae had approached Stirling to ask about acquiring their manager, Allan Moore. Unaccountably, Stirling were seeking compensation of, initially, £180,000, later reduced to £160,000. It was exorbitant for a part time manager with a year left on his contract.

Morton offered a more realistic £20-30,000 and the possibility of a deal collapsed. Moore was disappointed and said: "There's not much I can say. The clubs couldn't agree a fee. To be honest I think what Stirling were asking for was a bit over the top.

"Douglas Rae told me I was the number one choice and it would have given me the chance to go full-time. I am sure I would have made Morton a better team."

I commented: "To ask for that level of compensation was holding back a manager who had done excellent work for the club [Stirling] for seven years. It was almost inevitably going to be rejected."

Inverness then defeated Morton 4-1 at Tulloch Caledonian Stadium, Paartalu getting the solitary Morton strike but, despite that, Douglas Rae announced that he had decided to give James Grady the job full time on a contract until the end of the season when it would be reviewed.

The players were solidly behind Grady and Allan McManus who was to be his assistant. Grady commented: "I want to be successful as a manager. I am very ambitious and I know I have to be successful at Morton."

If he was inexperienced, he knew the players only too well. And he was no fool. He knew changes would have to be made to the squad at the end of the season.

Morton's injury-ravaged squad, by now down to 12 fit players, lost 2-0 at home to Partick Thistle, but there was a boost to the squad with the arrival on short term contracts of former Hibernian full backs David Van Zanten and Alan Reid. At last Morton had genuine full backs in their squad. Both Grady and McManus favoured a flat back four and it greatly increased their options.

Meanwhile the problem over the seemingly endlessly injured Dominic Shimmin was addressed. This young man had shown excellent ability whenever he had played, but there was clearly a personality issue.

James Grady said on the subject: "We have had a chat with Shimmin about getting fit again and we are going to give him a mini pre-season."

Without wishing to go into details on what, exactly, Shimmin's problems were, Grady continued: "It was a good, open, frank chat and we have told him that whatever happened in the past, it is now up to him to get himself fit. You don't play for Arsenal without being a good player. But we've let him know where we stand. He's taken it on the chin and it's now up to him."

The player's last appearance had been on 10th March, 2008. Shimmin was a complete enigma. Never have I come across a player of such obvious talent and such an evident lack of ambition. It was often as if he didn't care whether he played football or not.

Cappielow Park was then voted to have the best pitch in the First Division, testament to the excellent work of groundsman Mark Farrell. These awards were given on a league by league basis, but I doubt if there was a better playing surface in the whole country.

On Saturday 14th November, the long-suffering Morton support were given a huge lift when their side trounced Raith Rovers 5-0 at Cappielow, goals coming from doubles by Brian Wake and Peter Weatherson, and one from Erik Paartalu.

Morton were third bottom of the table, four points clear of Ayr and five ahead of Airdrie.

There was a revealing remark from Paartalu when he said: "At training we practise playing the ball out of tight situations. It's enjoyable. Under Davie Irons there was too much long ball."

There then followed a fine 4-2 win away from home to fellow strugglers Airdrie. After falling two behind, it was a vastly different Morton performance which saw them sweep past the Diamonds through goals from Wake (2), McGuffie and Van Zanten, the latter's a lovely curled effort from a quality player. The victory established an eight-point gap between Morton and Airdrie at the bottom. They were also six clear of second bottom Ayr.

Ryan Harding, who had joined Morton from Livingston in March of 2005, was meanwhile allowed to leave Cappielow, receiving a payment to compensate the few remaining months of his contract.

It was now Scottish Cup time, but a lacklustre and scoreless draw against Second Division Dumbarton at Cappielow resulted in a replay. At the second opportunity, Morton won through to a glamour tie with Celtic after Brian Graham's excellent downward header separated the teams.

Two league defeats followed – 3-1 at Ross County, Paartalu scoring, and 2-1 (Weatherson) at home to Queen of the South – as if to confirm that the Greenock men had not rid themselves of their irritating lack of consistency.

Against Queen of the South Dominic Shimmin made a comeback. Despite a lack of action for eight months, Shimmin strolled through the match in a virtually flawless performance in the centre of the defence. I wasn't sure whether admiration or exasperation was the appropriate response. Goodness knows what his manager felt.

Striker Iain Russell then returned to Greenock after his loan spell at Alloa to boost the numbers, but a disappointing 3-1 loss at Dundee left James Grady bemoaning his players' lack of mental strength. It was a recurring theme. There was no doubt that it was one which would be addressed when the season ended, should Grady still be at the club.

As the manager put it: "It's all about having the same objective and, if you can't win the game, draw it. It's about decision making and game awareness."

Grady was only too well aware himself that there needed to be major changes in personnel at the end of the campaign.

New Year, 2010, was brought in with a 1-0 defeat at Firhill against Partick Thistle. It was a game in which Morton enjoyed the bulk of the play with no reward. James Grady said: "We're away without any points from a game we bossed."

The transfer window saw David Van Zanten leave Morton on his way to Hamilton. It had always been unlikely that a Premier League quality player would stay at Cappielow.

Balancing that, however, was the arrival of former Celtic under-19 captain Michael Tidser. Once highly thought of at Parkhead, the youngster had been allowed to leave. A lack of pace apparently was the decisive factor in that decision, but the left-footed midfielder had good control and an excellent range of passing.

James Grady commented: "I'm delighted to sign him. I know a good number of people at Celtic wanted to keep him. He went away to Sweden, but we've stolen a march on a few clubs." It was an 18-month deal.

On Tuesday 19th January Morton had a chance to match themselves against quality opposition when Tony Mowbray's Celtic arrived at Cappielow for the fourth round of the Scottish Cup. Young Niall McGinn struck the only goal of the 90 minutes to take Celts through to the next round in what was a less than impressive performance from the Glasgow giants.

Once again Dominic Shimmin looked entirely comfortable at the back for a Morton side who fought valiantly but without the necessary class in the front half of the team. Grady was pleased and said of his players: "They gave us everything."

The concentration was now fully on league survival and, if possible, improvement. Peter Weatherson celebrated a new two-year contract with a double against Raith Rovers at Stark's Park, sufficient to give the visitors a 2-1 victory. Here was another player with the ability to play at a higher level in the game than he ever attained. I always felt he operated within his comfort zone.

Soon after Brian Wake was on his way to Conference club Gateshead, a move back to his own neck of the woods. He had been a good servant to Morton. His attitude was excellent and he was a very likeable young man.

He may not have had the greatest skill levels, but his workrate was never in doubt and he always managed to pop up and score key goals. Manager Grady commented: "Brian goes with our best wishes. He has been nothing but a model pro."

Moves to sign 34-year-old ex-Ranger Jonatan Johansson, the Finnish striker, failed to come to fruition. On the way in, however, on short term contracts until the end of the season were left-sided midfielder or full back Kevin McKinlay, formerly of Partick, and young ex-Coventry striker Donovan Simmonds.

The beginning of February also marked a sad occasion with the death of former Morton director Ken Woods. A popular man with a ready smile and kind demeanour, he had served the club over several years before stepping down to resume his interest as a season ticket holder.

Chairman Douglas Rae said of him: "He was a great Morton man over the years. His biggest strength was as a listener. He would listen very intently and invariably would then ask deep questions that got right to the point."

I always enjoyed Ken's company. He was a genuinely good man.

Next upon the pitch were Queen of the South at Dumfries. Since their return to the First Division, Morton had met the Doonhamers six times at Palmerston, five in the league and once in the Challenge Cup. They had won four of these games and drawn two. Coincidentally, the Dumfries club enjoyed a similarly good record at Cappielow.

Queens were going well under manager Gordon Chisholm but, once again, Morton had the upper hand, winning 2-1 with a brace by Stevie Masterton.

Masterton had been told he was free to find another club but, in his first appearance under James Grady's management, he clearly felt he had a point to make.

Morton were now nine points ahead of second bottom Ayr and 10 in front of Airdrie.

Midfielder Erik Paartalu then revealed that he had undertaken to return to Australia at the end of the season as the club began to look towards the final run-in.

In a dire display at home to Dunfermline, the Pars took all three points with a 2-1 win, Ryan McGuffie scoring the home goal. I reported: "Morton's sole redeeming moment in a mediocre performance was Ryan McGuffie's opening goal, a perfectly taken diving header from an equally well executed Stevie Masterton free kick."

Donovan Simmonds came on as a substitute while, once more, Dominic Shimmin impressed.

Shimmin was to depart at the end of the season, perhaps the most perplexing character I have ever come across in football. His talent was never in question; his performances were invariably exemplary, and always with the suggestion there was even more to come, but football almost seemed as if it were a vaguely interesting sideline to him; something to fill in the time.

CHAPTER FORTY-THREE

My final game covering Morton

By this time I knew my own career was coming to an end with the Greenock Telegraph. I was to be made redundant after 36 years of service, five years short of retiral. It was an odd feeling when I drove down to Somerset Park in Ayr to cover what would be my last Morton match.

In the event the game was disappointing. Morton lost 2-0 to their relegation rivals. Donovan Simmonds did well, so too did Michael Tidser, but manager James Grady summed up when he said: "They lacked support from experienced players."

The after-match press chat was predictable. When it finished I spoke to James Grady. He 'wisnae daft'. He knew there had to be a clear-out at Cappielow. He had clear ideas on what he wanted to do and where he wanted to go with Morton.

But at the end of the season, although Morton secured their First Division status, he found himself surplus to requirements. Allan Moore, Douglas Rae's preferred choice for the manager's post when Davie Irons was sacked, was appointed. The rest is history.

Six days after covering the Ayr match at Somerset I slipped out of the Greenock Telegraph office with my personal possessions in a bin bag. There was no presentation from management after 36 years of service. It wasn't quite how I had envisaged my career ending.

The day I left the Telegraph, the financial blow was softened by the relief I felt at leaving the newspaper. When I joined, in 1974, it was a great wee family evening newspaper, circulation 23,500. On one day it sold over 25,000 copies.

When I left I was one of two surviving editorial full-time staff to have served under the former Orr Pollock independent company. The atmosphere was totally different from the 'old days' of Orr Pollock. I disliked what the paper had become – a redtop tabloid, the front page of which invariably appeared to make Inverclyde out to be a centre of crime. The police had become 'cops', criminals were no longer sentenced to imprisonment – they were 'caged'; children were 'kids' and everything seemed geared to the lowest common denominator.

Big pictures and screaming headlines were the order of the day. Up-to-date national and international news, supplied via the Press Association, was excluded, a big mistake as previous market research under the old family firm of Orr Pollock had shown that, for sections of the readership, the Telegraph was their only newspaper. The management knew little about

Inverclyde, certainly didn't live there, and had little disposition to consult long serving staff members. Circulation plummeted to below the 14,000 mark, down 6,000 in a decade. They called it 'modernisation'.

Now, as I finish this book, the Greenock Telegraph has been subject to a management buyout. Dunfermline Press, of whom Clyde and Forth Press including the Greenock Telegraph were a subsidiary, went into receivership in March of 2012.

While the internet has affected newspaper sales, the decline of the Telegraph's circulation had much more to do with how the product had been changed. Those of us who came from the community, who lived and breathed it, were constantly subjected to complaints from our fellow citizens as to what the newspaper had become.

I recall former editor Ken Thomson saying that when you were appointed editor of the Greenock Telegraph, you became its custodian. It was a wise statement. The new management style demanded fundamental change which took no account of anything resembling market research. There is nothing wrong with change, but it must be managed carefully, especially when taking over a highly successful exisiting product.

But at the end of the day it was the customer who held the real power. A local paper has to be acceptable to all sections of the community.

No business should ever take its customers for granted.

CHAPTER FORTY-FOUR

Looking ahead

What now of Morton Football Club? In those 36 years of covering their activities, much has changed in this world of ours.

There has been a considerable depopulation in Inverclyde as the old traditional industries of shipbuilding, engineering, sugar refining and the woollen mill disappeared. The new computer industries which went some way towards replacing them also have suffered. That has obviously affected the club's fan base, but they remain one of those First Division clubs with genuine aspirations of mounting a return to the top table of Scottish football.

For too long they have underachieved, despite the commendable and not inconsiderable financial input of chairman and owner Douglas Rae. It is 24 years since the club played in the Scottish Premier League.

During Douglas Rae's term of ownership over 12 seasons, Morton have played five in the Second Division, one in the Third and five in the First; six including this season. Their best position has been sixth in the First Division. For all the resources that have been pumped in that is a very modest return. In the course of that period there have been seven managers, including current boss Allan Moore, plus one caretaker boss. These are statistics that should give cause for appraisal within the club.

My own feeling is that the lack at any time of a really experienced, proven, strong manager with First Division and/or Premier League nous, such as Alex MacDonald, John Lambie, Jim Duffy, Jimmy Calderwood or Jimmy Nicholl has been the single most important factor – someone who could have taken the club by the scruff of the neck, accepted nothing less than full control of the football side and commanded absolute respect. In saying that, there is a risk with every management appointment.

The aforementioned depopulation means that Inverclyde is less able to support a top quality First Division side; less able to provide a true challenge for Premier status. But ought Morton to be so inferior to the likes of Kilmarnock, Motherwell, St Mirren, Inverness, Falkirk or Hamilton?

They still have a respectable core support with a potential of 4-4,500 should they reach the SPL once more. Only once in the 24 years since they last competed in the elite league have they come close to challenging for a place at the top table.

For how long Douglas Rae and his family feel content to throw money into what is virtually a bottomless pit, time alone will tell. I estimate that the Morton chairman has already contributed well over £3million to the cause, probably closer to four. It is surely only a matter of time before part-time football becomes a reality in the First Division, unless dramatic restructuring takes place.

I believe there are far too many clubs playing in our senior leagues. Of the current number of 42, only 26 at the most have any real fan base. The recent liquidation of Rangers, and their consequent return as a newco in the Third Division of the SFL, has begun to concentrate minds. My own preferred solution would be for two senior leagues, the first of 16 clubs playing each other twice, the second of 10, meeting four times. Additional fixtures could be provided by reverting to the old League Cup section format at the start of the season. The rest of the clubs could form regional leagues.

But if the game itself requires restructuring, sport needs to be taken more seriously at a political level. School sport has taken a battering since the teachers' strikes of the 70s and 80s. I do not blame teachers for taking the action they did – indeed I sympathise with them – but at a political level it has been madness not to reintroduce meaningful sport within state schools. In my opinion it should be a core subject. Teachers should be paid, or given time off in lieu, to take charge of school teams playing on a Saturday morning.

Decent all-weather facilities and coaching should also be funded in every population centre. This would be expensive. Would it be more expensive than the burden we are placing on the National Health Service as generations of overweight children become obese adults? It would, into the bargain, have tremendous social benefits.

There are also jobs in sport, and who can quantify the benefit to business and society as a whole of the self-confidence which comes from sporting success? That applies as much to a nation as to a district within it. One only needs to look at the feel-good factor instilled by British success at the London Olympics.

I fear nothing substantially will alter, for the benefits of such change are to be found long-term, and politicians, by necessity as much as self-interest, are invariably motivated by short-term considerations. It would also take public pressure to concentrate the minds of our politicians and it seems to me that apathy has become the dominant attitude among the populace in general. One might ask who can blame them?

MY TOP TON TEAM

Finally, I decided to pick a top team of all the players I saw while reporting on the Greenock club during those 36 years from 1974 to 2010.

Goalkeeper: I would plump for the likeable Englishman, Roy Baines. Not the tallest, he was nevertheless extremely agile, a good communicator with his defence and capable of supreme athleticism. He was also good enough to win a transfer to Celtic before returning to Morton.

Right back and skipper: It has to be Davie Hayes. Strong in the tackle, hugely determined and a real driving force going forward. A never-say-die type of player who identified with the fans. A captain who led by example. A thorough professional.

Centre half: Joe McLaughlin. Dominant in the air, resolute in the tackle. He was a regular in the Scotland under-21 team. Won a move to Chelsea for a bargain fee of £90,000. Received a notable accolade from Alex Ferguson when manager of Aberdeen after one superb performance at Pittodrie.

Sweeper: Neil Orr. As former Dundee United boss Jim McLean once said, he was simply a class act. Read the game superbly, had a good range of passing and often broke forward to excellent effect. His long, loping stride disguised genuine pace. Was transferred to West Ham for between £350,000 and £400,000 after a Rangers bid of £150,000 was rejected. A regular in Jock Stein's Scotland under-21s and a Scottish League international, ironically he probably would have gone on to play for the full Scotland side had he gone to Rangers. The move to the Hammers was more lucrative, but once there he often found himself being switched from central defence to midfield, such were West Ham's needs and the player's versatility. This led to Willie Miller and Alan Hansen establishing themselves ahead of Orr as recognised sweepers.

Left back: Jim Holmes. Converted by Benny Rooney from a midfielder to a full back after being brought in from Partick Thistle. One of the best in his position not to be selected for Scotland. Excellent footballer and incredibly consistent. Great reader of the game and outstanding going forward. Had he gone full-time he surely would have played for his country.

Right midfield: Derek McInnes. Won a transfer to Rangers after many consistent performances for Morton over several years. True pro, he combined an inexhaustible work-rate with an excellent range of passing. He was also excellent at winning the ball back. He was simply a model professional.

Centre midfield: Janne Lindberg. Finland's captain while with Morton. Small, but very determined. Excellent work ethic and technique combined with perfect reading of game and top positional play. Like all very good players, he always seemed to have more time on the ball than others. A great support player and organiser.

Left midfield: Bobby Thomson. Tall, aggressive, strong, good pace and a true goalscoring midfielder. Fine header of the ball. A perfect complement to McInnes and Lindberg. His main flaw was his explosive temper.

Forward: Mark McGhee. Good enough to play for Newcastle, Aberdeen, Hamburg, Celtic and Scotland. Good close control, strength, pace and a nose for goal. Could play through the middle or on the right.

Forward: Jim Tolmie. Small and skilful with excellent pace, he was the scorer of some spectacular goals. Billy McNeill, an admirer of Tolmie's while manager at Celtic, brought him to Manchester City from Belgian club Lokeren. Could play as an out-and-out striker or off the front two. A very good footballer.

Forward: Andy Ritchie. Could play anywhere up front, or behind the front men. A wonderful natural talent. Great close control, top range of passing and a free kick and corner specialist. Scored an incredible number of spectacular goals. Probably the last of his type. I would ask him to run only if he were late for the team bus.

That leaves the side as (4-3-3): Baines; Hayes (capt), McLaughlin, Orr, Holmes; McInnes, Lindberg, Thomson; McGhee, Tolmie, Ritchie.

My subs' bench would be: David Wylie, George Anderson, Jim Duffy, Jim Rooney, Alan Mahood, David Hopkin and Derek Lilley. I know that's an extra two subs, but I couldn't leave one of these guys out. And it's my book!

I wonder what that little lot would command in today's transfer market!

Morton league placings 1974-2010

Season	Old First Division	Scottish Premier League	First Division	Second Division	Third Division	Manager
1974-75	17 (18 clubs)					Erik Sorensen, Hal Stewart *
1975-76			11 (14 clubs)			Hal Stewart *, Joe Gilroy
1976-77			4 (14 clubs)			Benny Rooney -
1977-78			1 (14 clubs)			
1978-79		7 (10 clubs)				
1979-80		6 (10 clubs)				
1980-81		8 (10 clubs)				
1981-82		7 (10 clubs)				
1982-83		9 (10 clubs)				Benny Rooney
1983-84			1 (14 clubs)			Alex Miller, Eddie Morrison *, Tommy McLean
1984-85		10 (10 clubs)				Willie McLean
1985-86			7 (14 clubs)			Allan McGraw -
1986-87			1 (12 clubs)			
1987-88		12 (12 clubs)				
1988-89			5 (14 clubs)			
1989-90			11 (14 clubs)			
1990-91			9 (14 clubs)			
1991-92			7 (12 clubs)			
1992-93			6 (12 clubs)			
1993-94			11 (12 clubs)			
1994-95				1 (10 clubs)		
1995-96			3 (10 clubs)			
1996-97			8 (10 clubs)			Allan McGraw
1997-98			5 (10 clubs)			Allan McGraw, Billy Stark -
1998-99			6 (10 clubs)			
1999-00			8 (10 clubs)			Billy Stark, Ian McCall
2000-01			9 (10 clubs)			Allan Evans, Ally Maxwell
2001-02				10 (10 clubs)		Peter Cormack, Dave McPherson
2002-03					1 (10 clubs)	Dave McPherson, John McCormack -
2003-04				4 (10 clubs)		
2004-05				3 (10 clubs)		John McCormack, Joe McLaughlin *, Jim McInally -
2005-06				2 (10 clubs)		
2006-07				1 (10 clubs)		
2007-08			8 (10 clubs)			Jim McInally, Davie Irons -
2008-09			6 (10 clubs)			
2009-10			8 (10 clubs)			Davie Irons, James Grady

* Denotes caretaker manager.

Lightning Source UK Ltd.
Milton Keynes UK
UKOW07f2358301117
313661UK00009B/647/P

9 780755 215133